PEOPLE AND POWER
IN THE
STEELWORKERS UNION

By John Herling

HARPER & ROW, PUBLISHERS

Grateful acknowledgment is hereby made for permission to reprint the following material:

Lawrence E. Spivak for permission to use portions of the transcript from "Meet the Press" in an interview with David J. McDonald and I. W. Abel.

331.88
H549r

To Mary, my dear wife

Contents

Foreword

This book is an account of the public and private life, the troubles and hopes, of one of the great unions of North America, the United Steelworkers. Spanning the years from 1952 to 1970, it is a personal, political, and psychological chronicle of how a union of more than 1,200,000 men and women was governed and sometimes misgoverned, directed and misdirected. It traces the key events leading to the selection and rejection of David J. McDonald, the union's international president for twelve years, one of the nation's most relentlessly advertised labor leaders. Out of the mouths of hundreds of participants and intimate observers of high and low degree, it seeks to explain how he managed to hold office during that time. It relates the moves and countermoves that led to his replacement by I. W. Abel, a man of another stripe, intent on another sort of leadership.

After a campaign of unusual proportions that culminated in McDonald's downfall, Abel and his associates undertook the dramatic task of transforming the relationship between union officers and the workers in the plants as well as with the community generally. They were to face new complexities and unexpected challenges. The breakthrough of minority workers, black and Mexican-American, into the life of the union became a force to be respected and reckoned with.

This book ranges beyond the orbit of a particular union, although its focus is clearly the Steelworkers Union itself. That colossal entity, with more than 3,200 local unions in 1964 (grown to 3,900 in 1970), is located in practically every state and province of the United States and Canada, from Puerto Rico to the Arctic Circle.

Through sheer size and function, the strategic placement of the union makes its political condition a matter of considerable concern for two nations. Its policies and the behavior of its leaders affect the daily lives of the families of its huge membership. They shape the relationships with the managers of the mighty aggregations of corporate power as well as of lesser enterprises. Obviously, the union's chosen leaders have to deal with the heads of U.S. Steel and Bethlehem and a dozen other great steel companies. But since their members are also employed in aluminum and can manufacturing, dig iron ore and copper, and work in a multitude of fabricating plants, union representatives must concern themselves with negotiations for more than two thousand contracts in almost as many communities.

This book is not primarily about collective bargaining but about how union leaders are chosen and how they carry out the responsibilities their members entrust to them. It records the growing awareness by ever larger sections of the union of how decisions are made and the heightened demand for accountability of leaders to the rank and file.

The turning point in the life of the United Steelworkers was the union's presidential election of 1965, the campaign that preceded it and the events that followed. Abel's challenge to McDonald started reluctantly; it was undertaken with considerable caution and a variety of misgivings. The campaign was mounted not in hot blood but largely as a result of cold exasperation. Some of its sponsors hailed Abel's campaign as a crusade, but his most influential backers wanted it to be a "quiet" one, not wishing to be embarrassed by an excess of unaccustomed fervor. For they were challenging the leader of the establishment whom they had largely sustained for twelve years, even as they were often dismayed by him. Over those years, they had stockpiled—or slag-heaped—their suppressed rages, their postponed indignation, their ulcerous frustrations. All of which ultimately served to fuel the open hearth of the political campaign.

At first, many viewed the election campaign as an awkward proceeding. By a considerable section of the "loyal" union cadres, it was regarded as an insurrectionary act, perpetrated by irresponsible types. While many had harbored the unspeakable thought that a change in top leadership should be attempted, they had developed a mode of accommodation to the vagaries of the incumbent administration. Permissiveness ran both ways. Under McDonald the district directors had exercised almost autonomous powers in their jurisdictions, in return for which the leader could function as he pleased. Such reciprocity was not the product of a formal compact, but the understanding was clear.

As for the federal government, the holding of a union contest of massive dimensions presented at the time a threat to the spirit of consensus. From the White House down, it was felt that a conflict in the Steelworkers Union would weaken the structure of the steel industry's labor-management relations and undermine the stability of the economy. For this reason, the immediate reaction in government circles was undisguised consternation. Was this imminent happening necessary? Couldn't it be aborted? Some of those who thought that they knew McDonald best felt certain that he would not undertake the endurance test of such a campaign. But the campaign and election did take place. It was accompanied by the direct and indirect influence of the federal government. The conduct of the union election is therefore followed here through the intercession of the governmental presence and the interplay of union and government political pressures.

The special character of the Steelworkers election activity is shown also in the extent to which the union's internal processes were revitalized and rectified. It thereby counteracted the creeping apathy that often characterizes many unions as well as many private organizational systems. The resulting upheaval evoked a comprehensive rethinking of the labor movement's conception of what union leadership should become. At the same time, it required managements to become more sensitive to their relations with union leadership. Management was generally disturbed at the prospect of disarray that could result from a large-scale election. Such an event would make it necessary to replenish its own arsenal of responses in the field of labor-management relations. At this point, management preferred to keep things and union leaders as they were.

But the dynamism of discontent in a union, as in a nation, often develops a life of its own. In the Steelworkers Union, the smoldering dissatisfaction in the union's political life exploded into the revolutionary act of compelling its top officers to compete for office. The events unfolded in this book, the collision of forces and personalities, took place in the context of a national polemic on the role and condition of the labor movement. The problem is how, in fact, to harness two sometimes alternating currents: the requirements of trade-union responsibility and the affirmation of democratic vitality in the life of a union. Nor does this imply that the burden of responsibility and the difficulty of greater participation fall on organized labor alone. They must be shared by management which becomes answerable for its own acts, and by government for its use or abuse of its interventional powers. But primarily this is a story of how an organization—economic, social, and political—moves toward a fulfillment of the needs and the changing demands of the people it is meant to serve.

Prelude: No Little Dictatorships

The last days of Philip Murray, president of the United Steelworkers of America and of the Congress of Industrial Organizations, were days of personal and political disappointment. He died suddenly on November 9, 1952, five days after Adlai E. Stevenson had been defeated for the national presidency. The Stevenson campaign had represented not only a deep political commitment for Murray but also a large-scale investment of money, energy, and union manpower. For both the CIO and the Steelworkers, the Stevenson defeat would require a period of radical readjustment. Now, under Dwight D. Eisenhower, would begin a life under a Republican administration—the first time this had been necessary for the CIO and its Steelworkers Union, which were begotten under the New Deal of Franklin D. Roosevelt and nurtured under the Fair Deal of Harry S. Truman.

While Murray saw possible dangers in the prospect of leading his people across this new political terrain, he was weighed down by a more intimate burden: the necessity of dealing surgically with an unpleasant personal problem at the highest level. Murray had already determined to remove the man who was more than the secretary-treasurer of the union, the post this man officially held. For many years Murray had regarded him almost as a son, whose career in the union he had launched and advanced but was now determined to halt. That man was David J. McDonald.

Murray had been raised in a tough school under a demanding headmaster, John Llewellyn Lewis, president of the United Mine Workers

1

and founder of the CIO. When in 1940 the time came for the most painful decision up to that moment in his trade-union career, Murray, chairman of the Steel Workers Organizing Committee and vice-president of the United Mine Workers, moved purposefully, if self-consciously, into the presidency of the CIO to replace Lewis, his mentor and sponsor. Locked in a feud with President Roosevelt, Lewis had threatened to quit the CIO presidency if the Republican candidate, Wendell L. Willkie, failed to defeat Roosevelt in 1940. Though the acceptance of Lewis's resignation would inevitably mean a parting of the ways, Murray received the gavel from a white-faced and shaken Lewis at a dramatic CIO convention. Again, early in 1948, when Lee Pressman, his general counsel and Machiavellian guide through the early years of the Steel-workers, placed loyalty to the Communist movement over that to the CIO and the Steelworkers Union, Murray dropped him fast and irrevocably. Months later, as at a wake, Murray sat with close friends all night and recalled how important a part Pressman had played and how he had depended on him. Murray wept while God-damning Pressman.

Now, in November 1952, he was preparing another decision: David J. McDonald was through; Murray had already informed his closest advisers that he planned to close those loopholes in the union constitution that seemed to have provided McDonald, as secretary-treasurer, with some legal basis for independent activity. There appeared to be incontrovertible evidence that McDonald was building a personal political machine geared to the day when he could succeed Murray.

Angered, Murray was determined to keep McDonald from succeeding him. Murray had gloried in union comradeship. His break with Lewis and his forced separation from the Mine Workers left wounds that had never healed. He had savored his relations with people, especially with his friends of mining days. The friendship of those miners who chose to stay with the Steelworkers rather than return to the United Mine Workers Union and John Lewis—men like the veteran Smaile Chatak —was especially precious to him. His own fierce pride in having won his place in the leadership of the UMW made Lewis's vengeful separation of him from that organization a haunting sorrow. Now on top of all that, the McDonald push for power—which Murray considered a push to hurry him into the grave—roused him to fury.*

* Some people think that Murray's disaffection with McDonald may have dated from the time that McDonald, a Catholic, divorced his first wife, Emily Louise Price of Cleveland, a secretary in John Lewis's office, in the summer of 1946. The divorce was granted in private chambers by State Judge Samuel Weiss. The matter became public and Murray, a devout Catholic, was incensed. "He had his own human side which made him very tolerant to other people," a colleague observed. "But he did not want them to be spectacles. As long as they did things discreetly and circumspectly, he had no great objection, but he became angry and affronted

A sense of purpose and moral earnestness often marked Murray's relationships, private and public. His office door in Pittsburgh was always open. Delegations of workers from the steel mills and old friends from the mines would come to sit with him to tell him what was on their minds and in their hearts. He knew the names of the messenger boys, the elevator men, and the secretaries in union headquarters. At conventions, the Murray presence seemed to suffuse the body of delegates, whether he spoke from the platform or walked confidently among them. By example and implication, he guided his colleagues along the paths of trade-union righteousness as he saw it. His closer associates confidently assumed that he would set them straight if they strayed. In turn, from him came the constant reminder that they, the delegates, the local leaders and staff men, were there in a representative capacity; they came there in behalf of the men who worked in the mills, and they were never to forget it. He had a natural, easy courtesy. His Scottish burr (especially pronounced before labor audiences), the glow of his eyes, their fire sometimes banked, sometimes flashing with anger or scorn, or with a sparkle heralding a quirky turn of phrase or reminiscence, the hold of his head, the rich baritone trained in outdoor meetings and hundreds of union halls, all constituted part of the instruments of his power over the membership.

In closing the May 1952 convention, Murray described the meaning of his comradeship with his union associates: "Certainly, no one derives greater satisfaction out of meeting people than I do. The little bit of strength and vitality that I have is what you have given me. The encouragement to do the things that have to be done comes from you. I derive greater satisfaction . . . out of mingling with you and the hundreds of thousands of people you represent than I do in mingling with the so-called big shots. I feel so much at home when I am privileged to have the chance of associating myself with you, and I find in you a greater sense of wisdom than I find anywhere in this country."

Having placed his confidence in a man, Murray assumed the existence of mutual trust. He was often suspicious of men whose intellectual and political commitments emanated from what he regarded as unfamiliar sources, which was to say outside the cultural life of the United Mine Workers.

With the creation of the CIO, Murray's own political understanding had quickened. An appearance before Lewis resembled an audience in a magisterial presence; Murray, on the other hand, invited conversation.

---

when he thought the union suffered as a result." In 1950 McDonald married his charming Washington secretary, Rosemary McHugh of Hazelton, Pennsylvania, who was related to Thomas Kennedy, secretary-treasurer of the United Mine Workers.

Murray had worked his way up in the political organization of the United Mine Workers through ability, struggle, and maneuver—always in the shadow of Lewis. The Lewis gesture and the Lewis tone often drew a responsive echo from Murray. After Murray and Lewis split finally in 1942, Murray continued to be self-conscious, reddening furiously in Lewis's presence. Lewis's glare, or his calculated air of supercilious indifference directed at one who had been a comrade in arms, would infuriate Murray to helplessness. His composure, seemingly absolute elsewhere, wilted under Lewis's lordly disdain.

Resolved no longer to pay homage to Lewis, Murray was determined to be and remain master in his own house. In this effort, he needed all the assurance he could summon. He found it in the company of those who chose to come with him rather than stay with the Mine Workers. McDonald—Murray's personal secretary for thirteen years, then secretary-treasurer of the Steel Workers Organizing Committee— was among those who joined Murray. Actually, as a practical matter there would have been no comparable place for McDonald to go. Nevertheless Murray was gratified.

Murray was inclined to be permissive, especially with people whose actions or ideas did not make him uncomfortable. McDonald and he worshiped in the same church, shared a common background—at somewhat different levels—in the United Mine Workers, and lived in its mythology. More specifically, both reacted from the Lewis experience.

In contrast to McDonald were men like Clinton Golden and Michael Harris. Golden, large-boned, big-voiced, in many ways the administrative architect of the Steel Workers Organizing Committee—the predecessor organization to the United Steelworkers—brought an immense faith in the labor movement and in the importance of the rank and file. He had little inclination to play conventional union politics. Assured in his own integrity and bound by a common purpose, Golden was ready to stand up *to* Murray as well as *for* him. But to stand up to Murray was also to run the risk of being considered a troublemaker. Golden nevertheless cared more for honest dealing than for personal power. He was the candid friend, but candor did not contribute to the leader's peace of mind.

In Golden and also in Michael Harris, a younger colleague whom Golden had brought with him into the Steelworkers after an aggressive career as an organizer in the Philadelphia trade-union movement, McDonald perceived the threat of serious competition. Their competence and diligence became his enemy. Neither man had a Mine Workers background but had joined Lewis and Murray on the eve of the creation of the CIO. A native of Pottsville, Pennsylvania, Golden had worked actively in the Machinists Union, had been a Socialist early in life, and later became manager and field secretary of Brookwood Labor College, a resident trade-union institution in Katonah, New York. His whole life was directed toward the revitalization of the union movement. In 1937, Golden, two years Murray's senior, became his assistant in the Pittsburgh office of the Steel Workers Organizing Committee.

McDonald, a scoffer at all isms, understood how to exploit Murray's frequent irritations with men who knew their own minds. Independence of mind was an almost unassimilable ingredient in Murray's leadership concept: his aim was to build an organization that was disciplined, responsive, and, above all, loyal.

After the break with Lewis, Murray was bent on achieving an organization able to withstand erosion or attack by Lewis, who for an interval had reaffiliated with the American Federation of Labor. To the outside world, it would appear to be weakness to have independent men around. McDonald saw that the strength of character and commitment of men like Golden or Harris could become the rock on which he could break them, and quite early he began to maneuver for allies inside the United Steelworkers. In Lee Pressman, McDonald found an ally of immense influence and guile.

Pressman's role in the late 1930s and the middle 1940s reached considerably beyond that of a legal adviser. He had developed a reputation as the gray eminence in the CIO and in government circles as well. Despite frequent charges that Pressman was a Communist—which years later Pressman admitted—Murray held on to him against all criticism, including Golden's. At the time of the Lewis split and despite Lewis's attractive counteroffers, Pressman stuck with Murray. Golden soon became aware that Murray, disregarding Pressman's party-line motivations, preferred the personal services of Pressman to the organizational commitment of men like himself. To the dismay of Harris, Golden finally resigned, with a heavy heart. His resignation came as the culmination of a long series of corrosive and abrasive encounters with the mutual-assistance program of McDonald and Pressman.

But Pressman's adherence to the Communist line now came in conflict with CIO policy. This became so obvious to Murray and to others in the CIO that Murray could no longer disregard it. Early in 1948 Murray finally discharged Pressman. He found himself leaning more heavily on McDonald who grew more aggressive in dealing with Harris, and those like him.

To Murray's easy permissiveness to those he trusted were now added other weakening factors. His own health was no longer robust; bouts of illness alternated with stirrings of passion and vigor. He was deeply immersed in the work of the CIO, and in governmental affairs following World War II and during the Korean War. As the Steelworkers' secretary-treasurer, McDonald readily relieved Murray of many administrative chores, which included the dispensing of funds and the appointment of staff representatives. So long as he had no serious reason to doubt McDonald's loyalty, Murray did not mind transferring to him the administrative authority over the Steelworkers Union, not excluding the power of the purse.

BOOK I

SUCCESSION AND

REBELLION

CHAPTER **1**

Ways and Means

Serene I fold my hands and wait.

JOHN BURROUGHS

Early in his life as a union functionary, McDonald learned the importance of the care and feeding of supporters at all levels. Over the years, McDonald had moved from attentive personal secretary to diligent apprentice. On the road to advancement—which for him meant succession to the presidency—he left little to chance. From the time he was elected secretary-treasurer in 1942, he sought to inculcate the staff, at headquarters and in the field, with a simplistic philosophy: loyalty to the future top boss.

Occasionally he was jarred by the refusal of some men to go along. Thus he had regarded Clinton Golden's resignation as a vice-president in 1946 as the removal of a formidable obstacle. This was soon followed by the Michael Harris case.

Harris had permitted a handful of locals in the Philadelphia district, for which he had rendered effective service as director, to nominate him for international secretary-treasurer. Such activity was considered almost subversive and intolerable. As a result, Harris was called into the international headquarters to explain. He protested, "Look, I'm not soliciting nominations. I haven't even thought of campaigning for this job. But what's wrong if some people want to send in some nominations?" Murray softly advised him that it would be much better if he did not run. But McDonald, a staff witness recalled, "crudely told Harris to get the hell out of the race. Tell 'em you don't want the nomination; tell 'em you won't take it. Issue a statement to this effect."

McDonald was determined to find a way of handling Harris's effrontery, and he found it. Only recently, a dues-checkoff system had been installed. Most people on the international union staff, including the district directors, held membership in the local of a plant where they had formerly worked, and many of them in plants whose locals they had helped organize. This situation was true of Mike Harris. Such men could not have their dues checked off by employers in the usual way because they were not being paid by the companies. They would submit their dues to the local financial secretary, who then forwarded them to international headquarters. Most of them, busy with union responsibilities, would normally send in a year's dues at a time. At one point, the time for the annual renewal of dues had arrived, a fact that Harris had apparently overlooked and of which he was not reminded by his local secretary. Suddenly this technicality of nonpayment of dues—of which Harris was apparently still unaware—was sprung on him in the executive board. He was informed by McDonald that he was not in good standing. One district director quickly pointed out that this was surely nothing but a slight technicality. He was certain, he said, that the local financial secretary would happily accept the dues retroactively and see that they were transmitted in the regular way to the international office. The legal point was then raised that this "restoration" to good standing could be accomplished only by unanimous agreement of the executive board. It was generally supposed that Phil Murray had no advance knowledge that this absurdly technical point was to be raised against Harris. But when it was insisted upon, Murray made a statement interpreting the constitution. Yes, he said, it certainly did require that members of the board remain in good standing; this was an important part of the responsibility for any trade-union member. He acknowledged that removal from the board was a harsh punishment, but a union member's first responsibility is to keep himself in good standing. Mike Harris had "lapsed," and he was dismissed.

While Murray had no intention of riding Harris out of the union, it was clear that McDonald had. Murray urged Harris to stay, offering him other jobs in the union. At this time, however, Clinton Golden, then engaged by the federal government to administer the U.S. program in Greece, offered Harris a job with the government. Harris took it. "So," remarked a close observer, "we lost the services of Mike Harris, who had committed the then unpardonable sin of permitting his name even to be placed in nomination by a few locals."

McDonald, always aware of possible opposition, had seen in Harris a comer. The best political insurance for him was to drive comers out of the organization. Alternatively, those who did not provoke McDonald's insecurity and who played on his team were rewarded with tangible expressions of gratitude. Sometimes these took the forms of merit increases in salaries, liberalized expense accounts, and the prospect of elevation to district directorships.

McDonald soon found himself coming up alongside two different types of men. One type was embodied by a young staff man named Otis Brubaker, who came to the Steelworkers Union right after World War II. In the fall of 1946, he began his service as director of the union's research department. At the time, Brubaker had been working as a labor specialist for the National Housing Agency; prior to that he had worked in the Philadelphia regional office of the tripartite War Labor Board, where he had come to the attention of union officials. Brubaker headed the union's research department for more than twenty years. An undergraduate at the University of Kansas, he had taken his doctorate at Stanford in 1940. He had worked his way there, taught, helped create a consumer cooperative in Palo Alto, and did part-time organizing work for the American Federation of Teachers.

Six years before his invitation to join the staff of the Steelworkers Union, Brubaker, with his doctorate in hand, had written to the union headquarters in Pittsburgh. Were there any openings for a fellow like him? Brubaker knew no one in the union at the time, and he never even got an acknowledgment. By 1946, when his abilities had been made manifest during his Philadelphia service with the War Labor Board, Brubaker was interviewed by Phil Murray and later, at Murray's request, by David McDonald in their Washington offices. He passed muster and went to Pittsburgh. In October 1946 he began preparation of memoranda for the steel negotiations of 1947. From then on he was in the thick of union negotiations. As Brubaker points out, these were the first real bargaining negotiations after the "quickie" contract following the termination of the War Labor Board, when everybody got an increase of 18½ cents an hour and ran.

By 1949 the management of U.S. Steel, on the alert for talent, became impressed with Brubaker's work as the union's economist. During hearings on the pricing policy of the steel industry, Brubaker had testified in behalf of the union while Roger Blough, then U.S. Steel's general counsel, spoke for the company. Later Blough invited Brubaker to lunch at the Duquesne Club, where the industrial elite of Pittsburgh met to dine. Brubaker, somewhat startled by the invitation, nevertheless went. Here is his account of the meeting:

"After exchanging amenities, mostly about my early life, which he had suddenly learned a great deal about, he said: 'Otis, we have something in common. I understand that we both grew up in the Church of the Brethren.' I said I wasn't aware that he was a member. Oh, yes. The church is prominent in central Pennsylvania where he came from. . . . After much of this, he told me that they had been watching me and were sure that I would go far, that I had a lot of ability, and so on. Then he asked: 'How would you like to work for the corporation?' I laughed and said I didn't think I was interested. Blough said: 'Now, don't turn me down before you hear me out. We can make a job which will be rewarding and interesting for you. If you want to work in industrial relations, that of course is the place where we know your abilities and where you obviously have had some experience. But if there's any problem as far as you are concerned in doing that—there might of course be an ethical problem.' That is, sitting on the opposite side of the bargaining table from which I had just sat.

"This indicated there was a matter of some delicacy to be considered, but as a matter of expediency, not as a matter of principle. Blough said that if there was a problem, they could find a job; in fact they could create a job if I would tell them what I wanted. Finally he got around to salary, at which point he disclosed that he knew how much I made and he knew that I lived in a modest home and against this background that they were prepared to make a substantial offer to me. As a starter, they were certainly willing to double my salary. He then elaborated on this. Of course, this still wouldn't bring me up, perhaps, to salary levels prevailing in the corporation, but I could expect rapid advancement. The whole prospect of membership in the country club, in the Establishment and the chance of influence in the community—it was all held out. Finally, he asked: 'How does all this sound?' I laughed and said it might be interesting to someone but not to me. He then wanted to know: 'Isn't this enough? I'm sure we can do better than this if need be.' Eventually, he said: 'Well, you don't like our proposal. How much would you want to come to work for us? You name a figure. I think we can meet it.' I told him that that really wasn't the problem. I frankly was not interested in working for the corporation. I had come to work for the union out of choice because I came from labor stock, if you will. I felt there was a tremendous service that could and should be served by the union movement and I wanted to make a contribution through that channel. I was not interested in making money for myself, and therefore was not interested in a job with the corporation. I laughed and said: 'I doubt that the corporation could make an offer of money that I would be interested in.' I was then told that while there might be some people who were not interested in making money, those were not very common; that for most people, over a period of time, some of the idealism wore off. Money is certainly the most important thing for most people, Blough said, and becomes increasingly that for most people. It will buy an awful lot of things, and it can be a tremendous force. . . . In his experience, he had found few people who were not more interested in making money for themselves than in anything else. 'Of course,' he said, 'many of us have great pride in our work and I'm sure you do, I've watched you. But there's no reason why you can't also make money while you're doing a useful job.' He said he had seldom seen people who were not willing to move ahead and make it for themselves. He asked me if there weren't a lot of things, really, that I would like, a better home, and so on. I said, I suppose foolishly, that I made more money working for the union than I had time to spend as it was. I was not making a munificent salary with the union, but it just happened I was then on a work schedule for myself, and I was largely my own boss and I was driving myself pretty hard, and I really didn't have that much time that I needed a lot of money; my tastes were relatively simple. So this type of thing did not have quite the appeal for me that it would have for many, the appeal of money. Finally, he urged me not to turn this down, to go home, think it over, and if I wanted, to talk it over with my wife and with my associates and counsellors at the union. When and if I decided I wanted to come back, give him a call, and 'we'll have lunch together again.' "

Brubaker returned to Phil Murray's office and recounted the details of the Blough conversation. Murray listened intently, his eyes flashing. He told Brubaker that he thought he had made a choice he would never regret. Then Murray let loose. "Why, that son of a bitch Blough, I'll give him a piece of my mind next time I see him—trying to steal my staff."

After Murray had left for the day, Brubaker was summoned to Mc-Donald's office. He understood, said McDonald, that Brubaker had had lunch with Blough at the Duquesne Club. "Oh, did Phil tell you?" asked Otis. "No," said McDonald with a slight smile, "I have my own sources of information." At that point nobody knew that he had been at the Duquesne Club except Murray, Blough, and whoever might have seen them at the club.

"You're a God-damn fool, Otis," said McDonald. "What did they offer you?" Otis replied, "Well, since you know everything about this, you must know what they offered me too." McDonald said, "Yes, I understand they offered you double your salary to start with. You know it will be a long time before you make that much here, Otis. And when you said you weren't interested, they kind of offered to let you name your own salary. You were smart to turn it down. You can do a lot better there. I know some people over there and, believe me, they will bid for this. This was a real good maneuver on your part. You just let me do a little bargaining for you and I can get you some real money. Fifty thousand is a cinch; and I think I can get you a hundred thousand."

Here Brubaker recounts the rest of the McDonald conversation. "I told McDonald I just wasn't interested, and that I had not come to work for the union to make money. Then he made some comments on his own philosophy about how I shouldn't be contemptuous about the power of money. He had long since discovered that most people could be bought for money and that he could buy and sell most of the people who worked for the union. And then he came with a real gem—for him at least—'I never could quite trust anybody I couldn't buy.' At this stage, I really laughed. 'What's so funny about that?' McDonald wanted to know. I said that it was just a little contradictory. I should think, I said, that the last person on earth you could trust is somebody you could buy, because he's for sale to the next guy who'll pay a little more. I don't think that quite got through. He did know even at that time that he could buy people as his own servants for his political and economic advancement—and he could do it cheap because he wasn't even using his own money; he was using union money. It wasn't as though really you had to take each of these people and say 'I'm buying you, you're now my slave.' You call a guy in, you flatter him a little bit and say 'I've been watching you and I want to encourage you. What are you making now?' He tells you. 'You ought to be doing better than that. I'm going to put through a thousand-buck increase for you.' Annual salary, that is; and in those days, that was a considerable amount of money. That was at a time when our District Directors were making only $8,000 a year, so a thousand bucks was a lot of money for somebody further down the line. This judicious use of the union's money can and did build a very strong machine of people who owed a lot to him, and therefore were loyal in their own way."

McDonald's push for power became more obvious in connection with James P. Griffin, the district director of Youngstown. The approach to Griffin took place in 1952. Griffin, then one of the younger directors, had come into the trade-union movement in 1933, as driver of an ice truck. He organized the first Teamsters local in Youngstown, Local 377. He gravitated to the steel industry when the National Recovery Administration came in and the Valley Ice Delivery Company made it too hot for him, but not before he had organized the "gypsy peddlers" and negotiated the first contract these drivers ever had. He reported the news to the membership from the back of an ice truck. In 1935, at the age of twenty-four, he went into the Youngstown Sheet & Tube mills, finally working his way up to the open-hearth furnace. His activity in the Steelworkers organization began in 1936, at a time when the groundwork was laid to capture the company union—the Employees Representation Plan (ERP)—which soon became part of the basic structure of the Steel Workers Organizing Committee. He held various local union offices and became president of the Mahoning County CIO council in 1940. As a result of an injury in the plant in late 1939, he went on workmen's compensation. Some of the motivation and deepened dedica-

WAYS AND MEANS | 15

tion to the labor movement came out of that injury—that plus the company's attempt to prevent his getting a compensation award. He argued his case before the Ohio Compensation Board, without an attorney, and won. He was the first worker ever to be sent to the Mayo Clinic in Rochester, Minnesota, under the Workmen's Compensation Law. He was operated on there and restored to health.

In the fall of 1942, Griffin's ability attracted the attention of the international union headquarters and he became an international staff representative. Four years later he became director of District 26. His election followed a hard-fought contest against the incumbent, James Quinn, whose aide he had been. Quinn was a close friend of Murray's. Griffin ran against Quinn anyway, because, he said, "No matter what you did for the guy, it didn't seem to satisfy him. He was hard on the guys he should have been easy with and easy with the guys he should have been tough on." As a result of Griffin's act of revolt, the district was thrown into turmoil. When Quinn fired him for insubordination, he went back into the plant and campaigned as a rank-and-filer. "Phil Murray," he said with a smile, "didn't do anything to help me." Griffin's effrontery angered Murray, whose whole background set him strongly against such acts of rebellion. Thus Griffin's unconventional success made him a marked man.

Early in 1952, McDonald sought to win Griffin over. He dispatched a fellow district director, George Medrick, to Griffin. According to Griffin, the emissary delivered this message: "If you are prepared to be a member of Dave's team, there will be no problems about your being elected District Director, or about your relationship with the international office." Griffin replied emphatically that he would not commit himself to McDonald as a future president.

After Griffin's sharp rejection of fealty, McDonald sent another messenger into the district. This time, Hugh Carcella of Philadelphia was sent to James McPhillips, a Griffin assistant, to sound him out on the possibility of running against Griffin with McDonald's support. Griffin soon got wind of this. At the next executive board meeting, he went up to McDonald: "Listen, bastard, I'll take you on, you son of a bitch, if that's what you want." Then Griffin informed Murray of the McDonald maneuver. "I was beginning to get along quite well with Phil in spite of my early rebellion. Then Phil died."

CHAPTER **2**

McDonald's Succession

The more things a man is ashamed of,
the more respectable he is.

GEORGE BERNARD SHAW

McDonald utilized Murray's illnesses in 1941 and 1948 to build up his influence. Then, 'during Murray's serious 1951 illness, McDonald took over the reins of union government and instructed his public-relations men to revise the Murray obituary. But Murray recovered and promptly learned of McDonald's meticulous preparations. He exploded to a visitor, "See what that dirty little son of a bitch has done to me. He's got me buried." For weeks this was Murray's constant refrain.

On January 3 and 4, 1952, a special two-day convention was held in Atlantic City to mobilize union support for basic steel negotiations at a critical juncture of the Korean War. By request of President Truman, the union leadership had agreed to continue work beyond the expiration of the contract on December 31, 1951. Since no contract, no work, was part of the union's traditional articles of faith, the membership assembled in convention was clearly entitled to an explanation. The convention agreed to continue working for forty-five days, while negotiations of a sort continued.

Having disposed for the moment of the external foe, Murray drew a long breath and glanced around the leaders seated on the platform and into the faces of the delegates. His face set and slightly flushed, his tone more deliberate, he spoke:

"Some day in the not too distant future we will be meeting you in National Convention again. That will be in May, when you have a Constitutional Convention. . . . You will have a great work to perform there,

I know, and I am going to help you perform some of that work in that convention because whatever life I have got shall be dedicated to bringing this organization closer to you. There are going to be no little dictatorships in this union, no connivances, no bribery. There is going to be no money used out of the treasury of this organization to buy the friendship of anybody in this union to promote any man to any office in this organization and you are going to help the officers of your union, when a Convention comes around, to see to it that you have the kind of a constitution that will permit you, the owners of this organization, to play a part in the operation of its affairs. That is a principle to which we adhere, and the bigger you get and the more responsibilities you assume, the closer you must live with the people who pay the taxes."

On the eve of the May 1952 convention in Philadelphia, the international executive board met to discuss the confrontation with the steel management and the union's equally abrasive internal situation. By word and disdainful gesture, Murray made it emphatically clear to all those assembled that McDonald's days as a power in the union were numbered. Emery Bacon, then the educational director, recalled the temper of the occasion:

"Everybody in the official family knew this was the end. McDonald was completely whipped and frightened. But he was unwilling to fight back at this time, although he had some very strong directors supporting him. Mike Walsh of New England, for example. Not so much because he loved McDonald but because he felt that Murray was going too far. Walsh was always opposed to total centralization of power. He went to McDonald; C. B. Newell, another director, went to him; a few others went to him. They said: 'Fight, if you don't fight you're going to be destroyed.' I remember late that afternoon. It must have been 5:30 or 6 at the Bellevue-Stratford Hotel. I was in the lobby with a number of District Directors, staff people, some local union people, some people from Pittsburgh. We were talking about the event, how Murray had really stripped David of all his authority. In fact, the constitution had not yet been changed. But it was accomplished already. Murray had that kind of power. There was no question about it. Everybody knew it. McDonald was disgraced and he refused to take Murray on. He showed how weak he was. Then McDonald came down the elevator. Generally he had with him a number of people in his retinue. That evening he came down alone. His own people had fled. He stepped off the elevator and all his old friends, cronies, were there, including some of the District Directors. They gave him a faint 'hello' but not a single person went up to him to shake his hand or leave the hotel with him. For some strange reason, never explained to me, he did point to me and say: 'I wonder if you would come with me.' I walked with him up to his own hotel. As we went down the street, he said, 'Wasn't that quite a show this afternoon?' and I said 'It really was!' I said, 'Why in the world did you stand there and take it? It would have been better if you had stood up and fought this. At least you would have the respect of the group and at the end you would have been a bigger man.' McDonald said to me, 'You've got it all wrong. Murray's not going to live.' I said, 'You're kidding.' 'No,' McDonald said, 'I know. He won't live. The chances are he won't live the year out. That's the reason why I took it. I'll inherit everything.' "

In the days following, the convention unanimously voted several significant changes in the constitution, all designed to subtract from the powers of the secretary-treasurer and to place them in the union presidency. First, the financial power of the secretary-treasurer was limited, so that the employment of staff representatives, even in the secretary-treasurer's office, was "subject to the approval of the International President." This brought the McDonald empire under Murray's direct control. Murray would talk witheringly about the "fellows in the backroom," meaning Howard Hague, McDonald's office manager.

Second, Murray was determined to break up the appearance of a duumvirate. Until then, the officers' reports made to the convention were signed by the president and the secretary-treasurer. The constitution was now changed to require the signature of the vice-president as one of the officers jointly responsible for the report.

Third, in the area of international union elections, the constitution was changed so that no paid staff representative of the international would be eligible for the office of international teller. Here Murray sought to prevent any McDonald appointee from occupying a decisive position in a referendum election—which had not yet been held.

Fourth, Murray sought to remove still further control of the election machinery from the secretary-treasurer's office. Henceforth, all "return sheets" from local unions were no longer to be forwarded to the international secretary-treasurer's office but to the "International Tellers, in care of the International Headquarters." In several other places, the international tellers acquired functions and responsibilities heretofore carried by the secretary-treasurer. Among these was the power to retain the services of the Honest Ballot Association or a similar organization to tabulate the returns.

Murray attacked McDonald's position on two levels by cutting down his power of appointment and by diminishing the influence of his palace guard. President Murray, not Secretary-Treasurer McDonald, was the man to look to. By reducing the secretary-treasurer's control over nomination and election procedures, Murray was arming himself against the possibility that McDonald might attempt to stage a contest in the forthcoming nomination period scheduled to start in November 1952, with the election to take place the following February.

For the next few months, most political activity in the union was held in abeyance because of the strike, which finally occurred, and the Stevenson-Eisenhower campaign. The union had contributed heavily to Stevenson. The day after the national election Murray stayed home, wounded in spirit and body. On Thursday he returned to the Pittsburgh office, disturbed about the state of the nation as well as of the union. He prepared to preside over the CIO convention a week later in Los Angeles, and on his way there he had arranged to address the District 38 conference in San Francisco. The evening he left for the train, Murray asked his secretary, Ann Benedict, to call Emery Bacon and Tom Murray, one of the most knowledgeable headquarters-staff employees and assistant to the secretary-treasurer, to come to his office. For more than two hours Philip Murray unburdened himself about the future and his decision to make very substantial changes within the union immediately upon his return from California.

He also confided that he was planning to "get rid" of Hague. His cleanup operation was to include the reading of McDonald out of the union, and replacing him with somebody who was concerned about the union and not about his own image. "Certain people," Murray said bitterly, had been "using the union for their selfish purposes—the wealth of the union, the power of the union."

Murray and his wife entrained for San Francisco. That Saturday night, November 8, after delivering a speech to six hundred delegates at the District 38 conference, Murray, obviously weary, went to bed. Walter J. Burke, then a district director, recalled that Murray spoke for over an hour but had delivered the speech in a low key "even for Phil Murray, who was not particularly high-key under normal circumstances. When I shook hands with him, I noticed he was trembling." Murray smiled cordially and said: "I'll see you down in Los Angeles sometime tomorrow, Walter. Good night, have a good rest." The next morning, as Burke was waiting for the elevator, staff man Joe Angelo came out of his room looking terrible and told him that Murray had died of a heart attack during the night.

McDonald recalled that he had solicitously "tried to persuade Phil not to go to San Francisco; it was too much. But he took the train. On Saturday, one of my aides got a plane and we flew to San Francisco where I was supposed to speak to the conference the following day. We went up to the Mark Hopkins Hotel; I found the airline had shipped my baggage to Los Angeles instead of San Francisco. There I was in a tan sports coat and a pair of green slacks. Mr. Murray was speaking across the street in the Huntington Hotel at the big dinner and I was ashamed to go to the dinner in the outfit I had on. Finally I was able to get a clean shirt somewhere and went over and sat at the back of the hall until he finished his speech and then went up and said hello to him and took a bow. The next morning I got this shocking news that Mr. Murray had died. I went down to see Mrs. Murray and asked if there was anything I could do; she said she'd like me to handle all the details. So I was able to get TWA to get an airplane for the whole crowd of Steelworkers who were there. We made arrangements with the Flying Tiger outfit to fly Phil's body back to Chicago. I worked all day on the telephone and made arrangements for us to be met in Pittsburgh. It was a foggy day in San Francisco, but sometime during the day we got out and the Constellation got into Pittsburgh."

Bacon recalls that Murray's coffin came back to Pittsburgh by train, having been transferred from the plane in Chicago. Both McDonald and the dead leader were arriving at about the same time: "There was quite an emotional problem—should one go to Pennsylvania Station to meet the coffin or to the Allegheny County Airport and meet the TWA charter flight. They both came in about nine or ten o'clock at night. This question worked away in most everybody's mind: where do we go, do we go out and meet McDonald, or do we go and meet the coffin. Nobody was told what to do. . . . I, myself, was terribly devoted to Murray but I did go to the airport to meet the chartered flight. I took my wife out . . . I suppose, mainly for the spectacle that was involved in seeing this flight come in—all of us sitting in the Ambassadors Club and getting reports on the progress of the chartered McDonald flight across the continent. Also, seeing all the people who would gather out there to welcome the new emperor and the retinue that would get off the plane and get into the limousines that were lined up. We did not go up and shake hands with David or greet him. We were sick, really sick, but we did watch what happened. Tom Murray, on the other hand, went to the railroad station and met the body. He did not go out to meet McDonald. Very few accompanied Tom. The king was dead."

The funeral arrangements were made and the eulogies delivered. McDonald moved confidently to win the board's agreement that he become acting president. The district directors—as members of the international executive board—deadened their remembrance of Murray's plans to drop McDonald. With Murray gone, the efforts made by McDonald over the years quickly paid off. He was ready to take over the presidency, which now embraced all the traditional powers of that office plus those heretofore resident in the secretary-treasurer. McDonald had indeed inherited it all.

One of McDonald's confidants at the time believed that McDonald fundamentally still had "grave doubts that he could swing it." But, he said, McDonald expected his friends to "respond to different kinds of bait or commands. Everybody was pretty well catalogued." Still, "Nobody really wanted him to be president. Even good friends didn't want him. The union had essentially been a social and economic crusade; they were afraid he would cuddle up to the companies."

McDonald's main objective was to keep the lightning from striking Vice-President James Thimmes. While the latter could hold on to that office, he lacked support for any other. Whatever influence he might have had was whittled down by McDonald over the years.

With Thimmes out of the running, Joseph Germano and others of the Western bloc of directors, having quickly concluded that there was no practical alternative to McDonald, sought now to push their candidate for secretary-treasurer. Directors in the Eastern bloc—Martin (Mike) Walsh of New England, Joseph Molony of New York, and William J. Hart of Pittsburgh—were enlisted in McDonald's behalf. At this time a bosom companion of McDonald's, Hart had set his sights for the job of secretary-treasurer. In effect, McDonald succeeded to the presidency because he was able to maintain a split between the Eastern and the self-styled Western bloc of directors, who could not get together on a common candidate.

The first name to come up prominently for secretary-treasurer was John Doherty, formerly director in St. Louis and more recently an international representative in the Chicago office of the Steelworkers. From time to time, when McDonald took off on foreign travel, Doherty had been called by Murray to act in McDonald's place. Like Murray, Doherty had come out of the Mine Workers and was a fixed part of the establishment. To Germano and others, he seemed the "least controversial." Germano and Al F. Kojetinsky, the St. Louis director, closeted themselves with McDonald to push Doherty, asking McDonald to "level" with them about his choice. McDonald promised to be frank, but subsequently a canvass of some of the directors closest to McDonald indicated that Doherty lacked McDonald's support.

"I had the votes," said Germano, "to take Johnny Doherty and beat any candidate that David put up. But I didn't want to do that because it's not starting out right, because it would be misinterpreted right away. This is the first mistake we made. If we would have done that to Dave McDonald and beat his ass at the time, we'd have made a better Dave McDonald."

Other names were suggested. McDonald preferred Bill Hart, director of District 19, although he avoided saying so directly. But the majority were adamantly anti-Hart. "Messengers" from McDonald reasoned with Germano: "Tim Flynn, then a staff representative, was sent to shove me around. 'O.K., Timothy,' I said, 'you got a job to do. Aren't you assigned to give Germano the working-over? Come on, Timothy. Beat the hell out of me.' They didn't have the guts to do it. As I say, the union could have been taken over by the board; they lost a golden opportunity."

At length Paul Rusen, director of District 23, pointed out the obvious to McDonald: if he persisted in naming Hart, he might split the board and perhaps make his own position less secure. Instead, Rusen suggested a fellow Ohioan, I. W. Abel of Canton, director of District 27, then forty-five, who had served on the board for ten years and would be agreeable to the sponsors of the other candidates. He was quiet, almost self-effacing in manner, with no active enemies. Besides, Abel was a Protestant, and it might be desirable to have at least one non-Catholic among the international officers.

At this point the United Steelworkers found itself, under the calendar of its constitution, at the start of a month-long nominating period. Theoretically, there was time for another candidate to be entered against McDonald. But who? Only the Western bloc could have been the source of such unprecedented insurgency. How to avoid such a development? To assuage the bruised feelings of the Western bloc and to abort the acute antagonism of its district directors, McDonald now proposed that James Thimmes, retained as the union vice-president, become the union's choice also as a vice-president of the Congress of Industrial Organizations (one of nine, the eight others representing other unions affiliated with the CIO), while McDonald would consent to take the lesser post as member of the more numerous executive board of the CIO. Thus Thimmes would acquire some additional prestige without diminishing McDonald's. The Steelworkers executive board had now arranged its trio of international officers, and the succession of McDonald was settled. In a self-congratulatory appraisal, McDonald marveled at "this stroke that I had. . . . It made Thimmes happy because as an officer of the CIO he thought it projected him nationally, and by agreeing to having Abel as secretary-treasurer of the union, it kept the others from being at one another's throat by eliminating a fight between Hart and Doherty."

In this way, a week before his fiftieth birthday, McDonald became the uncontested president of the United Steelworkers of America.

The First Year and the Men
Around McDonald

A man may be festooned with the whole
haberdashery of success . . .

RUDYARD KIPLING

About a month after he became president, McDonald invited a group of
union people to his home for a dinner party. With considerable serious-
ness, he told his guests he wanted to be a good president, a better president than Murray. In an unusual mood of self-criticism, he acknowledged
his weaknesses, his tendency to hedge and backtrack. But, he said, it was
up to the group with him that night to keep him on the proper track. Its
function was to meet once a week and make him do things he had committed himself to do.

"Well, he never held the first meeting of that group," Emery Bacon
said. "Very soon you couldn't talk to McDonald about serious things. He
devoted less and less time to the union. Other activities absorbed his
attention. The union was leaderless for long stretches at a time."

During the spring of 1953 McDonald began his first negotiations as
president. He wanted an early settlement before the reopening date of
the existing contract. Business conditions made spring a strategic time to
negotiate an increase.* The national economy was booming, and the
demand for steel was at peak levels. Companies were operating behind
schedule, their order books filled for four to six months.

* *Collective Bargaining in the Basic Steel Industry: A Study of the Public Interest and the Role of Government.* Directed by E. Robert Livernash. Department
of Labor, 1961, p. 284.

Despite this desirable bargaining position, McDonald was convinced that the membership, a year after the June–July strike of 1952, would accept almost any offer, relieved that they would not have to endure another work stoppage. Some of his colleagues, however, believed that he should not throw away his bargaining advantages by agreeing to a contract two weeks before the expiration date, which is what he did.

At the same time, the United Automobile Workers under Walter P. Reuther had won improvements from General Motors and Ford in a contract that still had two years to run. Prior to the UAW contract, the steel companies had protested that no mid-contract wage increase was justified, because the Consumer Price Index had remained almost stable. In the face of company resistance, McDonald "made no strike threats." But with the pressures of the UAW settlement, it became obvious that the Steelworkers could get something more, the only question being how much. In a mood of mutual gratification, McDonald and John A. Stephens, U.S. Steel's vice-president in charge of industrial relations, praised each other for their "statesmanlike conduct" and "honorable compromise."

A year after McDonald became president, a huge celebration took place in Pittsburgh. November 28, 1953, was proclaimed David J. McDonald Day by Mayor David L. Lawrence. The *Wall Street Journal* gave the event a send-off in a big page-1 story: PITTSBURGH BANNERED, LIGHTED AND BEDECKED, STAGING "DAY FOR DAVE." DINNERS, TELEVISED SPEECHES, FLOOR SHOWS TO HONOR STEELWORKERS' CHIEF MCDONALD. "More than 3,000 men and women from labor and industry, religion and education, politics and the professions, will turn out here tomorrow night to honor David J. McDonald as Pittsburgh's 'man of steel.'

"It will be quite . . . an elaborate testimonial for the 51-year-old leader of the CIO United Steelworkers. All downtown Pittsburgh buildings will be lighted from top to bottom.

"The Mayor-elect of New York City [Robert F. Wagner] and the chairman of United States Steel Corp. will speak at the main testimonial banquet in the William Penn Hotel. Their words will be piped to a satellite dinner in the Roosevelt Hotel several blocks away.

"General Chairman of 'David J. McDonald Day' is William J. Hart, director of United Steelworkers' District 19, . . . a dynamic labor personality who also serves on Pittsburgh's Board of Public Education."

To inaugurate the era of McDonald, district directors and staff representatives had assembled to pay tribute. Leaders of industry were given honored place. Ben Fairless, president of U.S. Steel, announced that labor and management are "inseparably bound together in a state of economic matrimony."

Some of the directors and staff men shamefacedly observed later that

Philip Murray would not have tolerated such a spectacle. But Hart said: "Look, we're going to give this guy everything he wants. If you call this brown-nosing, all right. I'm brown-nosing all the way."

Man of Steel

Several months later, a biography was published entitled *Man of Steel,* written by George Kelly and Edwin Beechler and published by North American Book Company of New York. It told of McDonald's rise from humble beginnings to present greatness. It related how he had attended night classes, first at Duquesne University and later at Carnegie Tech's School of Industries, to fill out his high-school credits. In 1922 he left his job in the storeroom of the National Tube Company's Continental Works and went to work in the office of the Wheeling Steel Products Company in downtown Pittsburgh, as a typist and switchboard operator. In the summer of 1923 a local UMW official took McDonald to see Murray, who gave him a job.

The purpose of the biography was not only to provide McDonald with a historic past, an impeccable genealogy as a trade-union leader, but also to bury all the stories of Murray's hostility to him. His biographers hailed McDonald as "the master mason of the pedestal that lifted the richly-gifted elder labor statesman, Murray, into the high public position that he won and held."

The book went on:

McDonald resembled anything but the popular conception of a labor leader. He looked more like a college football coach, big, broad shouldered, blue-eyed, handsome with wavy silver-white hair. Unlike the old-style labor leaders who thought the members wanted them to put up a "poor front," this man of steel dresses to fit the occasion and in keeping with the growing prestige of labor. While seeking the best possible in life for the steelworkers, he believes their officers should set the pace by putting their best foot forward. . . . Although favoring sports outfits and tweeds with bow ties, he wears "Brooks Brothers" business suits when conservative clothes are in order. His strenuous unending round of union business, civic, social and sports activities has kept his figure to a solid 200 pounds—plus.

However, heavy strain of the Steelworkers' presidency, unceasing demands in the banquet circuit and more worries than a big-league baseball manager are exacting their toll. Deep lines are etched on his Irish face and an occasional nervous twitch of the head shows the constant pressures under which he lives.

The biographers relate how McDonald modestly had sought to discourage their attentions. They caught up with him as he boarded the

United States on his way to Europe after David J. McDonald Day. One of them leaped onto a "lifting gangplank" to catch up with their reluctant subject. Once on board, the biographer managed to extract from the finally agreeable labor leader what he regarded as the quintessential McDonald: "Summing up his own career, the Man of Steel gazed out of a porthole and said: 'The greatest influence on McDonald has been McDonald. You have to believe things and feel things for yourself. My mother and father were greater influences on me than Lewis, Murray, Green, Gompers and all the others in the labor movement put together. . . . Lewis and Murray influenced my mind, of course. But they didn't change it one bit.' " The biographer concludes: "There isn't much more a man of destiny can say."

The biography was greeted with public laughter and embarrassment. Finally, orders went out to recall all copies of *Man of Steel*. One union official recalled with a grin: "There was a big expensive book burning."

McDonald's Men

The men clustered around McDonald were of various kinds and qualities. Some he had inherited from Phil Murray—such as Arthur J. Goldberg, the all but indispensable general counsel. For the negotiation and administration of contracts, he relied increasingly upon technical personnel, who were able to expand their responsibility under his permissive presidency. There were concentric rings of bosom companions, some of them dating back to his early days. Chief among these was Howard Hague, who was rapidly elevated to a special place. To this squad of cronies-in-waiting some were added or substracted, depending on the whim of their leader. A third category of diverse "experts" often performed as ambassadors to other exciting worlds that spun McDonald away from the boredom of the union's administrative activities. For a while, the most important among these was Phil Weiss, a man with a wide range of interests and contacts that McDonald found useful. Robert Post became McDonald's specialist in the promotional arts. Phil Regan, the Singing Cop, became a self-styled expert in human relations.

When Lee Pressman was dropped as general counsel early in 1948, Murray replaced him with Arthur Goldberg, recommended by Joe Germano. Goldberg was a member of a Chicago law firm with a general practice, in which he undertook union assignments that increasingly occupied the greater part of his time. In this capacity, he represented Germano's District 31. During World War II, he served in the Office of Strategic Services, as a contact man in Washington and overseas with foreign labor groups. He then became general counsel of both the Steelworkers and the Congress of Industrial Organizations.

For at least the two years between 1950 and 1952, both Vice-President Thimmes and Goldberg had expressed distress with McDonald's personal activities. Their reports to Murray, added to his own misgivings, caused an unexpected explosion on a day when Murray was being visited at his office by his four-year-old grandson, upon whom he loved to shower attention. Thimmes and Goldberg appeared on what seemed to be urgent business, so he settled the youngster on a couch to one side. When the vice-president and the general counsel reached a point that Murray decided required the presence of the secretary-treasurer, he summoned McDonald from his adjoining office. Their conversation soon turned into a disagreement and finally into a dispute. Murray's anger towered and his language to McDonald became so vehement that Murray's private secretary, Ann Benedict, quickly trotted the bewildered and forgotten child out of the room. When she returned, Murray was still storming. While he spoke, Thimmes and Goldberg became flushed; this confrontation between Murray and McDonald was more than they had bargained for. McDonald lamely tried to offer explanations and finally Murray dismissed him from his office. At that point, Murray wheeled on Thimmes and Goldberg:

"Why, you weak sisters. Here you have been feeding me stuff about this guy for two years, and when the time comes, you just sit there and let me do all the talking. Why didn't you talk up with McDonald here, as you do when he is not?"

When Murray died, Goldberg's relationship with McDonald was insecure. "Distrust and dismay" at first characterized Goldberg's attitude toward him. But Goldberg, said a district director, was a "good servant of the union and worked hard."

Not many months after McDonald became president, it was clear that his extracurricular interests had become dominant. Increasingly, he thrust important decisions onto Goldberg's shoulders, a burden that Goldberg did not shirk.

"While we often criticized Arthur, as we later criticized David Feller, his associate and successor, to an even greater degree for assumption of power, in many ways that charge was unjust," said a district director. "They were really filling a vacuum. McDonald just couldn't make any damned decisions. For a long time Arthur influenced the destiny of the union more than anyone realized."

Such active intervention by Goldberg enabled McDonald to reign as president. He had the trappings of status, the emoluments of office, and ready command of the union's treasury. While McDonald more than once might have felt irked at his dependence on Goldberg—or, more precisely, annoyed with the recognition that Goldberg was receiving—he recognized the reciprocal advantages in their relationship.

In the words of a critical board member, Goldberg finally "became a national figure through a chain of circumstances, starting off with the circumstance known as McDonald." McDonald had made Goldberg possible while Goldberg made McDonald viable.

The Coterie

On another level, McDonald enveloped some of his friends in a regimen of demanding social activities. Some balked. One staff member told why: "If you weren't at his house, you had to be at home, subject to a telephone call at eight o'clock in the evening or midnight. You were immediately supposed to go to his house. You had to be ready to travel with him if he wanted to go to New York or California, pick up his bag, pick him up, take him to the airport, be a companion. I couldn't stand it. But the individuals who did this had his ear. They were also subservient because everything they had depended on his whim. So long as they kept his good will, they prospered."

Such people usually had a title of some sort, with an office and secretaries. Generally they were required only to be the president's companions in waiting.

A pattern of behavior evolved to match McDonald's exalted station. A dramatic entrance heralded his presence. Outriders, a flying wedge of bodyguards, and a squad of protective staff representatives surrounded him as he and his men strode through a hotel lobby or down a corridor, proudly and purposefully, looking neither to the left nor to the right. Ordinary observers prudently pressed themselves against the walls to avoid being run over by the awesome aggregation.

When McDonald arrived at an airport, reception committees were expected. Late at night or early in the morning, the leader found staff men waiting to make him welcome and to make sure that he would be spared the chores usually attendant on arrival and departure. Taxis were for peasants; chauffeured limousines were in. His chief bodyguard, Charles Barranco, who received the salary of a top-level staff representative with expenses to match, often drove the presidential car.

McDonald disdained to ride an elevator in the company of the uninvited. Hotels were regularly alerted to the time of his arrival. When he rode the elevator, nobody else was permitted to use it.

An intimate group of attendants were allowed to ride the elevators with him: Barranco, Robert (Bud) Flannery, Clark Applebe, Johnny Cunniff, Robert Jahn, Edward Nassar, and after 1956, Maurice (Duke) Moran. All on the union payroll with generous expense accounts, these and others were deployed around various departments at the international headquarters. McDonald bestowed favors and then withdrew them.

They became so completely dependent that they seemed to lose all sense of their personal identification.

The chief steward at headquarters for McDonald's interests was Howard Hague. Among his other functions, he was reputed to run an internal espionage operation. In the surveillance of staff, beginning about 1955, McDonald and Hague had the support of Robert A. Maheu Associates, with offices in Los Angeles and Washington. Maheu or his representative would walk around the office, interview the staff, photograph them, ask questions, take notes on everything, and then report to Hague. As an ex-FBI man, Maheu brought with him the aura of authority. All in all, he was an unusual phenomenon in the internal life of a union. His special talents were later employed by the eccentric billionaire Howard Hughes.

Staff people and at least one international officer reported extensive wire tapping at home and office. One staff man said: "My own phone was tapped. To keep the stuff from being recorded we would turn on some electric equipment, like an air conditioner. . . . I went over to the Bell Telephone Company one time to inquire. I knew one of the officers there. I told him I heard that this was going on. They admitted it. Hague was responsible. But Hague did so many evil things. This was only one of them. . . . Hague tried to get something on everybody. . . . One man in a district who had fallen out of favor and was making trouble was doped, stripped with a woman, and pictures taken. It destroyed that man. He was completely innocent."

In Washington, Frank N. (Nordy) Hoffmann, a former Notre Dame football player, had become the union's legislative and political director. As the union's chief lobbyist, he maintained what took on the aspect of a McDonald embassy in the nation's capital. Thanks to an unlimited expense account, Hoffmann's well-tailored bulk made an impressive splash on Capitol Hill and in restaurants around town. He was an expansive host, and no one was faster in picking up the tab. He gave luncheons and dinners at the Touchdown Club, where he entertained those whom he and McDonald delighted to honor or sought to impress. During Phil Murray's day, Hoffmann imperiously stood guard at his hotel-room door, screening visitors. Under McDonald, he was transformed into a pillar of his personal establishment, became privy to his secrets, chartered private planes, and was a conduit of McDonald's wishes. At the union's Washington headquarters, separated by a floor from the Goldberg law offices, Hoffmann's activities were regarded with such profound distaste by Meyer Bernstein, the union's director of international affairs, that he disassociated himself by word and deed and gesture from the Hoffmann jurisdiction. For example, he insisted on having his own telephone line, separate and apart from the Washington headquarters switchboard. As one of the union's pioneer organizers and a man of almost quixotic integrity, Bernstein had attained respect and special status that even Hoffmann could not readily impair. Like the biblical Mordecai, Bernstein sat at the union's gates, and he and Hoffmann glared at each other.

Soon McDonald's own wide acquaintance with night spots began to produce a harvest of strange companions.

Robert Post, a combination of theatrical agent and film maker, came on strong after Murray's death. Late in 1953 he persuaded McDonald of the great value of filming the union's activities. The first large-scale effort was at the 1954 convention in Atlantic City, McDonald's first as president. McDonald announced exultantly that Post had eight hours of film "in cans" and that soon every local union could submit a filmed report of the convention to its membership.

Closest among McDonald's friends for a period of years was Phil Regan, who parlayed a tenor voice and a hail-fellow-well-met disposition into a formidable public-relations practice. A constant companion, Regan escorted McDonald in and out of the hot spots and introduced him to his network of friends in show business. In return, Regan gained access to a variety of industrial and political clients. As noted before, he went on the payroll of the Steelworkers Union as a public-relations adviser.

Regan's view of his role was not modest. (Later he represented National Distillers, Budweiser, and other companies.) He became known for opening and closing political and union conventions with "God Bless America" and Irish ballads. While still a singer in various night clubs, in Pittsburgh and elsewhere, he would bring notables who were present into the act: "And this song is dedicated to Ben Fairless, that great industrial statesman—hello there, Mr. Fairless." McDonald relished his friend's amiable exploitation.

Regan worked for McDonald and the Steelworkers Union from 1956 to 1963. As a "human relations" man, he claimed to have brought together President Eisenhower and McDonald in the closing days of the Taft-Hartley Act's injunction period of the steel strike of 1959–60. "I told Dave he ought to get together with President Eisenhower and iron the matter out. But he said he didn't think that was possible. So I called Tom Stephens, the President's appointment secretary. Stephens said he was sure that the President would want to see McDonald. Within five minutes the White House called and McDonald was told that the President would certainly want to see him."

Dismay turned into anxiety when McDonald's union colleagues contemplated his intimacy with Phil Weiss. Weiss seems to have made his first appearance before some of McDonald's union associates including Abel following a visit through the Great Lakes Steel Company plant, as part of the "labor-management" good-will tours in early 1954. When the union and company representatives had concluded their stroll around the plant, they repaired to McDonald's hotel suite for refreshment. As the ceremony was being concluded, McDonald said: "Wait a minute, fellows, I want you to meet a friend of mine who's right in the next room. Come on in, Phil." Weiss came in. "Tom," said McDonald turning to Thomas E. Milsop, then the chief executive of Great Lakes, "Phil here is an oil-and-grease man. I'd like you to buy some of his oil and grease." McDonald laughed.

The Weiss dossier had grown heavy in various investigative bureaus of city, state, and federal agencies. He had been arrested and convicted because of involvement in a big stolen auto-parts ring but kept pushing petroleum products "through his labor union sources." During 1953, McDonald was twice warned by authorities of Weiss's unsavory character; Weiss nevertheless showed up at the David J. McDonald Day dinner in Pittsburgh that November.

Weiss, reported in the press to be an intimate of the racketeer Johnny Dio, described himself as a "labor consultant." In 1960 the McDonalds tossed the Weisses a big wedding party in Alexandria, Virginia. When the marriage went on the rocks, Weiss boasted to his wife, according to her testimony in court, that "as long as Teamsters Boss James Hoffa and David McDonald, United Steelworkers President, are my friends," no court would force him to give her anything. Matters were patched up between them later.

In 1959 Weiss refused to testify before the Senate Select Committee to Investigate Improper Practices in Labor or Management, better known as the McClellan Committee, whose investigators were probing his relations with McDonald, Hoffa, and Charles Johnson of the Carpenters. Weiss had been charged with involvement with Johnson in a Yonkers Raceway payoff: in return for calling off a strike, a concession was reportedly granted in filling stations surrounding the track. At the same time, the *New York Times* also reported Weiss as head of a New York ore-products company, and of his boasting about "pull" at the White House. He was then free on $25,000 bond pending appeal from his conviction in Detroit. For his part, Hoffa denied that he had put the Weiss products on a "recommended" list for purchase by union truck drivers. "I wouldn't sell a gallon of gas or oil for Phil Weiss or anyone else," said Hoffa, who by then was preoccupied with his own involvement with the law. At that time, Robert F. Kennedy, the committee general counsel, asked Weiss, "Isn't it correct that you are probably the foremost in this country as far as selling your rackets connections, not only with racket labor union officials, but with racketeers in the United States?" Weiss took the Fifth Amendment.

Why McDonald should have persisted in this relationship with Weiss puzzled his friends. The fact was that Weiss provided steel on the gray market to hard-pressed buyers: "If a strike was going on and steel was hard to procure, he was able to get it for certain companies," his wife swore.

When McDonald was attending the AFL-CIO Executive Council meeting in Miami Beach in 1957, he and Weiss spent considerable time together and occupied neighboring suites. During these sessions, the AFL-CIO Executive Council was developing its Ethical Practice Codes. The secretary of the Ethical Practices Committee was Arthur Goldberg. It could not have been a comfortable duality for him.

At this time, A. H. Raskin observed dryly in the *Times* that McDonald "was a strong supporter for ethical codes designed to root out underworld influence in labor." How McDonald reconciled his ethical concerns with his relationship to Weiss was rather difficult to determine; the New York district attorney's office had already ticketed Weiss as a friend of underworld characters, such as Frank Costello and the late Abner (Longie) Zwillman.

During the same period, Phil Regan's assiduous cultivation of the great and near great helped McDonald as much as his "human relations" clients. It soon became apparent that McDonald's eagerness for social recognition was worth cultivating. Consequently, when Vice-President Nixon entertained Queen Elizabeth of England during her tour of the United States in October 1957, he invited McDonald as his "special guest." John O'Donnell, a New York *Daily News* columnist, noted that Nixon had passed over AFL-CIO President George Meany, Auto Workers President Walter Reuther, and other AFL-CIO bigwigs. McDonald began to talk about "my friend Dick."

In the practical life of politics and legislative maneuver, the influence and friendship of the Vice-President of the United States were hardly to be rejected. With his eyes on the 1960 campaign, Nixon was intent on mollifying the opposition of organized labor; union spokesmen, in turn, would not spurn the solicitation of a man who might one day become President.

CHAPTER **4**

First Open Challenge:
The 1955 Special Election

My friends forsake me like a memory lost.

JOHN CLARE

In March 1955, Steelworkers Vice-President James Thimmes died. McDonald was now determined to put his own man in. Eugene Maurice of District 13 was assigned to sound out sentiments of the other directors. By phone and in person, after a few preliminaries he would turn the conversation to the topic of filling the vice-presidential vacancy, suggesting that "The general feeling is that Howard Hague should get the job."

"What?" one district director said. "You're kidding. McDonald's male secretary? Why, the son of a bitch never saw the inside of a steel plant. He doesn't know the first damn thing about our union. What the hell are we making him vice-president for?" "Well, that's what the boys want and I just wanted to know where you stand when we take a vote on the board."

Maurice's inquiries spread consternation. The reply of Joe Molony, the director of District 4 covering New York, was direct: "All right, I'll tell you. I'll vote against the s.o.b. if no one else does. He would be a castastrophe."

Molony was determined to head off the maneuver: "I reached McDonald by phone in Miami Beach. He was out in his cabana. I summoned him from the cabana, which miffed him off. I said, 'Dave, I just got an extraordinary phone call. Maurice is conducting a poll of the executive board to determine if he can get Hague elected, and he's indicated to me quite clearly that Hague is your choice. I want to confirm

33

that—do you want Hague?' He said, 'Maurice has no right to say that I want Hague. Whoever the board wants is all right with me.' "

Molony persisted: "Well, do you approve of a director or board member polling the board instead of waiting until such time as we get together and can make some decisions?" "No," said McDonald, "I don't approve of that at all." "Well," said Molony, "call Maurice and tell him to stop bothering people and trying to put them on the God-damned spot." "I see," said McDonald. "By the way, Joe, how do you feel about Hague?" "How do I feel about Hague? I'll vote against him. Let me sum up my position for you so this will help guide you. I'm for any member of the international executive board—in fact for anyone for vice-president—with the exception of Hague and Molony."

Shortly afterward, McDonald called a meeting of the union's international executive board in Washington at the Mayflower Hotel, with Hague also present. To the full board, McDonald announced his intention to have Hague named acting vice-president. Molony was immediately on his feet. "All right," he said, "we'll have a little debate on this. First off: Hague here is not a member of the executive board. Out! He's got to leave the room."

"So," said Molony, "McDonald had to chase him out. Then we started into the God-damnedest battle you've ever seen or heard in all your life." Reporters waiting in the lobby could hear curses and roars of defiance.

As Molony recalled it: "Opposed to Hague were Jim Griffin, Tom Shane, Walter Burke, Larry Sefton, Bill Hart, George Medrick. The rest were less than enthusiastic but they were going along. We stood up and fought. This threw poor McDonald into a terrible tizzy. There were ten of us, bitterly opposed, out of the thirty-two or thirty-three directors on the board at that time. Oh, and Mike Walsh of New England; he was a gallant supporter of the anti–McDonald-Hague forces."

McDonald, however, maneuvered Hague's designation as acting vice-president. The board meeting broke up in confusion. "We who opposed Hague decided to have a caucus," said Molony. "Our hope was to strip the Hague appointment of significance. But McDonald had the bind on that. He announced an election would be ordered shortly."

A little later, McDonald met with Molony—just the two of them in a room. McDonald's jaw was working, his face twitching: "Do you know what you did to me down there in the board meeting, Joe? If you were in the United Mine Workers of America, you'd be dead now." Molony replied, "You silly son of a bitch, first of all we're not the United Mine Workers of America and I don't like people to threaten me, and don't you ever try it again." McDonald paled; slowly he reorganized his features. "Well, I'm just pointing out the difference," he said. He proceeded to apologize.

Molony left him and went to the caucus, which was in full swing with the purpose of fielding a candidate against Hague. Molony recalled the directors' psychological state at the time. "We had an interest in good well-paid jobs. We were all facing election as district directors in a little more than a year, late in 1956 and 1957. We were in no mood to get into a great battle. We had the feeling, as most trade unionists do, that such a battle could split our union. . . . Moreover, there was no real election tradition in the CIO, or the AFL for that matter, or the union which had such a formative influence on the Steelworkers—the United Mine Workers. No matter what the constitution said about electing officers, we were prisoners of our own tradition." A mere Gideon's band of district directors to start with, the opposition group proved to be a shaky constituency.

"As I was crossing the Mayflower lobby," recalled Molony, "Charlie Smith, the California director, who had not been at the board meeting, grabbed my arm and said: 'I just got a report on the whole thing. I want to shake your hand, Joe, and I'm with you 100 per cent. That no-good bastard of a Hague. We'll fight him.' " Molony replied, "Thank you, Charlie. By God, we'll fight him together," then he left, proud of this small band of brothers. Later that evening he was apprised of deterioration:

"I learned that Charlie had come out for Hague! My hand was still warm from his handshake—and I lose that particular s.o.b.! It took twenty-four hours more to lose Medrick. Shane abandoned us ten days later. We wound up with the hard core of Griffin, Burke, Molony, Walsh, Sefton, Bill Mahoney [the Canadian national director], and Bill Hart."

"No one wanted the job of running," said Molony. "Well, by a process of elimination—not acclamation—I was chosen, a most reluctant bride. I had no idea of what such an election might entail. So I am to run for the vice-presidency and these good friends of mine will get me the necessary nominations from the local unions. We'll plan a great campaign, and Jimmy Griffin will be my campaign manager."

The 1955 Vice-Presidential Election

When the campaign got under way, John Doherty, the prestigious international representative, became chairman of the committee for Howard R. Hague. In a letter to the hundreds of staff representatives, Doherty pointed out that Hague had been endorsed by McDonald, Secretary-Treasurer I. W. Abel, and the majority of the district directors. Doherty deplored the "disunity" resulting from the effrontery of Molony's challenge to the leadership. Then came the pressure: "An indication of your cooperation in this highly important matter would be most helpful." That indication was expected in at least two categories: a financial contribution to push the Hague campaign, and statements of support.

When nominations closed, Hague had received a total of 1,527 local-union nominations to 540 for Molony. The leadership of 75 per cent of the locals had backed the administration's choice, demonstrating that the staff representatives, under the district directors, had done effective work in getting around to the local union meetings at nomination time.

The campaign became nasty and violent. Molony's top-echelon supporters—the six directors who stuck with him—decided that to counter the overwhelming pressures of the international machine, they would really put their show on the road. Using trailers manned by Molony followers, the Rank and File Committee to Elect Joe Molony trekked from one district to another, venturing into hostile country.

At a conference of Hart's District 19, President McDonald pleaded for unity within the Steelworkers Union. He recounted in lurid color the story of internal fighting led by men of "low character" within the United Mine Workers in the 1920s, which, he said, almost wrecked the union. Hart stormed to the front of the platform and confronted McDonald: "In view of your account of the sad tale of these leaders in the Mine Workers—men who you say sold out to the companies, betrayed the union and ended up as a drunken bum, dope fiend, and a man who blew his brains out—are you suggesting that Mr. Molony, I, and other executive board members on this stage are sellout artists, traitors, or racketeers?"

McDonald backed away, saying that the answer to the question had been on the end of his notes but that he had slipped. No, he said, Mr. Molony and Mr. Hart were in no way similar to leaders of the revolt in the UMW.

The bitterness of the campaign intensified. In mid-September, a house trailer in which several Molony supporters were asleep at 3 A.M. near the Bethlehem plant at Irwin, Pennsylvania, deep in anti-Molony territory, was set on fire. Five Molony workers were severely beaten at the South Works gate of U.S. Steel in Chicago at the midnight shift, and their trailer was damaged. The unusual campaign took on an even uglier character. The president of Local 65 was charged with malicious destruction of property, a staff representative of District 31 with assault and malicious mischief. Molony, just arrived to open his Calumet region campaign, was beaten. The attackers, planted at the mill gate, had jumped onto the trailer in pairs, yanked out wires, broken headlights, and strewn Molony literature over the streets. After spending the night at the hospital and the Chicago police headquarters, Molony told reporters "the cowardly thugs" would not make him give up the good fight.

What did Molony mean by the "good fight"? In the weeks immediately prior to October 25, election day, the *Voice of Victory* and the *Molony Campaigner* explained the commitment to meet in Cleveland to formulate, for the first time in Steelworkers history, "campaign policies of a rank-and-file candidate for high union office."

They charged that unlimited funds were being squandered by Hague supporters to support lavish headquarters and full-time campaigners. Also, according to Molony's supporters, Hague backers had openly threatened that "staff representatives supporting Molony will be fired or transferred and charges will be filed against local officers and members who support Molony."

At the same time, Griffin recalled with pride that successful revolt against top leadership did have one precedent: in 1946 an incumbent district director had been overthrown in an election by none other than Griffin himself. If Griffin could challenge successfully in District 26, why couldn't Molony do it in the international union?

During the campaign, the Molony strategists threw their support behind a plan to organize a staff men's union so as to protect their freedom of action against threats of reprisal for supporting Molony.

"We Steelworkers have long been tired of one-man elections," declared the Rank and File Conference in Cleveland. "We want to choose our International Officers by contest between those who merely aspire and those who are fitted for such jobs. For the first time in our history, our members will have a choice through the secret ballot, and we feel it is a great step forward."

Of significance for future elections was the challenge to McDonald and the executive board at a one-day conference in Cleveland to establish a properly financed panel of "impartial observers," to be selected from the faculties of the University of Chicago, Pittsburgh University, Manhattan College, Notre Dame, John Carroll University, and similar institutions, "to view the actual election to see how our elections are conducted, and to make such recommendations to the International Executive Board and local unions that would, in their opinion, protect the democratic process in our union."

The proposal was ignored. The almost reflex response by the McDonald administration was that the constitutional provisions for election procedures were good enough.

As chairman of the Resolutions Committee, Walter Burke had presented the key resolution on "Union Democracy." What was involved here, he declared, was "whether our union is going to be dedicated to the type of democracy that is necessary to assure that rank-and-file, dues-paying members are to have the final say in shaping the policies of the organization. It is now questionable what sort of democracy we have in the Steelworkers, what with the beatings, arson, attempted murder, goon tactics, frame-ups or other crimes being committed against Molony supporters."

For Burke, the subject of union democracy was no academic matter. Not many weeks before, he had felt McDonald's pressure as administered by an old friend, John Doherty, now Hague's campaign manager. Doherty went to Milwaukee to "reason" with Burke as a friend. He said he was worried because "somebody else was scheduled to do the kind of pressuring I wouldn't want you to be subjected to." It was a full-scale warning delivered with benevolent insistence. Doherty made clear that Burke's rebellion might cost him his district. In his solicitude, Doherty went so far as to suggest that he bring Mrs. Burke to their dinner meeting to provide a fuller understanding of the risks her husband was taking. With considerable delicacy, as McDonald's ambassador, Doherty informed Burke that he wished to address Burke's staff the next day.

Burke had been told by Doherty, "You know who he's going to send in." The names of certain individuals were mentioned, people who were commonly known as McDonald's goon squad. "Surely you don't want these people around your district and I don't want you to have them, and I'm not threatening you that it will happen but it just might happen." All this was spoken in front of Mrs. Burke, but she said, in effect, "I agree with my husband; he's doing what's right."

When Burke stood up before the Molony conference, he was therefore bitterly aware of the personal alternative to union democracy.

Mike Walsh, the New England district director, saw the Molony campaign as the opening battle to restore the union to the members. In the next election, opposition candidates should be entered against all international officers and directors. In this way, he said, the will of the rank and file would be carried out.

The general uproar following the physical attacks on Molony followers demanded a response from McDonald, and he issued an announcement condemning violence—in a way: "We must remember that in the history of labor organizations, *agents provocateurs* are often utilized to bring discredit upon responsible people and elements in the labor movement by stimulating or provoking acts of violence to discredit the other side."

Molony was an open and active campaigner; Hague was not. Hague relied on the use of the union treasury and machinery, the staff representatives, and the majority of district directors, chief of whom was Joe Germano, who ran the Hague campaign from Chicago. Most of Molony's meetings took place in crowded back rooms of taverns in unfriendly districts. Efforts were made to address local meetings, but access was sometimes difficult when the district director or staff representative blocked the way. No law required them to step aside.

Once, in a meeting in back of a saloon when he was about to deliver his address, the cries went up: "Molony, go home! Who the hell asked you here?" "I've traveled five-hundred miles to speak, and God damn you, I'm going to speak," he replied. "I kept bellowing away. I venture to say there were twenty fist fights going on all over the place. It didn't make the slightest difference to me. There's always a couple of guys that'll sit in the front and listen. The cops came in and dragged them out. It was a great crusade, you see."

On another occasion, Molony addressed a mass meeting in Germano's district, which was "sewed up tight. I couldn't even get a guy in that district to act as chairman. I had to introduce myself. The meeting was packed with Germano's people, and Joe himself was there. When I introduced myself, I was roundly booed. I kept on talking. People are essentially decent and tried to listen. But Joe kept on interrupting. I'd answer him back.

"Germano said: 'You've been telling lies about our great President McDonald. I now challenge you to submit to a lie-detector test. I'll take the test, Molony; will you take a lie-detector test?' I looked at him and said: 'Germano, if you ever sat in a lie-detecting machine the damned thing would register TILT.' The whole audience burst out laughing. Germano lost complete control of his own damned audience. You know, there was great joy in this campaign."

The joy was qualified. Steel-industry management watched with interest. *Iron Age* for November 3, 1955, observed appreciatively that the election campaigns for district directorships (there were two by-election contests) and the vice-presidency reflected the professional touch. Campaign literature and tactics were, they said, on a par with those of a national political campaign. In general, however, steel management regarded the unusual event with Olympian amusement.

When the returns were finally published, Hague was credited with 400,017 votes to Molony's 184,542, the total representing about 55 per cent of the dues-paying members.* The average dues-paying membership in the July–December period was 1,057,359. The total vote, as recorded, was about twice McDonald's vote of 294,244 in the uncontested regular election of 1953.

Considerable doubt was raised about the honesty of the count. Several district directors reported they were "reasonably" certain that Molony had won. Molony himself never challenged the results. At a later convention, he announced that "I'd been defeated fair and square." Describing himself as the possessor of a cast-iron stomach, Molony commented, "it didn't bother me to say that. I felt I had to do that. What do you gain whining 'I was robbed'? Besides, there was then no machinery to correct the process."

* Lloyd Ulman, *The Government of the Steelworkers Union*, 1962, p. 139.

Molony was prepared to adjust himself to the overwhelming political reality that his group lacked sufficient strength. Nevertheless, the Molony-Hague campaign had set in motion a strong belief that international elections need not necessarily become an exercise in forced unanimity. The lessons of the 1955 campaign gave the membership something to talk about and the leadership something to think about. An election contest on the international level was no longer an unforgivable sin.

The contest had not raised questions of stability of labor-management relations. In fact, some company executives welcomed a certain degree of disarray that would make the union position a little less secure, less capable of resistance to a strong industry position. In the minds of the more Machiavellian industry experts, there opened up the possibility of new approaches to the union members over the heads of their leaders: the prestige of the union leadership might be lowered in the course of a knockdown-and-dragout political campaign. Alternatively, of course, some employers recognized the possibility that change in union leadership might become an adventure into the unknown. Under those circumstances, the company influence might be applied on the side of the incumbent union officers, who would not be ungrateful.

Despite the campaign threats, with the end of the special election the job security of the opposition district directors was not affected. Molony, Griffin, Burke, Sefton, Walsh, and the others in the "caucus" remained banded together. There was still the possibility that McDonald might turn openly vindictive and set up candidates against them in the nominations of 1956. If he couldn't beat them, he might at least scare them. McDonald did make several probing forays into districts of the dissenting directors, but in Molony's words, "Nothing came of it. Primarily, I think, because those of us who fought Hague, despite all our faults, were about the hardest-working directors in the union. We had good staffs who were loyal to us and we also had a good solid base in the local unions. McDonald's probes got him nowhere."

CHAPTER 5

The Rarick Interval

A poor relation is . . . a preposterous shadow . . .
a rebuke to your rising. . . .

CHARLES LAMB

So the political heaving inside the Steelworkers Union gradually subsided. The six directors who had dared to support Molony—all in their forties—represented a relatively new look; their total work experience was in steel, not coal. They lacked the traditional UMW background, but they had confident identification as steel workers. They had also worked with Philip Murray, and they did not depend on hearsay for their knowledge of the personal and political factors that shaped the Steelworkers Union.

Though keenly aware of the retaliatory powers of the union president, they were equally convinced that McDonald had his own fill of internal fighting. He was not inclined to stimulate or invite a chain of reprisals when, in the year to come, he himself faced the need to run for the presidency in the regular quadrennial election.

There was another matter to be reckoned with. McDonald found himself part of a bigger club—the newly merged American Federation of Labor and Congress of Industrial Organizations. One sure way for him to lose face and influence among the union leaders was to expose himself to the further necessity of suppressing insurrections in his own union. In this union and in its progenitor, the United Mine Workers, there was no tradition of union-wide electoral struggle; opposition had been smashed thirty years before, when, as secretary to Philip Murray, McDonald served as an apprentice in an election in which John L.

Lewis had been challenged by John Brophy, then a district director of the United Mine Workers. (See Appendix 1.)

Trouble came to McDonald not from the established leadership but from the lower depths, the rank and file among the local unions, a sort of Shays' Rebellion begun at the international Steelworkers convention in Los Angeles in September 1956.

The revolt was unexpected. Earlier that summer, the union and steel management had reached a collective-bargaining settlement considered highly satisfactory by the union. After a four-week strike, the industry agreed to pay during the life of a three-year contract about as much as it had offered, early in the negotiations, over the life of a five-year contract. The industry also granted a modified union shop, which it had resisted for years. Such a concession by the management meant not only that the union would possess more vigor in its representational capacity, but also presumably the regularization of a checkoff of dues and their systematic payment into the union treasury. In addition the union had won a cost-of-living provision.

Since the companies insisted on a long-term contract, Otis Brubaker of the research department had raised the question of "going the cost-of-living route"—a formula that the Steelworkers had rejected out of hand. McDonald in fact was originally indignant at the intrusion of the idea. "There's that Reuther bullshit," said McDonald, "and we're going to have none of that in our union." But Goldberg finally persuaded McDonald that the Steelworkers cost-of-living clause didn't look like the Automobile Workers clause. The companies went along.

As good as that 1956 agreement was, McDonald was determined to make it look even grander when he took it to the Wage Policy Committee for ratification. In accordance with standard procedure, Brubaker was requested to prepare a wrap-up of the benefits the union had gained.

Brubaker went to work on the "costing" and later told McDonald it was ready. "What does it show?" McDonald asked. Brubaker told him. McDonald reacted: "It isn't enough. Dress it up some more." Brubaker refused, informing McDonald that he "didn't really know but one way in which to calculate costs and that was by doing as honest a job as I could in making the figures honest, and be as careful as we could in making the assumptions about those costs. I felt we had to be consistent about this. During the bargaining we had taken positions that these costs were based on honest estimates. We thought they were honest then, and we think them honest now."

This refusal to dress up the figures annoyed McDonald, who then sent an aide, Bud Flannery, and Brubaker's own assistant of several years, Marvin Miller, to reason with Brubaker. Ironically, Miller had helped Brubaker prepare the calculations to which McDonald now objected.

The burden of their practical advice to Brubaker: "We really ought to raise the price tag on this settlement a little bit. Dave wants it higher and it really won't be a perversion of *our* integrity. He wants it."

Brubaker told Flannery to tell McDonald that if phony figures were actually presented to the Wage Policy Committee, he would rise in opposition. "Arthur Goldberg," said Brubaker, "gave the presentation to the committee, used part of my figures, swept over another part of them, and carefully avoided placing an exact price tag on them. He was fluid rather than precise."

During this extraordinary wrestling between the union president and his respected research director, McDonald began a process of undermining Brubaker. He drew away Miller, whom Brubaker had hired and trained. Once when Brubaker went to the presidential suite, McDonald "flaunted in my face the fact that he could buy people to give him the figures and facts that he wanted."

Later McDonald informed Brubaker that if he "didn't give him what he wanted, he could buy the whole bloody department from me, lock, stock, and barrel. Over a period of not too many years, he did exactly this. He just stripped from me every person I had in the department and threw this up to me on two or three occasions. He had bought these people, he said, and the price wasn't really too high."

The Los Angeles Convention

With the public plaudits for the 1956 contract still ringing, McDonald and his associates on the executive board believed that they controlled a tight and happy convention. But the mood of self-congratulation was transformed by two developments.

The first was brought about by the proposal of the Constitution Committee to eliminate the office of an elected national director for Canada. Under the constitution, the elected officials of the union were the president, secretary-treasurer, vice-president, the district directors, a national director for Canada, and the three international tellers.

Since the proposal to replace a national director elected by the Canadian membership with an appointed international representative had strong administration support, the leadership and McDonald were stunned by its violent rejection by Canadian delegates. To many Canadians, the national directorship was the international union's recognition of their national identity. In the trade-union movement as elsewhere, Canadian nationalism had already become an issue of sensitive political significance.

The Canadian delegates spurned the idea of receiving a proconsul from Pittsburgh instead of having a director of their own election. To remove a national director for Canada, warned one delegate, would be to play into the hands of the Canadian Manufacturers Association, which, he said, was using the slogan "The labor bosses from America dictate to the labor movement in Canada." Another delegate warned that the union's enemies—the Communist Party in Canada as well as "our opponents in the Chamber of Commerce and in industry"— would jeer at them.

On the floor, in bars, and in hotel rooms, the Canadian delegates mounted a lobby of the type which as seasoned politicians they were used to doing at Canadian Labour Congress conventions and in their political activities, but which in Steelworkers circles was unprecedented. The convention was by now heaving with excitement.

"Now there will be no booing, please," roared McDonald, his face a beet red. He was calling for the vote; the debate had gone on long enough. Then, as the situation became more difficult, he advanced the suggestion that "we should simply pass over this section for the time being." Again the audience broke in with yells for a vote.

Finally McDonald put the question to a voice vote of ayes and nays. Overwhelmingly, the committee's report was turned down. McDonald fought to control his discomposure: "Now let me remind you fellows who have had this bit of fun that you have bought yourself an obligation that I do not want you to hold me personally responsible for. I advise you, all of you who have had your moment of fun, to carefully read and carefully analyze the Audit Report."

Not only had the Canadians staged a little Boston Tea Party of their own; more significantly, for the first time in the history of the Steelworkers, a proposal of the international leadership was voted down.

Later that morning, the question of increases in the salaries of the international officers came before the convention. The Constitution Committee recommended that the president's salary be raised from $40,000 to $50,000 and that the other two international officers be paid $35,000 instead of $25,000. In introducing the subject, John Doherty, the committee's secretary, informed the convention that in proposing the increases it was risking the displeasure of the international officers, who had informed the committee they did not want a raise. But, he went on, "We feel the dignity of the office must be maintained and that the international officers could only maintain that dignity if they accepted that which we think is fair and just." Just before the convention voted the salary increases, however, one delegate sought to know whether they would have any effect on the rise in dues—a question that was soon to come before the convention. McDonald, who had yielded the gavel while the delicate subject of his salary increase was being discussed, moved forward to the rostrum, glaring at the offending delegate. "It has nothing to do with the dues increase and I don't want a wage increase. Is that clear?" The salary increases were approved.

At the close of a tough morning, the time had arrived for things of the spirit. McDonald introduced "the one and only, the great Phil Regan. . . . You have heard him on the radio, seen him on the screen, on television. He came down here because he is a good trade unionist. He gets $5,000 a performance. He doesn't get anything from us. He just came to say hello and maybe he will sing an Irish song."

Regan, not taken by surprise, was eager to please. Before rendering two selections, he addressed the convention as follows: "Dave and I have been friends for many years. Phil, before him, was a very good friend of mine. I would like to meet more fellows who refuse to take a raise. Would you mind standing up, fellows? I saw four hands. I have never seen that before."

By this time, when the question of an increase in dues was coming up, the atmosphere of the convention had become rancorous and boisterous. Preparations for a dues increase had been made, in a manner of speaking, through the usual channels. District directors and staff representatives had enlisted the support of more than three hundred locals which submitted resolutions favoring an increase, while twenty-five locals had sent in resolutions opposing it. Many local leaders were attracted by the idea because the constitutional formula for dues payments required that half the dues collected be returned to the local treasuries.

In the afternoon session, the Constitution Committee proposed that monthly dues be raised from three dollars to five. I. W. Abel, as secretary-treasurer, proudly declared that the Steelworkers Union had doubled its net worth in four years, to more than $21 million, but that the cost of running the international also rose. "Essential casual and part-time workers for limited periods, and salaries of staff representatives had to be raised. For a program of large scope and high caliber to maintain our place of leadership among the important unions of the world, this is the minimum support we owe our great President if we expect him to lead us effectively."

Despite the argument advanced by the generally respected secretary-treasurer, the attack on the proposed dues increase came full blast. While workers in basic steel benefited from the recent basic steel settlement, the workers in the fabricating sectors had hardly held their own. Now, said a delegate, "they will be confronted with a 70 per cent increase in dues. That is going to be hard to sell to people with families who have a take-home pay of less than $60 a week." This speaker urged that dues be paid on a sliding schedule, according to wages: "I am afraid that if this $5 goes across, there will be a wedge in our solidarity."

Other delegates spoke for the increase, advancing arguments that were greeted by booing.

McDonald angrily warned, "Once more . . . there will be no booing." Under the rules of the convention, he said, violators of decorum would be removed from the hall. Then, in one of the classic understatements in labor history, McDonald said: "There is nothing emotional about this subject. People may want to make it emotional, but it is not emotional. This is a question of hard-boiled facts—no emotions. I told you I didn't want that $10,000 increase in salary. It is only a penny a man per year, and I still don't want it. When you are voting on this, you are not voting a wage increase for McDonald."

From the very start of the convention McDonald had been sending out hints of his displeasure. "We understand," he said darkly, "that there are certain activities occurring in the foyer of this building which are detrimental to the policies of the United Steelworkers of America. We understand there is a certain kind of lobbying going on out in the foyer and it is being spearheaded by people who have never agreed at any time in their lives with the policies of the international union of the United Steelworkers of America. We know who these people are, and I suggest to them that they cease and desist in this iniquitous action, or if they don't, I will tell this convention who they are and let the international convention take appropriate action on these people." The delegates listened intently to McDonald's threat to unleash the power of the convention against some ill-defined enemy. They might have been impressed, but they were not deterred. Lines of delegates began forming at floor microphones, and McDonald ordered them back to their seats.

The language was acrimonious. The opponents were condemned as proof that "labor is often its own worst enemy." On higher ground, one delegate reminded the convention that higher dues were needed to enable the Steelworkers Union to support other less fortunate unions in their organizational drives, just as the United Mine Workers had come to the aid of the Steelworkers.

But current layoffs rather than past benefits were on the minds of other delegates. Some members, they said, were working only two days a week and "are not actually able to support an increase." Another delegate observed, with prescience that became hindsight for others in days to come, "I am looking forward to the day that the international union will take a constructive program whereby a man may be able to be educated toward a dues increase *before* he comes to the international convention. . . ."

District Director Paul Rusen scolded the delegates, who shouted back at him. "It is nice, boys. Go ahead and holler. I can holler as long as you can." Then he invoked the spirit of union past: "I wonder what Philip Murray would think of you if he were here today?" Then, "You put me in mind of a bunch of school kids. Now, I am going to tell you why a good many of you are opposed to a dues increase. . . . It is because of politics back in the local union. You are afraid if you go back somebody is not going to like it and you won't be elected again. . . . Well, it takes leadership. Delegates who can't sell their local members on the increase in dues should not be an officer of that local union."

Again the delegates stormed at the platform. At that point McDonald yielded to an "overwhelming demand" for the "previous question." "Does some delegate desire to move the previous question?"

In putting the motion on the dues increase, he first asked for a show of hands. The result was uncertain, and he called for a standing vote for the ayes and nays. As McDonald peered out over the convention, the tumult mounted. "The more noise you make, the more difficult you are going to make it for yourselves. . . . I think I know what I am doing. Take it easy, take it easy." The vote was close. Then he said: "There is no question but that the motion has been adopted by the overwhelming majority of the delegates to this convention." Now shouts for a roll call were raised all over the hall.

McDonald replied heatedly: "There are 2,671 accredited delegates to this convention. In order to have a roll-call vote we must have 30 per cent of that group, which is 801. Believe me, there were not 801 people who voted against that motion. Now, it is awfully nice for people to shout for a roll call, and you are going to have to sit in the confines of this convention hall with the doors locked and you are going to stay here all night. And you are going to stay here all day tomorrow if you want a roll call." Down came the gavel. The Steelworkers had never had a roll call and it was not to have one now. The dues increase was declared adopted. McDonald swept back his hair from a red and sweaty brow.

The press reactions all over the country, the hubbub in the halls, the long-night discussions in rooms and lobbies filled the air with foreboding. The mood of revolt was clear. Never before had there been such embroilment in a Steelworkers convention, so clear an open alienation of delegates from leadership.

In closing the convention, McDonald urged the delegates not to be "alarmed over the democratic demonstrations of yesterday. This is not the first demonstration which has occurred in the Steelworkers convention. Go back through the years and remember some things which happened. The record is filled with incidents. Remember the Boston convention in 1948 when some incidents occurred and the ushers had to take guns and knives away from men who were almost out of their minds with bitterness and hate. I witnessed divergent viewpoints. . . . This is a free union; this is a free country and people do enjoy the right to express themselves." Then in an onset of piety, "I ask you in a completely personal sense to remember me in your prayers, because I am your boy."

Despite McDonald's assurances that the decision on the dues increase was clear, A. H. Raskin reported in the *New York Times* that the outcome was in fact "still obscure." The next day, the *Times* reported that partisan feeling had run so strong that ushers had to take knives and guns from several of the delegates.

"We departed from Los Angeles," said a district director, "thinking, well, it was a little bit of a struggle but it's behind us, thank God. Then the moment we got home we were faced with open rebellion everywhere. Well, being good organization men, we went to meetings and gave reasons why the dues increase was necessary. Then Rarick announced."

This was Donald C. Rarick, a delegate from Local 2227, which represented the U.S. Steel Irvin Works in McKeesport, Pennsylvania. A grievance committeeman, he had achieved enough local prominence to win election as one of the eight delegates from that large local. In Los Angeles he was one of those lined up before the microphones to speak against the dues increase whom McDonald had ordered to take their seats.

Within a few weeks, more than fifty delegates from the Pittsburgh-McKeesport area gathered in the back room of Leonard's Café in McKeesport. In addition to Rarick, Frank O'Brien of the Homestead local and Nicholas Mamula, president of Local 1211, the Aliquippa local of Jones & Laughlin, then the second largest local in the international, provided the leadership of insurgency. It became known as the Dues Protest Committee—DPC. Rarick was named chairman.

The original strategy of the Dues Protesters was directed at persuading locals to submit petitions asking for a special convention to reconsider the dues increase. This McDonald's home local had already voted. Their stated objective was to amend the constitution to require ratification of all future dues increases by referendum vote of the membership rather than through convention action.

The dues protesters had already found a nucleus among those who had backed Paul M. Hilbert in his unsuccessful campaign in 1955 to become director of District 15, the district counterpart of the Molony-Hague special vice-presidential election the year before. Hilbert was now prepared to run again in the regular election.

The pattern of emerging revolt now began to be reported, almost on a local-by-local basis, by Charles H. Allard, the veteran labor reporter of the Pittsburgh *Post-Gazette*. In Philadelphia, a local district also called for a special convention. The press now reported a contagion of resentment against the dues increase in locals across the country. The triumvirate of Rarick, O'Brien, and Mamula, considered the brains of the operation, began to channel resentment that they could not have created. What they had going was a rank-and-file movement, a concept that for many of the top leadership bordered on obscenity and treason.

Confronting the Dues Protest movement was the problem of communication. Internal channels were under the strict control of the international office. While the offices of the district directors had the names, numbers, and addresses of all the locals, few if any districts distributed a directory of the locals, with meeting times and places, or lists of local officers. Such information was held back, presumably as a protection against industry infiltration or "dual movements" of any kind, either Communist-inspired or motivated by company unionism. Anybody bucking the leadership therefore would have to piece together the necessary lists over a period of many weeks. The process of instructing local union supporters to petition for a special convention was slow and discouraging work. There was no experience to fall back on. Accordingly, out of about seven hundred locals needed, no more than a hundred were reported officially to have petitioned for a special convention, but among them was the largest in the international union, Local 1014 of Gary, Indiana.

McDonald, who had preferred to ignore the revolt, now lashed out against the rebel leaders as dual unionists and threatened to bring them up on charges. Rarick promptly challenged McDonald to start proceedings. Though McDonald desisted from following through at that time, his threat started a debate between him, one of the country's best-known union leaders, and an unknown local union representative.

Shortly afterward, Arthur Goldberg, the union's general counsel, ruled that the locals' petition for a special convention was not in legal order. Allard reported in the *Post-Gazette* that Goldberg had characterized the petition movement as dual unionism and that he called a news conference to publicize his legal interpretation, which according to Frank O'Brien held that "a special convention would be called only for new business, and the raise in dues was old business."

The drive for a special convention collapsed, but the Dues Protest Committee began to experiment with a more daring thought: to enter candidates against President McDonald and his associates. Who was to take the lead in this larger endeavor? The first choice of the Dues Protest Committee was District 19 Director William J. Hart. But Hart turned the offer down. Hart's antagonism to McDonald did not blind him to the practical fact that the chance of success in such a campaign was slight. He was not prepared to sacrifice certain re-election to his district directorship to run for the highest office with the almost certain prospect of defeat.

At the urging of his associates, Rarick went to see Joe Molony. But Molony gave Rarick an emphatic "no." Such an act, he said, would have been "betrayal of my own kind." Molony later said, "I used the same God-damned expressions against him that were used against me when

I dared to run in 1955: 'What are you trying to do, destroy this great union?' "

In 1956, the union constitution required a candidate for international office to obtain at least forty local "nominations." Out of nearly 2,800 local unions then in the international, the DPC drive gathered sufficient support for Rarick to win endorsements of ninety-one locals against McDonald's 1,905. Newspapers announced this revolutionary development on page one.

The battle for Rarick nominations had been fought hard and bitterly. There was never any doubt that McDonald would outpace a candidate who lacked the open support of a single district director or any identifiable group of staff representatives, and who had emerged brashly from the great anonymous body of grievance committeemen.

Met at Midnight

Now McDonald and his associates hoped to dissuade Rarick from making the run. They were keenly aware of the pulling power of opposition to a dues increase. In other unions, it was not unusual for dues increases subject to approval by a referendum or even by a vote of conventions to be overwhelmingly rejected. Moreover, at the convention he had generated a current of hostility between himself and a large group of delegates who had carried that hostility and contempt home to their memberships. One other fact worried McDonald. In 1953 he had entered office by default; now a real live candidate, no matter how obscure, was undertaking to do him battle.

The tactics of dissuasion against Rarick now took a new twist, with Allard of the Pittsburgh *Post-Gazette* finding himself cast in an intermediary role in the effort to remove Rarick as McDonald's opponent.

"It was around Christmas time when I got this call from a taxicab driver named Armand Carlomango, head of the Yellow Cab drivers' union, a Teamsters local. They offered me $5,000 if I could get Rarick out of the race. They made this offer to me I guess because I was closest to the dues protesters.

"When I told him I wasn't interested, he said, 'Will you come and talk to another guy at midnight?' I wondered what the hell it was all about. So at midnight I met him. We go up to the Penn-Sheraton Hotel. This room was dimly lit. This guy was lying in bed. I recognized Phil Weiss. I said: 'What the hell do you want to get Rarick out of the race for; McDonald shouldn't be afraid of him.' Weiss replied: 'Well, there's a lot of important people interested in McDonald and they wouldn't like to see him embarrassed in any way.' "

Allard replied, "Well, so far as I'm concerned, Rarick will stay in the race and if he doesn't I'm going to find out why and I'll file a story."

Later Armand Carlomango called Allard again. "Can you arrange to let me talk to Rarick?" Allard agreed.

"We arranged this meeting up at the Penn-McKee Hotel up in Mc-Keesport," Allard said. "It was a bitter, snowing night, five or six inches already on the ground. Meanwhile I called Paul Hilbert, who was going to run with the support of the Dues Protesters against John Sullivan for director of District 15. I wanted him to be there as a witness in case anybody would challenge my account of what had happened. So Hilbert and I sat at a table off to one side and Armand and Rarick sat at another in the hotel grill. They talked for about three-quarters of an hour. When they got through, I asked Rarick, 'Did he try to get you out of the race?' 'Oh,' he said, 'he just talked.' " Carlomango drove Allard back to Pittsburgh.

According to Rarick, Carlomango continued to pressure him to withdraw from the race several days before December 31, the last day under the union constitution that he could withdraw. Like Allard, Rarick wished to make doubly sure that his meeting with Carlomango did not take place unobserved. He asked two local detectives, friends of his, to keep an eye out for him and to listen in to phone conversations at his home. During their meeting, Carlomango sought to assure Rarick—"You will have nothing to worry about." Rarick said he just listened and gave Carlomango his unlisted phone number, adding that it was too late to withdraw. But Carlomango persisted.

On December 31, the deadline day, Rarick took his car to be repaired at a garage in McKeesport. He found Carlomango waiting there. "Take a ride with me," said Carlomango. Rarick agreed, and soon they found themselves on Route 57. Carlomango insisted that he meet with McDonald. Rarick consented, and Carlomango phoned McDonald. They drove on to Beale's Motel, on Route 19, at Donaldson's Crossroads near Mount Lebanon, the suburb in which McDonald lived. Carlomango and Rarick got some beer, took a room and waited. A little later, McDonald arrived.

"Dave complained to me," said Rarick, " 'After all I'm doing for the union, and you're opposing me.' " McDonald kept urging Rarick to quit. Rarick said, "You've got to realize other guys are involved with me." "How many?" asked McDonald. "Eight or nine." "We'll take care of them too." It was now near six o'clock and dark. Rarick told McDonald he had to prepare for a New Year's Eve party he and his wife were going to. McDonald then urged Rarick to come to his own New Year's Eve party. Rarick said he would have to talk to his wife, and the meeting broke up. McDonald left first, observing that it would be better for him not to walk out along with the other two men, and got into a waiting car with a driver at the wheel. As Carlomango and Rarick left the motel, Carlomango turned to Rarick: "How much money do you want

—$5,000, $10,000?—this could be worth a quarter of a million dollars to you." The two men started back to Pittsburgh.

In the meantime, a deeply worried Mrs. Rarick had notified the Allegheny County police of her husband's absence since he had left the house to take his car to the garage for repairs. She also called Allard and told him that her husband had been gone all afternoon and that none of his friends knew where he was. Understandably, she was concerned for her husband's physical safety. Allard said later that his wife had been threatened by an unidentified caller because of some of his newspaper stories. He himself had been provided police protection. Just before eleven o'clock that night, Allard got a reassuring call from Rarick. The Raricks did not go to McDonald's New Year's Eve party.

On New Year's Day, Carlomango again got in touch with Rarick, trying to persuade him to quit: "You can't win, why fight?"

At the same time, Rarick's "team," candidates for secretary-treasurer and vice-president, had been named: William Klug and Edward Revack. They received sixty-one and sixty-two nominations respectively, as compared with Rarick's ninety-one, but still had more than enough to qualify. Pressures for withdrawal had not been directed only against Rarick. Howard Hague, still bearing scars from his doubtful victory in 1955, now found himself relieved of Revack, his opponent, who announced his withdrawal and attacked Rarick. In contrast, at the last moment, the office of the international secretary-treasurer, checking through the nomination papers, found that Klug had failed to fill out his form properly. Technically, Klug could therefore have been eliminated as a candidate. Instead, I. W. Abel, the secretary-treasurer, informed Klug that his form was not in order but that he would accept it if Klug would wire authorization of his signature before the closing hour. Abel's act of restraint and generosity was regarded by some of the constitutional "lawyers" among the directors and by Hague particularly as evidence of weakness of character.

Rumors began to circulate that Revack had been bought off. A few days later, news of the clandestine meeting with Rarick also had begun to leak out. On January 12, Rarick openly charged attempted bribery. McDonald the next day called it a "plain, unmitigated lie." All through the campaign, Rarick's supporters never let up on the charge. Just three days before election, on February 4, McDonald again found it necessary to make a denial.

On the surface, it was an uneven contest. McDonald had command of the full power of the union establishment and used it. Advised by the district directors that something had better be done to stem the growing rebellion, at Goldberg's suggestion McDonald called a series of six regional conferences made up of local union officers and staff representatives in different parts of the country. From the administrative point of view, such conferences could be technically justified as a means of developing closer communications between leadership and membership. But why so soon after the constitutional convention? In effect, McDonald had convened a series of six small conventions—a reply to the special convention sought unsuccessfully by the Dues Protesters and denied on constitutional grounds. Thus McDonald used the conferences to build up a counterfire to the rapidly developing Rarick movement. These specially called conferences cost an estimated million dollars. The dues increase was being put to work for the establishment.

The entire publicity machinery of the union was geared for the McDonald drive. *Steel Labor,* the official union publication mailed directly to the home of every union member, became the chief organ of the McDonald campaign. Its February 1957 issue was a sustained hymn of praise for McDonald; Rarick was not mentioned at all. The union paper printed no hint of opposition in the first contested presidential election in the union's history.

McDonald's conduct during the campaign met with the admiring approval of *Iron Age,* the industry publication, which said in its issue for February 11, 1957: "Dave is far more democratic than the late Phil Murray. He seldom cracks the whip. His reluctance to stir up a big deal during the campaigning and his 'apparent' nonchalance at Mr. Rarick's barbs were subtle moves."

In more than one district, the staff representatives had found their work cut out for them. As one said later, "We worked overtime, got tired marking ballots late into the night to make sure that McDonald came out of our district with a respectable majority." Their assignment apparently was not only to increase McDonald's margin but also in some cases to reverse the result *ex post facto.* By this time the generally soft-spoken Hague, McDonald's man-of-all-work, phoned his basking chief down in Miami Beach and told him sharply, "You better get the hell back up here if you want to hold on to your job."

Detailed charges of vote rigging were made by Rarick backers. Although Rarick claimed to have won at the U.S. Steel Local 1014 in Gary by 9,000 to 3,000, he said the count had been turned around through fraud. Rarick's charge was labeled "fantastic" and "sour grapes." But hardly two months before, this basic steel local had adopted a resolution supporting a call for a special convention to reconsider the dues increase.

"We knew there was going to be a hell of a lot of cheating," Allard said. "We wanted to get the returns reported as fast as we could. Speedy returns through the AP and UP would crowd the cheaters. The early returns came in showing Rarick doing very well. We began getting good reports from the West and Middle West. All of a sudden, a blackout. No more figures. Up in Clarendon, where our first report showed Rarick had won over McDonald three to one, they just switched the results. They threw the old ballots out, physically. A rebel got hold of them and dumped them on the lawn of a young attorney, James Ashton, who took on Rarick's appeal. They—the McDonald supporters— simply got a batch of new ballots and marked them for McDonald. You see, the ballots were not numbered; they're still not numbered."

Throughout February and March, while the international tellers were compiling the official tally, Rarick kept up a drumbeat of charges that the election was being stolen. Late in March, he wired AFL-CIO President George Meany, asking him to investigate. But Meany lacked the power or the inclination to intervene—traditionally the president of the federation would refrain from such intervention in the political affairs of an affiliated union.

The official results, as finally announced, were as follows:

	Number of Votes
President:	
McDonald	404,172
Rarick	223,516
Secretary-Treasurer:	
Abel	420,085
Klug	181,264
Vice-President:	
Hague (unopposed)	479,745
Blank ballots cast	about 150,000

McDonald had failed to defeat an inconspicuous local leader by even a two-to-one margin. Abel ran well ahead of McDonald, besting his opponent by considerably better than two to one.

The smell of near-success stimulated the Rarick forces. Officially defeated, they believed they had laid the groundwork for a continuing opposition. Rarick still raised the issue of election fraud. The AFL-CIO had already set up its Ethical Practices Committee, but the jurisdiction of the committee, though flexible, was not interpreted as extending to the internal government of affiliated unions. Counsel for the AFL-CIO Ethical Practices Committee was the versatile Arthur Goldberg, who had assumed this new set of duties in addition to those as general counsel of the Steelworkers Union and special counsel to the Industrial Union Department of the AFL-CIO.

Finally, Rarick and other leaders of the Dues Protest Committee protested to the McClellan Committee. After a preliminary investigation, Robert F. Kennedy, then the committee's general counsel, wrote letters to the 2,700 Steelworkers locals asking them to retain the ballots beyond the August 15, 1957, deadline set by the USW constitution. Although a question was raised concerning the committee's power to impound the ballots, concern for the complaint impelled Kennedy to do just that. Rarick charged that McDonald had used union funds in his campaign; McDonald denied the charge. Several weeks afterward, Rarick appeared before an executive session of the committee, headed by John L. McClellan, Democrat of Arkansas.

Allegations flew back and forth. In a letter to Rarick, Kennedy found they fell into two classes: (1) "allegations that the funds utilized by Mr. McDonald were drawn from the union treasury and that those used by you came from management sources"; and (2) "allegations concerning the tabulation and handling of the ballots themselves during and subsequent to the election."

Kennedy then asked Rarick to furnish an accounting of the amount he had spent in the election campaign as well as the source of any contributions he had utilized. In the ensuing months, Rarick and Ashton, his lawyer, were engaged in a series of pressure maneuvers to obtain more active intervention by the McClellan Committee.

The burden of Rarick's argument was that an investigation was justified for various reasons. No local-by-local report of the results of the election had been made available. Such a tabulation he demanded as a right under the union constitution (Article V, Section 18), which required that "votes for each District and of each Local Union within each District shall be tabulated separately and consecutively." But the language seemed sufficiently porous to enable the international union officers and their general counsel to decide they were not legally bound to make total, specific, and public disclosure, all of which recalled to many insiders the story of John Brophy, who thirty years before had fought John Lewis in a famous election for the presidency of the United Mine Workers.*

A cloak-and-dagger episode was added to this election story. Shortly after the election in February 1957, a man named Bill Staton went to Rarick with a hard-luck story of persecution by officials of the Steelworkers Union in California. Staton and his wife and children were welcomed into the Rarick group. In fact, he was so far on the inside that he became a member of the group that visited the Senate committee to complain about election irregularities. Then, after a national meeting of the Dues Protesters, Staton absconded with their records, including the list of participants and their plans. The documents wound up in the hands of McDonald representatives.

The international tellers submitted as their "complete report" the total votes for each candidate, without a breakdown by locals or even

* See Appendix 1.

by districts. Rarick argued that the constitution required a local-by-local tabulation. The union administration, its irritation mounting at what it called Rarick's harassment, felt that the publication of the local-by-local results would be only the first step in a series of demands yet to be unveiled by Rarick and his friends. Unused to such sustained protest and the considerable public curiosity aroused, the union officials sought to belittle Rarick's embarrassing inquiries as not being made in good faith. The officers of the international union also feared that the United Steelworkers would find itself subject to investigation in depth by the McClellan Committee.

The need to buttress the union against the erosion of suspicion required massive public relations. McDonald was easily persuaded to undertake a series of monthly television programs. Through a series of such "fireside chats," McDonald was presented as the concerned leader, earnestly addressing himself to the problems facing the union and the industry.

In the meantime, the DPC's pulling power over the nation had apparently been reduced, although individual rebel leaders were coming up in the local and district world. Rarick, for example, was elected president of his local, as was Frank O'Brien. Nicholas Mamula was re-elected president of the 13,000-member Jones & Laughlin local at Aliquippa. Anthony Tomko led a rebel slate in Local 1408 in Mc-Keesport; and interestingly enough, Thomas Flaherty, a strong DPC leader in California, was elected to the presidency of Fontana Local 2869.

By the middle of 1958, the excitement and novelty of bucking the establishment had generally lost their attraction. With his forces better prepared, McDonald now felt that he could move to prove that he was undisputed master in his house. But the election of Rarick and Frank O'Brien to local leadership carried with it a cutting edge. McDonald had hoped to defeat them. During their campaigns they had filed million-dollar libel suits against McDonald. Even though these sensational suits were later abandoned, they created useful publicity for the two rebel leaders in their local union campaigns.

McDonald persuaded himself that his TV appearances had begun to tranquilize the rank and file, but the attitude of his associate directors continued to deteriorate. Though the Rarick danger seemed to have been warded off, the restlessness on the executive board had begun to increase. In the summer of 1958, a *Fortune* article by Daniel Bell, then its labor editor, entitled "Decline of Dave McDonald," threw McDonald into a panic.

"In the last year or so," *Fortune* said, "McDonald has paid less and less attention to union affairs. When he has paid attention, he ignored the union's executive board. His actions have turned a majority of the board against him. The question is only whether the board, to stave off a rising rank-and-file revolt, will work to re-elect him and allow him to resign on a pension, or will oppose him openly. The district directors of the union, who hold the power, are convinced that McDonald, psychologically, will be unable to control the union convention and that only a statement by him that this will be his last term will stave off disorder." (*Fortune,* August 1958, pp. 169–170.)

The *Fortune* piece startled McDonald into action. He responded by charging that "curious sources" outside the union were making deliberate personal attacks on him; he accused the National Association of Manufacturers and the United States Chamber of Commerce of engaging in a plan to drive him from power and split the union. If employers were in fact the root of the attack, he nevertheless carefully avoided mentioning the name of any steel company as party to the conspiracy. A few days later McDonald said: "I am so conceited as to believe that if the United Steelworkers of America ever needed Dave McDonald, they need him more in 1959 than they ever needed him before."

He began a series of speeches to whip up support against the "menace" of a rebel uprising, ostensibly by the Dues Protesters. By a tour of the country, McDonald would make himself known to the local leadership and prove to the district directors, despite their limp pledge of allegiance, that he was very much in charge. Whenever his tenure seemed threatened, McDonald's diligence and attention to leadership responsibilities came on strong. Before an enthusiastic meeting in Cleveland, McDonald ominously emphasized the need to "root out this cancerous growth of treachery before it is too late."

CHAPTER 6

All Those in Favor?

Sock it to me.

ROWAN AND MARTIN'S LAUGH-IN

Interest in the internal life of American unions was stimulated in 1958 by a combination of factors. In Washington, the McClellan Committee had continued to hear testimony revealing a wide range of improper practices in labor-management relations, in which it bore down more heavily on labor than on management. In addition, the Rarick-McDonald election was still remembered by men concerned with union leadership.

In May the Fund for the Republic assembled a group of leading labor, management, and arbitration experts at Arden House in Harriman, New York. Among the participants was Arthur Goldberg, who delivered a paper from a "trade union point of view." He compared political democracy in our constitutional society with the structure of union internal life. He was firmly convinced, he said, that "democracy within the union institution is essential. By that I do not necessarily mean competitive politics, as in political government. . . ." He did not allude to the Steelworkers Union, which had just barely avoided a Senatorial investigation of its "competitive politics." A few days before the conference, the union was informed by the committee's general counsel, Robert Kennedy, that it need no longer hold the ballots of the 1957 election in escrow, and a deep sigh of relief ran through the international office.

While McDonald was always ready to give his elocutionary powers full play, he could employ a less grandiloquent approach. When a small group of newspapermen, at a golf party given by President George Meany, asked him whether he would quit the union presidency, he rejected the idea as absurd: "Now look, let's be realistic, fellows, where the fuck would I be able to get another job at $50,000 a year and all expenses?" At any rate, McDonald was prepared to make the 1958 convention the next scene of action. In the words of *Steel,* an industry magazine, "David J. McDonald's moment of truth is approaching. Next week he'll show the world whether he's still boss of the United Steel-workers of America. If Mr. McDonald routs the forces that opposed him in 1956 [and 1957], he won't have to prove anything during next summer's contract negotiations. He won't be under pressure to justify his existence through unusually exorbitant demands; his authority won't be questioned by steel industry negotiators; and there will be no doubt about his ability to get a contract ratified."

McDonald was kept aware of management's close scrutiny, and the considerable discontent among the district directors added to his uneasiness. At the convention, he sought to establish that he was in full control, in contrast to the near-runaway convention of 1956. He came from behind the parted curtains to the front of the stage, his hands upraised and the spotlight playing on his delighted face. The delegates roared; the band crashed out a football march. In his opening address, he invoked the spirit of Phil Murray, pledging that "I will not permit the enemies from within [i.e., Rarick, Mamula, and O'Brien] to destroy this union of yours." The excitement mounted rapidly. McDonald tied Rarick and his associates to every organization from the extreme Right to the extreme Left. "If you want your union to be clean and strong, don't leave it up to the Great White Father, as I am now being called in the South." A dramatic pause, then a shout: "Rip this cancer out of your bowels through your own doing and don't leave it to me."

He warned the now tense convention of the intentions of "those who masquerade under some sort of a title—the DPC, whatever that means —to fight the rules, the long-established rules of the United Steelworkers of America; to stir up racial antagonism. . . . They will use every iniquitous means that they can command here—the Communists, the Trotskyites, NAM agents, company agents. . . . They are going to fall back on the old Communist Party line which I first heard expressed in the United Mine Workers convention in the year 1924—the old Communist line that staff representatives must be elected.

"This is going to be their big fight now. . . . They have only a program of hate. They have only a program of greed—and when I say greed I mean the word 'greed' in all its connotations because the two top leaders now have filed . . . individual lawsuits totaling one million dollars each addressed at McDonald. 'Greed!' They want to dig it out of your pockets, dig it out of your treasury for their own personal use." When the delegates began to boo the targets of his tirade, the elated McDonald raised his hands. "No booing, boys, no booing! You will also find that they are going to hold caucuses. Yes, they are going to attempt to hold caucuses," he intoned.

Then a slight pause, a slight smile. "Now look, folks, I want a peaceful convention. I don't want any rough stuff here."

Then came the peroration. His arms outthrust, his bulk swelling, he exclaimed: "Rise up, you strong men of steel, rise up united, strong men of steel, and show America, show those who hate you and show all the people of the world the real tough metal of which you are made."

As if on cue, through the doors crashed a large group of McDonald supporters lined up in a mock funeral march. Pallbearers in mourning attire paraded a casket marked "DPC" while an organ resounded and McDonald feigned surprise. The charade was acted out without any real effort to stop it. McDonald banged his gavel against the uproar, then threw up his hands in a gesture of mock despair as the delegates, led by loyal staff representatives, snake-danced up the aisles.

Later that afternoon the delegates were brought to a shrieking pitch when Director Joseph Molony himself read the resolution in praise of David J. McDonald. McDonald announced, "I am proud but I am not vain." The resolution described all the virtues of leadership to him, with a fulsomeness suitable to a coronation. McDonald glowed wet-eyed. He was showing those bastards.

Adulation reached its apex when Al Whitehouse, director of District 25, began his own paean. A former minister who had worked for a while in a steel mill, he was now secure as district director of the smallest and least successful of the districts in the entire union. Whitehouse had now also become recognized as the union's chief voice on these occasions of personal adoration of the beloved leader: "I have a trumpet in my soul and I never get tired of playing it for my union . . . led by the greatest leader in the world today, David J. McDonald. . . . Let's throw the stinking stooges in our own ranks out on their ears."

The path toward expulsion of the rebel local leaders was now clearly marked. Should the convention throw them out forthwith, or find other means to take care of the unholy trinity of Rarick, O'Brien, and Mamula?

The convention broke into a huge demonstration. Carrying placards with printed slogans proclaiming their loyalty, the delegates stomped behind a brass band and moved up the steps of the stage to grasp the hands of their leader.

When the convention subsided from its paroxysm, McDonald resumed the chair. "You brought tears to my eyes and happiness to my heart." Suddenly, he said, "If there are some Jewish delegates present, happy New Year." The next day, following a speech by Arthur Goldberg, McDonald turned to the convention and said, "Yesterday when I asked if there were any delegates in the hall who were Jewish and wished them a happy New Year, Art came up and said, 'What do you mean, *if* there are any delegates? I am a delegate.' And he is right; he is a delegate. So, Art, a belated happy New Year." Goldberg and McDonald clasped hands.

At the end of the first day's proceedings, Rarick tried to catch McDonald in the corridor to ask for rebuttal time. Surrounded by his entourage, the bristling McDonald strode past Rarick without a word.

The next day the clamor rose again. Frank O'Brien, president of Local 1843, shoved a needle into the officialdom by recalling how he first met Joe Molony in 1955, when Molony was running for vice-president against Howard Hague. Some people in the Pittsburgh area "called Joe Molony nothing but a union-buster; if he is elected the union will be ruined." Now, said O'Brien, "I am accused of union wrecking." The officers and the district directors seated on the platform were not amused. Tempers mounted. Advice was shouted from the floor.

Some delegates appealed for moderation. From Mamula's Local 1211, delegate Mike Zahorsky arose to defend the "God-given right to express opinions. . . . This is not bad for our union. This is good for our union." He proposed that the subject be removed from the convention floor and hammered out in committee "to avoid spilling its troubles to the world."

But loaded for bear and wanting no behind-the-scenes settlement, McDonald declared his intention to "flush the matter out on the floor. I trust that critics and the enemies and the crybabies are in the room." He suggested a suspension of the rules. A key demand of the dissenters was the election rather than the presidential appointment of staff officers. On this sensitive issue, which McDonald knew would go nowhere, he recognized Rarick. To give him maximum exposure, the president inquired solicitously whether Rarick would like to come to the platform microphone. When many of the delegates started to boo Rarick, McDonald said, "Cut it out! Give the delegate an opportunity."

Rarick, usually voluble in smaller groups, did not do well in the larger arena. His inadequacy as a leader in any large sense seemed so clear that one wondered at the ineptitude of the union's officers in dealing with him. Constantly interrupted, Rarick shouted his defiance of the booing and declared his intention to keep talking.

As the discussion went on, McDonald stressed his readiness for a full debate. He was particularly aroused by the accusation made by Mike Zahorsky that hundreds of staff men were improperly seated as delegates. McDonald chided Zahorsky for making "vile accusations." He denied that this was a "rigged convention. . . . Believe me, I am your president, and I knew absolutely nothing about it until the boys began to march."

The administration lined up its speakers to present a full defense of McDonald. One delegate after another delivered his part of the script. Sometimes the delegates' anxiety to please the platform was over-extended, and McDonald, displaying generosity, would ask them to "knock it off."

At this point, a brochure entitled "The Mask of Deceit" was placed in the hands of every delegate. Based on material provided by Staton, who had infiltrated the Dues Protesters in 1957, it consisted of unrestrained vilification of Rarick and his associates. Smaile Chatak, Philip Murray's old rank-and-file confidant, a man of immense prestige who had lived and fought in and often reminisced about the militant atmosphere of the bare-knuckle, hard-fighting days, urged the convention to "give those guys sixty days to get out of this union or else we are going to kick them out." With Chatak on his side, McDonald had acquired a symbol of credibility, at least for the moment. Actually Chatak was defending his union rather than McDonald, whom he often spoke of scornfully as "Fancy Dan" among his friends.

When Chatak finished an emotion-choked speech, his words jumbling and tumbling, the convention roared. McDonald recognized Rarick, making the target visible once again. The booing became violent. Standing at a floor microphone, Rarick complained, "I am surrounded by a lot of hostile people." "I will give you my personal protection," said President McDonald, inviting Rarick to come forward to the platform. By way of preliminary, Rarick asked McDonald to request every staff man, every man on the payroll of the Steelworkers, and every committeeman to rise. Whereupon McDonald turned to the convention and said, "Will every accredited delegate to the convention please rise." Rarick protested he had asked only for "all of the staff men, not the delegates."

Glaring at Rarick, McDonald declaimed: "I am the president, I am the chairman of this convention. I arise now and I arise on behalf of all the staff men who have been elected delegates." Then this personification of the convention shouted, "Mr. Rarick is simply trying to make a play to the press! Go ahead, Donald." Again the delegates booed.

Rarick spoke, every few words punctuated by derisive shouts from the audience. For the last few days, he said, he, Mamula, and O'Brien had been "taken apart." He emotionally denied that he was a "union buster, a stooge of the companies"; on the contrary, "I know of people who are wholeheartedly with me who are scared even to talk because they are scared they will get their heads batted in. . . ."

Then he turned to the election of 1957. "A lot of people—223,000—voted for me in the last international election. I don't want to bring this out on the floor, but since some people are forcing me into it, I must. I have asked for a breakdown, which I think under the constitution provides for a breakdown local by local. . . . I am entitled to that. . . . I am asking for it again. In that way there would be no question as to whether I was elected or not. A question has come up as to where Rarick got his money to finance the campaign. I want to tell you this: he got his money from the mill gates. . . . If you want to, you can go back there and see where the papers . . . took pictures of the fellows collecting funds at the mill gates. . . . I tell you where I got money to come to this convention— I borrowed it from the credit union at the Irvin Works."

When Rarick finished at last, McDonald arose. Concerning Rarick's reference to having people's heads batted in, he said: "I don't know what more I could do for Mr. Rarick than offer him my personal protection. I watched him walk down the aisle. Nobody attempted to beat his head in. I wouldn't permit anybody to beat his head in. The ushers on the floor . . . would protect Mr. Rarick or anybody else."

As to Rarick's demand for a local-by-local breakdown of the votes, McDonald replied that the breakdown was in the sole possession of the international tellers. "I have nothing to do with the international tellers. They are elected by the rank and file. Nobody has gone to the courts of this organization nor has anyone filed an official protest about the vote." On the question of financing the campaign with union funds, McDonald cited the findings of the union's regular auditors, "who went over the union accounts with a fine-tooth comb, went over my personal accounts with a fine-tooth comb. The reports were sent to the McClellan Committee. Everything was found to be in order. There was not one single penny of the international union's money spent in the election campaign." In fact, the McClellan Committee had not declared "everything to be in order"; no hearing was held and there was no public scrutiny.

Then McDonald turned to Rarick's charge that the Dues Protest Committee had been infiltrated by an agent of the administration of the Steelworkers Union. "Staton," he said, "was never on the payroll of the Steelworkers." He implied vaguely that Staton was working for some investigating group. As to who put out "Mask of Deceit," McDonald became fervent: "I absolutely guarantee you—I swear to you by all that is good and holy, and I ask Mr. Abel to confirm it—I didn't know about the pamphlet. It was not paid for in any sense at all by the international union. It was not paid for out of the revolving fund of any district." He obviously had not exhausted the possible sources of subsidy.

McDonald sought to dissociate himself completely from responsibility for the pamphlet. The prospect of another libel suit was not pleasant. Moreover, the blatant use of union money in an internal campaign, although not yet specifically declared illegal by Congress, could have caused an investigation by the McClellan Committee. On the issue of election of staff representatives, the dissenters were overwhelmingly defeated.

The big McDonald-Hague campaign against the rebel leaders was still to get under way. The convention proceeded first to dispose of certain suggested election reforms, such as the numbering of ballots. More than eight hundred resolutions from as many local unions had recommended no change in the existing method of conducting elections for international officers, members of the executive board, and tellers. They rejected proposals to have observers at the counting of ballots, that the election report be detailed local by local, that authorized watchers of each candidate be present at each polling place. The time for change had not yet come.

When the subject of dues payments came up once again, the two years of pent-up official wrath poured down over the Dues Protesters. Again, a swirling cacophony of shouts, placards, slogans. Seldom had so many moved in on so few. McDonald banged his gavel, shrugging his shoulders in seeming helplessness as the convention continued in an uproar.

Rarick assured the delegates that he would "abide by the decision of this body." His assurance did not slow down the convention locomotive. The less conciliatory O'Brien, who had been re-elected president of his local union several months before, charged that many locals' presidents had been pressured into distributing Thanksgiving and Christmas hams and turkeys. Such political patronage became possible with the increase in the locals' share of the dues increase voted in 1956. "I don't intend to allow myself to become the president of a ham-and-turkey local," he said angrily. He then revealed that the May before, McDonald had warned him that he was subject to trial procedure. "If I am wrong, I should be brought to trial," said O'Brien defiantly, "but not in kangaroo court in Atlantic City." At this point, the convention began to shout.

Then Nick Mamula (on a point of "special privilege") declared that he had been threatened with bodily harm and deplored the "passions that have been stirred . . . and the minds inflamed." To those charging that the Dues Protesters were Communists, Mamula replied, "You lie in your beard and you lie in your bowels." Those who made the charge, he said, were duty-bound to report such charges to the FBI and the House Un-American Activities Committee. He heatedly rejected the charge of dual unionism, and pointed out that the Dues Protest movement succeeded in electing Paul Hilbert, director of District 15. By this time, the convention was no longer concerned with the question of the dues structure, but rather was intent on castigating those who had challenged the McDonald leadership.

A respite came when Senator John F. Kennedy of Massachusetts was introduced to address the convention. Active in the McClellan Committee, he had sponsored legislation, along with the late Republican Senator Irving Ives of New York, to correct certain malpractices revealed in the committee hearings. His speech was prepared after some consultation with Goldberg, on whose capacity and experience as a labor lawyer the Senator placed considerable reliance. Kennedy spoke impressively, emphasizing the ethical concern of the labor movement, which through the AFL-CIO had "thrown out hoodlums who had infiltrated into their ranks." He was referring to the expulsion by the AFL-CIO in December 1957 of the Hoffa-led Teamsters and two other unions. He invoked the memory of heroes past. "The heritage of Phil Murray and Van Bittner," he said, "will not be easily surrendered or squandered, nor will you be lulled into lethargy by those who say there are no longer any burning issues." For a while the convention's eyes were fixed on far horizons.

Unbeknownst to Kennedy, however, his speech became the prelude to expulsion proceedings. With the aid of the legal staff, McDonald himself was now ready to make the action "short and snappy." "Let's not beat a dead cat around any longer." The special resolution read by Molony, secretary of the Resolutions Committee, cited the Code of Union Democratic Practices, promulgated by the AFL-CIO and ratified by the Steelworkers Union, stating the right to voice views on the conduct of union affairs. (The language of the code had been largely the work of Goldberg in his capacity as special counsel to the AFL-CIO and secretary of the AFL-CIO Ethical Practices Committee.) But, said Molony, this "does not include the right to undermine the union as an institution, to advocate dual unionism, to destroy or weaken the union as a collective bargaining agency, or carry on slander or libel. We must regard the small group of persons . . . who, under the guise of protesting a constitutional dues increase, are in fact seeking to undermine the union as an institution. . . . There is no room in our union for traitors to trade-union principles." The local unions and the international executive board were to be instructed "in conformity with the rules of due process . . . to take prompt and vigorous action to eliminate from our ranks those guilty of these serious constitutional violations."

"There is only one thing left," said District Director Paul Rusen, chairman of the committee; "to go back to our districts and local unions, and anywhere they raise their ugly heads, file charges and let's kick them to hell out of this union."

His six-foot-four bulk trembling, looking directly at McDonald, Rarick denied any secret backing as charged by McDonald. "Mr. McDonald, you can laugh now, but you had better not laugh when it comes to the rank and file because they are not behind you, no matter what you get here. . . . There is nobody mysterious behind us. You, Mr. McDonald, know this because you sat down in a hotel in Pittsburgh with Frank O'Brien, myself, yourself, Ernest Nassar, your private attorney, and James Ashton, our attorney. . . . We didn't need bodyguards to protect us down in Florida, either, or anyplace we went."

The oratorical *coup de grâce* was delivered by Molony. "You would think no one else in this union has ever raised himself up and exerted himself and used his constitutional rights. Hell, we had rebels in this union before Rarick was a member. It is true that at one time I sought high office in this union. . . . I am sorry as hell I got beaten. . . . I was beaten by Howard Hague, and I recognize Howard Hague as the vice-president of the United Steelworkers. To this very moment, Delegate Rarick does not recognize President McDonald as president. . . . I will tell you something else. When I and the good people who supported me were beaten—and beaten fairly and squarely—I did not run to the McClellan Committee, I didn't sue my beloved union for a million dollars, and I didn't attack the character and the integrity of my friend, Dave McDonald."

Molony seemed furious over a possible comparison between his campaign and Rarick's. "There is no lynch law in the United Steelworkers of America. These people will be given a fair trial and, found guilty, will be delivered from our midst." Then in a mighty peroration, Molony said: "Messrs. Rarick, Mamula, and O'Brien—in advance of charges being filed, in advance of the findings of their local unions and the international executive board, and solely because of their conduct at this convention —I say, there is no place for you in the United Steelworkers of America." The convention hall roared approval. McDonald, his face shining, leaped up and said: "Brother Molony, I want to extend my sincere compliments to you for that marvelous statement." Only two votes against the motion were counted by the ushers.

In his closing remarks, McDonald said: "I tried to be democratic. . . . All allegations notwithstanding, I assume you delegates will agree with me that everybody had his say. . . ."

Phil Regan led the delegates in singing "God Bless America."

The next day a *New York Times* editorial described the convention as a "model of democracy." Two days later, the McKeesport, Pennsylvania, *Daily News* headed its editorial "Try 'Em, Hang 'Em." That same weekend, the McClellan Committee indicated that it would retain an interest in the way the United Steelworkers handled the rebels in the postconvention trial proceedings.

Second thoughts now began to prevail. The hothouse atmosphere of a convention, where manipulation of the proceedings generates a climate of security for the leaders was dissipated on the return home. Under convention instruction, however, the international officers were bound to move against Rarick, Mamula, and O'Brien, in accordance with the union's constitutional procedures.

These involved considerable time and manpower, with appeals, counterappeals, and finally a possible appearance before the convention two years later—in 1960. Under the union's constitution, even an expelled member would have the right to the platform at the succeeding inter-national convention. Consequently, the union leadership would find itself stuck on procedural flypaper, unable to step out of a situation that might deteriorate. After the convention, the union leadership—and Goldberg, its legal counsel—began to address itself to the question whether all this legal activity against Rarick *et al.* was necessary.

Inevitably, the proposed action against Rarick produced political reaction. The rough ride given Rarick, Mamula, and O'Brien redounded on the national leadership. The forms of democracy observed at the con-vention could not hide the massive vindictiveness. The arsenal of powers available to McDonald and the executive board could cripple the union's prestige and the morale of a significant section of the membership. Friends of the trade-union movement, Democratic and Republican alike, would find such a display of power against dissenters embarrassing, and perhaps indefensible, in discussions on labor legislation.

The convention had exposed the reality that the Steelworkers Union, unaccustomed to the expression of minority dissent, simply did not know, as an institution, how to handle disagreement with leadership except to treat it as obscenity bordering on treason. If the Rarick group appealed for the intercession of the McClellan Committee, Rarick could be made a "martyr" exploitable by antiunion forces in the face of im-portant collective-bargaining sessions coming up in 1959.

So the union strategists set about finding a face-saving formula that would uphold the convention mandate while taking into account the "total picture." The charges of dual unionism had to be processed by the local unions. The trial of Anthony Tomko, president of Local 1408 and a supporter of the Dues Protesters, was held in October; he was acquitted by his local union. In December Rarick was tried and ac-quitted. Nick Mamula, who was also exonerated of charges in his local union, received its all-out support; it ordered his accusers to pay the costs of the trial. The accusers, who were carrying out the convention directive, refused and were thereupon expelled from their local. Not until the con-vention of 1960 were they officially reinstated. However, in line with the "go slow" strategy, the acquittals of Rarick, Mamula, and Tomko were not appealed to the executive board. Instead, it censured Mamula—who had hired an attorney to defend him against the earlier charges—and the local's secretary-treasurer. Mamula appealed this somewhat less than harsh verdict to the 1960 convention, which upheld the censure. During the summer of 1961, Mamula was brought up on charges of misconduct in office. Part of the continuing pressure came from Kay Kluz, now the district director, whom McDonald had previously appointed to fill a vacancy caused by death. Kluz, a man with a ready command of lan-guage, saw in Mamula, as head of the Jones & Laughlin local, a considerable threat. Mamula's eventual removal by a vote of 161 to 144 at a meeting of his local—with a membership well over 10,000—was confirmed by the union's international board. He became ineligible to serve in office for a period of five years.

McDonald cracked down on rebel elements on the West Coast, notably on Thomas Flaherty, president of the Fontana local of the Kaiser Steel Company, whose activity in the Dues Protesters campaign had aroused the enmity of the staff representatives and the subdirector of the district, William (Billy) Brunton.

The McDonald course now zigzagged strangely. In preparing for the 1959 steel negotiations, McDonald suddenly announced the appointment of Rarick to membership on the U.S. Steel negotiating committee. To appoint the dual unionist of the year before to a prestigious committee seemed incredible to those who took such charges literally. But those on the inside understood that "dual unionist" was in fact a dirty epithet cast at any dissenter in the union. McDonald's enlistment of Rarick on the Wage Policy Committee was considered a clever move designed to divide and bewilder the Dues Protesters. Having been denounced as a traitor, Rarick was more than a little pleased to be brought into the decision-making apparatus of the contract negotiations.

Following the 116-day strike of 1959 and the settlement of 1960, mutterings and threats were revived in locals and districts. Considerable dissatisfaction arose from the fact that direct wage increases over a three-year contract amounted to no more than 34 cents as against the first report of 39 to 41 cents. This amounted to about a 3.7 per cent annual increase in total employment costs, as compared with an estimated 8 per cent annual increase under the 1956 agreement. It compared with other settlements made by the union with Kaiser of a 5 per cent annual increase in employment costs and the can and aluminum settlements of about 4.7 per cent. The workers got no wage increase the first year, although take-home pay was increased by the industry's agreement to pick up the full cost of insurance coverage. But the union agreed to give up 4 cents in cost-of-living escalation to which it would have been entitled under the expired agreement, with the strong possibility that the cost of the insurance program would eat up some of the putative increases. The government's Livernash Report described the result as a defeat for all concerned; it might have been possible to make the same settlement back in July as was finally made in January after a 116-day strike and the period of the eighty-day Taft-Hartley injunction during which the workers were compelled to work at the old contract rates.*

* *Collective Bargaining in the Basic Steel Industry: A Study of the Public Interest and the Role of Government.* Directed by E. Robert Livernash. Department of Labor, 1961, p. 307.

With the time for local union elections again approaching, the Dues Protesters, almost in the fourth year of their uneven, intermittent existence, met in May 1960 in Pittsburgh. About eighty rank-and-filers from eight states attended. They discarded the name Dues Protest Committee and arose, phoenixlike, as the Organization for Membership Rights. The group disdained the 1960 basic steel agreement as a "bag of crumbs" and charged that the end result hardly compensated for the four-month strike and its eighty day Taft-Hartley aftermath. It demanded that future strikes be called only after authorization by a referendum.

McDonald made a fervent appeal to Mamula's and Rarick's locals, now about to elect their officers, "to get these bedbugs put out of my hair." Disregarding McDonald, the membership re-elected them by large majorities. Tomko and O'Brien also won. At least two other members of OMR were elected local union presidents. In Fontana, California, four on the OMR slate were elected.

Still, the discontent that had churned up in 1956 and 1957 was no longer a union-wide phenomenon. Moreover, the long 1959 strike seemed to have drained off the political energy of the membership. Even more depressing was the fact that eight months after the industry-wide strike, steel production had fallen; 150,000 Steelworkers were out of work and 350,000 were employed only part time.

The 1960 Convention

The Atlantic City Steelworkers convention in September 1960 was the first one to be conducted since the passage of the Landrum-Griffin Act, which to an unprecedented degree affected the internal life of the American trade-union movement. Two of its provisions, in particular, affected areas of controversy inside the United Steelworkers: (1) its "Bill of rights for union members" (Title I) and (2) its section on "Elections" (Title IV). It provided rules and standards governing the increase of dues and assessments; forbade any labor organization "to limit the right of any member thereof to institute an action in any court, . . . or appear as a witness" in any proceeding, except that he may be required to exhaust reasonable hearing procedures (but not to exceed a four-month lapse) within such organization, before instituting legal or administrative proceedings against such organizations or any other officer thereof. Also, "no interested employer or employer association shall directly or indirectly finance, encourage, or participate in, except as a party, any such action, proceeding, appearance or petition."

In the conduct of union elections, the law (officially the Labor-Management Reporting and Disclosure Act of 1959) spelled out in considerable detail the rights of candidates for union office and the obligation of the organizations to see that such rights are fulfilled:

> Unions . . . must comply with reasonable requests of candidates to distribute, by mail or otherwise, campaign literature at the candidate's expense to members in good standing . . . and to refrain from discrimination in favor of or against any candidate with respect to the use of lists of members. . . . Every bona fide candidate shall have the right, once within 30 days prior to an election . . . to inspect a list containing the names and last known addresses of all members. . . . Adequate safeguards to insure a fair election shall be provided, including the right of any candidate to have an observer at the polls and at the counting of the ballots. . . . The votes cast by members of each local labor organization shall be counted, and the result published, separately. The election officials designated in the constitution and by-laws . . . shall preserve for one year the ballots and all other records pertaining to the election. . . .

On the first day of the convention, John F. Kennedy, Democratic candidate for President, addressed the delegates. But the praise bestowed on Kennedy became insignificant when the ever-ready Al Whitehouse declared McDonald the "greatest leader in the world today" and assaulted reactionary businessmen and their "stinking stooges in the Organization for Management Rights." Molony charged Rarick with attempting to undermine his leadership in the Carrier Corporation strike at Syracuse, New York, where Rarick urged the membership to set up an opponent against Molony as well as against McDonald. Molony roared: "I identify this traitor—Rarick, the strikebreaker." To the booing convention Rarick denied the Molony charges, explaining that he appeared at the Syracuse local on the invitation of the local president, obviously no friend of Molony. Smaile Chatak told the delegates that Rarick was like one of the "screwballs" of the 1920s in the United Mine Workers: "Let's pop them in the nose and kick them out." In anticipation of this advice, Anthony Tomko, president of the McKeesport local, was beaten up by four ushers; he had refused to stop circulating anti-McDonald literature on the convention floor. Then it was Rarick's turn.

The attack on Rarick had been too public to be easily brushed aside. It came after Rarick and his followers resumed their activity on the convention floor. Beside himself with rage, like Henry II with Becket, McDonald stormed around the platform and backstage. "Somebody get rid of that guy for me," he said. Several delegates followed Rarick off the floor and stalked him into the corridors and the lobby leading to the Boardwalk. Chief among them was George Elliott, a staff associate, who was recognized as a man talented in McDonald's service. As the group gathered around Rarick, Elliott grabbed hold of a reporter who had been talking with Rarick as he moved into the corridor. Elliott moved in hard and raised his fist. Wrong man! A combined operation of ushers led by Elliott then slammed Rarick against a wall, bloodied him up, and ripped his clothing. After Rarick had been severely worked over, Elliott was quickly removed from the Atlantic City jurisdiction and hustled aboard a private plane. Policemen arrived, but not before Rarick had suffered considerable physical damage.

One staff observer, convinced that this act of violence was not a simple spontaneous expression of loyalty for McDonald, went up to the president and berated him as responsible for the incident. "Look," said McDonald loftily, "go back of the stage and give the details to Arthur Goldberg." The staff man did. He recounted all the details to Goldberg, who took complete notes. Nothing came of it except a McDonald statement of exculpation to the convention, quoting Goldberg.

Rarick wired Secretary of Labor James P. Mitchell charging that he had been the victim of violence during the convention, in violation of his rights under Landrum-Griffin. Obviously, the assault at the convention that had just endorsed Kennedy for President and rejected Vice-President Richard M. Nixon had in itself disturbing overtones and possible repercussions. Rarick's appeal to Mitchell, who had been invited to the convention in his official capacity, gave the Republican Labor Secretary a text for his address to the convention—"which," he said wryly, "I know is a nonpolitical audience." It was "very unfortunate," he said, "that in a democratic union, such acts of violence as this take place."

Just before delivering his benediction in the concluding ceremonies, McDonald commented on the charges of violence during the convention: "I suppose, as Arthur Goldberg said, that in any city of 3,500 people almost every day somebody gets punched in the kisser and it is not a national story. But, as far as I know, there were three people punched; two outside the convention hall, and one poor fellow, a very good friend of mine. He was badly beaten up by some of my opponents, thrown out of the elevator in the Ambassador Hotel. We have made no point of that." Reporters could not determine where or even if the incident had occurred.

McDonald then confided to the convention a glimpse of his spiritual interior. "Every morning and every evening I say a little prayer to the Holy Ghost, the Third Person of the Blessed Trinity, for guidance and wisdom. It is a simple little prayer, and it goes like this:

Come Holy Ghost, Creator-blessed
And in my heart take up Thy rest.

> Come with Thy grace, Thy heavenly aid,
> To help this heart which Thou hast made.

I say that prayer for one purpose only, and that is to guide and help my Steelworkers."

Whether because of the efficacy of prayer or the rapid deterioration of Rarick's position in the postconvention period, Rarick failed to secure the forty local union nominations required to place his name on the ballot. In the 1961 election, Lloyd Ulman noted, "unopposed, McDonald polled 221,130 votes, in contrast to the 404,172 with which he had been credited in 1957." Thus in a no-contest election, no more than 20 per cent of the membership was recorded as participating in the referendum. The 1961 election was the first in which the votes were recorded and published on a local-by-local basis.

In the fall of 1960, the political energy of the Steelworkers Union was channeled into the campaign for the election of Kennedy. Rarick's fumbling alliances with certain Republican politicians alienated him from many of his previous supporters, while McDonald completely and deliberately identified himself with the Kennedy candidacy.

High Cost of Image Building

What McDonald lacked in charisma he had sought to make up in cosmetics. Image building came high. Part of its cost was revealed in the international's semiannual audit reports. When the dues were raised from three dollars to five dollars a month, the augmented funds provided a public-relations bonanza.

McDonald's monthly TV show began in 1957 and ran for twenty-four months. The theme song, "Strong Men of Steel," was sung by Phil Regan. In the October 1959 show, McDonald was shown seated deep in an easy chair, pipe in hand, reflective, the father image. He had received lots of mail, he said, from union members and their wives "troubled by rumors and reports." They wrote, he said, so "I could resolve their doubts." One of the correspondents wanted to know, "Why were you absent from New York during negotiations during August 1959?" At the time, there were widespread rumors that McDonald had disappeared in the midst of negotiations; nobody seemed to know where he was. Four months later, over TV, McDonald sought to explain his absence: "Where was I? I visited the local unions and the picket lines," he said in a pained, pious tone. "He must have gone incognito," one district director said.

Reels of the twenty-four TV shows were distributed widely—to local unions, to libraries, and to many colleges and universities. In most places this valuable contribution to higher education remained unopened. During this time, the union audit showed a rapid diminution in the amount of money spent for the international union's traditional educational activities.

In 1958, $958,000 was spent on dramatizing the McDonald image, compared with $10,300,000 for all other operating expenses of the international union that year. For the first half of 1959, the international audit report showed that $2,146,000 was expended for TV, radio, newspapers, and films, out of total international operating expenses of $7,724,000. For the educational program, the international office that half year expended $51,788. In the second half of 1959—the period of most of the 116-day strike—more than $860,000 was paid out for TV, radio, newspaper, and films, out of a total of $5,778,000 to cover all international office operating expenses. Thus for 1959 a total of $3,000,000 was spent on the Madison Avenue type of persuasion, and in 1960 a total of $1,100,000 was spent for the McDonald scenario.

Two weeks before the 1962 Steelworkers convention in Miami Beach, the imagery went sour. Phil Regan's close ties to McDonald got front-page headlines in New York papers. An investigator from District Attorney Frank Hogan's office tried to serve Regan with a subpoena; Hogan's office had been looking for Regan for two and a half months to get him to explain what he knew about an alleged $25,000 payment to an official of Mayor Robert F. Wagner's administration by an executive of the Duncan Meter Company to assure the firm a lucrative parking-meter contract. Regan was finally located in McDonald's twenty-first-floor suite at the Hampshire House, where a wedding reception for David McDonald, Jr., and his bride was in progress. The investigator seems to have waited discreetly in an anteroom, hoping to serve Regan without creating a fuss. But the senior McDonald took steps to protect Regan from the impending service. Regan moved to the terrace, the investigator ducked around McDonald to serve him, and Charlie Barranco, McDonald's premier bodyguard, moved on the investigator. The diligent rackets-squad man was finally "roughed up and thrown out" of the McDonald wedding reception.

The 1962 Convention

From the excitements of New York, McDonald and his retinue moved on to the union's September convention in Miami Beach. The mood was indigo. Instead of citing congratulations from the steel industry, Bishop Coleman F. Carroll referred to the pessimistic sentiments being expressed about the future of organized labor, specifically to several "popular as well as scholarly" pieces published in the weeks preceding the convention under such titles as "Is Labor on the Skids?," "Has

Labor Lost Its Punch?," and "Labor's Ebbing Strength." He came, said the bishop, not to bury the labor movement, but certainly not to flatter it.

Taking no chances on exposing his organization to an objective analysis, McDonald assured the delegates that the Steelworkers Union was a "great, progressive organization." He looked on the preceding two years and found them good. He could refer to meetings with President Kennedy and "our old friend, Arthur Goldberg," who had already served as Secretary of Labor and had just been elevated to the Supreme Court. In April of that year, the Steelworkers had agreed to an early agreement with U.S. Steel, which was then followed by the steel companies' announcement of a price increase, thus creating the steel crisis of 1962.*

In his opening address, McDonald again emphasized the importance of the Human Relations Committee, the group of management and labor that presumably would pave the "way to a new era of understanding with the American steel industry." At the same time the union, with a claimed membership of 1,250,000 members, had only 900,000 dues-paying members; the others were either unemployed or partially employed, or were working at jobs outside the union's jurisdiction. In basic steel, 100,000 fewer than in 1957 were employed as part of the industry's labor force. In five years they had gone, never to return. While the union had learned to live with the corrosive factor of reduced employment, this grim statistic settled over the convention like smog.

But union politics soon took priority. The Study Committee, authorized by the 1960 convention to revise the constitution, proposed several changes in the election and nomination requirements: instead of forty local nominations, this number was to be sharply increased. Henceforth the number of local union nominations required for a candidate for international office was to be determined by a new formula that would produce at least 120 nominations, depending on the current membership. A similar formula was applied to nominations for district director.

Opposition to this jump in the number of nominations came from the redoubtable Mike Zahorsky and from Rarick. Rarick decried the in-

* To President Kennedy, the action of the steel companies was a betrayal of an understanding that there would be no price increase. He pointed out that the Steelworkers Union had abided by their part of the bargain: agreement to keep the wage demands low, indeed well below the wage "guidelines" proposed by the Council of Economic Advisers. The resulting "steel crisis," with the confrontation of the President of the United States and the steel industry, became one of the significant political and economic developments of the year. As a result of the pressure by the Kennedy administration, the steel companies rescinded their price increases. But the role of the president of the Steelworkers Union in generating that pressure was almost imperceptible and, after a critical period of hesitation, only reluctantly audible.

creased requirement as undemocratic; the union was being put on the "road to destruction," a "determined effort by the few to nullify the chance of anybody running against them." McDonald pounded the gavel and demanded that Rarick apologize to the convention. He insisted that he had no fear of opposition and that the suggested change was not his personal recommendation at all. District Director Joe Germano asserted that it was only a matter of "proper representation." The change was adopted, to become effective for the next international election period starting in November 1964. Since Rarick had been unable in 1960 to collect even the forty nominations under the previous provision, the higher number now required (varying with the paid-up membership) diminished his remaining hopes for fielding a ticket against the McDonald administration.

Despite the change in nomination procedure, McDonald failed to obtain a proposed dues increase of $5 a month. The approach of the leadership was less direct than in 1956, when the rate went from $3 to $5, in that the additional $5 assessment was to be terminated when the union's net worth reached $25 million. Still, it was no go. The delegates reacted immediately—and negatively. For them, it was 1956 all over again. One delegate from the large Local 1222, an old Dues Protest center, dubbed it a "dues increase with a built-in escalator clause—a blank check." Another delegate called the approach poor public relations, the kind of charge that made McDonald jump. An unidentified Canadian delegate charged that such a dues increase device "will follow Parkinson's Law that if the money is available it will be spent."

As in 1956, McDonald called upon Abel as secretary-treasurer to "clear up the confusion in the minds of the delegates." Abel, a natural team player and the board's advocate, spoke half-humorously about the 1956 convention, where "we had quite a discussion and we had repercussions following it." The 1956 dues increase was justified by subsequent developments, such as the 1959 strike. Now as then, Abel said, the union was not poverty-stricken, but its leadership was concerned for the future. In 1956, Abel pointed out, the net worth of the union was $21 million, but the union—with its record membership of 1,200,000—required a net worth of at least $50 million to ensure its security. By 1959, the union's net worth had risen to just over $32 million. Demands of that year of the great basic steel strike spilled over to early 1960, and the union ended with a net operating loss of more than $6 million. For 1962, the membership figure was fluctuating between a high of 915,000 and a low of 837,000 dues-paying members.

As a consequence, the union's current net worth then stood at $21.8 million—of which $5.5 million was represented by loans to local unions, which repaid about $500,000 in loans that same year. Why then had the international union not invoked the assessment powers already permitted by the constitution during the 1959 strike? "Perhaps we should have," said Abel. "I am sure that with half a million members on strike the other half million wouldn't have objected to paying an additional five dollars to the winning of that strike in the advancement of the interests of our membership." But Abel explained that it was "the judgment of the Executive Board that the union was financially able to carry that strike without going to the membership for additional funds." Abel stressed that the self-restraint on the part of the executive board was due to a refusal to "willy-nilly impose additional dues upon the membership."

Although Abel's prestige with rank-and-file delegates was high and his knowledge of this problem intimate, the delegates seemed unresponsive. Unlike in 1956, McDonald did not try to bulldoze the dues change over the body of the convention. As he called on the delegates to be counted for or against the proposal, there was rising tension. The ushers counted and recounted while the opposition delegates hovered over the voting like hawks. McDonald, suddenly aloof, called on Abel to report the count made by the ushers. The dues change had been defeated, 1,532 to 1,454.

Furious in defeat, McDonald could hardly control his anger at the delegates, some of whom could not conceal their glee. "Maybe," he told them, "some of you feel elated over the outcome of that vote. Perhaps you voted against the motion because you didn't understand it. But this I absolutely guarantee you, my friends: as long as I am president of this union I am going to operate this union in the black. I will not operate this union if it is going to take loss after loss. I positively will not do it. I have been jovial and as kind as I can be up here." His half-smile became rigid. "I have no doubts but that in one or two years a lot of other delegates will be coming here with a lot of suggestions. A lot of local unions which are now broke will be asking the international secretary-treasurer to give them money or lend them money. I guarantee you are not going to get any loans. You are not going to get any grants. This international union is going to operate in the black." Then directing his words to some staff members who he felt had deserted the ship: "If this means a smaller staff, it means a smaller staff."

Then came the careless gesture, the toss of the head, playing it cool: "I kind of anticipated what was going to happen here today. We had a little joshing up here in front, good-natured joshing by friends of mine. They all have the right to speak their minds, to vote as they please." He glared at the assembled delegates by whom he felt betrayed. "Don't anybody leave here with the impression that your Constitution Committee, that your executive board, that your international officers have taken a tremendous beating . . . . You will be back and you will be asking for help, and we'll give you help. Remember this finally, we are going to operate in the black, so help me, we are going to carry out this program which we have outlined here . . . to the limit of our abilities. If our abilities are limited, you must understand why they are limited." Then he bore down on their base ingratitude: "Since 1956 the basic steelworkers have received new emoluments amounting to 30 per cent. Since 1956 not one employee of the United Steelworkers International Union has received a wage increase. The directors and the staff are working for what they got then. Everybody is working for the same amount of money, and they are your employees. You are the boss. You have spoken. So be it." McDonald stalked to the wings.

The atmosphere in the convention had become thick and black. The delegates sat silent under the tongue-lashing by their president. How could the convention be brought to an acceptable conclusion? Such a moment was made to order for a man like Joe Molony. He rose from his seat on the platform and strove to transform the convention's blow to McDonald's vanity into a record of a "great debate." He praised "our distinguished president for the calm and impartial manner in which he presided over the debate and the vote." Then, for the sake of the union, Molony sought to lift the McDonald persona above the battle. "You will note that President McDonald did not rise in support or in opposition to any particular changes." All the changes, he said, were offered by the executive board. To guard against unspoken accusations from McDonald or from his supporters, Molony said: "Confession being good for the soul, and in order to protect my own honor, I think I should tell you, seeing I didn't have an opportunity to speak for or against the changes in the constitution—I must report to you that I voted for the changes, and I believed in them." Then he concluded: "Let no one think for a moment that this represents a division within."

Molony's remarks were meant to remove the bad taste left by McDonald's savage rejoinder to the convention's action. The delegates instinctively understood and gave Molony a standing ovation. This spontaneous and unexpected tribute flooded up toward a man who was recognized as having made a gallant attempt to heal the wounded vanity of their president while spreading balm over the assaulted body of the convention, the stunned and bewildered victim of verbal aggression by its chief officer. By this time, McDonald was back from the wings and at his chair on the platform. He had decided not to abandon, after all, an ungrateful people to their own devices. With a rare display of insight, he said to the delegates: "I know you are tired, and if you are like me, you sure would like to have a beer. . . . The gavel is up for grabs!" He tossed it to the delegates.

Minnesota Vignette

Eyewitness stories of McDonald's extracurricular activities began to luxuriate. His press-agented familiarity with Zsa Zsa Gabor at "21" in New York was duly chronicled by syndicated Broadway columnists. Splashing around night clubs, however, was comedy relief; what began to stir annoyance in the union was his deportment on less private occasions, when he was expected to perform in behalf of the union.

Such an occasion was McDonald's visit in October 1963 to Duluth, located in District 33, which includes the series of northern iron ranges of Minnesota, northern Wisconsin, and the Upper Peninsula of Michigan. Earl T. Bester, director of the district, had urged McDonald to come there, on his first visit in six years, to participate in the climax of a dramatic campaign to keep the steel companies and thousands of jobs in Minnesota. The presence and voice of the union president were expected to add muscle to a touch-and-go effort.

The burning issue was the repeal of the Minnesota state tax on ore, levied for years on the steel and ore companies, which had exploited the rich and highly profitable workings. The tax, once a triumph of social legislation, had helped reduce the tax burden on the average wage earner. But as the rich ore began to peter out, the companies, feeling burdened by the tax, announced their intention to abandon the Minnesota ore fields; the financial returns apparently were no longer commensurate with their investment. The ghost of unemployment began to haunt the region. But while the rich iron ore was being exhausted, a low-grade ore, taconite, remained in abundance. It could be processed efficiently only by a technical plant that needed a huge outlay of capital. The companies made it clear that such an investment could be made only if the tax on ore was removed. They put it bluntly to the state and to labor: "Either the tax goes or we don't develop the taconite operation here. We'll move it to South America or Labrador." With McDonald, the companies employed gentler tactics: they argued that their campaign was in effect an extension of the Human Relations Committee approach, by which he set such great store.

The McDonald visit of October 1963 remains vivid in the mind and memory of one union participant:

"Well, we had some agonizing reassessments and Earl Bester and his constituents made them. To save steelworkers' jobs, they decided to stump the state in behalf of tax repeal. The whole lobbying campaign was timed to reach a crescendo about the time of the District 33 conference. Neighboring district directors were invited and McDonald's speech had been elaborately researched, polished, and refined for weeks.

Shortly after, the state legislature was to vote on the tax repeal. Other segments of the labor movement were against the repeal because they weren't going to be benefited directly and they were sure their taxes were going to go up as a result of ore tax repeal. But the Steelworkers Union and steel management were working on this together. Company representatives were invited to the District Conference banquet, an unusual fact in itself. So, in this strange and difficult crusade, Earl was relying heavily on McDonald and his speech to clinch the thing.

"Arrangements had been made for saturation TV and radio coverage throughout the state. You never saw so many TV cameras and mikes short of a national political convention. . . . The banquet committee began to get antsy when by 6:30 McDonald hadn't put in an appearance. We knew he had spent some time out on the Range visiting some mines and taconite installations, but he had returned to the hotel hours before. Where was he? The dinner began, without the guest of honor. Finally, a rustle and a bustle in back of the hall. In comes Earl Bester, some of his staff, and a couple of members of McDonald's entourage, and the man himself. I took a quick look at David and I immediately realized the worst was about to happen. Flushed, slack-lipped, he was literally carried up to the dais with a guy under each arm, propping him up the two, three steps, and they set him in his appointed place. Earl was absolutely livid. I said, 'What's the matter?' 'You can see. The dirty, rotten so-and-so is drunk. I can't believe he'd do this to me. Look at him, look at him! I don't know whether he can even speak.' By this time, McDonald began to eat. He dug into the shrimp cocktail and he was so loose at the joints, he was weaving sitting down. I thought, 'My God, help us in this hour of need.' Finally, the television boys are waving and pointing to the watches. Prime time had arrived. Earl said, fearfully, 'Dave, we've got to put you on. You won't be able to finish your dinner.' 'S'all right, s'all right. I don't care. Let's get this show on the road.' Earl got up and made a nice introduction: 'I give you the international president of the United Steelworkers, my great friend and yours, David J. McDonald.' Wild applause. Dave got up. 'Where's the speech? Where's the God-damn speech?' Earl's secretary, Sophie, said, 'What's that in your back pocket, Mr. McDonald?' He clutched at his hip where the speech had been stuck. He lurched toward the podium and dropped his speech. The pages fluttered to the floor. McDonald and Bester—all this on camera—stooped at the same time to pick it up. They bumped heads; apologized; stooped again; got a hold of the same sheet and managed to tear it in two. McDonald finally set his speech down on the podium, and started reading, plunk in the middle of it. Under the weather though he was, he seemed to realize something was wrong. All of us were praying for the earth to open up and swallow us. The cameras were winking away and finally he set the script aside and said, 'I'd like to speak off the cuff. I don't like these stereotyped speeches.' He proceeded to deliver the most rambling, incoherent diatribe about nothing at all I ever heard in my life. He finally ground to a shrieking halt. The cameras clicked off, and so ended the day.

"You know, it was not the drinking. It's the fact he didn't deliver. There's a time and a place for getting your shoes full, but not at a time like this."

BOOK II

THE UPHEAVAL: THE GAVEL IS UP FOR GRABS

CHAPTER 7

Start of the Action

Nemo me impune lacessit.
(No man provokes me with impunity.)

The beginning was no bigger than the enthusiastic shout of a single local union, No. 1123 in Canton, Ohio, I. W. Abel's home local. He had served it in all elected capacities from the time of its organization in 1936. The members were employed by Timken Bearing Division of U.S. Steel. Named the Golden Lodge in honor of Clinton S. Golden, then assistant president to Philip Murray, the local prided itself as the first in the Steelworkers Union to build its own headquarters.

Iorwith Wilbur Abel, one of four children, was born in Magnolia, Ohio, on August 11, 1908, the son and grandson of blacksmiths. Grandfather Abel had come to this country in the last century from Alsace-Lorraine, then part of Germany; Abel's mother was of Welsh mining stock. Abel attended grade and high schools there in Magnolia and went on to a business college in Canton. By the time he had finished high school, he had worked in a brickyard as a stoveman, plumber, mud mixer, and brick carrier. An impatient boss decided that his Welsh first name was too hard to handle: "We'll call you Abe." From that time on, he was Abe to everybody but his mother, who always called him Iorwith.

After leaving school, he worked in the shipping office of the American Sheet & Tin Plate Company, later part of U.S. Steel. By the time he was a husky and raw-boned sixteen, he had established himself. He became a "boomer," a man with a trade ready to travel where the work was. From the Canton Malleable Iron Company he moved on to the Timken Roller Bearing foundry. In June 1930, at twenty-one, he was married to Bernice Joseph, of nearby East Sparta, Ohio. Six months later Timken closed down the foundry and the young Abels began celebrating the familiar rites of the Depression. For a while he got a job firing kilns in an Ohio brickyard at sixteen cents an hour, twelve hours a day, while his wife worked in a tile plant at a cent an hour more. About this time, he also got his first political job, on election day, working for the Democratic Party in Republican Magnolia.

During the next five years, Abel had channeled his rising discontent. Back at Timken in 1936 he joined the Steel Workers Organizing Committee, the predecessor of the United Steelworkers. After helping organize Timken, Abel became shop steward, grievance committeeman, vice-president of the lodge, and, in 1938, the local's president. Philip Murray appointed him a staff organizer in 1939, and his heavy-muscled frame and rumbling baritone began to be seen and heard in labor circles. In 1942, Murray appointed him district director of the SWOC. That same year he was formally elected to that post by the founding convention of the United Steelworkers. He was henceforth a member of the top leadership.

For the next ten years, Abel led Steelworkers Union organizing drives and was an active officer of the Ohio Congress of Industrial Organizations. In the postwar 1940s Abel engaged in negotiations with the management of Timken Roller Bearing, whose board chairman, William Unstadt, was known by steelworkers as "the Prussian general." In the immediate postwar period, this district became the scene of several long strikes. Abel became more generally known to the local leadership and his fellow district leaders on the international executive board, which in 1952 chose him secretary-treasurer to succeed McDonald.

The Abels had bought a house in Bethel Park, a Pittsburgh suburb where they lived alone—one of their two daughters was married, the other working. His house sat atop an abandoned mine, where legend had it that Phil Murray once dug coal. At Deep Creek, in western Maryland, he had built a summer house in the mountains.

When Abel became secretary-treasurer, his friend John S. Johns succeeded him as director of District 27. While Abel remained tight-lipped in public, Johnny Johns was considered somewhat more outspoken. By 1964, he was convinced that McDonald's time had come and that Abel was the man to replace him. Abel hung back, rejecting attempts to push him into open contention. He was not inclined to campaign simply on his own dissatisfaction with McDonald, the frustration of his life under him, and the intramural mutterings of several dissatisfied district leaders.

What Abel couldn't or wouldn't do, his friends—among them Adrian J. Clark, then the local's president—did. In May 1964, an article in the *Golden Lodge News* became a trial balloon for an Abel candidacy. Encouraged by the response, the local's newspaper ran an editorial demanding the start of a drive to draft Abel for president:

Phil Murray, President of the Steelworkers, died more than a decade ago. A man of vision and determination, he led the S.W.O.C. through its formative years. The Steelworkers today need a leader to maintain and preserve the union that men like Murray, [Van] Bittner and Golden built. Rumblings of discontent among union men grow louder day by day.

This union will elect International Officers in 1965 and there is a man available who can lead this union in the direction those old-time mine workers first started it. This man will probably have to be drafted. It is now time for all Steelworkers to start insisting that I. W. Abel become President of the Steelworkers. Steelworkers now need a leader such as he, before the harshness of their historic past becomes the prophecy of a bleak and bitter future.

This union must have a President who will command respect from others and lead his own with dignity and honor. This union needs such a leader if it is to survive and flourish. We are comprised of dirt, sweat and toil—not perfume, cake and tea. Iron and steel we know—not penthouse clubs and fancy social affairs.

The rank and file must start a DRAFT ABEL FOR PRESIDENT drive. Steelworkers, tell him plain and direct: ABE, YOU ARE THE MAN—YOU CANNOT REFUSE.

The Golden Lodge stories, picked up in newspapers throughout the country, were regarded with incredulity in some places and hope in others. Even Abel's close friends in Pittsburgh and Washington, in districts he had visited, considered it an enthusiastic compliment paid to a favorite son rather than a lively possibility. Nevertheless, the *Golden Lodge News* kept up its barrage.

Abel seemed to pay only limited attention to the call from Canton, though an echo also came from the Fontana local in California. Ever since the Rarick contest, steelworkers of some standing had approached him privately, asking: "Abe, why don't *you* run?" "How about it: why don't you take him on? It's time to do it." Abel would shake his head. Even close friends came to believe that he lacked the stomach needed to mount a campaign.

By the summer of 1964, however, Abel had begun to think of it more seriously but still tentatively. During August—just a month before the Steelworkers convention—Jacob Clayman, an old friend from Ohio and administrative director of AFL-CIO Industrial Union Department, found that Abel's thoughts were directed toward his future role in the union. "You know, Jake, some of the fellows want me to run against McDonald." "Are you?" Clayman asked, recalling previous suggestions Abel had brushed off. "I'm giving it serious thought." "I'm not sure you are," Clayman teased. "No, no," Abel said, "I'm really thinking about it very carefully."

He always proceeded cautiously. He did not practice risk politics. But this time his habitual restraint no longer blocked his political thinking. For several years now—some of his friends placed it somewhere in the post-Rarick period—his heartache took the form of bitter observations about what was going on, so much so that he seemed to be undergoing a personality change. Theoretically the No. 2 man in the union, he had been fenced out of all sectors of decision-making. Matters of prime union concern were often not known to him until he read about them in the newspapers. Although his office was just a few feet from McDonald's, communication between the two was practically nonexistent. Not only was he bruised and angry because of slights systematically administered by McDonald and some of his staff associates; he was increasingly distressed about the kind and amount of expenditures he was required to honor. Since bills were paid only on the president's approval, what McDonald ordered paid was paid out of the office of Secretary-Treasurer Abel. Psychologically and functionally, Abel was trapped. He could quit, refusing to take it any longer, or else hang on. Actually there was no real alternative; his union activity was his whole life.

Abel's isolation became intensified during the period of increased importance to McDonald of the union's general counsel, Arthur Goldberg. There were distinct efforts to downgrade him, partly out of Goldberg's loyalty to McDonald and partly out of the natural tendency to preserve his own growing strategic role. After Goldberg left to become Secretary of Labor, the tendency to diminish Abel was accentuated. David Feller, as general counsel, himself often distressed with McDonald, would say, "Abel doesn't count for much. All he does is beef."

As the summer of 1964 began, several of the directors—Johns, Germano, Rusen, Schremp, Molony, and Hart—started a campaign in the local unions of their districts to submit amendments to the constitution to require compulsory retirement of officers at a certain age. Hundreds were submitted in advance of the convention. In this indirect way, they reflected the growing conviction that McDonald, then past sixty-two, should make his exit, with the compulsory-retirement route giving him and the union an easy way out.

On Saturday, September 19—the weekend before the official opening of the convention—Joseph Murray, a staffman and Phil Murray's foster son, had thrown his modest hat into the vice-presidential ring. He hoped now, he said, "to become a rallying point for the rank-and-file members dissatisfied with the conduct of union affairs by its present leaders."

While the Joe Murray announcement caused a mild flurry of talk, neither his ability nor his lack of it was likely to attract support, either from the disaffected Rarick followers, a fragmented group by this time, or from the larger sectors of the union seeking responsible alternatives to the McDonald establishment. For his presidential running mate, Murray announced young David Wilson, chairman of the grievance committee of Bethlehem Local 2609, in the Baltimore district.

In the meantime, a more significant development revealed a clearer political determination. Just two weeks before the September convention, a letter recapitulating the sentiments of the first Golden Lodge editorial was sent to the officers of the larger locals in the international union. In Cleveland, when queried by a reporter about his possible candidacy, Abel made a noncommittal reply. Upon Abel's return to Pittsburgh, McDonald stormed across the corridor into Abel's office and demanded that he disavow any thought of running for the presidency. Abel refused.

Rumors of contention exploded. One district director, Kay Kluz, a strong McDonald supporter, drove in from Ambridge, Pennsylvania, headquarters of District 20, to find out, he said, what the hell was going on. He went directly to Abel's office. As they talked, McDonald burst in. Kluz recalls that McDonald was almost beside himself, cheeks puffing, chin out, jaws clenched, nostrils flaring. "There's a helluva show on the road," Kluz blandly told McDonald. "It wasn't me that started it," said McDonald. After some muttering and God-damning, McDonald left and Abel said to Kluz, "You see what I have to put up with?" After leaving Abel, Kluz touched base with McDonald, who asked anxiously, "Did you talk him out of it, did you talk him out of it?" Kluz urged McDonald to go down the hall and talk directly with Abel. "We've had enough of this estrangement," he said. But McDonald said, "I've got my pride."

The week before the convention, McDonald announced to the executive board that he himself was going to propose a comprehensive compromise amendment to the constitution. He was speaking, he said, for the three international officers. Immediately, Abel flatly denied that McDonald was speaking for him. Abel's open rejection of a McDonald proposal—more than of the proposal itself—provided fresh evidence that their relationship had changed and hardened irrevocably.

What McDonald had proposed and Abel had rejected was a "study commission" to prepare constitutional amendments for the 1966 convention two years later. While several district directors like Hugh Carcella, William Moran, William Mahoney (the national director for Canada), and James P. Griffin favored such a delaying tactic, John S. Johns of Abel's own district and Joseph Germano of District 31 were opposed, despite McDonald's passionate plea against an unprecedented retirement amendment.

The major fight in the executive board was now concentrated on the specific issue of compulsory retirement: not *if* but *when* it was to go into effect. Although Abel had apparently played no part in initiating the retirement resolution, he was now urged by Germano, Molony, Johns, and others to take a strong position for a compulsory retirement recommendation. Abel agreed. No man, he informed the board, was indispensable; this union had survived the passing of some great leaders and it could do so again. The board was divided.

The night before the convention, rumors flew around hotel bars and up and down the Boardwalk. In his hotel suite, McDonald grieved on the base ingratitude of some of the directors and their followers: "They want to discard the man who knocked himself out for them."

Prior to the convention, McDonald had flown to Washington in a private plane to whip up top-level government support for his convention build-up. In view of the uncertainty about his own political future, McDonald required something special from the White House and his friend, Lyndon Johnson. In response to a White House request, the Labor Department dispatched a representative as an advance man for the President's appearance at Atlantic City. What McDonald wanted especially, he told this representative, was explicit praise from the President of the United States, something to overwhelm the delegates and slow down those elements which had created this unpleasant climate of insecurity. As McDonald phrased it, he wanted the President to "blow smoke up my ass. . . . If he does that, then I'll be in control." Checking around, the advance man got wind of the dissension within the union. The White House was informed that under the prevailing conditions some restraint was advisable, even from a grateful President.

Hubert H. Humphrey, Johnson's running mate, also strongly advised against unqualified praise of McDonald; some of Abel's friends had told Humphrey that it would have the effect of taking sides in the union's internal affairs. These men regarded McDonald's exploitation of the union's support of the national Democratic ticket for his own private political purposes as an additional affront. Several directors, such as Germano and Molony, were themselves already fully involved in the Johnson-Humphrey campaign. Important Democratic politicians in their own right, they were furious that McDonald had "the gall to go down there and talk to the President or his people and try to persuade him to intervene on his behalf. And yet we are the people who will elect him in Illinois, in New York, and other places."

In opening the convention, McDonald made his pitch for the loyalty of the delegates: "I have stood upon convention platforms before, and I have used the words of Al Jolson, the singer of many years ago of great fame, great ability: 'Stick with me, kids, you ain't seen nothin' yet.' Stick with me, kids, you ain't seen nothin' yet! Because I am going to start with you, with your help, with your loyalty, your devotion, something which has never been done on a large scale in our land, either in the United States or Canada. We are going to devise something way beyond what we created in '36 and '53. We are going to start a campaign to bring the members of the United Steelworkers of America what I choose to call 'Total Job Security.' "

Then he pointed the moral: "If you are with me in a determination to achieve these aims, we must not permit petty politics of any sort inside our Union to thwart our ideals. To start down this road we must have here in Atlantic City a completely united Twelfth Constitutional Convention . . . and over and beyond you and I, we must have a united membership determined to move ahead."

Fully aware that the talk about Abel's candidacy could harden into reality, McDonald sought to placate those directors without whom an Abel candidacy could be only an electoral exercise. Of all the district directors, Joe Germano was obviously the key. He was the leader of the district with the largest membership. His vote on the executive board carried the weight of the membership in his district, and his voice and personality had power beyond it. When, therefore, McDonald introduced him to the convention as chairman of the Committee on Officers' Report, he pulled out all the stops. Germano, he said, is "one of the oldest friends I have in this organization . . . since July of 1936. We have remained personal friends through these many years. Every time the going was rough . . . he has always given me a hand. . . ."

Not to be outdone, Germano replied to McDonald in kind. Spontaneous, emotional, effervescent, Germano delighted to indulge in oratorical arabesques. He proclaimed himself as good a friend of McDonald as McDonald was of him. Since "sincerity comes from the heart," said Germano, "it is not hard for me to say here . . . how I feel about Dave McDonald, how I feel about the secretary-treasurer of this organization, how I feel about the vice-president or members of the international executive board. Neither is it hard for me to express how I feel about the members of the United Steelworkers of America." At this point, he recalled Murray's words at that special convention of January 1952 where he proclaimed the importance of the rank and file as the ultimate source of strength of his leadership. To be reminded of these words, which had become a sort of litany recited at conventions, could not have given McDonald unadulterated joy: they had been uttered by Murray as a reproof to McDonald.

Germano pressed on: "There is nobody going to destroy this organization—outside of the organization. If it ever is going to be destroyed, it will be destroyed within this organization. . . . Let's cut out this monkey business, because the Goldwaters are not going to destroy us. I know what is going on. I love this union and I love you. I love Dave McDonald. I love the officers of this board and I love all the people of this organization." Such an all-embracing gesture by Germano seemed to signal a cessation of the anti-McDonald campaign and the drive for Abel. The cannier delegates thought that maybe some deal had been made in return for which Germano was ready to give McDonald a reprieve from competition.

When Lyndon Johnson appeared the next day to a standing ovation, the words he uttered were an appeal not only in behalf of himself but also for the support of the union president: "Under the presidency of Dave McDonald this union has charted a path of progress and has brought strength to all the American people. . . . Your Human Relations Committee has established a fruitful pattern of day-in, day-out relations between employer and union. You have moved steel toward an era of creative, constructive bargaining, recognizing that labor and management have a common stake in each other's welfare, and in the health of the entire economy." Such words from the President of the United States were jeweled support for McDonald's shaky crown.

When the convention reconvened that afternoon, District Director James P. Griffin, chairman for the first time of the Constitution Committee, brought in a unanimous report on changes in the constitution. Unanimity was reached, he said, "after negotiation and consultation with representatives of the other point of view on the matter of suitable retirement age for officers, appointed officials, and employees."

The supposed compromise actually would permit McDonald's tenure to be extended two more terms. Specifically, it provided that "no member shall be eligible for nomination or election to an International office, if upon assuming office, he would have attained the age of 68 years." Germano, an originator of the early retirement movement, agreed to recede from his position and the formula to extend McDonald's tenure.

Abel was furious. Having been urged to challenge McDonald openly, he felt that he had gone out on a limb and was left hanging. This was the last trip to the altar he was going to take with these characters, he said.

Many of the delegates regarded the "compromise" as a surrender to the McDonald forces, and dissenters took to the floor. Rarick insisted on sixty as the cutoff age, making McDonald ineligible for re-election. Several other delegates, including Archie Broadfoot of Local Union 1104 and Mike Zahorsky of No. 1211, made two points: "It's sixty-five we want, strictly concurrent with Social Security; nothing more, nothing less. When Social Security goes down to sixty, then it will be sixty"; and, "Indispensibility is a lot of hogwash."

Although no admirer of McDonald, Lawrence Spitz, subdistrict director in New England, rejected compulsory retirement for union officers as inconsistent with union principle. Since 1950, opposition to compulsory retirement had been the union's policy in collective bargaining. "You cannot," Spitz said, "draw an artificial line between advocating and adopting a compulsory concept as it applies to our organization and then lining up against the concept as it may apply to our rank and file."

Germano arose to support the committee compromise, thus making it clear that a switch had occurred. But he denied that there was any other motive in the resolutions on compulsory retirement than to establish the principle of retirement itself. Indeed, it was an error to assume that Germano had suddenly decided to abandon a cause to which he had privately committed himself and others. Later both Molony and Walter Burke explained that it was simply a matter of counting noses; they had found that McDonald and Griffin had managed to swing enough district directors to the side of the eventual compromise. While the chances of victory would have been better than slim if they had in fact carried the issue to a fight on the floor, Molony and Germano did not think, on balance, that this was a sensible convention pursuit. Moreover, they had established the *principle* of compulsory retirement for officers. Despite the general impression to the contrary, the compromise did not carry with it the obligation of men like Molony or Burke or Johns, or Germano, to support McDonald for president. They could live with a compromise, but this did not mean that they agreed to a commitment to live with McDonald for another term.

The Constitution Committee had decided to recommend, later in the convention, an increase in the district directors' salary from $16,000 to $20,000 a year. Since the compromise retirement applied to them as well, this meant a proportionate increase in their pensions. Thus, at the time of the convention the attitude of at least a majority of the district directors, eight of whom were retiring after the next election, was, "What the hell, we might as well go along."

Though McDonald had clearly won something of a victory, Germano's enthusiastic but Aesopian remarks hinted at something else. Germano had not made McDonald the sole object of his affection and esteem. Several times he pointedly referred to the fact that officers were elected at the ballot box, not the convention. Germano was not normally one to encourage election contests. But as postconvention developments began to unfold, Germano's convention remarks came to be considered a "sleeper." Whether by plan or by a fortuitous choice of words, his freedom of action was not inhibited when the time came to consider the nomination and election of international officers. Convention rhetoric would not obstruct the thrust of political realities.

At one point, McDonald informed the convention that he was sixty-one on his last birthday, which was also memorable for another event: "On November 22, 1963, one of the greatest tragedies in the history of America occurred. I was sitting in the kitchen at the table having a glass of beer with three of my friends. Neither the radio nor the television were turned on, and suddenly my wife answered the phone and came into the kitchen almost unable to speak. She was overcome with the news which she had just received of the assassination of President Kennedy. He was a great man. He was a personal friend of mine. . . . President Kennedy never considered himself indispensable, and I think it was demonstrated that there was a man who replaced him and rose to greatness."

When the time came, McDonald gave strong support to the increase in salary of the district directors. Both present and prospective district directors thought it was justified, especially since, as McDonald pointed out, they had not received any salary increases at all since 1956, while members in basic steel had won increases amounting to about 30 per cent. But vigorous opposition came from at least one delegate, who argued that the leadership of the Constitution Committee was disregarding the recommendation that an increase in salaries of the district directors be accompanied by a reduction in the number of districts.

The next day, delegate Paul Piccirilli from the Jones & Laughlin plant in Aliquippa complained that many delegates desiring to speak had not been recognized. As for himself, he opposed the salary raise for directors. "The rank and file sent me here to express their views on the subject. . . . I don't want to have to go out of this hall saying that David McDonald railroaded anything through." To this complaint, McDonald explained that under the rules he was required to close discussion because the question was called. But he assured the troubled Piccirilli that he, McDonald, had lots of friends in Aliquippa and that he shared Piccirilli's concern for the opinion of his local membership.

The convention went on, and grievances of another kind were aired. Some delegates demanded that locals be made "contracting parties" in negotiations, that no company contract be signed before agreements were reached on local plant conditions and that the international headquarters make more technical assistance available to locals.

Behind this request was deep-seated dissatisfaction with the lack of participation afforded local unions in determining the character of the contract signed by the international, which ultimately binds the locals and their members. Other unions, said one delegate, take cognizance of local situations and adjust their ratification procedures. "We negotiate," he said, "and we settle the master agreement and then sit down for two or three days to settle local conditions. The company stalls and stalls, and finally we have to sign."

To curb further discussion on this subject McDonald said sharply: "Let me put the record straight. You in this convention have already approved the election of an international Wage Policy Committee. You have given that committee its authority. . . . This matter was disposed of on Monday. It is all over. It is finished. I don't think the members of the international Wage Policy Committee are in a mood to resign. Are you ready for the question?" Bang went the gavel; change was rejected.

McDonald was now presenting himself as the figure of the leader and as a responsible negotiator; he would brook no nonsense that would jeopardize that role. Not many months later, when the negotiations in basic steel were opened and he was being challenged for the presidency, McDonald softened his position, incorporating in his platform a plank giving priority to the settling of local issues affecting local conditions.

The convention now throbbed with the repetition of the unity theme. In speech after speech, McDonald and his supporters pursued his identification with the great of the land. But in the midst of all this name-dropping, something else was quite noticeable. McDonald had followed a course of studied neglect of Abel, disregarding him on the platform, refusing to call upon him for anything but routine announcements, even barring him from making the union's financial report, a standard feature of union conventions. McDonald was taking no chances: if Abel made his usual comprehensive report, the occasion might turn into Abel's political advantage. McDonald and Hague blocked every opportunity that the convention normally afforded to bring the secretary-treasurer to the attention of the delegates.

Jimmy Jones, the veteran Negro international union representative who had access to the platform, observed Abel sitting to one side. "How are you doing?" asked Jones. Said Abel, "I don't know how I'm doing. By the way, you'd better be careful. You're sitting with a guy who can get you into trouble." "I looked at him," said Jones. "I thought he was kidding me. But I saw he was not." Then Abel spelled it out for Jones: "Well, you see no one sitting around me and you also see I'm not making my report."

In contrast, special emphasis was again given to an unusually long resolution of tribute to McDonald, read with oratorical flair by Molony. The supporting speeches, delivered, as one observer remarked, by a cast from the "lily-gilders union," were led by District Director John Grajciar and Al Whitehouse. Grajciar urged McDonald "to come to the front of the platform and get the ovation and the accolade so richly deserved." The leader came forth and faced, unflinchingly, a standing ovation. A little later the usual resolution in praise of all three international officers—McDonald, Abel, and Hague, as well as the international executive board—was offered. This time Grajciar discovered that he had failed to ask the convention for a vote on the previous resolution devoted to McDonald alone. To correct this oversight, he asked for the formal vote: "Stand up and give him another ovation."

So Abel was shunted aside. Similar treatment was being dealt to anyone who was a friend of Abel. For example, a veteran steelworker and staff man, Nicholas Zonarich, the popular director of organization of the AFL-CIO Industrial Union Department, was called upon to discuss the resolution on organizing. Zonarich was given an affectionate reception by the delegates. As he began to speak, McDonald became restless and obviously distressed. Not only was Zonarich a friend of Abel; he was also an officer of the AFL-CIO arm, then headed by Walter Reuther. Striding up and down the platform, McDonald progressed from silent but noticeable gestures into loud imprecations. The platform microphone was open, and the delegates heard him curse as he told Zonarich, "Knock it off, knock it off. You're killing me." Finally McDonald began to yank at Zonarich. Zonarich turned in bewilderment and humiliation, and could only attempt a dignified conclusion with a few face-saving words: "President McDonald, I know we are pressed for time." He fled the stage and wept.

When the convention adjourned the next day, Emery Bacon, the union's educational director, approached Abel and said: "Abe, let's try to forget this whole rotten business and sometime next week, let's our families get together for dinner." "Somebody else may forget it, but I'll be damned if I will," Abel replied.

After the first day's remarks, neither Germano nor any of the other district directors went beyond the merest formal necessities. Joe Germano might love Dave McDonald the first day of the convention, but by the end of the week he was tight-lipped. For Abel, this convention marked the end of his long forbearance. He was no longer restrained by the tradition that loyalty to his union required a surrender of self-respect. He never felt more clearly and more passionately that the future of the union demanded a halt in its deterioration under McDonald. It was time to move.

CHAPTER **8**

Commitment to Battle

Once to every man and nation comes
the moment to decide.

JAMES RUSSELL LOWELL

The fires of union politics were banked for a while. For with the adjournment of the convention, the main order of business became the Johnson-Humphrey campaign. The time, attention, and money of the union leadership in the United States, from international headquarters down to the smallest local, were concentrated on the priority of sinking without trace Barry Goldwater, the Republican candidate. Abel traveled with Hubert Humphrey as visible witness of the interest of organized labor in a confirmed friend of labor.

The storm clouds of an international union election fight, moreover, appeared to have been scattered by the unity theme stressed by McDonald, Griffin, and even Germano. The feeling grew that the union's disagreements ought not to be permitted to interfere with its effectiveness in the Presidential campaign. So it appeared that 1965, like 1961, was after all to be a no-contest year in the United Steelworkers. But John S. Johns, director of District 27, thought differently. He was convinced that McDonald had made a serious error in his convention maneuvers. In his opinion, if McDonald had agreed to the resolution that would have permitted him as incumbent to hold office for only four more years, it is unlikely that a contest would have resulted.

Despite the first pull of the Johnson-Humphrey campaign, union politics soon became a major preoccupation among the Steelworkers' upper echelon. Kay Kluz was worried. A presidential contest might well mean that within his own district, opposition, never far from the surface, might again rise against him, because of his clear identification with McDonald. He told friends he was convinced that Abel could win over McDonald.

At about the same time, in Canton, Ohio, Johns responded to a call from Director Paul Rusen of District 23: "Abe and I want to come up to see you." Johns, now convinced that Abel would run, became the first director to announce publicly for Abel. Paul E. Schremp of Cleveland followed. The movement was under way.

More than any director, Johns had been privy to Abel's state of mind. Abel's personal frustration was only one aspect of his discontent. His job at headquarters had become distasteful and almost meaningless. He often said that hell, all he knew about the union was what he read in the newspapers; that McDonald would talk to the press before he would talk to him. Certain staff people would make union policy during McDonald's frequent absences from Pittsburgh without consulting with Abel, the senior officer at headquarters.

But the lack of aggressive bargaining had turned off a good part of the union. After the creation of the Human Relations Research Committee, following the 1960 contract, McDonald was being hailed as a labor statesman. He won kudos for pioneering an era when strikes were on their way to becoming obsolete. This publicity had been a shot in the arm after the disastrous re-election of 1957. The wide backing for Rarick in that year jolted many of the directors, who became aware that McDonald's weakened hold might impair their support in their own districts. McDonald, increasingly morose, had talked about "ungrateful people who don't appreciate all the tremendous personal sacrifices I had been making for them over the years and—the hell with them." At one time, Arthur Goldberg reported to a friend that McDonald had informed him that "he wasn't going to take this shit any longer; he'd had enough of it; if they wanted the union, they were welcome to it. He was going to look out for Dave McDonald."

The Human Relations Theme

Where did the highly controversial Human Relations Committee concept come from? It began with the vague formula of "mutual trusteeship" that McDonald introduced as "something new" to the 1954 convention. After a four-week strike in 1956, he reactivated what Otis Brubaker called the "sweetness and light theme" with the words: "We have opened up a whole new area of effective teamwork between union and management." The union was still nursing its wounds in the aftermath of the strike when McDonald saluted "the forward-looking leaders

COMMITMENT TO BATTLE | 97

of the steel industry who fully accept our union as . . . a constructive force for the betterment of relationships that would otherwise be chaotic."

The industry leaders had said nothing of the kind, but they did not reject whatever noble sentiments McDonald cared to attribute to them. Shortly after, McDonald orbited rapidly, proclaiming that "mutual trusteeship" had ushered in "people's capitalism."

Later in the rebellious 1956 convention, Goldberg added a special twist. Sensing, however, that a mood of self-congratulation had not enveloped the delegates, Goldberg complained to the convention: "We have just negotiated a very great contract and frankly, fellows, after watching the convention . . . I am beginning to feel that the Steelworkers are beginning to act like the fellow who says, 'What have you done for me yesterday?' I haven't seen too much reaction to this contract." Then, turning to the union president, "Dave, maybe it was too good." To which McDonald agreed, "Could be."

During the next two years the companies' spokesmen, especially for U.S. Steel, issued warnings that the next negotiations were going to be tough. In 1959 came the 116-day strike in basic steel. With the settlement of the strike early in January 1960, McDonald transformed "mutual trusteeship" into "human relations."

In early postsettlement meetings, the Human Relations Research Committee—its original name—excited more enthusiasm in McDonald than in management. In fact in its annual report to stockholders in 1960, U.S. Steel failed to mention the "human relations" plan. But by the end of that last year of the Eisenhower administration, the industry found the Human Relations Research Committee useful for application under the incoming Kennedy administration, with a Secretary of Labor who had just left his post as general counsel of the Steelworkers Union.

Several subcommittees of the Human Relations Research Committee were set up as a result of the 1960 agreement to "study and recommend solutions of mutual problems" and "guides for the determination of equitable wage and benefit adjustments." The industry representatives, however, had rejected all union-suggested criteria in determining wage and benefit adjustments. "Without an agreement in this basic area of economic criteria," said Brubaker, "all the rest of the Human Relations Committee operations have been a sham, an elaborate charade. . . . It didn't face our mutual problems. It ran away from them."

Brubaker was particularly scathing in his analysis of the "hurriedly early" contract settlement of March 1962: "The agreement brought no wage increase, but was made up of a package of fringe benefits . . . priced at ten cents an hour." He figured this was equal to 2.4 per cent of the industry's employment costs. Industry estimated the cost of the settlement at "about 2.5 per cent." This package came to only three-fourths of the 3.2 per cent wage-guideposts figure developed by the Council of Economic Advisers—a figure that the labor movement had rejected as inadequate.

The settlement was applauded by the *Wall Street Journal* as the "cheapest labor peace in eight years, the most modest" steel labor pact since 1954. *Iron Age* found it came "closer to the company position than any recent settlement," and "the union seemed to have given more ground than the mills."

This agreement, in Brubaker's words, the "first fruit of the HRC's updated mutual trusteeship concept," brought no wage increase. It also dropped the truncated cost-of-living clause that had been machined into the 1960 agreement. As a result, he said, by 1962 the rank-and-file steelworkers suffered a cut in real wages because of the rise in the cost of living.

In fact, the 1962 settlement became the prelude to the "steel crisis" of that year. The union and U.S. Steel had reached an early agreement —three months before the expiration of the contract—under the urgent persuasion of President Kennedy and Secretary of Labor Goldberg. Despite the union's concessions and the "cheap settlement," Roger Blough, U.S. Steel's president, announced a price increase of $6 a ton. An angry President Kennedy reacted swiftly. He called the company action a "shocking double cross." The union had shown "restraint"; industry's management had not. But McDonald preferred to play it cool. He sent word to the AFL-CIO headquarters that he hoped nobody would use too strong language in condemning the steel-price increases. "After all, I have to live with these people." Later in the morning after the Blough announcement, however, AFL-CIO President George Meany hit out at U.S. Steel's "price-gouging." That afternoon came President Kennedy's tough attack on the steel companies at his news conference. McDonald then joined the chorus of disapproval of the price increase. Subsequently, through diverse pressures, President Kennedy succeeded in getting the steel companies to cancel the price increase and the "steel crisis" of 1962 was over.

It became increasingly clear that the "human relations" concept was used one way by steel management and another by union leadership. Many felt that labor had been hoodwinked. Although Professor Philip Taft of Brown University observed at this time that "union leaders should not be expected to behave as if they were members of the Council of Economic Advisers," the union officers had held their agreement well inside the Council's guidelines and had thus begun to look like "patsies" to their rank and file.

Undismayed, some weeks later McDonald said that he regarded the "negotiations which we have just concluded with the basic steel companies . . . the healthiest and most fruitful in years. . . ." By the following year, in Brubaker's opinion, the situation worsened:

> In 1962 there was at least the pretense of going through the procedures of the union's Wage Policy Committee prior to the early settlement—even though its recommendations were almost totally ignored in the settlement. In 1963, the pretense was dropped. No Wage Policy Committee meeting was even called. The Human Relations Committee became an open substitute for the union's regular procedures. There were no open demands. The contracts were not reopened. No contract termination date was set. No use was made of the union's bargaining power. A deal was made in secret HRC sessions. Then, and only then, a Wage Policy Committee was called "to ratify" the agreement. Last minute hitches over details, however, kept the Wage Policy members, the executive board members, and the "official" Negotiating Committee standing by in the wings as outsiders, while someone else negotiated a deal. . . . What happened in 1963 was not *collective bargaining*. It was *collective begging*.

Later, the 1963 settlement again won praise from the *Wall Street Journal* as "the lowest cost settlement since 1944." *Iron Age* complimented the union's leadership and concluded that "this contract . . . made a success of the Human Relations Committee . . . a triumph of Human Relations bargaining."

"This is quite an endorsement—and all from industry sources," said Brubaker bitterly. "With a few more such triumphs, we could lose the entire war—and our union as well."

Under the HRC, the union, he said, achieved the following:

1. Two of the cheapest settlements in our union's postwar history.
2. 'Real' wage cuts for our members.
3. Secret dealing by a palace clique instead of collective bargaining.
4. Bypassing of our union's policy body, the Wage Policy Committee.
5. Deliberate and determined non-usage of the union's only bargaining power—the threat to strike, if all other recourse fails, in support of its demands.

"This is no good," Brubaker declared. "This whole HRC mutual trusteeship is alien to all that is good within the trade union movement. It must be destroyed."

"Ecrasez l'infâme!" Brubaker's strongly held belief was now shared in considerable degree by the directors who now supported Abel. Their words were less dramatic, not so unqualified. But the issue of the Human Relations Committee—which in effect had become largely the work of several staff members, notably Marvin Miller and Ben Fischer of the union's Arbitration Section—rapidly developed into an issue of high voltage. While publications like the *New York Times* praised the Human Relations Committee for what it termed its creative impact on labor-

management relations in the steel industry, in the vehement opinion of Abel and his supporters the HRC was draining away responsibility and recognition from the elected leadership of the union.

Inside the union, dissatisfaction with the results of the 1962 and 1963 agreements was spreading. The first agreement had been processed through Secretary of Labor Goldberg. The second followed the same pattern. At one executive board meeting, John Johns arose and, armed with a set of figures and analyses provided by Brubaker, delivered an aggressive attack on those "human relations" contracts. The slightly built and quiet-spoken Johns was not given to spread-eagle oratory. Therefore his remarks created a deep impression. His verbal punches hit so hard that Vice-President Hague challenged him to physical combat, whatever that might have amounted to. To Hague, Johns's analysis was treason. Undeterred, Johns repeated his attack before the larger Wage Policy Committee. Dissatisfaction with the 1963 contract ran so deep that it had required all the union's presidential power to ram it through; in the public press McDonald had been praised for achieving another statesmanlike agreement. Under such conditions, McDonald was not disposed to lose face with the employers, with the publicity media, and with what he said defensively was an obligation to a friendly national administration.

Early in October 1964, Abel took practical steps. He went to Milwaukee to see Walter Burke, director of District 32, to sound him out further. A few days later, Abel, Molony, and Burke met in Pittsburgh at Klein's Restaurant.

Abel expressed his flat intention. "Joe," he said to Molony, "I'm going to run for the presidency and I'd like you to run for that job you ran for once before. And Walter, I'd like you to run for secretary-treasurer." Molony spoke first: "Abe, I'm glad to hear that and I'll support you, but I'm not running for the vice-presidency." Burke took about the same position. The three men parted, with an "admonition" from Abel that they think some more about it.

When Molony returned to Buffalo and told his wife that he had turned down Abel's offer, he later recalled, she "hailed my decision with wifely pride. She's glad she doesn't have a nut for a husband, and thank God, I do think of my family once in a while." But Marguerite Molony, as the wife of a veteran labor man, regarded her husband's information as a not too distant early warning.

Later that October, McDonald convened the union's steering committee of basic steel, made up of some of the chairmen—all district directors—of the negotiating committees for U.S. Steel, Bethlehem, and the other large companies, to discuss conditions surrounding a new contract. (The current contract was to expire the following May 1.) Among those present were Joe Germano, James Griffin, Molony, Abel, and the staff technicians. McDonald announced that steel was in a "helluva shape": unemployment and foreign imports were threatening American production; profits were down and liable to slide further. With such an unpromising prospect, McDonald guessed that the membership was in no mood to face a strike; assembled district directors nodded agreement.

In view of these considerations, McDonald said he already had met with R. Conrad Cooper, the U.S. Steel vice-president in charge of industrial relations and the acknowledged spokesman for the industry as a whole. He was hopeful, said McDonald, of reaching an agreement before the first of the year. "You know," he said, "we might have it for Christmas!" One union negotiator thought that was a nice sentimental touch. Then somebody else piped up, "How about those local issues?" "We'll work them out," McDonald said grandly.

Molony listened carefully. Then:

"I said, 'Dave, you say you're meeting with Cooper. God bless you! Do what you can with him.' Then I threw the grenade: 'When are you going to reopen the agreement?' He looked at me with absolute hatred. 'What do you mean, reopen the agreement? You want us to go down that road again like 1959?' 'I don't know what the hell you're talking about. Aren't you going to serve notice that we're going to reopen the contract?' 'No, I'm not.' 'God damn it, how are we going to apply maximum pressure to get the best possible settlement unless we have some threat hanging over these people? The only damn weapon that's useful to us is not reason or persuasion; it's the strike threat, whether we use it or not. Furthermore, something has been said about local issues. We've got to settle those damn things. I notice that Walter Reuther is settling them.' "

Around this time, the Auto Workers had settled with General Motors. When Reuther's name was mentioned, McDonald leaped from his chair. "Are you suggesting, Mr. Molony, that I get myself into the God-damn mess that Reuther is in?" Then Molony jumped up. "I wish to Christ we were in that kind of a mess now. That's the kind of a mess I'd like to be in right now. Sixty-five cents an hour increase! There's a real damn mess, McDonald. Let me tell you what the people in Lackawanna [near Buffalo] are saying in the saloons. They're saying they wish to Christ Reuther was president of the United Steelworkers. That's what they're saying in Lackawanna."

"The whole God-damn meeting broke up," Molony related. "I met with Burke and Abel that evening, instead of the next day, as we had planned. I told them I would run. I was so God-damn mad that again we were about to go through this bullshit . . . passing papers back and forth between Cooper—'old Coop'—and McDonald, that we will not use the only weapon that a poor workingman has to get justice, and maybe a little extra. By God, this tipped the scales. I had no particular stomach for another damned campaign, but this was too much, so that's when we told Abel we'd run. I went home and told my dear wife and she forgave me. I felt good."

Obviously, the support of at least some of the key district directors was indispensable for success in a campaign against McDonald. Joe Germano, head of the largest district—as McDonald triumphantly pointed out when he introduced him to the September 1964 convention —exercised considerable influence. All three men—Abel, Burke, and Molony—talked to Germano. Whatever pangs of hesitation they had suffered in deciding to run were diminished when Germano indicated his support. Since votes were what would count on the executive board just as in an election, the support of the leader of the largest district, with that district's organizational apparatus, could prove a tremendous asset. Burke later said, "It was a tremendous shot in the arm to hear from Joe's lips: 'Yes, I will support you.' " Still, Germano insisted on deferring a public announcement.

Nailing down the support of the mercurial Germano was important. On October 24 there was to be a gathering in Milwaukee of some friends of Walter Burke's to attend his daughter's wedding. Both Molony and Jimmy Griffin, who over the years had been close to Burke and was godfather to Burke's son, were going. The day before, October 23, Molony stopped off in Chicago, to determine again, for himself, whether Germano's previously expressed support represented hard political currency. Germano pledged his support. Again they both agreed that they shouldn't talk about it—and for the time being not even tell Abe of Germano's commitment.

Since Griffin was to be a member of the wedding, Molony hoped that it might be possible to persuade him also to go along. He had to proceed cautiously. Jealousy between Griffin and Germano had become so intense that if Griffin was urged to "join us now, Germano's with us," Griffin might have frozen. At the reception, Larry Sefton, director of District 6, covering Canada from Toronto west, began talking union politics with Griffin, Burke, and Molony. They then told Griffin that they were going to run. Griffin replied: "You guys are crazy. You can't win." "Well, that's the chance we take. We took it before, Jim; you were with us then in 1955." "You can't win," repeated Griffin; "furthermore, I happen to know a few things. That son-of-a-bitch Abel is going to back down."

Finally Molony said: "Now look, Jim, I don't want to be vice-president. Why don't you run?" Burke also offered to step aside for Griffin. Griffin did not budge. "We're trying to cleanse the union," they told

COMMITMENT TO BATTLE | 103

him. "We want you with us." By this time Molony was sure that Griffin was fully aware of what was at stake, especially for Burke. It seemed their close friendship no longer was a tie that bound. Of the three candidates, Burke was taking the gravest risk. At 54, he was the youngest of the three. If he was defeated, he would have to wait six years for a pension. In the meantime, he would be out as district director and finished inside the union. Molony, 58, had only two or three years before being eligible for his pension. Abel, by running for president, was risking the loss of a bigger salary than Burke or Molony, but he also would receive a bigger pension if he lost, and could better afford to wait for it.

The stubborn Griffin had his own ambitions to consider, and his own grievances: Burke and Molony were now in alliance with Abel—Abel, who years before had blocked his way to political leadership in Ohio, and who was now possibly in cahoots with Germano, for whom his distaste had grown. On the positive side, there was the possibility that his friendship with McDonald might lift him ultimately to the union presidency. His friends were convinced that McDonald had promised him as much.

Griffin now began a campaign to win over Sefton, head of the second largest district in the union, to McDonald's side. Sefton had not yet committed himself. But he played hard to get—first because he was deeply involved in negotiations, and second, because, like most of the union's Canadian officials, he felt somewhat aloof from what appeared to be a disagreement primarily confined to the United States. During this period of noncommitment, Griffin arranged a meeting between Sefton and McDonald, who offered him the place of secretary-treasurer on the McDonald ticket.

The last days of October continued uncertain. While Griffin was trying desperately to disparage and discourage the campaign against McDonald, the tactless behavior of the union president managed to make the contest all but inevitable.

The scene unfolded in Chicago, where a huge rally for President Johnson on the twenty-ninth was to be followed the next day by the conference of delegates of District 31. On October 29, when Johnson came to Chicago for a great campaign windup rally, Germano—intense, voluble, proud of his political power—was on deck. The steelworkers of District 31 had contributed heavily to the campaign. Of his relation to Chicago's Mayor Richard J. Daley, Germano proudly said, "We don't agree on everything but we're very good friends." For the Johnson meeting in Soldier Field, the mayor made sure that Germano was rewarded with ringside seats: "When he gave me those tickets, I told him that Dave was in town. The mayor understood. He gave me two beautiful tickets for McDonald. I was to be sitting right next to the President and Lady

Bird. The tickets he gave me for Dave were right behind us, in the next row." Germano called McDonald at his Hilton suite to tell him of his good fortune and ask him to come on over. At the other end of the wire McDonald seemed to be in no condition to appreciate the honor: "Oh, it's your party, Joe, I'll see you tomorrow."

Germano was furious. He felt McDonald once again was upstaging him: "He didn't even say, 'Joe, look, I want to see you for breakfast tomorrow.' Or 'I want to talk to you.' Or 'I'd like to talk to your staff for breakfast.' Nothing like that. No effort to express appreciation." The next day, McDonald made his entrance into the District 31 conference in the Hilton Ballroom to the applause of the assembled delegates. Despite his anger, Germano managed to maintain the decorum required to introduce his international union president. His differences with McDonald were known only to a few of his aides. In presenting McDonald, Germano praised him: "He has done a good job for us. I have always liked to feel that I was his friend and that he is my friend." Then Germano moved over to play some notes in an ominously lower key. Facing McDonald, he said: "I feel that I have had differences from time to time with you. I said at the [September] convention that the United Steelworkers of America from District 31, in spite of what some may say, have proved themselves to this organization, loyally and financially. . . . I have said that if Joe Germano is a great director it is because the membership made him great. I say that always about any leader. No leader is greater than the membership makes him. I have been the kind of man that likes everybody, the kind of man that expresses the wishes of my membership." He then added cryptically: "The kind of a plan that I am very seriously carrying out is in accord with the thinking and desires of the great membership of District 31. And, as I have said, I have always been proud to present to this great organization our great president, David J. McDonald."

The delegates rose and applauded. McDonald moved forward to the rostrum. Arms outstretched, he addressed "Director Germano, Vice-President Hague, District Directors of the United Steelworkers of America, the staff assigned to District 31, the delegates to this great conference, and my friends." His reference to the "staff assigned to District 31" conveyed a special message. McDonald thereby reminded them that, under the constitution, they were employees serving at the pleasure of the international union president, that they were therefore not to regard their organizational relationship within a district as an irrevocable tie to the district director.

"Friendship is a many-splendored thing," McDonald began. "It is absolutely wonderful to hear a man like your great director, Joseph Germano, stand here this morning and express his friendship for me.

And his friendship for me is just as splendored as my friendship for him." This sonorous ambivalence was greeted with hearty, innocent applause. Then McDonald moved quickly:

"Somebody said to me: 'Were you out with the President last night?' I was not. I was not at that meeting. But," he rose to his toes in exultation, "I spent a half hour with the President of the United States in his own bedroom last night, and with several of his aides, before he went out to that great meeting. And I want you girls particularly to know that before I left I kissed Lady Bird. So, you see, friendship is a many-splendored thing." McDonald grinned triumphantly. Kissing Lady Bird represented higher status than seats in the row behind the President, the mayor, and Germano. Germano caught this piece of one-upmanship with a fixed grin.

Having established his intimacy on the highest levels, McDonald moved on: "I want to start off with what I have to say . . . by a very, very simple statement: I AM A CANDIDATE FOR THE PRESIDENCY OF THE UNITED STEELWORKERS OF AMERICA. AND I INTEND TO BE ELECTED. [Applause.] And I want to tell you something else, there are a few other people who have already announced their candidacy. They have said they were going to run for the presidency of the United Steelworkers of America.

"Well," roared McDonald, "whoever these candidates are, *whoever they may be,* I am going to be rough, and I am going to be tough, and I am going to be mean, and I am going to run over these candidates just like you and I ran over the steel industry in that 116-day strike in 1959. [Applause.]

"Am I bragging? I am not bragging. I have a few years on me, but I am still young, and I am still hard, and I am still tough, and I still have a good left hook. Does anybody want to try it out? I am ready."

Thus McDonald hurled defiance at his enemies. "We cannot permit petty internal politics to interfere with our aims and our desires. . . . I have seen petty politics played in unions. I saw petty politics played in the United Mine Workers of America. And I saw the leaders who opposed John L. Lewis, who opposed Phil Murray, and the United Mine Workers, play their politics . . . for their own selfish desires. And what was the end? The Mine Workers Union was destroyed." (McDonald was referring, among other matters, to the internal UMW struggle culminating in the Lewis-Brophy election contest of 1927.) "It was destroyed. And what happened to those who were the leaders of the group who played petty politics? What happened to them? I will tell you what happened to them. The principal leader of that group died as a boozehound and a dope addict; and he is lying in a grave not very far from where we are today . . . just a bunch of bones with six feet of mud on his kisser. And one of the other leaders died in jail . . . because he made immoral advances to a twelve-year-old boy. And he died in jail. And he is lying down in the state of Kansas in a little old box . . . whatever is left of him . . . and six feet of mud in his face. . . .

"If we want to see the United Steelworkers of America torn asunder, if this is what you want, go ahead and play petty internal union politics. Oh, I don't deny the right to be ambitious. . . . I don't deny anybody this right. I encourage this right, but, I am telling you something, I do not believe that in achieving this ambition, one should tear down those who are trying."

McDonald now adverted to charges that he had handed too much power to the union's technical experts. But, turning to the directors on the platform, he said that the technical problems now facing the union were far too complicated for them. He singled out perhaps his most determined admirer among the district directors as an example of inherent inadequacy: "Can you imagine a big flatfooted steelworker like my friend Al Whitehouse, who is sitting here—and he refers to himself as a big flatfooted steelworker, he always uses the word 'dumb,' which I eliminate—being able to compete with the statisticians, and the experts in pensions and insurance experts who are employed by the companies? Do you imagine that he could compete with them by himself? Can you imagine him competing with the legal brains? . . . This is ridiculous! So we employ people; many of them have come up from the ranks, others we have obtained from government; others from universities—lawyers and statisticians, experts of all kinds, so that they are working for you and with you, and are able to meet the brainpower which the various corporations can hire."

Since the conference was preparatory to the contract negotiations not many weeks off, McDonald referred to "one thing which is bothering the steelworkers quite a bit—what is known as local plant conditions; we fought for 116 days in 1959 to prevent the companies from destroying local plant conditions. I am not looking for a fight. I want a peaceful agreement. I want to go into negotiations with the basic steel industry and other industries in friendly and peaceful fashion. And this I absolutely guarantee you, that every member of every negotiating committee is going to have his opportunity with his boss to try to straighten out his own local plant conditions."

In a belated effort to mollify Germano, he concluded with the hope for "many years of continued close association with him," and emphasized the importance of the November 3 national election the following Tuesday: "Lyndon Johnson is fighting our fight. The big issue is peace and patience." Then he said: "As corny as it may be, and if I may sound like a high-school cheer leader, I am going to sound like one: YOU GOT

TO WORK—YOU GOT TO WORK—YOU GOT TO FIGHT—YOU GOT TO FIGHT —YOU GOT TO FIGHT—AND WE WILL WIN—AND WE WILL WIN—AND WE WILL WIN." The audience rose and applauded.

With deceptive mildness, Germano assured McDonald that "these people in District 31 are intelligent. . . . They know and appreciate from time to time that we must hire people because of special assignments. But the membership of District 31 feel like I do, that we are the organization, that the leadership of this organization is elected by the people and we service the people. In the great words of our great leader, Phil Murray, 'the membership is the organization.' And the membership makes the policies of this great organization. [Applause.] David, we want you to hire the best to do the job assigned to them by this union. I say that because I don't want any misunderstanding in the minds of any-body. And you can rest assured, so far as members of this District 31, nobody is going to destroy this union."

Meanwhile, down Baltimore way, Donald Wilson of Local 2609 at the Bethlehem Steel plant at Sparrows Point had confirmed his intention to seek the nomination for the presidency with Joe Murray for vice-president. The latter, exiled to the Florida subdistrict, was almost con-sumed with hatred for McDonald, who had humiliated, ignored, and insulted him in public. Wilson, age thirty-three, and Murray, who had been a staff representative for a quarter of a century, did not exactly represent an overwhelming political force, but they constituted a symbol of discontent. Moreover, Frank O'Brien, president of Local 1843 at the Jones & Laughlin local in Pittsburgh, was announced as coordinator and campaign manager for the Wilson-Murray ticket. Since O'Brien had gained a certain reputation in the Rarick campaign of 1956 and 1957, both Wilson and Murray hoped they could talk up a Rarick-size storm. Moreover, the Landrum-Griffin Act, enacted since the earlier contest, could perhaps block wholesale stealing of votes. Such minor acts of daring won some brief attention in the union as long as the more significant candidates had not surfaced.

The day after Johnson's election, rumors of larger happenings turned into practical certainty. Under a Pittsburgh dateline of November 4, the *Wall Street Journal* reported that a "movement is growing . . . to run I. W. Abel . . . in opposition to David J. McDonald." Abel maintained public silence.

For the *Journal* and steel management generally, an Abel candidacy was significant because of the "rather severe implications for the next round of basic steel industry negotiations. A hot union election cam-paign probably would divert some attention from the bargaining."

While reporters were busily attempting to verify rumors, McDonald was nowhere to be found. Vice-President Hague, however, was prepared and available. He said, first, that he was going to run for re-election, as was McDonald. He flatly denied a rumor that McDonald was being considered for a federal appointment. As to whether Abel was to run for re-election as secretary-treasurer, Hague replied stiffly that it was a question for Abel to answer.

At the Irvin Works of U.S. Steel, where in June 1964 Donald Rarick had been elected president of Local 2227, Rarick said he wouldn't be surprised if Abel would run. "Abel," he said, "knows local union conditions better and would give local unions better representation than they've been getting under McDonald."

McDonald played it cool. At a press conference called the afternoon of November 4, he would admit that all he knew of a movement to run Abel for president was what he read in the papers. He repeated his intention to run. He laughed off reports that he might be interested in a government post. The ostensible purpose for the press conference was to announce a meeting of the union's executive board on November 10, to set a date for the meeting of the 163-member Wage Policy Committee. He expressed the hope that in his campaign for re-election "I will be as victorious as Lyndon Johnson was yesterday." He then said jokingly that the only government job he ever considered was the Vice Presidency of the United States. So far as he was concerned, he said, repeating the Hague line, Abel was still on his slate of officers as candidate for re-election as secretary-treasurer.

Barely suppressed excitement spread through the offices of the international union, but Abel and his assistant, John Rooney, a close friend from Ohio days, kept their counsel. Carefully avoiding the use of the union's office facilities and personnel and possible infringement of the Landrum-Griffin Act, the three candidates and Germano decided to hold the "hoopla to a minimum."

The announcement of the candidacies finally came in a one-page mimeographed news release run off outside the office premises. After hours, afternoon and night, Abel, Rooney, and their wives got together in the Abel kitchen, stuffed envelopes, did them up in batches, and sent them on to Burke and Molony for redistribution from their offices, to the more than three thousand local unions.

A covering note from the three candidates, dated November 5, was sent to "Dear Sir and Brother: We intend to seek nominations for International Office . . . We are hopeful that you will give consideration to our efforts. Our only purpose in seeking office is to preserve and protect our Union, to give it new vitality and sense of direction. Our decision to run is made at the request of a great number of our fellow members."

Releases for November 6 went to the press and to the field staff.

McDonald's associates now sought to build up opposition candidates to those district directors up for re-election who were considered most likely to support Abel. The target districts were those in which the directors had had opposition in the past and whose tenure might be considered shaky.

In their decision to hold off their public announcement until after Election Day, November 3, the Abel-Burke-Molony group ran the risk of a late start and of the consequent impairment of their own campaign. Under the union constitution, the nominations were to start November 11 and to continue for a period of thirty days. In effect, the Abel forces therefore had only a weekend in which to signal the start of the campaign for nominations among the local unions. The drive for nominations became the first arena of competition between the Abel and McDonald camps.

McDonald now had to face up to a fact. Abel was in the race.

CHAPTER 9

The "Primary"

Nor shall my Sword sleep in my hand,
Til we have built Jerusalem . . .

WILLIAM BLAKE

The action now centered at the local level, where the process of nomination for international union offices began. It was to last for thirty days.
A local union meeting takes on the aspect of a badly attended town
meeting, except in the event of a hotly contested local election. The
poor attendance is due to many factors: meetings may conflict with work
shifts; members may live too far away to attempt a trek back to the
union hall; they may be baffled by parliamentary procedure, or lack the
ability or inclination to do much speaking; and in some locals, they
may lack fluency in English. Meetings occasionally become disorderly,
and discouraged steelworkers who are shouted down are not inclined
to charge the parliamentary barricades more than once. In addition,
there may be competing entertainment, such as TV or bowling; or religious, social, or family obligations.

The consequence is that the core of attendance is usually made up
of the local union officers, who are elected every three years by the
membership of the local at large. In such triennial elections, however,
more than half of the membership may come out to vote. At other
times the members normally are content or at least are reconciled to
have their local's business carried on by the elected officials, who consequently become the power structure of the local union at monthly
business meetings.

Nomination Procedure

In 1964 the schedule for the international union election began to operate on October 16. As secretary-treasurer, Abel sent a letter to all district directors, with a list of the locals and the number of dues-paying members as of June 1964. At this time Abel had not yet announced his presidential candidacy. Each director was instructed to have each staff representative check the total number of members in each local union under his jurisdiction, this information to be returned to the international headquarters by November 1. On November 9, nomination certificates were sent out to local secretaries.

Each local union, whatever its membership, had an equal constitutional right to make a nomination for each international office to be filled: president, vice-president, secretary-treasurer, and three tellers. Within each district, the local unions also made nominations for the district director, with the names appearing on the same ballot as the international officers. After the local meeting, called with proper advance notice, the local union officers were required to indicate opposite the name of each person nominated the number of votes cast *for* and *against* his nomination. After the vote, the printed nomination certificate, sealed and signed by the recording secretary, was to be mailed to the international secretary-treasurer. Strangely, the certificate provided space for the name of the successful nominee only; although the number of votes against him was required to be entered on the certificate, there was no room to enter his opponent's name. The deadline for return of certificates was December 11.

Within ten days after the receipt of the nominations from the locals and their validation by the international tellers, the secretary-treasurer was required to inform the nominees of their designation. They had until December 31 to accept or reject their nominations. But once the nominee filed his official acceptance—properly attested by the officers of his local union—he could not withdraw his name. Appeals had to be submitted to the international executive board by December 26. Thus, within the range of fifty days—from November 11 to December 31—there was room for considerable maneuvering, for bargaining, for second thoughts.

In the election of 1965, a new constitutional method of nominating candidates was in force. Two years before, the convention had voted to raise the number of nominations or endorsements required for international officers from 40 to an estimated 125 local unions.

McDonald strategists now developed a series of countermoves. Several pro-McDonald district directors, headed by Griffin and Hugh Carcella, began planning tactics of diversion to undermine the Abel presidential candidacy; they encouraged local unions to nominate Abel for secretary-treasurer. In this way they hoped, if not to eliminate Abel as a presidential candidate, at least to confuse his supporters. Since internal communication depended in considerable part on the staff representatives under the guidance of their district director, the membership of many local unions in certain districts could be kept off balance about Abel's true intentions. Added to this McDonald ploy, rumors began to circulate of the possibility of intervention by key Washington officials. Who knows, it was surmised, friends of the union at the highest echelon might work out a solution and avoid a bruising contest for the leadership.

For thirty days the union vibrated on different levels. The day before the nomination procedure began, the international executive board convened. This meeting was in effect a testing of strength for both sides. Who would stick? Who would quit? The memory of the special 1955 vice-presidential election remained vivid and relevant. It was recalled how several district directors, under pressure from McDonald, had slipped away from the Molony candidacy despite their fervent assurances of support.

James Griffin had still gambled on enticing a strong candidate for secretary-treasurer on the McDonald ticket. But by the time the executive board had completed its sessions, he reluctantly had to settle for Al Whitehouse, perhaps the weakest of all the directors. Whitehouse headed District 25, the smallest in the United States, registering a consistently large deficit and a huge expense account. His reputation was based solely on his oratorical extravaganzas in praise of McDonald at conventions and at other gatherings.

A burly native of Louisville, Kentucky, Whitehouse, originally a steelworker and an active churchman, was one of the directors elected during the founding convention of 1942. After the AFL-CIO merger in 1955, he had served as director of the Industrial Union Department until he was ousted from that post by the IUD president, Walter P. Reuther. He was also chairman of the union's American Can Company negotiating committee.

Whitehouse, once a vice-president of the National Council of Churches, was now at fifty-nine about a year away from voluntary retirement. He had resisted the political assignment. Since Griffin, desperately trying to enlist a candidate with more prestige and drawing power, had not yet given up on Larry Sefton, Whitehouse was assigned a double role as stand-in and fallback.

The November 10 meeting of the board was called upon to fill two vacancies for international tellers. The first test of strength developed between Steve Caruso of Cleveland, who was the Abel nominee, and Guido Palumbo of Aliquippa. Caruso won by a show-of-hands vote of 16 to 13, with all the Canadian directors voting for him. Their vote dashed the hopes of the McDonald forces that they could exact some form of neutrality from the Canadian sector. Moreover, John Shipperbottom, a local leader from Larry Sefton's District 6, was named to fill the second vacancy. This was a great satisfaction to the Canadians and was considered an additional advantage for Abel.

While most board decisions were taken by a majority vote of the board members, a roll-call vote could be demanded by any board member on any question. In such a proceeding, the voting strength of each member of the international executive board was weighted according to the paid-up membership in his district, by the formula of one vote and one additional vote for each thousand members or a majority fraction in his district. The national director for Canada carried the voting weight of the number of members equal to that of the Canadian district director with the largest membership. On a roll-call vote, each of the three international officers was entitled to a vote equal to that cast by the board member representing the district with the largest membership. In effect, this meant that three international officers—president, secretary-treasurer, and vice-president—each carried the same number of votes as Joe Germano, head of the district with the largest membership, while the national director for Canada voted the numerical strength of District 6, headed by Sefton.

The weighted vote gave McDonald 441,500 and Abel 479,500. Fifteen directors were pro-McDonald. Abel had the support of fourteen. Abel's advantage lay in the fact that his backing came from several of the larger districts. At this early stage, William Moran of District 9 and Charles J. Smith of District 38 were thought to show signs of weakening in their support of McDonald, but Griffin managed to stiffen their wavering resolve.

The tactics of confusion were carried on more intensively among the locals. In districts headed by McDonald directors, staff representatives were instructed to cool off enthusiasm among the dissenting pro-Abel elements. Both Abel and McDonald began to seek out possible candidates to oppose incumbent district directors who were unfriendly to their respective causes; the objective was to concentrate a director's concern on his own re-election. Even where the likelihood of defeating an opposition district director was slim, a contest for district office could tend to bring a larger participation in the district that might not otherwise be available to Abel or McDonald.

In the Philadelphia district, the diversionary movement to draft Abel for secretary-treasurer was carried on with determination. Here Director Carcella, an aggressive supporter of McDonald in close rapport with Griffin, was busily engaged in "drafting" Abel, while Abel and his friends were kept busy disowning the "draft" movement, assuring various local leaders that he was indeed a candidate for international president. Contradicting a Carcella rumor that a deal was about to be made, Abel wired one local union officer on November 23 that "no deal can or will be made. Offer of meeting for such purpose tendered last Friday and rejected by me. I am candidate for office of president and will not accept nominations for secretary-treasurer. . . ."

Over in District 15, headed by Paul Hilbert, who was originally elected with Dues Protest Committee support and was now pro-McDonald, the stratagem to nominate Abel for secretary-treasurer took a new turn. There Anthony Tomko, president of Local 1408 of the National Tube Division of U.S. Steel, with about five thousand members, wrote Abel on November 19 informing him that the members of his local were nominating the incumbents "in their present jobs in hopes that you may iron out your difficulties and come to a mutual understanding." This letter from a veteran rebel who had been beaten up by ushers at the 1960 Steelworkers convention surprised Abel. It became clear that the line of dissent could waver.

In Atlanta, headquarters of the Southern district, M. C. Weston added his support to the drafting of Abel for secretary-treasurer. Halfway through the nomination period, Abel warned a friendly Southern staff representative that "Weston is attempting to give us the business down there."

In Tennessee the 4,500-member Aluminum Company of America local, the largest in the district, nominated Abel. This became a critical battlefield. McDonald promptly ordered Horace Brock, a staff representative friendly to Abel, out of the area and assigned him to the Florida subdistrict, where his activities could be supervised by a director friendly to McDonald.

In his own district, Griffin worked the draft-Abel theme to considerable effect. When presidents of twenty-eight locals in the Warren, Ohio, area "resolved" to push the incumbent international officers, again Abel insisted that he would accept only nominations for the union presidency. But Griffin refused to acknowledge Abel's negative. He expressed the pious belief that when "I. W. Abel receives an overwhelming number of nominations for international secretary-treasurer he will, as a good trade unionist, bow to the wishes of the membership and run for re-election to the office he now holds." Then came the snapper: "Such voluntary action on Abel's part will end the power struggle that he has started."

Concurrently, Griffin sought to give the impression that a deal could be made. If enough of the district directors who had announced their support of Abel would renege or even appear to hesitate, Abel would be left more or less in the position of Molony in the 1955 campaign. McDonald could not lose by Griffin's maneuver. It might stiffen the spines of some of the wavering local leadership and reassure those who might have believed that Abel rode the wave of the future. For Griffin, the immediate target was to gain the psychological advantage of winning more nominations for McDonald than for Abel. He hoped to steam up the McDonald people who were shaken by the prospect of an unfamiliar type of campaign, while injecting among the membership a distaste for Abel's "senseless power struggle." This appeal helped establish the pattern of the McDonald campaign.

But Griffin was himself under fire. He now found himself opposed as district director by Russell Thomas, subdistrict director for Warren, Ohio. Quite simply, the creation of opposition in a district election was meant to throw the incumbent—in this case Griffin—off balance and stimulate the turnout of those opposed or uncommitted to his leadership. Griffin was the special target because his was clearly the dominant will behind the McDonald candidacy. With Griffin as McDonald's campaign manager, the Abel-Molony-Burke team believed it essential to divert him from the national campaign by keeping him busy putting out fires in his own district.

For his race against Griffin, Thomas could expect considerable support from Abel's Ohio supporters—after all, Abel's former District 27 adjoined Griffin's—and within District 26 itself. As a subdistrict director, Thomas could almost be assured of the nine local nominations necessary to qualify for the candidacy in the district.

Within several days after the close of the nominating period and before the deadline for withdrawal, Thomas proposed with tongue in cheek that Griffin quit the race. Since Griffin was chairman of the U.S. Steel Negotiating Committee, said Thomas, he could hardly give that important assignment the required attention if he devoted himself both to his personal re-election campaign and to managing the McDonald campaign. Thomas claimed that he himself had received nominations from locals with almost two-thirds of the membership in the district. In all, Thomas had received 30 nominations and Griffin 71 out of the district's 131 locals. Bitterness increased as the campaign developed. The *American Metal Market* observed that while the top executives in the industry preferred McDonald over Abel, most of the steel executives in the Youngstown area detested Griffin, "mainly for his extra-curricular activities, especially in politics." But one local leader in a large Republic Steel plant analyzed the political situation in District 26 in a letter to Abel: "I work in the transportation department and come in contact with the rank and file of all departments. In talking to these people, I know James Griffin does not have control of District 26 as he says he does. I don't know if Mr. Thomas can win the election for District 26 director. . . . I do know that you, Mr. Abel, can carry our district for the presidency of the union."

CHAPTER **10**

Rugged Preliminaries

All our past proclaims our future.

ALGERNON CHARLES SWINBURNE

To the management of the steel companies, an election in the international union was an unattractive nuisance as well as a risky venture into the unknown. While most steel officials carefully refrained at that time from publicly expressing their opinion on an election campaign, they privately feared that it would result in distorting the Human Relations Committee pattern, which they had confidently expected would continue to give direction in the 1964–65 contract talks.

In Washington, when rumor of Abel's candidacy became a fact, the concern of the Johnson administration bordered on consternation. The administration's main immediate objective was to fend off what could prove a serious embarrassment through complications in the steel negotiations. In the brainstorming that went on at various levels in the Labor Department and the White House, one government official suggested how to solve the problem: why not persuade both McDonald and Abel to withdraw from union office at the end of their current terms? Whereupon they would be named to important posts by the head of a grateful administration, in addition to which they would be eligible to collect handsome union pensions. Alternatively, if such a solution was not acceptable, both officers should be persuaded to agree to extending the existing steel contract well beyond the union's election period, to avoid interference with the negotiations and jolting the economy. For slightly differing reasons, therefore, both management and government deplored the holding of a union election on such a scale and at such a time.

116

After several days, however, word came that the administration on "the highest level" had decided not to intervene in any way. But Justice Arthur J. Goldberg had apparently begun to move somewhat obliquely and remotely to effect a reconciliation or to contrive some formula of solution. AFL-CIO President George Meany was approached with the suggestion that he might assemble an unpublicized conference to include Secretary of Labor W. Willard Wirtz, McDonald, and Abel to discuss alternatives to an election contest. When the proposal was put to Abel, he flatly refused.

Abel felt that such a conference could be transformed into the application of pressure on him to withdraw. His vehement rejection of the stratagem was intensified by the timing. Since this suggestion was made during the thirty-day nominating period, even the rumor of such a meeting could slow down his campaign, no matter how tight the security. The McDonald strategists had already planted stories that the Abel flurry would soon subside. The slightest hint of Abel's encouragement of a Goldberg-Meany-Wirtz meeting would only play into McDonald's hands. However lofty the sentiments of the prestigious personalities outside the union, the effects of such a conference would constitute an attempt to abort an exercise of trade-union democracy.

In the meantime, other feelers flowed from McDonald quarters. If McDonald withdrew, would Abel agree to the establishment of a new office of president emeritus for McDonald with special financial arrangements? To this Abel replied dryly that the $25,000 pension available to McDonald on his retirement would be ample and constitutional.

McDonald was putting on a bold front and bargaining hard. His object was to prove he was the man in charge. First, he had announced to the board that he planned to call together seven hundred local union presidents in the eleven basic steel companies to determine the needs of the rank and file for a new agreement. Such a session was to be followed by a meeting of the 170-member Wage Policy Committee in early December. It was clear now that McDonald had abandoned all thought of an early agreement. Both McDonald and Abel had declared publicly that the impending election would not affect the course of collective bargaining, but the interweaving of the two was inevitable.

Asked whether the election campaign might drive McDonald to demand broader gains from management to ensure his re-election, Abel said in a conciliatory tone: "If we come up with a good settlement, I don't think one man can be credited with its achievement. All components of the union structure—the Human Relations Committee, the executive board, the Wage Policy Committee, and local officials—will all have a hand in reaching an agreement." Also talking with newspapermen, McDonald said that the Wage Policy Committee would decide if and when the contract was to be reopened, and whether negotiations would be held before or after the union election.

To the outside world, there was little indication of the tension building up—the dagger looks, the angry words, the heavy sarcasm, the loss of self-control.

McDonald sought higher ground. The day after the meeting of the union's executive board, he and R. Conrad Cooper, executive vice-president of U.S. Steel, pledged their intention, as joint chairmen of the Human Relations Committee, "to solve our problems cooperatively and in timely fashion." Meetings between management and union representatives in each of the eleven large steel companies were to begin about the middle of December.

While McDonald was appearing with Cooper before TV cameras and newsmen, in Chicago Joe Germano announced his support of Abel: "I hereby serve notice upon all elements of management, labor, and the nation that any election which may develop within the United Steelworkers of America will not bespeak any internal rupture within the organization, or any internal disagreement as to the basic collective bargaining and organizing functions and goals of this union. We stand entirely united in such matters, and shall firmly and unanimously oppose any organization or employer who threatens to weaken, disrupt, attack, or destroy our union or any portion of its membership."

Other district directors began to surface with pledges of support. For McDonald, a joint statement by James P. Griffin (District 26), Eugene Maurice (District 13, covering the Donora-Monessen-Johnstown area in Pennsylvania), and Charles Smith (District 38, covering the Pacific and Western states) seemed to balance Germano's declaration for Abel. The combined membership of their districts just about equaled that in Germano's sector.

Over in District 20, embracing the Beaver Valley-East Liverpool area in Pennsylvania and Ohio, Kay Kluz, who finally came out for McDonald, was confronted with the prospect of opposition from the respected veteran unionists: Michael J. Zahorsky, sixty, the recording secretary of the Aliquippa local, covering more than eleven thousand Jones & Laughlin workers; and Michael Katchur, sixty-two, a subdistrict director in Akron, Ohio. Their support for Abel was part of the "off-balance" technique that both sides employed to slow down district directors who had announced for the other side.

Both sides spent the November weekend after the Abel announcement in feverish meetings. The next order of business was to be the gatherings on November 16 and 17, in New York, of the seven hundred local union presidents from basic steel, the 170-man Wage Policy Committee, and the thirty-three members of the executive board. This could be the first important sampling of the most influential sector of union personnel in an electoral struggle.

In advance of the big meeting, McDonald issued a blast in reply to criticism that he had lost contact with the rank and file. He appeared angered by talk that he spent too much time at his second home in Palm Springs, California. "I have every right as a citizen to invest in a piece of property anywhere. I bought the house for $28,000 with a $6,000 down payment I borrowed from a bank and a twenty-five-year mortgage."

In an interview Abel stressed that "real issues" existed between him and McDonald. "But we don't intend to burden the public or press with our problems." By seeking to keep the campaign within the confines of the "union family," Abel hoped to counter McDonald's contention that such a contest would undermine the union's bargaining capacity.

The meeting of the local union heads represented a considerable organizational structure. McDonald presided over an opening session of more than a thousand people (including staff) at the Hotel Biltmore. The assemblage seethed with political tension. When Abel entered the Biltmore room, which was closed to the press, he was greeted, according to a delighted supporter, by a "terrific ovation." During this meeting, which was devoted to reciting demands and grievances, both sides studiously avoided any mention of the political contest.

McDonald at once made it explicit that there would be no automatic extension of the current contract. He had bowed to the pressure of the executive board on November 10 against such an extension. After the Biltmore meeting, the hundreds of local union presidents broke up into eleven groups—representing each of the companies involved in the basic steel contracts—in five different hotels. The following afternoon they reassembled at the New York Hilton to permit the local leadership to sound off on what they considered the main order of business—collective bargaining.

Organization of the Staff

While the McDonald-Abel confrontation was the main subject of discussion in bars and lobbies, another important development was taking shape: the organization of more than eight hundred staff representatives. During the 1955 Molony-Hague campaign, the proposal for an organization of staff representatives, strongly advocated by forces supporting Molony, was angrily opposed by McDonald. After Molony's defeat, McDonald curtly ordered staff members who still harbored the idea of a staff organization to "knock it off." Now, nine years later, the McDonald strategists saw in such an organization a political weapon for the coming campaign. He now favored an organization that would give staff representatives security of tenure no matter how the election turned out. By approving a union of staff representatives and pushing for its recognition, he sought to pick up support among representatives even in districts whose directors were pro-Abel.

The field staffers are predominantly recruited from those who have served as elected local union officers. While the initiative in selecting a staff man is usually taken by the director of a district, officially he must obtain the approval of the president to put a man on the staff. Staff representatives are responsible for implementing the union's policies and orders between conventions. Altogether, the international union must negotiate and police more than three thousand contracts, the vast majority of them small-scale agreements involving a local union. Typically, a staff representative will serve several local unions in their negotiations, in helping them deal with grievances, and by participating as union spokesman in the political and civic activity of the area.

Although the larger local unions have substantial treasuries to pay full-time officers, the majority of local unions do not. Thus for a large section of the membership, the only paid person is the staff man. Most locals, however, have treasuries—built up from the 50 per cent of the dues of their members, the portion returned to them by international headquarters—adequate to compensate various members for time off taken from their work to handle grievances or to participate in arbitration proceedings. In addition, the local treasuries pay a part of "lost time" expenses incurred by delegates to conventions or other conferences called under union auspices and set aside sums for defense and strike funds.

Leading the drive for staff organization were George Kutuka of District 13—the Donora-Monessen-Johnstown area, of which Eugene Maurice was district director; William Mooney of District 15, the Homestead-Duquesne-Clairton, Pennsylvania, area headed by Paul Hilbert; and Andrew Kmec of District 16, the Southside-Westend area of Pittsburgh, headed by Paul Normile. These three district directors had already declared for McDonald. The staff representatives in their districts now sent letters to staff men in other areas inviting them to join the staff union by payment of a ten-dollar initiation fee. With a political campaign of unprecedented significance and uncertainty under way, the position of staff representatives inside the international union had become a political issue. At stake was the deployment of the union's international top-level personnel in the coming campaign. The staff representatives found themselves able to bargain for their tenure, no matter who was elected.

The first call for the staff men's union was couched in pro-McDonald terms:

As staffmen, our only purpose is to protect our great organization, fashioned by Phil Murray and David J. McDonald. It has been programmed and

nurtured to full growth and worldwide respect by President David J. Mc-
Donald. His program of "total job security" is for all employees. It dovetails
with President Johnson's "great society." Neither must be allowed to be
sabotaged.

The staff men supporting Abel promptly announced an organization
of their own, a modern SWOC—the Staff Workers Organizing Committee—headed by Mike Matsuka from Buffalo, New York, in Molony's
District 4. Infighting among the staff representatives clearly presented
the danger of a nasty struggle.

The sponsors of the first staff men's group, having second thoughts,
declared in a second letter that their pro-McDonald statement was not
meant to be partisan and, taken all together, was a mistake. They proposed, they said, to steer strictly clear of the campaign. On the advice
of the union's general counsel, a card check of their claimed membership
was conducted by Dean N. T. H. Moor (Ret.) of Trinity (Episcopal)
Cathedral in Pittsburgh, who found that the original staff group had the
majority. On December 17—several days after the close of the nomination period—McDonald recognized the first group, the Staffman's Organizing Committee (SOC), as the exclusive bargaining agent for the
staff assigned to the districts in the United States. Through this unilateral
action, McDonald gained a certain political advantage, although constitutionally his decision would require the approval of the international
executive board, whose meeting was weeks away.

The day following, Andrew Kmec, acting chairman of SOC, met with
McDonald and Hague.

While a staff organization of field representatives was new to the
Steelworkers Union, more than 250 employees of the international headquarters in Pittsburgh, Washington, and Chicago had long since achieved
union representation, through the organization of a local union of the
United Steelworkers—No. 3657. The field staff, though pushing for
similar union representation, considered it desirable to be organized as
an entity apart from the United Steelworkers. Complications began to
develop when the contract for the Pittsburgh, Washington, and Chicago
headquarters and clerical staff now came up for renewal. By agreement,
the economic aspects of the contract were postponed until the steel-
contract negotiations had been completed. But McDonald supporters
on the Negotiations Committee of Local 3657 proposed a number of
changes to guarantee union employees against discharge or demotion in
the event of an Abel victory. At the same time, without any announcement, McDonald pushed through a series of salary increases for his most
trusted friends on the staff or those he hoped to win over or neutralize;
he added staff members, and in general sought to bolster his forces
through his hold on the organization and its finances.

McDonald opened his New York meeting of the seven hundred local union presidents to formulate demands for the contract talks. Murray Kempton then of the New York *World-Telegram* reported, "The union's most powerful district directors have either declared for Mr. Abel or are lagging distressingly in oaths of fealty to Mr. McDonald." He continued: "It is a tragedy for anyone not born rich to look so much as if he were. He had wanted to leave the union in the 30's and become an actor; he lost heart and trailed back to his job there. Now he is in the pathetic position of being in danger of losing a job for which he never had much respect in the first place. . . . To the steelworker he must look like one of those men the company decides would be better salesmen if they toured the plant once or twice."

Editorially the *New York Times* expressed the theme for McDonald's campaign strategy—that under McDonald's leadership, peace and statesmanship had come to the union and to the industry:

In the last four years, the establishment of a Human Relations Committee representing the union and eleven major companies has taken the crisis element out of bargaining in steel. Top leaders on both sides have met on a year-round basis to discuss the complex problems of changing technology, foreign competition and worker needs. Agreements have been made without the pressure of strike deadlines *at levels well within the Administration's guideposts for curbing wage-price inflation.* [Italics supplied.]

Now there are indications that the Human Relations Committee will be pushed out of any role of consequence in the wage talks scheduled to begin January 1. The union bargainers will be under strong rank and file pressure to bring back contract improvements at least as big as those won in this year's negotiations by the United Auto Workers—improvements that far exceeded the anti-inflation guideposts. Also there will be pressure for the same kind of concentration on in-plant grievances that shut down General Motors for a month and is now cutting deeply into production at Ford.

Both factions in steel have pledged that they will not let their internal differences obstruct the bargaining process, but the temptation will be strong to hold out for dramatic gains. A reversion to the old wage-price spiral and the climate of the perpetual strife would damage the steelworkers as much as it would the industry and the national economy.

To the Abel supporters, these were clear signals that "public opinion" was shaping up. Yet McDonald understood that he had to win inside the union. He directly assured the steelworkers' representatives that the first order of business in the contract negotiations would be the painful subject of "local issues." Discontent with nearly a decade of summit bargaining was mounting. Prior to the middle 1950s, the international union had frequently convened pre-bargaining sessions when the leaders at the lower levels sounded off on local problems. In the last few years, however, the international leadership had relied increasingly on reports from its districts and its professional staff for pre-bargaining background. As time went on, even the district directors were not seriously consulted in negotiations.

Prior to the New York conference of local leaders, McDonald protested that the locals had in fact been permitted a voice in formulating demands. He denied that their interests had been ignored. But the rising chorus of disapproval among the local leadership had led McDonald and his supporters to assemble the local union presidents. There was political advantage in such a meeting. He could use the occasion to placate the anger of the local leadership. Presiding over the meeting and surrounded by the apparatus of the international office, McDonald could also buttress his position against challengers, now led by Abel.

Local leaders emphasized that union workers in basic steel—about 425,000 compared with some 525,000 members employed in other areas of the union's jurisdiction—had not received a wage increase since 1961. Wage increases were therefore a No. 1 demand. They demanded a reduction in the amount of overtime work, tighter curbs against contracting-out work that steelworkers could perform, more seniority protection, security against job and wage losses as new steelmaking processes were installed, and opening up incentive pay to more workers. Grievances had been piling up at many plants. Caucuses of U.S. Steel local unions called on the international to bargain for an end to no-strike clauses in contracts, to make it possible to call plant strikes where the grievance machinery had stalled.

The industry began a build-up of steel inventories. For employers, stockpiling was not only a means of protection against the possibility of a strike, which could not take place before May 1; it was also a psychological weapon to strengthen the companies' bargaining position.

The steelworkers viewed stockpiling as evidence that they might have to be forced out on strike, since the companies, with warehouses bulging, could reject the union's demands while continuing to supply their customers' needs. While the members might temporarily receive additional wages as a result of working overtime to meet the inventory demands, they were in effect provisioning the company to last out a period of nonproduction if a strike should actually take place.

Because of the Abel campaign, it was anticipated that McDonald might take a more militant stand. Management circles began to sympathize with the course McDonald might now have to follow. The union leadership was working on two levels: political and collective bargaining. The first nomination returns were coming in, with a significant pro-Abel margin. All indications now revealed demands that the Wage Policy Committee would be expected to approve. The controlling fact was that in the last two contracts the rank and file had not received a wage increase. Instead, they had settled, in 1962 and 1963, for certain fringe benefits—some of them important, such as the thirteen-week extended-vacation plan. The last wage increase, 7 cents, became effective on October 1, 1961. Grumbling had increased. At the September 1964 convention, promises were made that union negotiators would press the companies for substantial wage increases. The wage demand would have been on the agenda even if there had not been an election contest.

Predictions of the shape of the new demands were being made. An increase of fifteen cents an hour considered likely because this was the pattern established by the United Auto Workers several months before. The UAW's three-year settlement, which, with the inclusion of its auxiliary benefits, seemed to have exceeded the anti-inflationary guideposts of the President's Council of Economic Advisers, attracted sympathetic attention, especially at the lower levels of the Steelworkers Union.

The issue of the role of the Negro members in the United Steelworkers now came into the open. While exact figures were lacking, it was estimated that about 16 per cent of the basic steel labor force was black.* In Detroit on November 27, a group of fifty-eight Negro union members from various districts in ten states endorsed Abel, with a scattering of "no" votes.

The meeting was chaired by W. A. Davis, president of the American Radiator Local 1199 of Buffalo, New York, located in Joe Molony's District 4. Davis made it clear that the group was not a formal organization: "We weren't elected by anyone to come here." He explained that the fifty-eight were leaders of a drive to strengthen the Steelworkers "by working for civil rights and democratization within the union." Matter-of-factly, Davis said that Negroes didn't feel that they could expect more from Abel than from McDonald, but while McDonald's record and that of his staff on civil rights "in the community isn't bad, in the union it stinks." Boyd L. Wilson of Pittsburgh, a member of McDonald's staff, pleaded against the endorsement of either candidate, placing his objection on high grounds: "I'm tired of seeing lily-white slates in election after election in the union. Why should we endorse either slate? There's not a Negro on either." The group decided to send a group of ten to meet with Abel formally to "ask him what he intended to do for the Negro membership in the United Steelworkers."

In the meantime, McDonald attended a White House meeting of the twenty-one-man President's Advisory Committee on Labor-Management Policy, of which he was one of the seven labor members. Before the committee convened, he made public a letter to Secretary of Commerce Luther H. Hodges, chairman of the committee for 1964, urging a large-

* *The Negro in the Steel Industry,* by Richard L. Rowan. University of Pennsylvania, 1968.

scale "concentrated effort of industry, labor and government agencies" to prepare workers for new industrial developments.

Meeting in advance of the union's Wage Policy Committee on December 2, 1964, the executive board issued its proposals for consideration by that committee. "Total job security" keynoted the list of demands. In specific terms, the union's demands included a "substantial" wage increase, the first since a seven-cents-an-hour increase on October 1, 1961; a restoration of cost-of-living adjustments that had been phased out under the 1960 contract, as a result of which the steelworkers claimed that they had suffered a 4 per cent loss of buying power; a cost-of-living formula as protection against future increases in living costs; pension improvements with increased incentives for early retirement (the union believed that this could be accomplished by payment of full pensions for early retirees, at the age of sixty-two, three years before the normal retirement of sixty-five); and income protection for senior workers against layoffs and loss of pay resulting from automation, recession or sickness.

In the area of grievances, the union demanded that companies be compelled to settle more quickly. As a prod, local unions would be empowered to strike when efforts to solve important grievances peacefully were blocked by the management; under the prevailing procedures, the union locals were locked in by a no-strike clause. Some union bargainers, however, appeared reluctant to press this demand. McDonald feared that the grant of such contractual power would open the door to walkouts such as occurred in major auto companies after national agreements had been signed.

Psychologically, the timely adjudication of local issues was the important noneconomic demand. Abel supporters now insisted that the union negotiators demand that such local issues be attended to prior to signing of the basic agreement. A section entitled "Greater Dignity and Justice on the Job" called for changes in incentive-pay programs to eliminate inequities, for increased compensation for craft and maintenance employees, and for the companies to follow seniority in training workers to man new equipment and to bar the hiring and training of new men for these jobs. One district director claimed a backlog of 540 grievance cases over such matters as incentive-pay rates and work-crew sizes, which he insisted would have to be resolved as part of any settlement. The list of demands of the United Steelworkers, now determined to "bargain out" a contract, came to twelve pages.

McDonald refused to place a price tag on the package of demands, but he declared that he did not feel bound by the Johnson guideline that would limit contract-settlement costs to the estimated 3.2 per cent annual increase in national productivity. In an attempt to soften the union's apparent divergence from the President's official wishes, Mc-Donald wrote a letter assuring the President that he "understood his position."

Abel declared his satisfaction with the Wage Policy Committee statement. Some union officials wryly attributed the committee's prolonged discussion to fog. This was not entirely a figure of speech; a heavy fog had literally closed Pittsburgh's airport. "The guys knew they were going to be stuck here anyhow, so maybe they figured they might as well keep on talking."

As the nomination period came to a close, efforts in the McDonald camp to abort the election became more frantic. Griffin and General Counsel David Feller were seeking to slow the Abel drive and alternatively to enhance the McDonald position in the campaign.

In the effort Feller enlisted the support of Drew Pearson, perhaps the most widely syndicated columnist in the country. Through a strange coincidence, Pearson, Griffin, and Feller now developed a concurrence of interests. According to Griffin, several months earlier Pearson had become involved in a local political campaign in which he supported an opponent of the veteran Congressman Michael J. Kirwan, who had long represented the Youngstown district. Over the years, Griffin's political influence, his prestige as a district director, and his considerable organization had been enlisted in Kirwan's behalf. Pearson, however, was now feuding with Kirwan through his "Washington Merry-Go-Round" column, downgrading him and extravagantly praising Bob Hagan, his potential opponent. This exercise of partisanship, however, suddenly took another turn when Pearson, after appearing in Youngstown at a kickoff campaign dinner for Hagan, turned to attack Griffin. He announced that the local Catholic leaders—the Youngstown chancery in particular—were now supporting Hagan. Whereupon Griffin, as a leading Catholic layman, went to the chancery to apprise Auxiliary Bishop James W. Malone of the rumors and of Representative Kirwan's anxieties. The bishop, said Griffin, emphatically declared that neither Hagan nor his campaign manager should be making such statements. Word of Griffin's visit with the bishop soon spread.

Shortly afterward, Pearson ran an account according to which Griffin had been so impertinent to the bishop that the angered churchman had ordered Griffin out of his study. "Pearson portrayed me as a sort of goon and tried to get me in trouble with the Catholic trade unionists, and it was damaging," Griffin said. At the time the column appeared, the bishop was in Rome attending the sessions of Vatican Council II, so that Griffin was unable to reach him quickly for a denial of the story. Griffin thereupon announced he was going to sue Pearson for libel. At this point Feller, who over the years in Washington had gotten to know

Pearson, sought to calm matters down. A meeting of understanding was arranged. Not long afterward, Pearson ran items in which he described Griffin as a devout Catholic—one of his daughters was a nun, another taught in a parochial school—and indicated he had received assurances from the bishop that Griffin was always welcome in his church. Pearson also turned off the heat under Kirwan. Griffin withdrew his threatened suit after Pearson printed his placatory columns. (Later on Griffin said, "In spite of all that, I wish I had sued the s.o.b.")

Pearson's column, which appeared in newspapers in most steel towns, was now enlisted in the McDonald campaign. After receiving a full and highly sophisticated briefing from McDonald representatives, Pearson reported:

A bitter battle is raging inside the Steelworkers' union that may affect the economy of the nation. President Johnson is watching it carefully. Some advisers would like to have him intervene to prevent a serious round of inflation. The battle is between his friend David McDonald, now president of the steelworkers, and I. W. Abel, the Union's secretary treasurer. . . .

Both sides are doing some colorful name-calling. The opposition to McDonald is calling the handsome, silver-haired steelworkers' president a "frustrated actor who enjoys glamor more than the grime of the rolling mills." They assert Dave spends more time in Palm Springs, California, or the "21" Club in New York than in Pittsburgh or South Chicago. . . .

What McDonald's critics overlook is that he has done one of the most outstanding jobs in the trade union movement by setting up the Human Relations Council [sic], which has ironed out labor disputes without strikes. However, this type of bargaining has taken McDonald out of the rolling mills and into the Duquesne Club, the sacred inner sanctum of the steel executives. As a result if Dave walked through one of the plants outside Youngstown or Chicago today, few of his men would recognize him. This is what his opponents are making the most of. They are led by Joe Germano of South Chicago and Joe Molony of New York, both close to the picket line and both backing I. W. Abel.

Then Pearson shot this torpedo:

Abel has the reputation of being a troublemaker, and in his campaign literature against McDonald he promised union members that he will give jurisdiction back to the locals. This means more likelihood of strikes. This is where President Johnson is deeply concerned. It isn't merely that McDonald happens to be a friend who went down the line for him in the recent election. It's also the fact that either a steel strike or a wage boost would almost certainly lead to an increase in the price of steel. . . .

The President may be forced to throw his weight behind McDonald and make clear the reasons he supports him—namely, that another round of inflation would mean depreciation of labor's pension values, an increase in the price of labor's food, and an increase in the cost of housing. Furthermore, it would affect the pocketbook of every citizen in the nation.

Such a powerful statement in McDonald's behalf, the belittling of Abel, and the recurring emphasis on the close tie between Johnson and McDonald, the friend of the President, became an important McDonald campaign document.

Less than a week later, Pearson's column of December 14 wrapped up in one day's package an apology to Kirwan and a pat on the back for Griffin:

The steelworkers' battle to unseat Dave McDonald has started some unfair backlash against some of Dave's friends, among them James P. Griffin, for 22 years director of Youngstown District 26. Griffin has done a great job not only for labor but also for the community, is chairman of the Mahoning County Community College, on the Advisory Vocational Committee of the Ohio State Board of Education, and Bishop Emmett M. Walsh pays sincere tribute to him for his work among Catholic men. So does Auxiliary Bishop James Malone.

In content, Pearson's column was timed to synchronize with two other developments: the close of the nominations period—December 11— and a special poll by the Oliver Quayle organization of political sentiment of the Steelworkers Union. In the meantime, unofficial returns indicated that Abel had passed McDonald by several hundred nominations out of the 3,200 locals in the international union. These results caused considerable nervousness in industry circles. But the *Wall Street Journal* for December 11 accurately observed that "nomination results don't necessarily reflect rank-and-file sentiment in the union because each local, regardless of its size, is counted equally. . . . Turnouts at local nominating meetings have been low, often totaling less than 5 per cent of a unit's membership. In Chicago, for instance, only 168 members cast ballots in a local that represents some 18,000 workers at the big Inland Steel Company plant. . . . Most of the nominating sessions were conducted by a standing vote instead of the secret ballot that will be used in the February 9 election. . . ." In Fontana, California, Verne Maxie, vice-president of Local 2869, which went for McDonald 90–68, predicted that "a lot of guys will vote differently in a secret election."

The First Quayle Poll

Griffin and Feller continued their effort to impress Abel with the futility of pursuing his candidacy in another way: through a Quayle poll.

At the time, Quayle was generally considered Lyndon Johnson's favorite pollster. Thus his results might carry weight in administration circles, and if widely publicized counteract the effect of the Abel majority over McDonald in the number of nominations. McDonald's strategists planned to announce the results of the Quayle poll at the close of the nomination period.

As general counsel, Feller was caught between his responsibility to serve the entire union and the knowledge that he was employed not by an abstract entity, known as the international union, but by President McDonald. As successor to Arthur Goldberg, he also found himself caught up, willy nilly, in the politics of the union. In discussing Feller's role, labor lawyers closely observing his involvement raised the hypothetical question of what Goldberg would have done. Answers usually simmered down to two: it was Goldberg's good luck that he was not still the union's general counsel; alternatively, he would have successfully contrived to call off one side or the other. Feller tried desperately to prevent the contest, not only because he was convinced that the campaign would interfere with contract negotiations but also because he would necessarily have to side with McDonald, whose legal adviser he was and of whose administration he had been an advocate. He had no obvious alternative. Feller's acute mind was often wired to a sharp tongue, and too often in his sponsorship of McDonald's interests he failed to endear himself completely with other officers—including Abel.

After consulting Henry Fleisher, a respected veteran public-relations man in the labor and political field, Feller arranged in mid-November for Quayle to conduct a survey of opinion among the steelworkers. It was understood by Quayle that this would be the first of a series of such analyses.

The poll, based on six hundred interviews with Steelworkers members, was conducted on November 30 and December 1.* In the first results of the poll, issued by Griffin from Youngstown, McDonald was given more than 58 per cent of the steelworkers to 41 per cent for Abel.

Quayle made the pollster's usual cautionary observations:

While this is not, and cannot be, considered anything like a prediction of the final outcome, it is an accurate report as of the first of December. President McDonald goes into this campaign with a commanding lead. With almost 59 per cent of the vote . . . , he has a larger margin than Eisenhower got in either the 1952 or 1956 National Elections. McDonald is now just two points behind Mr. Johnson's landslide figure of 61 per cent recorded last month. Mr. Abel must make up a great deal of ground if he is to make this a close contest. Should he achieve a come-from-behind victory, it will be only after a long uphill struggle. He is an old, well-liked and respected officer of the union. However, President McDonald's present lead indicates no widespread dissatisfaction with the present leadership and direction of the Union's affairs.

The processing of the report then began. The major part of it was released. Pleased with Quayle's findings, Griffin uttered a note of controlled enthusiasm: "The results of the poll are gratifying. The results are sufficiently close that we will not be overconfident."

* Appendix 2.

According to Feller, he personally advanced about $8,000 for the payment of the first Quayle poll. He was convinced, he said, that an election contest waged during a period of negotiations with the basic steel industry could do considerable damage to the pattern of union-management relationship that had developed under the Human Relations Committee. Moreover, the election campaign carried on in almost every state and province of the United States and Canada would require the deployment of considerable union manpower. In addition—and this, said Feller, was what worried him especially—large amounts of money would have to be spent on both sides. No candidate, he believed, could run his campaign out of his own salary or that of his followers, so he feared the threatening possibility that "outsiders" would be brought in as contributors. Just who these outsiders were, Feller would not say. At this time there was considerable talk and rumors of help from non-union sources and of conveyances through vague twilight zones of influence. With the use of funds from outsiders, Feller feared that the moral position of the union would be threatened, along with a likelihood that federal laws might be violated.

CHAPTER **11**

On Two Fronts

> Oh, ye'll tak' the high road,
> and I'll tak' the low road.

ROBERT BURNS

As the negotiators met in Pittsburgh on December 14, there was confident talk that a strike could be avoided despite the likelihood of long-drawn-out bargaining sessions. McDonald and Abel, as president and secretary-treasurer, sat with other union negotiators at the Penn-Sheraton Hotel, the traditional site of many bargaining sessions. The format of the afternoon's opening session brought together the chief negotiators of each of the eleven companies and the eleven district directors who were the union's chairmen of bargaining committees representing the workers of the companies.

On the union side, Griffin, director of District 26 (Youngstown), headed the negotiating committee for U.S. Steel and Molony that for Bethlehem Steel. Thus the union's two leading negotiating chairmen confronted each other as political antagonists: Griffin as McDonald's campaign manager and Molony as the vice-presidential candidate on the Abel ticket.

As was anticipated, the companies resoundingly rejected the union demands as "unfair" and expressed disappointment with the union call for a reopening of the contract, which established a strike deadline of May 1. The companies had hoped, they said, that the union would not expose the country to the disturbance of a potential crisis date, because "the union must know that reopening notices will not induce the companies to grant demands that are economically unsound."

Under the new conditions it was uncertain what role the Human

Relations Committee would play, although there was little likelihood that it could supersede the bargaining machinery as it had in 1962 and 1963. At a press conference of the committee, Cooper and McDonald sat together at a long green felt-covered table, flanked by their associates; four from the companies and ten from the union. But the meeting was only ritual.

Within the next two days, the union and the companies staged a press-release duel. The companies issued a reply half the length of the Wage Policy Committee's statement. McDonald regretfully noted that the companies "have seen fit to issue a set of statistics concerning their profits and steelworkers' wages on the eve of the opening of negotiations. The union intends to do its bargaining at the bargaining table, not in the press . . . but through free private collective bargaining."

In the meantime, the sessions of the eleven separate companies with the union were being attended by the top company labor-relations officers, the union's district directors, and the representatives of many plant and local union officers. For example, the U.S. Steel Corporation meeting, held in the ballroom of the seventeenth floor of the Penn-Sheraton, was attended by 225 company and union men. Meetings of other companies were held at the same time in other large rooms on the same floor, attended by smaller groups. Despite the companies' strong six-page rebuttal statement to the twelve-page Wage Policy Committee document, and McDonald's retort to the companies, the *Wall Street Journal* of December 16 noted hopefully that both sides displayed "marked cordiality."

While diplomatic niceties were observed, inside the union tensions were mounting. Soon, companies and the union had agreed to postpone formal negotiations from Friday, December 18, to Tuesday, January 5, because of the Christmas holidays. The holiday interval was welcomed by the union contestants impatient to get on with the election business of official reports of the nominations, establishing campaign headquarters, assembling election staff, and decisions on strategy.

McDonald also announced plans, comparable to those in basic steel, for an early January New York meeting of local union presidents in aluminum and the steel-fabricating and -finishing industries, for which contract negotiations were scheduled later in 1965. As president, McDonald could quite plausibly turn union occasions into political opportunity. In this instance, union funds could be used to pay the travel and living expenses of hundreds of key local leaders brought to the meetings. Similar conferences at an estimated cost of a million dollars had been held in 1957 during the Rarick-McDonald contest.

McDonald determined to ridicule the Abel campaign as an inept enterprise without a serious future. Abel was scheduled to address a December 11 meeting of a local union in Indianapolis, where, according to the local press, Abel was to "launch" his campaign. The meeting was poorly attended. Photographers took shots of empty seats, giving the scene a look so forlorn that the budding crusade would seem already to have withered. Abel's "kickoff rally," Griffin announced gleefully, was a "flop."

In contrast, McDonald appeared on December 13 at a dinner in Cleveland to participate with industrial men of distinction such as Frederick R. Kappel, board chairman of American Telephone & Telegraph, for the presentation to Thomas Patton, head of Republic Steel, of a Brotherhood Award sponsored by the National Conference of Christians and Jews. The conjunction of the event itself with the general awareness that McDonald was on the eve of an election battle, developed strong emotional overtones. Kappel declared that businessmen who serve community needs will be identified with "the leaders in achieving good human relations inside the business itself." * McDonald directed his remarks to Patton and other steel executives with whom he was to meet the next day in Pittsburgh both for the opening of contract negotiations and for a session of the Human Relations Committee: "We need a revival of the spirit of brotherly love . . . which is exemplified so emphatically in our testimonial here this evening. . . . It takes more than applause and participation in testimonials . . . to understand fully the meaning of brotherhood or mutual trust. . . ." Turning to the president of Republic Steel, McDonald said, his voice trembling: "I swear to you, Tom, to resolve our differences, whatever they might be, not with conflict but with intelligence. I think that brothers have a right to disagree. We will eventually agree; brothers usually do this."

Abel's Campaign Opens

As the first contract sessions were moving toward adjournment, the announcement was made on Thursday, December 17, that Abel would formally open his campaign in Chicago two days later, December 19. That Saturday morning, Drew Pearson's column released the results of Quayle's poll, which reported McDonald nearly nineteen points ahead of Abel. Describing Quayle as "one of the most accurate pollsters employed by President Johnson," Pearson did not add that Quayle had been hired by McDonald supporters to make the survey.

The Abel news conference was held at the headquarters of the International Committee to Elect Abel-Burke-Molony, at 316 West Randolph Street. Aiding Joe Germano as the committee's secretary was Alex Fuller from Detroit's District 29, headed by Charles Younglove, with Tom Murray treasurer of the committee.

Abel now made his first appearance as a full-fledged candidate:

* Cleveland *Plain Dealer,* December 14, 1964.

Never before has the American trade union movement produced a parallel for the campaign we are about to undertake.

For several years I have been urged by many members of the Steelworkers board of directors and others in the union leadership to seek the presidency of our great union. This is not news to most of you. This time, however, I have accepted.

It is with a mixture of pride and humility that I formally announce that I am asking my coworkers to choose me for their president and formally open our headquarters here in the center of the American continent.

Two of the most respected members of our international union are also seeking top leadership posts as part of this crusade. They are Walter J. Burke of Milwaukee, director of District 32, who seeks the office of secretary-treasurer, and Joseph P. Molony of Buffalo, director of District 4, who seeks the vice-presidency. Among those most conversant with the interior structure of the United Steelworkers, there can be little doubt that both of these gentlemen will be elected.

All of us have tried our very best to carry on the great democratic union traditions established by our founder, the late, beloved Philip Murray. We have decided to seek this change in the leadership because it has become clear to us it is essential to the welfare of the union and the well-being of the million-plus people who look to their Union for the greater security and a fair share of the good things of life.

This is not a matter of personalities, but of politics and principles.

Abel then read off an eight-point platform:

1. The basic democratic traditions of our union have been subverted over a period of years. To an ever greater degree, the decision-making processes have been concentrated at the top. Our constitution gives the members the right to regain control of their union by electing officials responsive to their needs and desires. *We intend to restore rank-and-file control over basic policy.*

2. We intend to restore the bargaining table to its rightful position, as the proper place for collective bargaining. We intend to return the Human Relations Committee to its original function—that of fact-finding, and discontinue its encroachment on the policy-making function.

3. We intend to recognize local agreements as a vital part of the collective bargaining process. All too often what appears to be won in master negotiations is lost in the local application. As a result, many plants have a disgraceful backlog of unresolved grievances, grievances affecting the well-being of hundreds of thousands of individual members.

4. We intend to work for industrial peace by providing management with a clear understanding of the collective bargaining responsibilities of both sides of the bargaining table. Under our present bargaining formulas, management cannot always know clearly the degree to which rank-and-file needs and desires are being represented. Nothing is more likely to produce needless conflict than management's miscalculating the depth of the union's dedication to the principles under discussion.

5. We intend to seek more meaningful answers to the problems created by

automation. Too many of our members have been "human engineered" to inferior positions. Too many know the gnawing insecurity of holding jobs destined for elimination, with inadequate access to suitable future employment.

6. We intend to contribute to American prosperity by seeing to it that Steelworkers get their fair share of the fruits of technology. Since October 1961, our members have not had a general wage increase.

7. We intend to utilize fully the abundant manpower resources of our international union. We have a staff of field representatives second to none, but many are unhappy because of the gradual change in our operating methods. We intend to give our staff members the opportunity to be of maximum service to the membership, the job to which they aspire.

8. We intend to provide full-time leadership that is always accessible to the rank-and-file members for the solution of their immediate problems.

In summary, we present the rank-and-file members with a clear choice—between conscientious trusteeship, a devotion to the self-interest of the entire membership, and so-called "mutual trusteeship," in which the union presumes to solve its problems while also serving management.

So long as management is primarily concerned with profits, the interests of management and labor cannot be identical. We have great faith in the ability of management to analyze its own problems and propose intelligent solutions, and while we will not be unsympathetic, we believe the primary function of the union must be to represent the membership.

With unofficial returns from locals now indicating a wide margin of endorsements for Abel, the McDonald strategists sought to minimize their significance. They understood that local nominations provided a meaningful index of support of key officers and activists in the local unions. It was they who regularly attended local meetings, they who would distribute the literature, mobilize the voters, and, above all, man the polls. Back in 1955, Molony, running against the administration, had called in vain for an outside group to supervise the election. Then and in 1957, McDonald supporters controlled the election machinery. But in 1964 this was no longer true; at best McDonald could command half the organizational structure, which in itself could not be relied upon to deliver support automatically. As a defensive act, he and his supporters began to raise questions about the honesty of the forthcoming election and, by creating doubt and uncertainty, to lay the groundwork for investigation by the government.

Griffin and Feller announced that McDonald intended to ask the international executive board to enlist the services of the American Arbitration Association in the forthcoming election. This, in effect, would superimpose a new structure over the election machinery. On the basis of the past attitudes of the executive board, they knew there was little likelihood that it would agree.

At this time, Feller himself was deeply involved as the attorney for James B. Carey, president of the International Union of Electrical Workers, whose re-election was being challenged. Because Paul Jennings, Carey's opponent, had charged fraud, the case was hung up in the courts, and the ballots—under the IUE constitution all ballots voted in the locals were shipped to the international office for counting—were sealed by court order. Arguments before the federal district court and later the Court of Appeals in Washington, D.C., had sensitized Feller to the availability of legal alternatives that a contestant in an election might invoke. His legal astuteness, coupled with a flair for the uses of publicity, provided Feller with an arsenal of weapons he might borrow in the Steelworkers election contest.

To force Abel on the defensive, McDonald issued a statement justifying his intention to ask for the employment of the American Arbitration Association:

. . . While I have the greatest confidence in the integrity and honesty of the Steelworkers local union officials and the members who will conduct the balloting, it would be a tremendous calamity if the Steelworkers' election were tied up in court or even in proceedings before the Secretary of Labor after the election has been concluded.

To insure that our Union members do not lose because of this election, it is my strong recommendation that we engage the services of the American Arbitration Association, a respected and qualified organization, to assist us in the conduct of this election. . . .

This statement was followed the next day by the announcement that McDonald had written to Abel, challenging him to participate in a series of debates.

The campaign you have launched to attempt to take over our union may endanger our ability as a union to present a united front in the fight for further economic benefits and adjustments. We must clear the air before the members and the general public, so that everyone will know the United Steelworkers is still the most progressive union today.

It is with their deep human interests at heart that I issue you this formal challenge to state the issues upon which you intend to base your campaign and to face me personally before the members of our union and debate those issues before our membership. . . .

Almost immediately, Pittsburgh radio and TV stations began to offer facilities and time "for your debate with your opponent, as a public service." McDonald was confident that his presence, his voice, his total configuration would give him great advantages over Abel, whose diction was not so precise, who was not at ease before a microphone or TV camera, and whose features were not smooth.

Abel derided McDonald's "gimmickry." He "questioned the motive" of the challenger whose office was a few doors from his yet who was

never available for normal communication. Debates, said Abel, rather
sententiously, should be held within the family rather than in public. As
to the AAA's supervision of the February 9 election, Abel pointed out
that the decision belonged to the executive board, to which McDonald
had directed his request. The board was not scheduled to meet until
January 4.

On December 21, the TV program *Meet the Press,* through producer
Betty Cole, had formally invited McDonald and Abel to appear on a
"split" program in which each man would be interviewed separately by
the same panel of reporters, headed by Lawrence Spivak. The date proposed for the program was February 7, 1965, the Sunday before election. McDonald was ready, but Abel's acceptance of the invitation hung
fire for several weeks.

The publicity given McDonald's challenge to debate failed to blank
out the news of the confirmatory official report of the three international
tellers, released on December 21: Abel had received the nominations of
1,310 locals for president as against 904 for McDonald. Several hundred
nomination certificates had been rejected for technical reasons, among
them failure to include the number of votes cast for and against, as provided in the constitution since the 1962 convention. Had these been included, Abel would have been credited with 223 additional nominations
and McDonald 144; in that event, the totals for Abel would have come to
1,533 nominations, for McDonald 1,048. About ninety others were disqualified for other technicalities. Out of approximately 3,200 locals,
2,692 had made nominations.*

Thanks to the last-ditch diversionary campaign engineered by Griffin
and Carcella, Abel had received 378 nominations for secretary-treasurer
with Whitehouse receiving only a few more—395. Hague and Whitehouse lagged considerably behind Molony and Burke. Molony's nominations total exceeded Abel's, with Burke only a little behind. Support for
the Abel-Burke-Molony team was strongly rooted among the local leadership. In contrast, it was clear that McDonald could not rely on the pulling
power of his associates; he would have to develop additional political
resources. From the start, this was Griffin's estimate of the situation; he
realized that Hague and Whitehouse were negative factors. He would
gladly have sacrificed both of them, he said, if he could pull McDonald
through. Moreover, it would have given him a special satisfaction to see
Burke and Molony elected and Abel left in defeat.

While the heat mounted, the administrative responsibility, under the
constitution, for setting up the election machinery rested with Abel as

* Official nomination results:
For President .... Abel 1,310; McDonald 904
For Secretary-Treasurer .... Burke 1,273; Whitehouse 395 (Abel 378)
For Vice-President .... Molony 1,319; Hague 780

secretary-treasurer. The day following the tellers' report on nominations, all recording secretaries of the local unions were sent the "official circular" with six pages of rules to be "strictly followed in order to comply with the applicable provisions of the International Constitution and policies and the Landrum-Griffin Act."

But there was still another period of theoretical uncertainty: under the constitution, the candidates had until December 29 to accept or reject their candidacies. Neither McDonald nor Abel was now about to give way. Abel simply indicated officially that he was not available for his old job.

Operating in full cry in Chicago as campaign manager, Germano hailed the nominations report as demonstrating that Abel would surely be elected and that "as president he will have a working majority on the executive board when he assumes office June 1." He based this confident assertion on the fact that all the district directors supporting Abel were sure of election because they were unopposed; more accurately, no opponent of a pro-Abel director had received a sufficient number of nominations to qualify as a candidate. On the other hand, five district directors supporting McDonald were compelled to face opponents committed to Abel. For Germano, the nominations report was "proof that a majority of the rank-and-file members of the union support this quiet crusade to put men dedicated to trade union principles into control of the union. The nominations have always been an accurate barometer of the feelings of the rank-and-file members." All of which the McDonald supporters now denied. They argued plausibly that the number of locals nominating a candidate did not reflect the number of votes that would be polled in the February election. At the same time, while expressing confidence that this preliminary round meant final victory, the Abel strategists understood that their index of advantage could prove only temporary.*

* The staff representatives could become the muscle of organization. Of the 664 staff representatives—not counting the employees in the Pittsburgh headquarters and the Washington and Toronto offices—350 worked in districts whose directors had announced their support of McDonald and 314 in districts headed by directors who had come out for Abel. Eighty of the staff representatives were in the three Canadian districts; these were late starters in the campaign and generally would reflect Canada's general aloofness to the international union election. Abel could count on not more than 234 staff representatives in U.S. districts headed by his friends among the directors. In contrast, McDonald's directors, all of whom headed districts inside the United States, could tick off at least 100 more staff representatives; that is, if all those staff representatives stuck with McDonald. Actually a significant minority of staff representatives broke away in five McDonald districts— Nos. 1, 16, 21, 26, and 30. In these districts five active contests for the directorship took place. In each of them, the opponent to the district director or nominee favored by McDonald was a staff representative or a subdirector who carried on an aggressive political campaign. They recruited the support of other staff representatives and officers in local unions who felt no allegiance to the establishment as represented by the incumbent or retiring district director.

Abel, "enormously gratified," saw in the preponderance of support for his ticket a "great demonstration of support for the union principles which this leadership team symbolizes. . . . My opponent has been basing his campaign on the claim that this is no time for a display of disunity. It seems the shoe is now on the other foot." Along with Germano, Abel claimed that his mandate from the majority of locals reflected "a clear lack of confidence in McDonald's leadership." Then Abel plunged the needle deeper: if McDonald was seriously concerned, let him accept the nomination results and at once relinquish the presidential reins. To Abel's suggestion that he now retire, McDonald replied: "Retire? Hell, I've just begun to fight. My opponent has already left his fight in the gym."

Despite his public statements depreciating the significance of nominations, McDonald began to lay the groundwork for a possible challenge to the nominations report of the international tellers. On December 23 he wrote to Abel as secretary-treasurer, asking for the "complete report of the International Tellers. The document submitted to me is completely insufficient." Aroused by what he regarded as innuendo in McDonald's inquiry, Abel dispatched on December 28 a certified "Dear Sir and Brother" letter to his opponent, several feet away in the union's executive suite. In accordance with the constitution, wrote Abel, "the report was made by the Tellers" to him as international secretary-treasurer on December 18, 1964. "Their report was in the same form and content as in previous elections for International offices. I furnished a copy to you and to Vice-President Hague and later sent a copy to each District Director. Such copies are exact copies of the report furnished me."

Having taken care of the technical side of the response to McDonald, Abel then bore down on McDonald:

This is the second time recently that you have, in my opinion, cast reflections upon the International Tellers. It is recalled that on November 9, 1964, you stated to them that you wanted to "protect" [the International Tellers], and under the guise of so doing you suggested that an employee of the International Union, a person other than an elected International Teller, "assist" them in their work.

Each of the three International Tellers informed you that they resented the implications in your remarks, as did I. I particularly resented them since the person you mentioned had already been "macing" other employees of the International Union for substantial contributions for your campaign.

It becomes increasingly obvious that, in addition to holding the International Tellers in contempt, you now want "to change the rules of the game." You have publicly stated that you believe the International Executive Board should employ the American Arbitration Association to conduct or supervise our International election.

Abel then cited Article V, Section 17, which provides that the international tellers should retain the services of the Honest Ballot Association or, should it not be available, a similar organization that would tabulate, under the supervision of the tellers, the votes cast for the various nominees and then file the report with the tellers.

By now fully alert to the developing strategy in the McDonald camp, Abel raised another point:

When you informed the public news media that you were suggesting the employment of the American Arbitration Association, you indicated that you were doing so to avoid the possibility of legal challenges concerning the election. I am sure most people were curious as to what prompted your remarks. I am even more curious now since certain recent activities of at least one member of the law firm which is retained as General Counsel for our International Union clearly indicated that he is not neutral in this election but, in fact, seems to be preparing to represent your personal interests.

Abel thus served notice that Feller could no longer be considered impartial.

In the meantime, McDonald and Griffin were planning to press the AAA proposal before the executive board. Bernard Kleiman, attorney for District 31 and *de facto* counsel for the Abel-Burke-Molony ticket, relayed to Joe Germano a lengthy analysis of the McDonald proposals in a series of questions and answers. Summed up, it was a sharp rejection of the proposed AAA supervision of the election as a violation of the union constitution and hence, by inference, the Landrum-Griffin Act.

As experienced union politicians, McDonald and Abel were keenly aware that the nomination and election procedures were the first battleground even before the campaign was fully under way. Better than most, they undestood that elections are often won or lost in the arrangement of the nuts and bolts of election machinery, at the local or precinct level.

The District Terrain

While McDonald and Abel maneuvered for position and waged psychological warfare at headquarters, the effectiveness of their campaigns could be proved only in the field.

Considerable time and attention were now paid to the mobilization of forces in the districts headed by friendly directors and the stimulation of opposition in districts led by unfriendly ones. In friendly districts, the candidate could count on the director and the majority of staff representatives; in unfriendly districts, he waged a form of guerrilla warfare, seeking out a discontented staff representative here, encouraging disgruntled local leaders there. The candidates had to deliver speeches, but the operations at the local level were much more critical. But how to activate the precincts, how to develop a sense of concern and a mood of participation among the rank and file? At least one method was clear:

light fires under the opposition. Wherever possible, encourage the nomination of opponents against unfriendly incumbent directors.

With this end in view, Vice-President Howard Hague maneuvered with frantic intensity. Reports began to circulate that Hague was ready to hand out favors to those who would come under the McDonald standard. In some places he sought to collect on past political debts; in others he exploited old animosities and revived latent ambitions. He tried unsuccessfully to persuade James Cuff O'Brien, a young staff veteran who had recently been assigned to work with retired members, to run against Director Paul Schremp, an active Abel supporter, in District 28. During the McDonald-Rarick campaign, O'Brien had worked in the district with proved fidelity; he was generally well liked and could have proved an attractive candidate. Despite ambitions cherished over the years, O'Brien rejected the offer. With O'Brien unavailable, Hague proceeded to encourage Joseph J. Kender, president of Republic Steel Local 2265 in District 28, to push his appeal to the International Executive Board for a place on the ballot against Schremp.

In District 33 Hague outmaneuvered himself. Just before the opening of the nomination period, he had heard that staff representative Gene Saari, well known in the Upper Peninsula of Michigan and in nearby northern Wisconsin and Minnesota, planned to run for the vacancy to be created by the retirement of District Director Earl Bester, who had already chosen his assistant, Glenn Peterson, as his successor. Hague persuaded Saari to call off his campaign. Through this intervention, Hague hoped that he would make a grateful Bester an active McDonald adherent, or at least neutralize him. But by the middle of November it became clear that Bester was neither committed to McDonald or neutral; his own cumulative experience with McDonald, the humiliation he had suffered in McDonald's pratfall in Duluth, and the opposition to McDonald of directors in neighboring districts—Joe Germano, Walter Burke, and Larry Sefton of Canada—had definitely brought him to Abel's side.

Hague was furious. He sought to relight the fires of political ambition under Saari, but Saari rejected Hague's alternate threats and blandishments. Thus in the Northern Peninsula, Glenn Peterson was given a free run without opposition. For his timely sacrifice, Saari was assured of suitable recognition in the event of an Abel victory.

Concurrently, the Abel strategists went shopping to set up opponents to McDonald-oriented directors. In several places, such as the West Coast District 38, their movement got under way too late. An opponent to Charlie Smith, whose district throne had long been tottering, might have generated enthusiastic support for Abel as well as for himself. But the effort to find an opponent had proved abortive. Internal communication in so large a district, scattered over many large states, was difficult to establish quickly. Smith could run for re-election unthreatened and presumably would now be in a position to steer the entire district organization to McDonald's cause. In two Southern districts, Nos. 35 and 36, two directors were retiring; both they and their heirs presumptive played it cool. Until the nomination period was concluded, they exuded an aura of neutrality. By mid-December, when the threat of qualified opponents had failed, they felt it safe to announce allegiance to McDonald.

Active elections for directors were therefore to take place in five U.S. districts. In District 30, Harry Dougherty, tapped for the succession by the retiring James Robb, an aggressive McDonald supporter, was opposed by Robert E. Washburn, who was regarded as pro-Abel. In District 21, William Nicholson, designated for succession by John Grajciar, the retiring director and the paymaster or treasurer for the McDonald campaign, was opposed by Ray F. DeMay, with Abel support. In District 16, Paul Normile, long known as a member of the McDonald coterie, was opposed by Walter Bachowski, a staff representative. In the Youngstown area—District 26—we have noted that James P. Griffin was opposed by Russell Thomas, a subdistrict director. And in New England—District 1—the incumbent director, Roy H. Stevens, was to be opposed by Lawrence N. Spitz, the subdistrict director for Rhode Island. The campaign in District 1 was to develop into perhaps the most intense of the district struggles.

CHAPTER **12**

Into the Campaign

> If the trumpet give an uncertain sound,
> who shall prepare himself to the battle?
>
> I CORINTHIANS 14:8

While both sides clearly understood that their attention had to be placed on the internal organization of the union, they were equally convinced of the need for an auxiliary public-relations apparatus to push their candidacies. Internal communication was not enough. To the Abel forces, it was obvious that McDonald was already receiving considerable attention through the advantage he enjoyed as president of the union. The Quayle poll, the Pearson columns, the stories often planted here and there in newspapers, magazines, and the trade press—all indicated that this election could not under any circumstances be a privately conducted family affair despite Abel's protestations.

Ray Pasnick, editor of *Steel Labor,* the union publication received by every dues-paying member, was openly identified with Abel. Because of the Landrum-Griffin Act, his official position would limit his campaign activity. The Abel campaign committee decided to call on "outside publicity."

On its behalf Pasnick engaged Charles (Chuck) Baker of Toledo and his Burr Communications Agency. Baker was thoroughly acquainted with the trade union movement and its personality conflicts. He had considerable experience as an "election specialist," most recently in the 1964 Ohio senatorial campaign when Democratic Senator Stephen Young won an upset victory over Robert A. Taft, Jr. Before that he had helped "handle" the 1958 anti-"right to work" campaign in Ohio, where the trade unions defeated a referendum drive to outlaw the union shop. More to

143

the point, Baker understood McDonald's role in the labor movement; he had knowledge of the intricacies of the politics of the labor movement in general and of the Steelworkers in particular. Baker's function, however, was auxiliary to a campaign committee already in being.

Early in December, several caucuses of Abel supporters—district directors and staff representatives—had created an International Committee to Elect Abel-Burke-Molony. To his "fellow campaigners" Germano had reviewed the plans "to remind each of us of the obligation and responsibility we have voluntarily undertaken. We have our work cut out for ourselves, and the sooner we tackle the job in a coordinated way, the greater our success." The emphasis on the "obligation" was to buttress their commitment. The memory of violated promises, especially during the 1955 campaign, was vivid in the minds of men like Molony, the victim of sudden abandonment by several directors. Nor was anybody quite sure just where and how, and to what effect, unanticipated pressures might yet be brought to bear.

Germano was determined to bring efficiency and certainty into an *ad hoc* campaign organization, with its headquarters at 316 West Randolph Street, Chicago.

Campaign buttons were ordered; literature was in preparation; mailing lists were being compiled for a communications network. Plans were being made to establish a number of field headquarters and a speakers' bureau, and to map detailed plans for obtaining the maximum vote.

The immediate needs were two: money and communications. As to finances, Germano confirmed that the budget, as agreed upon, was to be initially $100,000, to be raised by seeking "voluntary contributions"— $200 from each supporting staff man and $2,000 from each endorsing director and the three top candidates.

Additional funds were to be raised from the local unions. This was the responsibility of the cooperating district directors. Checks for the International Committee were to be sent down to Tom Murray as committee treasurer, at a special post-office box in Pittsburgh. Although funds raised for area or local purposes were to be retained in each locality, Germano asked that he be kept informed of the amounts collected and the names of the contributors. For the communications network, he considered it imperative to receive as quickly as possible the names, the numbers, addresses, and sizes of the local unions that nominated or were supporting the Abel team. Every effort was made to avoid the use of facilities of the international union. Under the constitution and in conformity with the Landrum-Griffin Act, each side would have equal use of all facilities. What was made available or denied to one side would have to be made available or denied to the other.

Germano urged the compilation of lists of key local union people and staff men ready to work for the Abel cause with their names, addresses, and home telephone numbers. In hostile districts they would be supplied with reports and literature.

Within this comprehensive setup, the public-relations aspect of the campaign would have to be worked out as soon as possible on the basis of consultations in the Abel camp. Baker summed up his impressions in a confidential "Battle Plan for the Abel-Burke-Molony Campaign," for possible use during the five weeks preceding the election.

As Baker saw it, he had to perform the function of the candid friend. While the Abel campaign funds apparently would not permit the hiring of a pollster as an offset to Quayle, two Baker associates—Eugene P. (Pete) O'Grady and Elgin A. Whiteker—carried on forays into some of the steel towns. In a hasty, unscientific sampling of men around steel-town bars, they found that in some basic steel towns in Pennsylvania the current was running pro-McDonald.

"Because the USWA election procedures leave so little time for actual campaign," Baker informed Germano and the candidates, "a premium is placed on quick decisions. Time has prevented as thorough a research job as we would like. We have, however, established some operating premises, and if there is any disagreement on them, we should know about it quickly and adjust our thinking accordingly." These were some of the "premises":

PREMISE No. 1—The *rank-and-file* workers are not opposed to a change, but do not know why they are being asked to make this leadership change at the top. In . . . a series of 100 interviews in enemy territory in Pennsylvania, a few on the West Coast, and some in friendly territory, we found a great gap between the rank-and-file understanding of the issues and that existing among the leadership.

We must provide a good fast answer to the question: "Why change now?"

PREMISE No. 2—*This is essentially a negative campaign.*

USWA rank-and-file members recognize I. W. Abel as a good union man, . . . but . . . they are more inclined to be anti-McDonald than pro-Abel.

PREMISE No. 3—*The Abel forces have enough negative material on McDonald to assure his defeat,* but are reluctant to use it because of the damage it would do the union.

By and large, the USWA leadership has done a pretty good job of covering for McDonald. Much of what the leadership knows about McDonald, the rank-and-file does not. This poses a delicate equation which we will have to work out as we go: Losing the election would damage the union. Throwing too much dirt also would damage the union.

A decisive Abel victory, on the other hand, would be extremely beneficial to the union. Being too gentlemanly, obviously, is not in the long range best interest of the union because it will not produce a big enough winning margin and could cost us the election. How far do we go?

PREMISE No. 4—*McDonald will have no scruples* about the devices he will use to seek victory, and will place his welfare above that of the union.

He is likely to presume that you will use rougher material than is planned and will gauge his campaign accordingly.

PREMISE No. 6—[McDonald] will be supported by industry, and will have plenty of money for a radio, TV, newspaper, advertising campaign. *A blitz scare campaign* is in the future:

a. A vote for Abel is a vote to go on strike.

b. Campaigning for Abel will reduce what members can get this time around at the bargaining table.

PREMISE No. 7—*The side which takes, and holds, the offensive is the likely winner.*

a. Either the Abel forces or McDonald will make capital out of Executive Board meetings. If we don't, he will.

b. Ditto for negotiations.

c. This involves reaching USWA members through the public media.

PREMISE No. 8—*You can't rebuild union spirit in a month, so we have no choice but to appeal to the self-interest of members or to convince them something they have now is threatened.*

PREMISE No. 9—Walter J. Burke and Joseph P. Molony are "in" and, while association with the winning candidates is good, the effort should be concentrated on I. W. Abel.

PREMISE No. 10—We need to step up the image of I. W. Abel from being a good reliable secretary-treasurer to being an effective No. 1 man, symbolizing the union. . . .

We're now in competition with McDonald for comment on national and collective bargaining matters. While we don't have to chirp at every development, we have to make some substantive comment on matters of key concern to members.

PREMISE No. 11—McDonald will attempt to hamstring our grass roots efforts by keeping district directors involved in negotiations and other business.

a. The extent to which he does so could determine the outcome.

b. If we have 350 reps [staff representatives] devoting nights and Sundays to the Abel campaign, we are getting the benefit of about 7,000 man hours a week. If he [McDonald] has 250 reps devoting the *bulk* of their efforts to the campaign, he is getting the benefit of about 13,000 hours a week.

PREMISE No. 12—We have, in a sense, two campaigns.

a. The headquarters campaign out of Chicago which is the fountainhead of materials and advice and the place to call with gripes, etc. and the source of some press releases, etc., and

b. The *roadshow* involving appearances of key spokesmen in key places on key occasions, and keeping pace with day-to-day tactical developments.

PREMISE No. 14—It is essential that we reach the members in "enemy" territory.

The bigger the fire we build in the enemy backyards, the less time they'll spend igniting wood sheds in friendly territory.

PREMISE No. 15—ONLY A USWA REPRESENTATIVE CAN DO AN ADEQUATE

JOB OF PUTTING TOGETHER ORGANIZATION IN OPPOSITION DISTRICTS. WE NEED A STAFF OF ORGANIZERS.

PREMISE No. 16—Convincing "opposition" international [staff] reps that McDonald is going to lose can reduce the amount of grass roots effort they will exert on McDonald's behalf, and this would be greatly to our logistical advantage.

PREMISE No. 17—We must exploit our opposition's weaknesses, and these include:

a. Two long, costly strikes.

b. Two recent, inferior settlements.

c. An identification with the management elite (the so-called Tuxedo image discussed below).

d. Living a plush life at union expense.

e. Failure to meet with the rank and file.

f. His vanity. He can be led into exposing himself as a pompous stuffed shirt, but, in doing so, it would be a grave error to underestimate his shrewdness.

g. He has made many enemies, in the press, within the labor movement, etc. . . . h . . .

i. Local union problems have been ignored and this IS resented.

j. The grievance machinery apparently is not working well.

PREMISE No. 18—McDonald will attempt to exploit our weaknesses, and these include:

a. A fear on the part of many rank-and-file members to do anything which will displease the man at the top.

b. UNION TRADITION. Steelworkers nearly always vote for the incumbent, and, at least on the record, *always* have voted for the incumbent top officers.

c. Lack of organization in many areas, particularly Pennyslvania and the West Coast.

d. Reluctance to get involved in any kind of byplay which will damage the overall image of the Union.

e. Probable monetary disadvantage.

IN SUMMARY OF THE ABOVE—We need to project an image of McDonald as a man who has lost contact with the rank-and-file, as a man who places himself above the union and who, as a result of his desire to acquire great status, has connived with management in ways which are harmful to the individual steelworker.

We can project this as *Tuxedo Trade Unionism*. We need a phrase which capsulizes the message, and the above seems to me to do the trick.

Likewise, we must be projecting an image of I. W. Abel as a distinguished trade unionist who has kept up with the times, and who decided to make the run for the Presidency in 1965 because he is deeply convinced the present leadership is out of step with the times.

I think we can capsule this as *Progressive Trade Unionism*.

Through this survey, Baker prepared an agenda for the four weeks between early January and the first week in February. But more important than the publicity apparatus—as Baker himself recognized—was the fullest possible use of organizational structure, the stimulation of supporters and the psychological attack on the opposition. This was to be stressed as a quiet crusade, not a grab for power.

In this endeavor, Baker believed in wasting no time. As a technician he was concerned with how well Abel would perform before TV cameras and the press generally. Later he recalled Abel's appearance at the December 19 campaign opening, when his hands twitched below the podium as he began reading his statement. "I have never seen anybody develop so fast," Baker said. "By the end of the campaign Abel was really a pro on camera. Dave had challenged Abe to a TV debate because he felt he could here have a clear advantage. Dave was a trained actor, felt that his appearance was all in his favor, that Abel could not come through well, and remember—Abel looks older than McDonald in many ways, even though he is six years younger. McDonald is a very handsome man. I didn't know whether Abel could take McDonald on or not; I'd never heard him speak. I knew about McDonald's training. I'd read *Man of Steel.*"

Baker believed that his first task was to combat overconfidence on the part of Abel forces. They were overconfident because they had counted the house, so to speak; they had the majority of the local nominations; the fourteen pro-Abel board members represented the majority of the union membership. Moreover, they thought they understood McDonald's weaknesses. But to judge by the modest samplings, attitudes among the rank and file seemed to be pro-McDonald. Baker carried on what he called an internal public-relations campaign to convince the Abel power structure that "you damn well could lose." As the campaign developed, they found that McDonald had press support, especially in the Gary-Hammond-Chicago area.

Abel's early decision against appearing in TV debates, according to Baker, was based sincerely on the thought that the debate might result only in mudslinging, which he felt might contribute to the entertainment of the public and the glee of management and antilabor elements rather than the improvement and enlightenment of the Union.

The McDonald Publicity Setup

By mid-December, Griffin decided that a publicity bureau was needed as part of the McDonald campaign. Since he was caught up in a contest for the retention of his own job in Youngstown, Griffin needed help in Pittsburgh.

On the recommendation of Elliot Bredhoff, Feller's partner, Griffin hired Stephen Wexler, a young attorney then working for the Labor Department who had before that participated in an acrimonious presidential campaign in the American Federation of State, County and Municipal Employees. Lively and articulate, quick to understand political intricacies and intrigue, Wexler knew his way around Washington.

Feller and Bredhoff had assured Griffin of Wexler's competence to handle "certain internal union problems." On arriving in Pittsburgh the second week in December at the conclusion of the nomination period, Wexler met with Vice-President Hague and Griffin, with whom Wexler had talked only by phone.

Wexler recalled later:

I had no contact with them before this. I just came in cold. The campaign organization was Griffin and me. I expected a going organization, but all they had was four empty rooms on the second floor of the Penn-Sheraton Hotel. That night we had a meeting with Dave McDonald—that was the first time with Dave—Griffin, Hague, Al Whitehouse and a fellow named Bob Maheu who was a friend of Dave McDonald and a public relations man.

I read every single line of the Steelworkers minutes of the Executive Board from the time of the SWOC. They're good minutes. Talk about interesting reading! One thing that did come out, actually from the time Phil Murray died until 1960, I think that if anybody ran the union, it was probably Arthur Goldberg. The same means that were used to screw Rarick and screw Tony Tomko [who once ran for district director]—the same means that forced us to lose the election . . . were instituted by Arthur Goldberg—his rulings in those meetings. The right to know the charges before you go into a full session, which are just standard ethical things, don't apply in the Steelworkers. They don't because Arthur Goldberg, years ago, said they didn't. . . .

Robert A. Maheu, with offices in Washington and Los Angeles, took part in the early strategy session. Maheu's operations included "security work" for another client, Howard Hughes, the mysterious billionaire, a role that later expanded with the expansion of Hughes's business and financial interests. To Wexler, Maheu seemed an "empire builder." As a "friend of Dave's," Maheu quite early tried to take over the management of the campaign, but Griffin was not interested in accepting that much help from an outsider despite his intimacy with McDonald. Griffin did not want a "private eye" operation. Maheu's chief aide was Walter Fitzpatrick, in charge of his Washington office.

Nevertheless Maheu's operatives arranged for printing bumper stickers and for planting editorials through a special "blind" service—in Wexler's words, "black propaganda." "We had no control over them." Wexler termed the relationship between McDonald and Maheu personal, and to him obscure. Griffin took a dim view of Maheu's operations.

Word of Maheu's influence circulated around international union headquarters. Wexler noted: "I have no idea who was paying the Maheu outfit. . . . Just that Maheu was another one of Dave's friends. Maheu himself was very personable . . . but we just didn't work with him. . . . We couldn't. We were opposed to them in many different ways. . . ."

Several days in Pittsburgh convinced Wexler that the campaign head-quarters needed its own publicity expert. His friend Ross Thomas, an experienced publicity man and writer, had been associated with him in the Arnold Zander-Jerry Wurf campaign in the State and County Union. At one time Thomas had worked in Europe in public relations for the advertising firm of Batten, Barton, Durstine and Osborne for whom he was also on assignment in Nigeria.

Thomas arrived in Pittsburgh a few days after Wexler. His function was to put out campaign newspapers and write speeches. "It was also decided," said Wexler, "that none of our names would appear on any stationery. We were staff. . . . Then Joe Angelo, subdistrict director from Oakland, California, took a leave of absence from his job in Dis-trict 38, and came to work for McDonald as chief of the field operation. . . . A little after New Year's a fellow named Herschel Johnson, a Negro [from District 13], was hired. He did an excellent job in organizing the Negroes and the so-called minorities. He was right out of a steel mill."

Wexler and Thomas operated as a team. Over the period of less than three months, Wexler said they were paid $5,000 and $6,000 respec-tively, plus all expenses.

The smart and cynical Thomas mounted the counterthrust to the Abel strategy. He edited the campaign newspaper *Unity News* and wrote McDonald's basic campaign speeches. He became McDonald's mentor, escort, and psychological guide.

As the campaign developed, McDonald's home in fashionable Palm Springs, California, had become a part of the alienation-from-rank-and-file theme used by the Abel campaign. To counter this, Thomas made much of the fact that Abel had a rather comfortable fishing shack on a lake in Western Maryland. Whether Abel's fishing shack was the moral or physical equivalent of a Palm Springs home was a question, but some retort was regarded as better than silence.

Thomas told of his use of media:

"We bought radio in certain markets. . . . About $45,000 worth cover-ing Chicago, New York, Baltimore and Pennsylvania areas. This, in the last week or ten days of the campaign. . . . We timed it or tried to buy the time to coincide with the plant breaks when the members were in their cars or going to or from work. . . .

"As to TV, NBC and CBS sent their men—Herb Kaplow (NBC) and Stan Levey (then of CBS)—they traveled around. Their camera crews . . . got McDonald at the plant gates; they got him on his Chicago tour, start-ing at the hotel, traveling out into the boondocks that surrounded Chicago, Gary and so forth, where he called on various families, sat down and ate enchiladas. . . . Mostly it was planned under my direction, but using the local union people to set up the individual houses and have him meet some of the workers. . . . We got him to use his Spanish a little bit in the Chicago area . . . and a little in California. . . . He doesn't have a lot of words but the words he does know come out quite well. . . .

"Joe Angelo took over the contact for the locals and districts because he was a Steelworker. We had to have him or people like him. . . . Angelo ran the finances, Steve handled the legal work and the office management and I handled the public relations. . . .

"I traveled with Dave to Washington, to Chicago, to Canada, throughout the Pennsylvania area and Ohio. I must have spent two weeks on the road . . . in a six-week campaign two weeks on the road was quite a bit. I tried to stay in the office as much as possible . . . an 18–20 hour day job. . . . We received very little help or advice from any of the staff of the United Steelworkers. It was strange that [McDonald] should have been in office so long and should not have acquired a loyal cadre that would be at his beck and call in the face of a campaign like this. Apparently the cadre, or a number of them, had been siphoned off by his opposition. . . . This told me that McDonald had not expected opposition. . . . On December 11, I guess, McDonald faced up to the fact that he did have opposition. . . . Jim Griffin was, as I understand it, trying to maneuver it so that McDonald would have one more term without opposition. . . . On the last day of the campaign McDonald told me that his single purpose in running this time was to throw his weight to Griffin for the next election. Griffin had the ambition to be President of the United Steelworkers. . . . He told me so. He made no secret of it.

". . . We didn't go on the offensive until the last two weeks of the campaign. The "Tuxedo Unionism" charge and McDonald's so-called penchant for high living and for Zsa Zsa Gabor and what have you was picked up by the opposition and spread about. . . . They used that as their basic campaign issue, other than the fact that he had grown away from the members. . . . Our campaign was based on the record of the considerable accomplishments of the McDonald administration, which we spelled out in the literature. . . . I thought their issue that our man had drawn away too far from one million members was a little phony. To run a million-member union, I don't think that he could spend all of his time going to local meetings.

"McDonald did like to talk about the big people he knew; a hell of a name dropper. There was one time when he was debating whether to go to a party of somebody important or to a rather large union rally that was being held for him. We had to convince him that the rally might be more important. . . . He would always turn to the amusement page first and read the gossip columns. . . . He was quite interested in what went on on Broadway and in Hollywood among his acquaintances there.

"But he had something else. He had the ability when he wanted to relate to a group of Steelworkers . . . and the ability to read a speech as well as anybody I ever knew, and I've met quite a few. . . . He had a terrific stage presence. I think while he was making a speech, and if the audience was responding, he was as happy as he ever was in his life. But he didn't much like the mixing and mingling that sometimes comes after a speech, the sleeve-tugging of members who wanted to talk to him about what he considered minor grievances. . . . I think he was tremendously bored at the end. . . .

"We got a good break in Drew Pearson's columns, saying that the odds were in our favor. . . . Freddy Sontag claimed that he was able to kill a story in *Time Magazine* which carried the theme that 'David McDonald is confronted by two enemies, I. W. Abel and I. W. Harper.' This was a crack going around at the time, but I'm not convinced that this mysterious Mr. Sontag killed it out of type in *Time Magazine* as he claimed. . . . I suppose we got at least ten memos a day from him, 10 or 15. . . . Maheu paid Sontag. (Who paid Maheu?) I think that's still debatable. I don't think Jimmy Griffin did. Jimmy was presented with enormous bills. (Griffin said "Maheu was one of Howard Hague's operations.") There was something else they did. There is an outfit . . . which provides an editorial service to the more conservative newspapers, weeklies and dailies. For $5,000 you can buy yourself an editorial. . . . Fitzpatrick [Walter Fitzpatrick of the Maheu firm] bought one for Dave McDonald. It was written by a man who opposed repeal of 14(b) and favored right-to-work laws. He wrote the editorial and then he sent it out as part of the package of editorials that these papers subscribe to. Now how many other business firms or organizations around the country avail themselves of this service I have no way of knowing. But it is an interesting commentary on the American press that you can buy an editorial for $5,000 which appears in maybe 50 papers. . . . I was against it. I thought it was a waste of money, for one, because I didn't think the Steelworkers were going to read the editorial and if they did, they'd wonder what this paper which had always fought unions was doing coming out for Dave. . . . I also made the point that this was not exactly ethical and I didn't think it would do any good. . . .

"During the campaign I did everything in my power to tell Dave that he was losing or that he was going to lose. If I didn't do that he would have slacked off. I kept scaring him or trying to scare him and the rest of us did the same thing. . . . We were running him scared. . . .

"[Among the] district directors, I would say that Dave had attracted the majority of the passive ones while Abel for some reason had attracted the aggressive ones . . . with the exception of Jim Griffin and Hughie Carcella, the gentleman from Philadelphia, who was quite an operator in his own right.

"With a few exceptions I was working rather as an autonomous public relations director of a million-member union, with no staff, with a lot of money and with almost a free hand to do whatever I wanted to do. . . ."

CHAPTER 13

First Days in January

You ain't seen nothin' yet.

AL JOLSON

After the Christmas holidays, the practical politicians on the executive board were primarily concerned with establishing or disentangling their political lines inside the international union and between districts. The testing ground was the meeting of the executive board beginning January 4. Under the constitution, the board was required to make decisions about the challenges of the McDonald and Abel supporters arising out of the tellers' reports on the nominations. The eyeball-to-eyeball phase of the campaign had begun.

The day before the board meeting, Abel supporters from three Ohio districts staged a rally in Youngstown to launch the presidential campaign behind the lines in Jimmy Griffin's district. They sought to establish the fact that Griffin now would have to fight for his political life against Russell Thomas, the acknowledged candidate of the Abel forces.

In the heart of Griffin's district, Molony belittled the McDonald proposal that the American Arbitration Association oversee the election as a "stunning insult" aimed against the integrity of the international tellers and every local union officer and local union teller.*

In reply to the McDonald charge that a campaign in the midst of negotiations would hurt the union's chances of winning a good contract, Molony declared the opposite to be true. In previous negotiations, he said, settlements were made clandestinely at the summit. Now, under pressure, McDonald had announced that local issues would be the first order of business, rather than be submerged or shunted aside. In addi-

* *Steel Valley News,* January 4, 1965.

tion, said Molony, recent settlements had "flash, rather than substance"; it had been years since the union members had won a real wage increase. Steelworkers suffered, he said, in comparison with the gains "Walter Reuther won for the auto workers."

To all this, Germano added that McDonald had offered him the post of secretary-treasurer but that he had chosen instead to manage the Abel campaign. Why? He drew the edge of his palm across his forehead: "I've had it—up to here."

Russell Thomas deplored specifically the motives behind Griffin's appointment, "after long delay," of the two Negro staff representatives, which had been announced that same day, as an obvious attempt to win the votes of black steelworkers.

Thomas now charged Griffin with ineffectiveness. He had, he said, failed to organize two major firms in Youngstown "because he hadn't worked enough with the people in those plants."

"He voted for me years ago," added Molony, recalling Griffin's active support of his candidacy against Hague. "Now he's working for the same man I ran against. That's another reason why Abel is extremely anxious that you elect Thomas."

Attention now shifted to the Pittsburgh meeting of the executive board, which had to deal with McDonald's proposal to have the American Arbitration Association supervise the February 9 election. The Abel forces understood the possible attraction and appeal of having an outside agency ensure the "integrity" of the count, and some district directors were encouraged to inspire sentiment against it. A conference of Abel supporters in the Texas region excoriated McDonald. They were "shocked that the President of the International Union would suggest we violate our constitution by permitting outsiders to conduct our elections. We're shocked that he proposes to squander an estimated $1 million from our treasury for his operation 'Eagle Eye.' "

The Steelworkers election procedures, they said, provided "iron-clad guarantees for honest elections. Never has a breath of scandal touched our union elections. McDonald has been elected four times by the identical process which he now distrusts." The last sentence certainly was true. The previous sentence, however, could have been written only out of innocence or dead-pan partisanship.

In a stormy two-hour executive board meeting, McDonald was defeated in the "first test of strength in his battle to retain control." * His defeat occurred the day before he was to lead the union negotiators in a resumption of contract negotiations with company officials. To reporters, McDonald heatedly denied it was a test vote: "I'm still going to win this election." But the board's vote was certainly a blow to his self-esteem,

* Charles Allard in the Pittsburgh *Post-Gazette,* January 5, 1965.

and his entrance into the meeting with the industry representatives would lack some of the lordly assurance he usually affected.

The Abel campaign committee promptly stressed the political meaning of the defeat "to change the international election procedure." If McDonald had been able to carry the executive board, said Abel, "he would have plunged the union into an election debacle which would have taken months to straighten out. . . . His proposal clearly violated the USWA constitution and the Landrum-Griffin Act."

McDonald hit sharply at Abel: "The opposition to the motion, . . . led by the union's secretary-treasurer whose office has complete control of the Union's election procedure, . . . has to be branded a cynical disregard for the welfare of the union members." Outside supervision of the balloting would "have insured an election above reproach. . . ."

In the meantime, negotiations resumed at the Penn-Sheraton. Quite obviously, the minds of the negotiators were hardly fixed on collective bargaining. The sessions recessed early to permit the union officials to pick up where they left off in the executive board meetings. On the second day of a three-day session, the board worked late into the night to act on eight complaints from would-be candidates for district directorships.

The significant complainant with staying power was Kender. He charged Schremp, the pro-Abel incumbent director, with having obstructed his efforts to obtain the eight nominations necessary to qualify in this district for a place on the ballot by denying him the use of the mailing list of union members, while making use of it at union expense to further his own campaign. Kender claimed that he had been barred from speaking at local union nominating meetings. Despite all such obstructions he claimed he had received nine nominations, one more than the minimum needed to get on the ballot. But four of these were ruled invalid by the Abel majority in the executive board. When the dust settled, all complaints were disallowed by the executive board. Having exhausted internal grievance procedure, however, Kender kept his case alive, at this stage, with support of the McDonald strategists, who urged that he resort to the provisions of the Landrum-Griffin Act. They cared less about Kender than about the case's nuisance possibilities for later litigation in behalf of McDonald. Kender, however, needed no special urging.

As a result, on February 1, 1965, Kender finally submitted a six-page bill of complaint to the Secretary of Labor to halt the Steelworkers election. He charged that union officers had violated the union constitution, misused union funds, and conducted themselves improperly in the pre-election proceedings. Specifically, Kender charged he had been denied a place on the ballot by the Steelworkers executive board against Schremp, the incumbent director. Having exhausted his remedies under the union constitution by appealing to the executive board, he considered his case now properly before the Secretary of Labor Willard Wirtz.

To the members of the executive board, seemingly dealing with technicalities, this infighting was critical.

Conflict continued over the still unresolved question of recognition of a staff organization. The two organizations competing for recognition were the Staffman's Organizing Committee (SOC), which was organized by staff men friendly to McDonald, and the Staff Workers Organizing Committee (SWOC), which had the backing of the Abel camp. On December 17 Andrew Kmec, SOC's chairman and, of course, a McDonald supporter, claimed that it had enrolled a majority of the staff representatives and therefore was entitled to exclusive recognition by McDonald and other top union officials.

FIGHT RAGES OVER USW STAFF UNION ran the front-page headline in the next day's Pittsburgh *Post-Gazette*. Anticipating the McDonald move, Abel did not oppose the principle of recognition of a union of staff workers. His supporters raised the point, however, that there were two competing staff groups. The Abel men on the executive board, as the majority, refused to recognize SOC as proposed by McDonald.

Immediately after adjournment, McDonald, as international president, dispatched an official memorandum to staff representatives, pointing out that whereas he had readily recognized SOC on December 19, the international executive board on January 6, 1965, "refused to approve this action."

Thus, McDonald sought to strengthen his bid for support of staff representatives by establishing himself as their friend and protector. Instead of gaining reassurance, however, many staff men now saw their hopes for recognition as a group mangled in the political campaign and with it the possibility that a change of administration might endanger the job tenure of individual staff men.

But the resolution of the international executive board ". . . had called for the establishment of a commission to consult with the staff men on the nature and scope of the organization they wished to represent them."

The commission, headed by Canadian Larry Sefton, director of District 6, included directors from both sides. After promptly hearing spokesmen for both SOC and SWOC, the Sefton group recommended the recognition of a staff organization. This the board agreed to on January 14, and it recognized and certified SOC as the sole collective bargaining agent for the 675 field representatives in the United States and Canada.

Both SOC and SWOC committees agreed jointly that the new staff organization "shall not and must not participate *as an organization* in any election within the International Union by endorsement, statement or otherwise."

Here was the make-up of the lame-duck executive board between January 4, when it ruled on the nomination contests for district director, and June 1, the day the new administration was officially to take over:

	PRO-ABEL			PRO-MCDONALD	
District	*Director*	*Votes*	*District*	*Director*	*Votes*
2	James Nicholson	7	1	Roy H. Stevens	30
4	Joseph Molony	52	7	Hugh Carcella	54
5	Pat Burke	21	8	Albert Atallah	31
6	Lawrence Sefton	86	9	William Moran	42
19	William J. Hart	26	13	Eugene Maurice	29
23	Paul Rusen	36	15	Paul Hilbert	33
27	John S. Johns	36	16	Paul Normile	19
28	Paul E. Schremp	29	20	Kay Kluz	25
29	Charles Younglove	26	21	John Grajciar	17
31	Joseph Germano	115	25	Al Whitehouse	14
32	Walter J. Burke	31	26	James P. Griffin	45
33	Earl Bester	20	30	James Robb	23
34	Al F. Kojetinsky	31	35	Lorne H. Nelles	17
37	Martin Burns	24	36	R. E. Farr	32
National Director of Canada			38	Charles J. Smith	58
	William Mahoney	86	President David J. McDonald		115
Secretary-Treasurer I. W. Abel		115	Vice-President Howard Hague		115
"Abel" total		741	"McDonald" total		699

The Abel forces now exulted in this confirmation that, at least on the executive board, they had a bandwagon rolling. But to the New York *Herald Tribune* (January 5, 1965) McDonald said: "These are only directors voting. There are about one million steelworkers who will have their say February 9." The *American Metal Market,* an industry publication, saw in "the vote by the executive board . . . a stunning victory for Mr. Abel."

In these first days of January, spokesmen for employers seemed anxious to provide what aid and comfort they could to McDonald's cause. On January 6 Walter F. Carey, president of the United States Chamber of Commerce, called upon the "labor establishment to resist pressure from the 'new breed' leaders now bidding for rank-and-file support. . . . It will be up to the labor establishment to withstand these pressures from below if the American economy is to continue its steady growth with price stability." Later Carey sought to "clarify" his position as not intended to refer to the election struggle inside the United Steelworkers. Despite Carey's disclaimers, more cautious representatives of steel management shuddered at what was considered ineptitude in the manner and timing of his remarks. Carey's attack was to be used by

Abel to support the charge that McDonald was the preferred candidate of the industry.

Battered by defeat on several key issues inside the executive board, McDonald now sought to recapture the public-relations initiative. He announced that he would start bargaining January 20 in New York with American Can and Continental Can "for total job security, pay increases and dignity and justice." The can companies had remained in production as a result of a contract extension from September 30 of the year before to March 1. At the time the decision was made to delay the talks in can manufacturing, union negotiators had regarded the steel industry as "a better first target [for 1965] because of its strong sales and earnings position." But the unexpected election contest made it clear that a quick settlement in basic steel was out of the question. Consequently, can negotiations were also bound to be affected by the fact that basic steel negotiations would be continued at least until May 1, the date of contract expiration.

Heading the union's can negotiating committee were District Directors James Robb, a strong McDonald supporter, and Al Whitehouse, McDonald's candidate for secretary-treasurer. Under such friendly political auspices. McDonald announced a meeting of local union officers and staff representatives in the can industry, on the eve of the resumption of can negotiations in New York late in January. More immediately, McDonald called a meeting of local leaders and staff representatives in the aluminum industry for the following Friday and Saturday—January 8 and 9—ostensibly to consider bargaining issues. Since the aluminum contracts did not expire until July 31, more than six months later, McDonald was clearly making use of the collective bargaining apparatus as a political peg. As part of a comprehensive plan, Griffin also had urged that a similar meeting be held for local union officers in the steel-fabricating and -finishing industries for Chicago on January 14 and 15.

Upon adjournment of the executive board, McDonald distributed a program under an inclusive title: "Let's Soar Through the Sixties." His proposals, said McDonald, "will enable the United Steelworkers of America to soar through the Sixties, not sink back to the Thirties." They amounted to a compendium of economic, social, and political goals for the nation and for the union, starting with "total job security."

But McDonald's program received little attention at his news conference. Before television cameras and a forest of microphones, he disregarded the elevated tone of his platform. He charged that Abel was seeking "to vilify the staff, damage the union's reputation, and hinder its effectiveness at the bargaining table." Newspapermen reported an "angry, fighting McDonald who emphasized his points by fist-shaking . . ."

McDonald continued, "I am not going to be backed or maneuvered into a strike by either I. W. Abel or the industry because of this politics in this union." By this time, rumors had been mounting that the bargaining sessions, which had been resumed earlier in the week, would be recessed again, possibly until after February 9, election day.

McDonald spent considerable time replying to charges made by Abel that he had permitted the staff specialists too decisive a role in the administration of the union and in collective bargaining, frequently supplanting the function of elected district directors and local officers. He characterized Abel's charge as a "falsehood designed to divide this union."

At his own news conference, Abel responded to McDonald's attack. McDonald, he said, was trying to turn the forthcoming election into a "public circus." He therefore rejected McDonald's proposal that they appear in a joint TV debate. He proposed instead that "the best interests of our union would be served by each of us taking a page in . . . *Steel Labor,* which goes to the home of every member. . . . To the fullest extent possible, the debate should be kept within the union family, and the logical way of doing so is in the union publication. . . . This method . . . will help promote a feeling of unity while making sure that the election strengthens our Union."

By this time, any hope of keeping the election "within the family" was pure illusion. Abel sought to contrast his determination to hold the election campaign within certain bounds with McDonald's predilection for the microphone and the camera. Willy-nilly, a public exchange, formal debate or no, was actually under way.

Regardless of who won, Abel said he was convinced that the union would come out of the campaign more unified than it had been in recent years. In the three months before May 1, the date of contract termination in basic steel, "we will be able to meet our collective bargaining agreement in a rational, responsible manner."

He emphasized that McDonald had called an "unprecedented series of meetings" to acquaint the local union leaders with collective bargaining processes and to obtain their views. This, said Abel, was the result of the same rank-and-file pressures that led to the Abel-Burke-Molony candidacies. And thus, thanks to an election campaign which McDonald deplored, "there will have been a greater rank-and-file participation in the bargaining process than at any previous time since President McDonald took office."

Abel replied to McDonald's slashing attack "in temperate, measured language." The only harsh remark made by Abel, reported Charles Allard in the *Post-Gazette,* was that the union president's statements "sound like the rantings of one suffering from complete frustration." Abel attributed the immediate cause of this frustration to his opponent's defeat in the executive board, and the now mounting certainty that the companies were seeking a recess in the collective bargaining until after the election. Abel himself favored the postponement: "It might be in the best interests of all concerned."

The prospect of a recess in collective bargaining had at first not been to McDonald's liking. By holding bargaining sessions, however perfunctory, McDonald would enjoy a clear publicity advantage through constant exposure before cameras and news stories: McDonald with the leaders of the industry; holding news conferences; checking in with the rank and file to report back to the collective bargaining conferences; McDonald, the diligent union leader, being harassed by an office-seeking politician.

Despite the advantages McDonald might gain by a continuation of the bargaining sessions a month prior to the election, the industry executives were apprehensive over what such a continuance might entail. First, it was clear that effective bargaining could not be carried on under McDonald's disputed leadership. Since his opponents as union officers would also participate in the negotiations, the internal struggle—no matter what the efforts at self-restraint—could sharpen the union position vis-à-vis the companies. Second, McDonald might no longer be an effective president after the February 9 election. Third, the meetings of the executive board just concluded showed that McDonald no longer controlled the old board and would not control the new board.

At the very hour Abel was holding his news conference, industry and union negotiators assembled to discuss the possibility of a recess. McDonald was present; of course Abel was not. Later that evening, word leaked out that the union and the eleven basic steel producing companies would jointly announce a negotiations recess until February 15. The next morning, January 8, when the joint announcement was made, McDonald implied that management, not he, was responsible. The suggestion for the recess had come from U.S. Steel's R. Conrad Cooper, chief negotiator for the eleven steel companies. He quoted Cooper as saying that "the union cannot conduct major bargaining in its present disturbed form, that companies would not make agreements at this time and that most of their answers, even on local issues, would be 'no' until after the union's elections." McDonald then added that he and other union officials present at the meeting had "reluctantly" agreed to Cooper's suggestion for a recess (*American Metal Market,* January 11).

Cooper, displeased with McDonald's version of events, called his own press conference to reply. He emphatically denied that the industry negotiators had forced a suspension of negotiations. He asserted that the steel companies had asked the union "to restore integrity to the 120-day period provided for the negotiations" by extending the termination date of the contract to a period 120 days after the February 9 election day, and that the union representatives refused this request. Whereupon, Cooper said, "we offered the union the alternatives of suspension until the air is clear, or continuing next week. The union elected to suspend."

At his news conference, McDonald pointed out that when the top negotiators met the afternoon before, Abel was engaged in a press conference. He implied that Abel by his preoccupation with politics was responsible for the halt in negotiations.

In every section of the country, these moves were watched closely by the local leadership. They traced and evaluated subtleties of maneuver that were lost on the general public. Whatever McDonald's ostensible position, the recess in negotiations gained him necessary time for the rigorous campaign his advisers were now urging upon him. McDonald was clearly the only articulate spokesman for his own cause. Al Whitehouse was neither popular nor widely respected. Howard Hague's abilities were confined to headquarters planning, or, as his enemies put it, plotting. On the other side, for Abel, Burke, and Molony, a day-and-night speaking schedule lay ahead.

In the next three weeks the campaign would take shape. The recess in negotiations denied McDonald the publicity and status exposure he had banked on. Determined to gain the initiative, he and his advisers now embarked on a program of conferences of local leaders as well as of executive board meetings. With McDonald presiding over such proceedings and pro-McDonald staff representatives politicking in the lobbies and hotel rooms, the backbones of local supporters could be stiffened and backsliders might be brought around.

Buttressing McDonald's position of a "strike-happy" Abel, Thomas Campbell, publisher of Iron Age, now predicted that if Abel were elected, a steel strike would surely follow: "The average steel worker is much smarter and able to think better than most union officers or company officials give him credit for. The workers do not want another 116 day strike and they are not interested in power politics." While Abel's supporters cited Walter Carey's and now Campbell's observations as further evidence of their claims that management was backing McDonald, such a solicitous attitude on the part of management spokesmen would not necessarily impair McDonald's standing except perhaps in certain sophisticated sections of the union membership. On the other hand, many McDonald supporters would consider management's warning against Abel as a reasonable political dividend collectible under the "mutual trusteeship" or "human relations" plans. Throughout the union, however, the news that Abel now commanded the majority vote on the executive board signified that a transfer of power was imminent.

Quayle's Waves

Oliver Quayle's services now became an instrument for McDonald's campaign. The first survey in November had provided initial information for the development of the McDonald strategy, and the covering of Quayle's findings by the media gave McDonald status. His re-election had been predicted by President Johnson's favorite pollster, which would impress LBJ now and at a later time.

With bargaining in basic steel suspended until after the election, Quayle in his "second wave" of interviews saw the way opened to McDonald for a "massive, full-time campaign down to the wire," though he must "run scared."

The Abel campaign did not make use of sophisticated polling techniques. One reason was lack of finances; the other was skepticism of their value in a union election. To Abel and his associates, moreover, a Quayle poll provided further proof of expensive McDonald gimmickry.

According to Quayle's first poll, McDonald entered the campaign with a "substantial lead of 58.6 percent of the vote," but, McDonald was warned that the outcome could go either way. "An incumbent has an advantage in early polls by virtue of that incumbency," Quayle reminded his client.

Quayle had found that three out of every four voting members considered that the choice between McDonald and Abel made a real difference.

This is an asset for Abel. The burden on him is to make the race. He must come from behind. He must persuade members it is in their best interest to lift the mantle of leadership from President McDonald and transfer it to Abe Abel. He can do his best in a climate of real interest in the election. In times when members are casual or disinterested it is easiest for an incumbent to remain in office. This does not mean that David McDonald will lose. It does mean that Abel has an opportunity to win. David McDonald is in a fight for his life. He must be prepared to go all out. We speak of personal effort. Seven or eight, or even ten hours a day will not be sufficient. It will require 15 to 16 hours daily and seven days a week. If David McDonald invests anything less in this campaign, he courts defeat. It is that simple.

In the second wave, Quayle said, his smaller sample carried less statistical reliability, and the ballots were not taken in secret. The "undecided" had jumped from 1 to 17 per cent, but without them the standings were virtually the same as the month before: McDonald far ahead.

Under these conditions, Quayle found the burden resting on Abel. Although the challenger appeared not to have made headway during December, his campaign had stepped up. "Countermeasures by President McDonald become urgent," Quayle prodded.

In the races for vice-president and secretary-treasurer, Quayle found that about 50 per cent of those polled were undecided. Quayle's stern conclusion was that McDonald must go it alone. "We feel it would be a mistake for the McDonald campaign to make any great expenditure for Secretary-Treasurer." Alas poor Whitehouse! *

Quayle found that members between twenty-one and thirty-four years old were strongest for McDonald. Thus, campaign literature, he said, had to be prepared with a special appeal to young voters. At the same time, more Abel supporters attended union meetings regularly—54 per cent as against 46 per cent for McDonald, who was doing best with members who "rarely or occasionally attend union meetings."

Quayle made much of this finding. How to overcome the supposed advantage Abel had among the more seasoned members? Quayle advised: "Fewer meetings at union halls and more shaking of hands at plant gates. Literature going directly into the homes rather than handouts. Telephone messages. The McDonald people should be well organized on telephoning the day before the election, that evening and during the day. . . ."

On the matter of religion—McDonald a Catholic and Abel a Protestant—Quayle suggested: "McDonald must make his religious affiliation known, but it is not necessary to stress it."

On the matter of civil rights, Quayle drew this conclusion: "Members of the United Steelworkers reflect remarkably national thinking. . . . The race issue in this campaign can be dangerous. The more it is brought front and center, the greater the risk of alienating the almost two-thirds who have some reservations on the issue. Rights for Negroes is not a presently working factor in this election, and it will be to McDonald's advantage if the issue remains that way."

Quayle suggested that campaign literature identify McDonald with the great of the land through the use of photographs taken with "President Johnson, the late Mr. Kennedy, former President Eisenhower, and other easily recognizable Americans."

Then Quayle produced a "profile" of Abel based on interviews with members: "He is surprisingly well known. Of all the comments made about Abel, 85 percent are favorable. He is liked mainly for the job he has done. He is thought to be very strong for the individual working

* Quayle provided this statistical picture: in the South, McDonald led Abel by 74 to 26 per cent; in the East (including eastern Pennsylvania and eastern New York), 60 to 40 per cent; in western Pennsylvania and western New York, it was even; in the Midwest, McDonald was given the edge, 52 to 48 per cent; in the Far West and the West Coast, McDonald led by 65 to 35 per cent; and in Canada, McDonald was running away by 77 to 23 per cent. By industrial categories, Quayle showed McDonald leading Abel 51 to 49 per cent in basic steel, while under "Miscellaneous" McDonald was given 65 per cent to Abel's 23 per cent.

man. He is straightforward. He would be a change from David Mc-
Donald. He has handled finances well and come up the hard way. People say he is experienced and a man who fights for what is right. There
has been little or nothing said against Abe Abel."

Consequently, Quayle said, it would be a big mistake if McDonald
launched personal attacks on Abel. Rather, he said, "McDonald's attitude can be more of a bemused 'he's a nice fellow and I like him, too.'
In striking this posture, McDonald must be careful not to be looking
down his nose or acting haughty but he must make it clear that Abel is
just a lightweight. . . . By indirection, McDonald must raise doubt as to
whether Abel is heavy enough for the job, without criticizing him as a
person."

Quayle found McDonald's "job rating" 56 per cent favorable to 44
per cent unfavorable. Fully 17 per cent declared he was doing a down-
right poor job, while only 2 per cent said that about Abel. At this point,
Quayle offered balm to the slightly battered "profile" of his client in
these words: "A union president, just as much as the Governor of a
state, can suffer the ravages of incumbency. In truth, David McDonald
comes off very well. He has had to make enemies. Over the years,
while he may have rubbed some the wrong way, he has gotten the job
done."

Quayle reported that while some found McDonald "domineering and
arrogant," "completely missing are any comments about his various
homes, lunches at '21,' or even about his divorce. David McDonald is
not hurting about the image of a man who is living off the fat of the
union."

Nevertheless the Quayle report offered these sharp observations:

McDonald's big weakness is that union members feel he has lost touch
with them. McDonald is somehow operating at an entirely different level, and
one that leaves him completely removed. It is not that members *object* to
their President functioning at this level. They are even *glad and proud*. What
they do object to is that he remains exclusively in this exalted atmosphere.
How can he represent the people if he does not spend more time with them?
David McDonald has neglected his public relations. Even as a member of
Congress must keep in touch with the home folks, so must a union president
stay as close as possible to his constituents. This, plus a "safe" Abel, makes
many union members think it is time for a change.

"We are not sure this aspect of the McDonald image can be refur-
bished in a month, but a mighty effort can be made—and must be
made," Quayle warned. "That is why McDonald must spend a month
with the people. He is not going to win this election with long speeches
and articles that people won't read. They think he has done a good job.

Now he must remind them that Dave McDonald is also a 'good guy.' He needs exposure."

Quayle now discussed "issues" McDonald could turn to advantage. Quayle found in the "strike issue" a potential comparable to that found by President Johnson in the "finger on the trigger" issue against his Republican opponent, Barry Goldwater. Quayle had elicited the finding that the "fear of strike" theme might hurt Abel. Properly exploited, this would clearly made Abel less "safe." McDonald and his associates had already begun to charge that Abel was "strike-happy," and they leaped on any Abel statement to buttress the point.

McDonald, said Quayle, should hammer away at Abel's refusal to debate in order to make McDonald come through as a heavyweight against Abel, a lightweight fearful that his weakness would be revealed in a debate. Thus, said Quayle, this theme would emerge: "McDonald is the strong man in this election. Do the members want to take a risk of giving up strong leadership? The debate issue needs constant repetition in this context."

Quayle urged that McDonald issue two direct mailings to the members' homes. "No matter what we say, we know the first piece will range over all the issues. There must be a second one that is very short and very simple and which talks only about the *best issues.*"

Quayle's early January "confidential" analysis ended: "There is majority support for all the projected McDonald campaign arguments: (1) 'The Human Relations Committee has improved bargaining in steel'; (2) 'David McDonald is best qualified to deal with important people'; (3) 'We have achieved prosperity under McDonald'; (4) 'McDonald would be a stronger man than Abel in bargaining'; (5) 'McDonald would use more modern methods in bargaining and running the union'; (6) 'David McDonald would be better than I. W. Abel on job security'; (7) 'I. W. Abel is not as strong a man as David McDonald.' "

This second Quayle report included ideas gleaned from McDonald's advisers—men like Griffin, Dave Feller, and Howard Hague—who hoped that McDonald would pay more attention to Quayle than he might to them.

Quayle's insistence that the race issue be avoided was ignored later on by the McDonald campaign headquarters, and by McDonald himself. Politically it seemed too easy, too tempting. The final Quayle survey came three weeks later.

At this point, McDonald announced a "first major breakthrough toward job security." This was the tentative agreement between the union and the Alan Wood Steel Company, which he proclaimed comparable to the program inaugurated in January 1963 in the Kaiser plant at Fontana, California. Alan Wood is a one-plant operation in Conshohocken, Pennsylvania, with 2,500 workers, located in District 7. The willingness of the company management to announce the plan a month before election day was tribute paid to the mutually satisfactory relations developed over the years between Director Hugh Carcella and Harleston R. Wood, president of Alan Wood. The company was not concerned that the announcement brought political advantage to the union president. If it fitted in with the plans of the McDonald supporters, that was merely a nonfinancial contribution to closer relations with the district director, the man with whom it had to deal in negotiations and adjustment of grievances.

A few days later, Wood released a more modest version of the plan: "We're anxious to obtain better operating costs by getting cooperation from the union. . . . Total job security, in a company our size," he said, with a bow to the larger steel corporations, "will have no impact on steel prices. We're a single integrated plant operation. The total job security plan . . . is an enlargement of the supplementary unemployment benefit fund to do a little more effective job than it has been doing."

At any rate, McDonald exulted that under his leadership there was first Fontana, now Alan Wood, and next year? Such agreements, he said, taken together could constitute a forerunner of "total job security." "All of us are greatly interested in advancing a total security program for our membership. If it is possible to achieve security for the kind of money [an estimated two to seven cents an hour in new money], perhaps others can do it too."

Armed with a "few more details," Abel later belittled McDonald's claim. He attacked him for "substituting hot air for solid progress." On January 23 the Alan Wood newsletter cautiously explained to its stockholders what the agreement was all about: "We are in agreement on the proposed plan which is designed to expand social security benefits within the existing SUB [Supplementary Unemployment Benefit] Program, and this agreement will embody some of the features publicized in the press." The plan, the management said defensively, was designed to "improve the earning power of our company." All in all, Abel said, the company's restrained claims indicated that you "can't buy Utopia for 2 cents an hour," the price tag the Alan Wood spokesman had placed on the plan. "This may turn into a contract advance," Abel said, "but I object to Mr. McDonald trying to turn a tentative agreement, one not yet signed by local union officers and probably not applicable to more than one local union, into some sort of mysterious package that would apply nationwide."

In Coatesville, Pennsylvania, he reminded the steelworkers that in 1962 "McDonald brought home a no-wage-increase pact, which contained some fringe improvements and also some hot air," which was cheered by the *Wall Street Journal* as "The Cheapest Labor Peace in 8 Years." In 1963, Abel added scornfully, McDonald followed the same pattern: "Some fringe improvements and no wage increases but more hot air. This one was tagged by the *Wall Street Journal* as 'one of the cheapest settlements in 20 years.' Now, in the Alan Wood agreement, we have McDonald taking a modest fringe improvement, plus a plan which could eliminate incentive pay for reassigned workers plus some hot air and coming up with what he claims would be a great package."

Indirect support for McDonald now came from another source. Monsignor Charles Owen Rice, known in the Pittsburgh area over the years as the "labor priest," deplored the "power struggle" (Pittsburgh *Catholic*, January 14). He had found it "impossible" to find "real divergence between the participants in the Steelworkers' melee." The "reluctance of Abel to debate McDonald," he said, only contributed a lack of clarity. In November, he had urged Abel to withdraw from a "power" contest with McDonald. Monsignor Rice, who usually exerted more influence over the rank-and-file Catholic membership than over the leadership, seemed to the ordinary workers to speak with the authority of the Church. His formulation pleased the McDonald camp. Abel's criticism of McDonald's way of using staff experts, according to Father Rice, smacked of "anti-intellectualism." But to the Abel side, the Rice utterance amounted to a political caricature of Abel's position. In the thickly settled steel districts where Father Rice's words were read by his parishioners, Abel feared he would be hurt.

In mid-January the focus of union attention was the Chicago meeting of the district directors, assembled as the international executive board at the Conrad Hilton Hotel. With them, McDonald also brought in the Wage Policy Committee from all parts of the United States and Canada. Both Abel and Germano berated McDonald for "assembling needless and expensive meetings" as publicity springboards to further his campaign. Bringing in the Wage Policy Committee for a mid-January meeting lasting only a few hours cost the union between $50,000 and $60,000. His reported intention to add meetings of local leaders in the fabricating industry for January 14 and 15 would have cost the union about $1 million. McDonald denied that he ever had such a plan and Joe Germano called him a liar.

For McDonald, Chicago was going to be the big kickoff, right in the heart of Germano territory. Germano would presumably have most influence on the staff; the McDonald strategy was aimed at enlisting the support of local dissidents inside Germano's District 31. For example, former President Mark Tincher of Local 1014, the huge 15,000-member local at the Gary plant of U.S. Steel, was placed in charge of specific activities. McDonald men, reported to be flashing an impressive stack of bills, were now becoming active in the saloons near the plants, buying drinks for the house. In enemy territory, McDonald's campaign now began to take on the pattern of politicking familiar to state and national office seekers. Rather than confining himself to speaking at the usual meetings at union halls and shaking hands at plant gates, McDonald was cast in the role of the eager campaigner, the outgoing candidate. He was followed by a train of reporters.

January 15 was bitter cold. Snow fell on the frozen crescent of steel plants along the lake front which stretched from Chicago to Gary. The full press and TV coverage, the high-pressure public-relations approach used by McDonald, contrasted with the restrained, pedestrian approach of the Abel team.

Chauffeured by his bodyguard, Charles Barranco, and accompanied by an entourage of media representatives, McDonald moved rapidly to the various points on his schedule, stopping for brief chats in the homes of three steelworkers: Harry Gensell of Hessville, Indiana; Clarence Winfield of Gary; and Humberto Lira of East Chicago. In Lira's home, TV cameras and newspapermen were ready. When the candidate arrived, he "paused long enough to eat some enchiladas and tacos and sip a glass of ginger ale. In true presidential tradition he kissed Lira's three-year-old daughter. . . . Taped to the wall above the unlighted dining room fireplace, behind McDonald's chair, was a campaign picture of the union leader. . . . Lira's beauty-prize-winning daughter, Hortensia, 19, radiant in a cranberry-red dress, waited on table." Lira, a second helper on an open-hearth furnace, said he was proud that McDonald had stopped by. "All the way, I want him to be president of our vast union," he said in a helpful echo of "All the way with LBJ."

McDonald then took off to the meeting in the high school auditorium in East Chicago. There he and Minnie Minoso, a former Chicago White Sox star and local hero, were awarded plaques from the Steelworkers local. Joseph de Rosa, the local master of ceremonies, "reminded the union chief that he was using the same lectern that President Johnson had used not long ago." Then de Rosa, with a sideswipe at Director Germano, said that "everyone who had turned out for McDonald did so because they wanted to, not because they were ordered."

That night at Germano Hall in East Chicago, Abel, addressing an overflow crowd, replied to McDonald's "strike-happy" charges: "My position is that the union must strike if it is necessary to do so, and if we need to strike this membership will respond as in the past." Also, Abel recalled that it was under McDonald that the steelworkers had been "forced" by management into a six-week strike in 1956 and a 116-day stoppage in 1959–1960. Abel struck a responsive chord in the audience when he declared that young leaders must be helped to rise within the union. He scornfully referred to McDonald's "chronic" absenteeism from his union responsibilities.

The two men were now slugging in earnest. McDonald alternated between painting Abel as "power-mad" and "strike-happy," or as a "nice enough man, whom he would trust to borrow his tools, but that he was really no more than a competent clerk who was good at reserving hotel rooms." By now he had begun to absorb some of the tactical guidance provided by Oliver Quayle's "second wave" analysis of the campaign.

Retorting, Abel professed confusion: "Last Saturday, I read that Mr. McDonald said that I am a nice enough man and that he would trust me to borrow his tools. That's real neighborly. Then the next day I read in the Sunday *New York Times* that Dave calls me 'a damned liar.' That's kind of confusing. Now, Dave knows I got all the tools I need. Dave knows I know how to use tools. I used them for many years in the plant. Incidentally, something Dave never did."

The humor was heavy but the thrust was hard, both ways. McDonald's appearances in Chicago were derided by Germano: McDonald's "expensive build-up, including slick two-color advertisements in the area papers," sought to "lure the crowd with a huge variety show, including Latin American and U.S. orchestras." He jeered at McDonald's "rally in a junior high auditorium . . . for the entire Chicago area." The hundred-member choral group the McDonald forces relied on was canceled when the Musicians Union pointed out it was a nonunion enterprise. When McDonald got up to give his recitation, he had, "by actual count . . . 52 persons on stage and 396 in the auditorium, including 161 women and children." In proud contrast, Germano reported that in East Chicago the meeting was strictly devoted to union business: "I. W. Abel spoke to 500 union members on a snowy, blustery night, and then shuttled over to Gary—Walter Burke and Joe Molony covered East Chicago—for a speech before 950 union members at Philip Murray Hall." Then Germano advised the "brothers" that "If the McDonald forces try to stage a rally in your area without benefit of dancing girls and an orchestra, they're discriminating against you."

With Johnson's inauguration a few days off, McDonald again stressed his identification with the President and other exalted government officials. By now those who attended the meetings of the candidates— at best a small portion of the total membership—knew that Abel was pointing with pride to his acquaintance with the rank and file, and how he had worked with them throughout his twelve years as secretary-treasurer. McDonald in turn indignantly denied that he had "lost touch" with the membership—a denial that he felt constrained to repeat.

Among the more than 115,000 eligible voters in Germano's District

31—at least 10 per cent of the international union—McDonald was determined to pry away from Germano's influence as large a chunk of the workers as possible. In the Chicago area, he had made appeals to minority groups, not only to Mexican-American workers but also to Negroes, some of whom were quick to believe charges of racial discrimination against Abel, which had begun to circulate by word of mouth.

With three weeks before election day, McDonald was working to hold on to the presidency as he had never worked before.

CHAPTER **14**

Three Weeks to Go

Rank by rank again we stand.

WELSH STUDENT HYMN

While McDonald attempted with pyrotechnical displays to blast away at Joe Germano's District 31, where disaffection in several large locals was a normal state, Germano, running unopposed, was determined to prove that his political prowess remained unimpaired. With great confidence in his highly skilled assistants, Lester Thornton and Samuel Evitt, Germano was certain that he could carry the district for Abel by a sizable margin. McDonald's operation against Germano was a personal counterpart to Abel's attack against James Griffin in District 26, with the important difference that Griffin, McDonald's campaign manager, faced an opposition candidate sponsored by Abel.

After Chicago, McDonald failed to make a campaign appearance in Johnstown, Pennsylvania. "More of McDonald's chronic absenteeism," said Abel supporters gleefully. McDonald's people explained that bad weather had kept his plane from landing, but his opponents said that more likely he had feared a poor attendance. Actually, McDonald was busily engaged before TV cameras in Chicago and in Pittsburgh.

That Sunday night, McDonald appeared over KDKA-TV in Pittsburgh. He assumed the "bemused" attitude toward Abel that Quayle had advised. He told the audience that Abel had been his "personal choice" for secretary-treasurer in 1952: "I was somewhat disappointed in him. But he did take good care of the books." In a tone of pained objectivity McDonald said that, on the basis of close observation, he did not honestly feel that Abel had the qualities to make a good president of the United Steelworkers. That same Sunday, in a lengthy interview with

172

Rosemary McDonald, Vera Glaser of the North American Newspaper Alliance syndicate portrayed her as a busy, happy wife, excited by the drama of her husband's position. "One night we're in Washington dining with President and Mrs. Johnson. The next I'm back in my own kitchen in Bermuda shorts, peeling potatoes. I never know what tomorrow will bring." When the reporter asked her what she regarded as the greatest experience of her life, the wife of the steel union's president replied: "The first time we dined at the White House."

On the same day, election forecasts began to crop up. The Chicago *Tribune* believed that it would be "close, but David McDonald will keep his post." The Gary *Post Tribune* opined that Abel showed the "slightest of margins."

Abel, still backing away from TV programs, returned to Chicago on January 18 to address the Steelworkers seventh annual Illinois state political education conference. He received a roaring welcome from six hundred delegates representing one hundred and fifty Illinois locals.

While Abel continued politically active in the Chicago area, McDonald appeared in New York for a strategy meeting on the can industry negotiations, scheduled to reopen on January 20. In one sense, this was friendly territory. The cochairmen of the can negotiating committee were James Robb, retiring director of District 30, who was a McDonald man, and Al Whitehouse. More than two hundred local union officers had gathered, representing an estimated 45,000 workers in the can companies.

McDonald's appearance in New York as president, rather than as a candidate, afforded him "high-level" publicity. Since the basic steel negotiations had been recessed because of the election, McDonald stated that the contract pattern to be set in the can industry could possibly apply to basic steel; "total job security" was the prime objective. He again pointed to the tentative agreement with the Alan Wood Steel Company, which had become an all-purpose campaign tool.

The next night McDonald appeared in Baltimore to address a rally in District 8, headed by Albert Atallah, whose support Abel had once hoped for. Instead, the Abel supporters now charged that the race issue was being used against Abel by word of mouth. As a result, a large number of Negro members attended the McDonald meeting. Adopting a new note, McDonald threatened: "If I am re-elected, Abel will have to go job-hunting. I have no job for him. He can go fishing or he can go to work for the Government if he wants to, or he can stay in the union and go to work back in some plant." This brought the hoped-for laugh. "He's a nice enough fellow, but sometimes given to exaggeration. In tough negotiations, he is a little out of his depth. He's been a pretty good bookkeeper. At least our general audit has always checked out with his figures." In a more menacing tone, he warned that in the event of his re-election, the staff personnel supporting Abel would also be fired. It was a threat that Abel and his supporters turned against McDonald.

Over in District 32, in Waukegan, Illinois, Walter J. Burke's native town, the major, Robert Sabonjian, presided over the meeting at the Steelworkers' John F. Kennedy Memorial Hall. As a former worker at the Cyclone Fence Company and the son of a steelworker, the mayor described himself as "a fellow steelworker." Because of this inheritance, he said, "I feel it's important to commit myself in this election." He deplored McDonald's "departure from close relationship with the membership"; it was time for a change. The talk was wildly applauded, with no question being raised about the propriety of a city official's intervention in a union election. (Two years later, the mayor embarrassed his union friends by opposing the re-election of Senator Paul Douglas because of his liberal civil rights position.)

As Abel entered the hall, a member demanded to know why "we can't have accord in the official family, and isn't this campaign bad for the United Steelworkers?" Abel reviewed the steelworkers' struggle over decades and how finally, through a union, they found a way "to have a voice in determining their own destiny . . . in a constitutional organization." "For the first time in the history of this union, three individuals from the ranks, out of the mills, the factories and foundries, have become candidates for this union's top offices." All three, he noted, could have held on to their previous jobs without fear of replacement; they had job security. What impelled them to run was the belief that they had to challenge decision-making by clique, operating under McDonald, and McDonald's deliberate disregard of the union's elected representatives on the executive board and on the Wage Policy Committee. Abel recalled how the 1963 settlement was first reached by a small "top group," the Human Relations group, after which the Wage Policy Committee and the negotiating committees were called in for "consultation." Some local leaders refused to sign these agreements: not a single local union officer signed the Jones & Laughlin agreement or the Pittsburgh Steel agreement, and more than half the local union officers refused to sign the Republic Steel agreement.

The refusal by local union leaders to sign such contracts, agreed to in their behalf by their top leaders without adequate consultation, created a core of discontent that had impaired the morale of the union: "This method of negotiation, or of relationship, has failed to bring benefits to the Steelworkers comparable to the benefits won by other trade unions."

In the next three weeks of the campaign, warned Abel, an effort would be made by McDonald forces to "scare the daylights out of the membership of this union and the general public." The leaders of several basic steel companies were participating in this campaign of fear and misrepresentation, Abel charged, "because they want to retain their cozy little deals and not run the risk of honest-to-God collective bargaining—which means sitting across the table conducting affairs on the basis of fact, of mutual respect, but maintaining our position at arm's length." Pressed for details concerning management's involvement on McDonald's side, Abel replied: "I am told Edgar Kaiser of Kaiser Steel is interested and I can understand why" (Pittsburgh *Post-Gazette*, January 21, 1965). It was clear that McDonald sought to give that impression.

But Abel continued to resist the TV debate to which he had been challenged by McDonald: "From the outset, we have wanted to discuss our problems within the family of steelworkers. We did not want to engage in any public circuses and debates and television shows like some people are clamoring for."

Abel concluded with a plea "to get out the vote—to see to it that the vote is recorded and safeguarded." Both sides constantly warned their followers that the "integrity" of the ballot had to be observed. The memory of the shenanigans in the contests of 1955 and 1957 stimulated lively apprehension about the procedures in the coming election.

The Importance of January 20

The distribution of ballots through the mails began. The secretary-treasurer was responsible, under the constitution, for dispatching the official printed ballots to the recording secretaries of the local unions "in sufficient numbers to supply each member not later than two weeks prior to the election." As the incumbent secretary-treasurer, Abel also distributed to each district director a set of three-by-five cards showing the name and address of the recording secretary of each local union in the district and the number of ballots sent to them. Responsibility for the actual shipment of ballots rested with the Cornelius Printing Company of Indianapolis, the official printer of the international union and its publication, *Steel Labor*. In his letter to the directors, Abel pointed out that "should any of your local unions claim they have not received the ballots, you will be able to immediately check your cards and advise the local union to whom the ballots were sent." Staff representatives were to be instructed by each director to check receipt of the election material—which included also tally sheets, a return sheet, and an envelope in which the return sheet was to be enclosed. All staff representatives were supplied with a copy of the letter of instruction sent to each district director to enable him to follow the procedure and ensure or verify the timely receipt of ballots.

That same day, Abel's campaign headquarters office blasted McDonald's reported threat at the Baltimore meeting to fire him and the staff personnel supporting him. Abel described his opponent as a "desperate and frustrated man, flailing about in all directions. Just a couple of weeks ago he was bragging about his recognition of a staff union. The inference was made that the staff wanted a union because it was afraid of what would happen if I am elected. Mr. McDonald's remarks last night clearly should indicate to the staff of whom they should be afraid. After all, I was once a staff man in this union of ours. Mr. McDonald never was, just as he was never a local union officer. He doesn't think—he is incapable of thinking—like a local union man or a staff man—and he has now admitted that he doesn't believe in democracy."

While the constitutional procedures were being carried out at union headquarters, the candidates were covering the Pennsylvania districts. McDonald spoke in Braddock, while Abel and Walter Burke, accompanied by Director William J. Hart of District 19, the only one of the seven district directors in Pennsylvania supporting Abel, spoke in Johnstown.

Bill Hart's campaign activity seemed to be hurting Abel more than it helped. Ten or more years before, his adoration of McDonald—climaxed in David J. McDonald Day in November 1953—had turned into contempt. Over the years, he continued to be renominated and reelected as district director without ostensible opposition. But he had a wide circle of enemies as well as friends. As head of the AFL-CIO Allegheny County Labor Council, he had become the target of criticism and of charges of election malpractice. He boasted openly of considerable private assets. Politically allied with the Republican Party, he was jeered as "Steamboat Willie" after a cruise with Republican Governor William Scranton. Thus, in the minds of many, Hart's espousal of Abel was no recommendation. Hart was charged with listening too responsively to the special requests of the management of Allegheny-Ludlum, for example, in making adjustments downward from the general basic steel contract.

Thus when Abel supporters were asked, "How come you can be with Bill Hart?" the practical answer—reminiscent of all political campaigns—was: "Hart is not the candidate. But give the guy credit. He's for Abel. Whatever his reasons, he is doing right this time." But the animus against Hart was high. Lacking the inhibitions of Abel, Burke, and Molony, Hart one day at a campaign rally embarked on so vituperative an attack on the internal life of the McDonald administration that he aroused his audience to open hostility. Joe Molony, the main speaker and no mild critic of the McDonald regime, sought to undo the damage. Later on, the displeasure of the majority of the members in Hart's district was visited upon Abel. Hart, while unopposed for district director, was unable to carry his own district for Abel.

In New York, with preliminaries out of the way, the can negotiations had begun under the cochairmanship of Directors Robb and Whitehouse. Whitehouse was clearly anxious to come up with a "pattern-making" agreement well before the expiration date of March 1. Politically, considerable advantage could be extracted from an agreement, which could also affect the negotiations in basic steel when they were finally resumed. The winning of a good contract would redound to the political benefit of the McDonald group, and of course to the candidacy of Whitehouse himself.

At this point, the Abel strategists sought to develop a bandwagon psychology, by emphasizing once again that when the new executive board convened on June 1, the directors supporting Abel would control the majority vote no matter who won.

Moving into the Hazelwood section, McDonald's old neighborhood, Abel spoke on the union's objectives and the probable impact of the election contest on the collective bargaining goals. "Within the ranks of the United Steelworkers," he said, "there is not now, and for many years there has not been, any fundamental disagreement over what we want to achieve. The real question before our members is not where do we want to go, but how best to go about getting there." The "best interests of our rank-and-file members will be better served if we: (a) involve all of the leadership the members elect to represent them in the collective bargaining process, instead of trying to make it a one-man show, (b) tell the rank and file the true state of affairs and the actual scope of collective bargaining gains, instead of relying on trick phrases and gimmicks to obscure the truth, and (c) elect top leadership pledged to these reforms."

In Monessen, Pennsylvania, where eight hundred workers of the Pittsburgh Steel Company jammed the high school auditorium, McDonald declared that he was outdrawing Abel six to one in his stumping tour by running on his record. "Abel," said McDonald, "wants to go back to the good old days, while we want progress . . . we have no fear of the future." He compared Abel and his alleged "good old days" theme with Senator Goldwater—"another guy who ran around the country talking of good old days." The comparison of Abel with Goldwater, always good for a laugh, also fitted in with the McDonald effort to identify himself with President Johnson and his massive victory.

In Homestead, Abel spoke to about four hundred union members in the Carnegie Library. At the door he was greeted by some McDonald followers—this was District 15, headed by Paul Hilbert, a McDonald director—with a leaflet referring to the postponement of negotiations, entitled "Who Switched Signals, Mr. Abel?" Abel exhibited the leaflet as an example of McDonald's "ranting." The fact, he said, was that he had been informed by McDonald only an hour before the announcement was made that the talks were to be recessed. Apparently both McDonald and Abel considered the negotiations "recess" a significant issue. By it, McDonald sought to prove that the election contest had interfered with negotiations, while Abel indicated that the decision to postpone had been decided upon by McDonald and the steel management without adequate notice to the board.

Abel attacked McDonald for exaggerating his claims for the 1963 negotiations out of which had emerged the "13-week extended vacation plan." He considered it "morally wrong for President McDonald to tell the union at the time that the plan would create 25,000 additional jobs; this amounted to holding out a false hope to thousands of our seniority members on layoff who thought they would be recalled when other members were taking their extended vacation. But we didn't get that kind of replacement. In many plants, schedules were shifted about, or workloads increased, and as a result, while we cannot tell how many jobs were created, we know that the total is less than half of what President McDonald said it would be." Because of the inroads into jobs arising out of automation and the introduction of new methods, such as the basic oxygen furnace, Abel pressed his concern "not for just our present members, but with their sons and younger brothers, the younger people about to enter our work force for whom no jobs exist. No one program, no single contract is going to solve the entire problem or provide enough jobs for every member and where the member's grown sons can also be employed at a decent wage. . . . It certainly cannot be done by one man . . . short-circuiting the collective bargaining process."

CHAPTER 15

Struggle in New England

A fierce unrest seethes at the core.

DON MARQUIS

The campaign in New England was sulphurous. It was highlighted by a clash of personalities in the race for director of District 1 between Roy H. Stevens, the incumbent and a McDonald supporter, and Lawrence N. Spitz, strongly pro-Abel. In this district, three-quarters of the members were employed in a diversity of metal-fabricating plants; there is comparatively little heavy industry in New England steel. One of District 1's five subdistricts was headed in Providence by Lawrence Spitz. For several restive years, Spitz had served under Stevens, who in 1960 had been named acting director by McDonald on the death of Martin (Mike) Walsh, an independent character with a sailor's background who was never a McDonald admirer.

From the start of his labor career, Spitz was a passionate and articulate believer in improving the human condition, with the trade-union movement as the natural instrument in such a cause. While in high school he worked as a volunteer in some neighboring textile strikes, which made him the young agitator in a local feature story that brought about his expulsion from high school. Spitz went to work in a textile mill, and subsequently helped organize what was called the Industrial Trade Union—the ITU—a sort of free-lance operation unaffiliated with either the AFL or the CIO.

When Spitz returned from the army in 1946, Walsh, the Steelworkers district director, renewed an invitation for Spitz to join with the Steelworkers organization, for assignment to the Providence area, at that time sparsely organized. Two years after becoming a staff man Spitz

179

was enrolled, under the GI Bill of Rights, at Brown University, from which he was graduated three years later *magna cum laude* with a Phi Beta Kappa key.

During those three years, Spitz kept working at his union job with little time off. President Henry Wriston and Dean Patrick Kenny of Brown made this off-beat student's academic life as viable as possible: his class schedule was often geared to meet his working schedule. "Some days I was in a picket line at five in the morning," Spitz said, "then would hustle over to the campus, study until my first nine o'clock class, perhaps attend another and then rush back to the office and when negotiations were underway, work until God knows what hour."

Walsh leaned heavily upon Spitz. They were fellow crusaders. In the Hague-Molony election campaign of 1955, Walsh had angrily rejected Hague for the vice-presidency. With his own background of dissent, Spitz required no special urging to enlist in the Molony crusade. As an appointed staff representative, however, he was vulnerable to the displeasure of international headquarters in a way that his superior, Walsh, an elected director, was not. Under the constitution, the international president had the power to hire, fire, and reassign the union's employees. Late in September 1955, Spitz received a wire from McDonald ordering him to appear in Pittsburgh. "Just go and see what he has to say," said Walsh.

Spitz was ushered into McDonald's office. Surrounded by several associates, McDonald charged Spitz with speaking "unfairly" about him. Spitz acknowledged that he had repeated stories that had already been printed about McDonald in magazines in general circulation, and that they were being used by management to undercut the union's organizational drives.

Several staff representatives who had been transferred out of Spitz's subdistrict had happily carried stories of Spitz's criticisms of McDonald. Throughout the proceedings, McDonald kept reminding him of the president's punitive powers. What bothered Spitz especially was that McDonald had used the testimony of at least one staff representative who, it was known, had received money from an employer. The latter subsequently boasted to various gatherings that he "could buy any Steelworkers' staff representative for $300." When Spitz indignantly confronted the employer, the latter produced checks, ostensibly for loans. When Walsh heard about this, he arranged with Abel as secretary-treasurer for the repayment of the money to the employer by deductions from the salary of the staff representative. The staff representative was switched out of New England into the Johnstown district, headed by Eugene Maurice, a McDonald intimate. But when the Molony-Hague campaign got under way, the discredited staff man reappeared in New England, flashing campaign money for Hague.

As the session waxed hotter, Spitz told McDonald that perhaps he had best take the matter up with Walsh, his director, and with the representative of a Staffman's Union, for which about three hundred out of the seven hundred staff men had then signed up. Whereupon McDonald triumphantly announced that the "man who is your chief steward for the Staffman's Union in New England" was in the next room. "He's one of the men who signed the charge against you." Apparently, said Spitz, the man had been playing a dual role: presumably supporting Molony and Walsh against Hague, but actually working with Hague and McDonald. As the session ended, Spitz said that McDonald could take any measure he wished. After Hague's victory, however, McDonald failed to follow through on his threats.

Spitz's grievance against the McDonald establishment had increased over the years. At international headquarters, he had found an atmosphere of toadyism: even some staff experts of considerable technical competence were all too anxious to prove their loyalty to McDonald by taking it out on those who dared to be his critics. Most of them avoided even greeting Spitz when he was summoned before McDonald. By now, Spitz was also appalled at McDonald's loading the payroll with a considerable number of men with doubtful qualifications.

Despite his reservoir of resentment against McDonald, Spitz supported him against Rarick in the 1957 campaign; Rarick's incompetence seemed so obvious that it would have been a mockery to back him for union president.

Following Mike Walsh's death in 1961, McDonald moved promptly to prevent Spitz from making a bid for the directorship. He agreed to Hague's suggestion that he appoint Roy Stevens, and summoned the New England staff to Pittsburgh to announce Stevens's appointment as acting director. He made a point, however, of polling the staff individually to elicit their reactions. Spitz's comment was that McDonald might have done worse because there were so many incompetents in the room, but then added that he could have done better—by appointing Spitz. Thereupon McDonald said, "Well, you have a sense of humor, I must admit that." In June 1961, a special district election was held and Stevens was elected without opposition.

Outside his regular duties, Spitz kept an observant eye on union political developments. He recalled a 1960 meeting when Abel came to New England to address a Steelworkers conference. Walsh had privately urged Abel to run for the presidency; Abel evinced some willingness but—recalling the defection of the district directors in the Molony campaign—expressed the opinion that the right time to run had not yet arrived.

All of which supported Spitz's observation that many of the directors had been turned into "capons" by McDonald's willingness to permit generous expense accounts and all the perquisites of "an easy life, good job, financial rewards, no inordinate demands." In return, McDonald continued to enjoy tenure. Abel's let's-wait-and-count-noses stance was interpreted by some as proof that Abel lacked courage or else that no challenge to McDonald could be mounted successfully.

With the onset of the Abel movement, Spitz began to break out of his "self-isolation" in District 1. He was not exactly hermetically self-sealed. In addition to his absorption in the union, he was active in community affairs. Under Walsh, Spitz had found himself frequently at odds with Stevens, then a fellow subdirector. Walsh would send Spitz to work the union out of a sticky situation—sometimes even in Stevens's subdistrict in Worcester, a practice that naturally did not inspire Stevens's affection for Walsh or Spitz. When Stevens became director, Spitz no longer was able to maintain easy contacts with the rank-and-file members or local union officers in other sections of New England. Aside from his own subdistrict, Spitz could expect little support. Only in the North country— New Hampshire and Vermont—had he kept strong and even affectionate relations with groups in the Scott & Williams local at Laconia, New Hampshire. A decade before, Spitz had gone there to assist in a strike that had begun to fall apart. He raised enough money from the areas to see them through the strike and into a settlement. He was remembered as being the only person outside their area in the Steelworkers who brought them help in a time of their serious trouble. Another area of friendship that could perhaps materialize into political support was the local of the Joy Manufacturing Company, the second largest local in the North Country, at Claremont, New Hampshire.

Abel's announcement of his candidacy on November 6 came as no surprise to Spitz. A week or ten days before, at the Penn Statler, in New York, he had run into Nicholas Zonarich, IUD's director of organization. With great urgency, a highly keyed-up Zonarich asked him to sit down for a talk that lasted late into the night. Zonarich relived with Spitz the Pittsburgh "star chamber" proceedings against the New Englander in September 1955, when only Zonarich of all the staff men dared to come over and greet him. He also told him how frequently since then Abel had declared his admiration for Spitz for having stood up to McDonald, and, indeed, confessed how uncomfortable he and several others were made to feel because they remained silent. At Zonarich's urging, Spitz agreed to call Abel and ask him to run.

After Abel's announcement, the first act of New England District Director Roy Stevens was to call a "crisis" meeting of the entire staff. In advance of the meeting, Stevens expressed the hope that Spitz and his associates would not support Abel. Stevens argued that he had not heard Abel talk up to McDonald in board meetings or speak critically of anything, that he did his grumbling in the men's room. Moreover, Stevens charged that some of the staff, such as Marvin Miller of the Human Relations Committee, Ben Fischer in the arbitration department, and General Counsel David Feller, were being criticized in anti-Semitic terms by Abel forces. To which Spitz heatedly replied that he had heard to the contrary; that it was being hinted in certain McDonald-controlled areas that Abel—despite his Welsh-Lutheran background—was in fact Jewish (witness his nickname "Abe"). To which Stevens pointedly remarked, "You and your friend Sam Angoff [a labor lawyer] should of course be interested in this facet of the campaign." At the formal staff meeting, Spitz stated that he inclined to support Abel and he urged Stevens to consider doing the same. He referred to rank-and-file dissatisfaction, and the disaffection of some staff men with McDonald, and recalled that Stevens had once permitted himself to be highly critical of McDonald. "That's true," replied Stevens, "but after all, he appointed me and I'm beholden to him." Following his return from the November 1964 executive board meeting called in Pittsburgh, Stevens announced his commitment to McDonald. Spitz confirmed his intention to support Abel. To this, Stevens replied: "I wish you wouldn't because you must realize the full consequences if you do." Spitz said: "What does that mean?" "McDonald is going to win and you will be out of a job," said Stevens evenly. Spitz replied, "I'm sorry to hear you say that, Roy, but I don't think that's going to change my position."

With the exception of the six staff men from the Providence subdistrict, the majority of the staff now echoed Stevens's support of McDonald. Some staff men, in addition to upholding their director in his decision to support McDonald, introduced a motion to support Stevens for reelection, a move designed as a test of staff loyalty.

Responding to these maneuvers, Spitz declared his willingness to support the resolution on the directorship, but wanted it clearly understood that he intended to support Abel. Stevens then uttered an edict: "The most that I will permit you to do is to support Abel in your own subdistrict. I hereby forbid you and your staff to campaign on his behalf outside your subdistrict." Before a tense gathering, Spitz promptly refused to accept Stevens' restriction against his campaigning, although he did not dissent when the staff finally passed a resolution supporting Stevens.

The next day, Spitz called Abel who told him that Joe Molony had been trying to prevail on Stevens to support Abel, under the impression that he was still susceptible to such approaches. Abel told Spitz he was convinced that Stevens was leading Molony on. He then said, "Larry, I think you should run for director there." Although such a thought must have crossed his mind more than once, Spitz now told Abel that he really had no desire to run, and that moreover he had not dissented from the motion to support Stevens. Abel was not impressed with this technicality, awkward though it was for Spitz. "I've gotten letters from the rank-and-file in New England areas outside your own subdistrict expressing . . . widespread discontent with Stevens. I think you should run." Apparently reluctant, Spitz told Abel he would continue to try to work out an understanding with Stevens that would permit him to campaign for Abel throughout New England.

In response, Abel told Spitz to avoid the exercise in futility that Molony was still undergoing with Stevens. While Spitz agreed that Molony was wasting time in his effort to sway Stevens from McDonald, he called Stevens again. This time Stevens informed Spitz that though he would not support Molony for vice-president or Burke for secretary-treasurer, he would not oppose them as he would Abel. To Spitz it became clear that Stevens was following the strategy already laid out by Griffin and Carcella: concentrate the attack on Abel and let events take their course insofar as Burke and Molony were concerned in their contest with Whitehouse and Hague for the other two offices. What Stevens wanted, said Spitz, was a "nice quiet campaign in District 1. If necessary, let this nut Spitz, who's going to get his head chopped off anyway, run around his own subdistrict until it's all over." A "quiet campaign" would blunt the Abel thrust; by using a conciliatory tone with Molony and Burke, who would have strong pulling power among Irish Catholics, Stevens might be able to garner a large percentage of votes for McDonald. Abel sensed all this. He told Spitz, "This guy is stringing us along; the son-of-a-bitch is no good."

When Spitz finally agreed to run against Stevens, he asked Abel to send him a telegram urging him to run. Abel said that he would sign such a telegram, as would Burke and Molony. Almost half the nomination period had gone by. The day before Thanksgiving, Spitz telephoned Stevens and informed him that he had decided to run for director. Silence. Then Stevens angrily exploded: "Well, if that's the way you want it, Larry. But I told you before what the consequences could be. Now it goes double. You're not only supporting Abel, you're running against me. This means your job." Spitz had already gathered as much.

He now received a call from Molony, who told him that Stevens had asked Molony to dissuade Spitz from running. Molony questioned the political utility of dispatching the formal telegram of support that Spitz had requested. It might, he said, set an awkward precedent for other districts where directorship contests might occur. Molony's argument against open support for Spitz was partly rooted in the union tradition of "senatorial courtesy" that one director did not cross district lines by interfering in the internal workings of another's barony. You did not campaign against a fellow member of the club. Thus, if word got out that Abel and his associates were pushing for Spitz against Stevens, an incumbent director, then directors favoring Abel might fear that the McDonald forces would retaliate by instigating opposition against them. In some districts this was already happening. Such an intervention was regarded even by some friendly directors, said Molony, as a precedent that would "haunt us for years to come." Spitz replied: "I am not at all opposed to this type of intervention; I could think of many situations where open and active commitment was not only necessary but long a crying need." In a three-hour telephone conversation, the two men covered the political ground and tested the booby traps. Later that afternoon, Molony gave Spitz the reassuring news that he had informed Stevens directly that he was fed up with him.

On November 25, Spitz received this telegram signed by Abel, Molony, and Burke: "Our union must be returned to the membership. The candidacies of Abel, Burke and Molony are designed to do this. We are advised that the director of District 1 is opposed to this program. Because of this we urge that you run for district director on our slate and help accomplish this important goal." The telegram became Spitz's indispensable credential from a new national leadership to conduct an effective campaign in the New England district.

With the Thanksgiving weekend largely a period of preparation, Spitz had roughly eleven days to collect nominations. As evidence of his own strength, Stevens announced that he had received a $10,000 campaign contribution from McDonald. To "organize the unorganized" in the district. Stevens assigned local union presidents to "casual work" and "part-time work" for the ostensible performance of additional union duties, and authorized payment for time "lost" from their regular duties. This sudden flood of authorized dollars from local union treasuries stiffened the loyalty of their hesitant officers. What Stevens did in New England was standard operating procedure in other districts. It follows the traditional use of public—in this case, union—funds for building a political machine.

The struggle for nominations became for Spitz a battle to obtain basic information to enable him to reach the local unions: the location of their headquarters, the dates and places of their meetings, the names and addresses of recording secretaries. He had to operate largely in the dark, so far as information about subdistricts other than his own was concerned. He wrote to Abel in his capacity as secretary-treasurer for an up-to-date list of the names and addresses of local unions. Abel replied that the secretary-treasurer's office possessed only a list of the recording secretaries of the local unions. Such a list did not often indicate clearly the location of the plant covered by the locals. District 1's 152 locals were spread widely over five states. At this point, Spitz wrote to Stevens directly for the names and addresses of local unions, which he knew were kept in the district office. As a candidate, Spitz believed that he had equal right of access to such information. Lacking such basic data, an opponent to an incumbent was engaged in uneven combat. Stevens did not reply.

Pressures were obviously heavy. A close friend of Spitz's, a Steelworkers lawyer in the district who had urged him to run, went on an early vacation to Florida. Stevens retained the advantage of access to the legal staff of the international union. Nevertheless, Spitz found sources of information outside the union. Several of his volunteer supporters extracted the names and addresses of local unions and their officers from the reports filed in the Boston regional office of the U.S. Labor Department under the Landrum-Griffin Act. Spitz phoned and visited friends in the North Country. At the Scott & Williams local, in Laconia, New Hampshire, a good five hours of hard driving from Providence, young Maurice Goyette, president of the local, and George Lynch, its vice-president and a veteran of the Molony-Hague campaign, helped Spitz and his associates gather indispensable names.

Through intensive coverage of local union meetings by telephone and in person, Spitz won forty-two local union nominations, far above the minimum number of eight required for the district. Stevens, whose nomination drive had been under way for two weeks before that, made good use of the district machinery—staff representatives and local union officers—and accumulated the formidable number of seventy-two nominations. Little time elapsed before Spitz and Stevens collided.

Stevens saw the contest as a battle for his life. Then fifty-two years old, he had joined the Steel Workers Organizing Committee (SWOC) at the age of twenty-three, and became the local's financial secretary when he worked at the Reed & Prince Manufacturing Company in Worcester. He was blacklisted for his activity in a two-month strike of eight hundred employees. The strike was broken. Stevens got a construction job, and later went to work at the U.S. Steel plant in Worcester, where he again became financial secretary and a member of the local's grievance committee. After the Supreme Court upheld the constitutionality of the Wagner Act in 1937, Stevens returned to Reed & Prince as a matter of principle. When efforts to revive the local there failed, Stevens returned to his job at U.S. Steel. In 1942 he was appointed to a staff job by District Director Mike Walsh. After the war, he was made subdistrict director in the Worcester area, the site of several basic steel plants. "On Mike's death," said Stevens, noting only the mechanics of the process, "I was appointed and subsequently elected unopposed in a special election in June 1961 to fill out Mike's term." Thus the contest of 1965 was his first test by referendum of the district's membership.

The election campaign of 1964–65, Stevens admitted, "became a very dirty one." By way of justification, he noted that Spitz was sharp-tongued and made people butts of jokes. The whole staff, except for those he appointed and who were under his control, knew him as a man who was "absolutely ruthless."

Throughout his campaign Stevens tied the "Commie" label to Spitz. "Did you charge him with the Communist affiliation when he was present?" "I believe it was mentioned," Stevens said with a slight smile. "He denied it." Why had Stevens not brought charges against Spitz under the constitution—since Communist affiliation would have barred him from union membership, not to mention union office. "I didn't hire him; I inherited him," Stevens replied testily.

Stevens sought to hit Spitz where he thought he was most vulnerable. He cultivated the prejudice in some New England areas where suspicions could be roused against a Jew and an intellectual. Immediately after the nominations, on December 15, Stevens launched an all-out attack on Spitz at Windsor, Vermont, at what was meant to be a regular meeting of the Northern New England Steelworkers Council, made up of delegates from the local unions in New Hampshire and Vermont. Maurice Goyette, in a letter to all local union presidents and recording secretaries, informed them of "serious allegations and insinuations" made by Stevens about Spitz. Spitz, he noted, had not been invited and was unable to reply to "vicious filthy rumors."

Because of the "serious nature" of the Stevens statements, Goyette called a special meeting of the council at Windsor, Vermont, for Sunday, December 20, which both candidates were invited to address. He was blocked in the effort by Thomas H. Breslin, the subarea director in the North Country and a supporter of Stevens, who refused to provide him with names and addresses of local union officials on the technical ground that no regular or special meeting might be called without his permission, which he refused to give. Breslin was regarded highly in and out of the union as a deeply motivated man, but Goyette saw in Breslin's refusal evidence of the "kind of politics we as officers and delegates and rank-and-file members can expect from the Stevens supporters."

The next day Breslin, under Stevens's instruction, dispatched a letter from his subdistrict headquarters in Concord, New Hampshire, informing all "presidents and recording secretaries" that his office did not "approve" the meeting. Since a regular council meeting had already been held on Sunday, December 13, he could see no reason to have another the following Sunday "except that the group elected as officers now want to use the Council as a political forum for the candidate they support as

Director." He conceded that "brother Stevens in his role as Director of this District was accorded an invitation . . . to address the delegates and in doing so made some political remarks in regard to his own candidacy and in reference to his opponent. But, two wrongs don't make a right and I for one am not going to see the Council used as a political football in the coming election campaign." He added the threat that if "this is the intention of the newly elected officers of the Council, then this office will withdraw its support and disband the Council. The Council has no official position within the Steelworkers organization and only exists at the direction of this office and the International Union." If such a meeting did take place, he warned that expenses incurred would not be paid out of Council funds.

Despite Breslin's interdiction the special meeting was held, with all the local leaders supporting Spitz on hand. "You did a remarkable job," Goyette wrote to Spitz the following week (December 28), and "the only regret I have is-that every steelworker in District 1 could not have heard your rebuttal to Brother Stevens' remarks." Plans were being made, he said, for a large delegation to attend a meeting in Boston that the Spitz campaign committee had organized for January 9. They were coming down from the North Country in two buses they had hired. They promised to have "sled dogs at Faneuil Hall" to dramatize their wintry locale. Goyette enclosed a check for $119, the proceeds of a local collection, for the Spitz campaign kitty.

In Bridgeport, Connecticut, on December 16, Stevens again attacked Spitz at a regular membership meeting from which Spitz and his followers were barred. Police were called in by Stevens supporters to debar Spitz, who had been invited by local union representatives.

Stevens now showed how an incumbent could use his office for political purposes. On December 22 he addressed registered letters to forty-odd unions affiliated with the Providence Union Area Relief Committee, notifying them that he had found it "necessary" to take over its administration and forbidding local unions to make further payments to the committee, "because the committee has refused to cooperate with the auditors appointed by the United Steelworkers in connection with their audit of union funds. Since it is believed that this Fund exceeds $150,000, you can see the importance of my action in safeguarding the interest of your Union and its members in the Fund which I intend to turn back to the Local Unions as soon as a proper accounting has been obtained. The siphoning off of local union funds from the control of the Union and its members must stop."

By the same mail, he ordered Spitz as field representative to secure compliance with his orders by December 30. Spitz telephoned Stevens and told him to go to hell.

Local unions in the Providence area defied Stevens, declared themselves "satisfied with the administration of the Fund . . . and questioned his motives for taking an action which is unjustified, immoral and disgusting. We want no part of it." More than twenty local leaders from Rhode Island picketed Stevens's office in Worcester, demanding that he keep his hands off their fund, built up by members' contributions of a quarter a month.

More formally, on January 9, the officers of the Union Area Relief Committee denied Stevens's allegations and officially explained the structure and administration of the fund. Aside from the fiduciary obligations, the fund was subject to federal disclosure laws, administered by the Bureau of Labor-Management and Welfare and Pension Reports of the Department of Labor. Union auditors regularly checked through the funds of all districts. On January 6, I. W. Abel, as international secretary-treasurer, informed Stevens that an international union auditor would appear in District 1 to audit the books of the district office as well as of the subdistrict offices. Stevens angrily wired Abel his objection to a district audit until "after February 9 in order to avoid claims and charges of political activity." To this Abel replied stiffly: "The audit of your District funds has nothing to do with the election of February 9. The Labor-Management [Landrum-Griffin] Act requires the full reporting of all funds of the International Union annually. . . . This is not subject to either your discretion or mine."

While Abel sought to maintain a clear line of demarcation between his responsibilities as the union's secretary-treasurer and his role as a candidate for the union presidency, such an exercise could not have been simple, especially since he and Joe Molony were scheduled to campaign with Spitz throughout New England over the weekend of January 9 and 10.

Abel and Molony in New England

The theme of the Abel-Molony-Spitz tour was the pledge to "return the union to its members." In New Haven, Abel and Molony learned at first hand of the "gutter level" of politics. The New England campaign was operating on two levels—personal vilification of Spitz and the issue of responsibility of national and local leadership. From the New Haven area, Abel, Molony, and Spitz reached Boston in time for the start of the Faneuil Hall meeting. Buses loaded with steelworkers from the North Country and Providence had already arrived. Fulfilling a promise, Goyette and his followers trucked in a dozen huskies. The dogs and sleds did not make it into the jammed hall, but the effort contributed to the excitement. For Spitz, Faneuil Hall, the "cradle of liberty," became the symbol of his campaign.

Added to the occasion was coverage by a crew from the Columbia Broadcasting System, which invaded part of the sacred precincts. A large mural inside the hall portraying a gathering of Revolutionary patriots provided the speakers with a backdrop with the bold slogan "Save the Union." The speakers considered this a sign from heaven, a happy historical coincidence that made them followers in a great tradition. It had been here that John F. Kennedy concluded his campaign on election eve in November 1960.

Outside, Stevens supporters busily distributed anti-Spitz flyers. Inside, Spitz charged Stevens with being an "absentee director" and for failure to organize workers in "Electronics Alley," the complex of industrial plants that had sprung up along Route 128, Boston's circumferential highway. "That's where Stevens ought to be passing out leaflets!" Spitz shouted. He complained that under McDonald's presidency New England members of the Steelworkers Union had become second-class citizens, in that most of the members in fabricating plants remained "untouched" by benefits won by national bargaining in the basic steel industry.

An outside observer with a management background, Professor Herman Gadon of the University of New Hampshire, who had brought a group of his students to Boston to witness a union political meeting, later gave his estimate of the performance: "Abel sounded like the Rock of Gibraltar, if it could talk. He was strength. He looked like a basic trade unionist; lines in his broad face. He came across like somebody you could count on. . . . Molony . . . was not only a marvelous phrase maker, he looked like the solid citizen. He was a guy who could be your neighbor too, and go have a beer with. Then Larry [Spitz] got up as the fireball, the guy who was to rid the district of oppression. He talked in a kind of general and abstract level. He related his candidacy to the team concept of Abel, Molony and Burke. He talked about them at great length. When he is talking to a local union and he's attacking the company, he talks differently. He's hitting you in the gut there. In Faneuil Hall, I didn't think he came through quite that effectively. He spoke on higher ground."

The day after the Abel-Molony tour, Stevens obtained a court order freezing the funds and records of the Union Area Relief Fund, but the temporary order was dismissed the next day. Stevens had informed the court, in his capacity as "administrator" of the fund, that he had removed its three officers. In the suit, Spitz, himself not a member of the fund committee, was alleged to be in control of a sum of money on deposit in a special account and to have "blurred the clear purposes of the fund money." Spitz angrily charged that Stevens was "trying to shake the faith of people in this area in my candidacy for the district directorship. He won't succeed; I helped them get this fund started and encouraged them to the point of self-sufficient administration under the provisions of our union constitution." He denied that Stevens could properly assume the post of administrator. Spitz then explained that the "special account" of $2,000 was not related to the fund but was used for subdistrict office expenses. The relief fund, he said, contained $170,000 in all. Its administrative committee also maintained a fund of about $27,000 for scholarships for children of union members; at the time, twenty-four students at Providence College, Brown University, Pembroke College, and the University of Connecticut were receiving such scholarship aid.

An official protest was now telegraphed by the officers of the Rhode Island Area Fund to the international union headquarters in Pittsburgh. They questioned Stevens's right to "establish himself as administrator, to proceed without charges, hearings, or due process, and to go to court without exhausting his remedies within the Union as the Constitution requires." The committee requested the executive board to instruct Stevens to withdraw his court action, which "on the eve of an election is an abuse of our rights and of our International Constitution."

McDonald now entered the picture, though he never appeared in New England in person during the campaign. On January 23, 1965, he telegraphed that on March 24 and 25, 1964—ten months before!—the fund's committee had not made available to the auditors the minutes of its meetings, the financial reports that had been distributed to affiliated local unions, and the fund's by-laws. This refusal of the fund's committee threw suspicion on the integrity of the fund, said McDonald. In addition, he remarked acidly that the committee's insistence on the "provisions of the Steelworkers Constitution" represented a "change of position" on its part.

To both of McDonald's observations, the angry committee made a strong reply on February 2: the change was spurious, the auditor had access to the minutes and financial reports distributed to the local affiliates, and although the minutes were not made available to the auditor until some time later they "ultimately" were sent to the international union. If Stevens had found anything amiss with the fund, he had not said so, in writing or orally, from April 1964 to the time the campaign started. The committee found it "even more disturbing . . . that you have lent yourself and your office to this type of action." McDonald did not reply.

In addition to characterizing Spitz as a man of doubtful political character, a "security risk," Stevens, himself a non-Catholic, was able to make an even more direct appeal for support, especially among the Irish Catholic groups in Massachusetts. To emphasize his own political respectability, Stevens circulated an undated statement issued by the Holy Cross Institute of Industrial Relations of Worcester, in connection with

its award to him fourteen years before of a Labor Plaque "for distinguished service in the promotion of sound industrial relations." At that
time he was serving as staff representative under Mike Walsh. With the
date omitted, Stevens gave the obvious impression that the plaque was a
blessing recently bestowed. Stevens visited active Catholic members to
warn them against Spitz. To counteract the Stevens innuendoes, Spitz
came up with a contemporary photograph of himself with Monsignor
William J. Carey, Rector of Saints Peter and Paul Cathedral (Providence
Bulletin, October 21, 1964). Reassurance concerning Spitz's character
was cited in a letter from Reverend Edward Brock, formerly head of the
Social Action Institute of the diocese.

Stevens revived attacks on Spitz made during a strike he led in the
1950s at the Nicholson File Company. At that time the Providence
Journal investigated and dismissed as ridiculous the charges made against
Spitz as well as those against the district director, Mike Walsh, as one
who was financed by employers' agents and was not an Irishman but a
Russian-Jewish Communist whose original name was Walsinski. Another
attack on Spitz as a Communist had its origins in the 1930's. At that
time, after an investigation, the American Legion's Americanism officer
finally declared, "We have nothing against Spitz!" Twenty-seven years
later, Stevens raised the same charges of Communism and subversion
against Spitz that the American Legion had rejected. Spitz carried press
clippings and letters, some of them going back almost thirty years, up to
the North Country to counteract Stevens's charges.

Throughout the campaign Stevens, or someone speaking for him,
would throw off the line "I'm not saying he's a Communist, but ask him
who Joe Caldwell is." Caldwell, long since dead, who once served in the
Atlanta Penitentiary with Eugene Victor Debs, was a veteran Socialist
bearing something of the aura of the town radical, a thorn in the side of
the Communist groups as of the conservative Rhode Island establishment. At the same time, Stevens alluded darkly to foreign trips, planned
by Spitz but not taken because he was denied clearance by the State
Department.

Then the Committee for the Re-election of Roy H. Stevens issued a
leaflet captioned "Security Check," which tied together implications of
misuse of the Union Area Relief Fund and allegations of political subversion. Spitz was described as "a very clever operator, who now wants
to put his fingers on an even larger pot, has been trying to get out of the
country for some time. . . . The Philippines, Japan . . . you name it. We
don't know exactly why his papers haven't come through. But we get
little cold shivers every time we think of Larry Spitz with access to a fund
built out of per capita payments from *the whole district* (little Rhode
Island put $250,000 in it all alone), then taking off for the Orient while
the Union auditors are refused to look at the books."

In places like Worcester, Boston, and the Connecticut area, where Spitz was less known, the leaflet produced an impression that where there was smoke, there must be fire.

With the distribution of the "Security Check" leaflet, Spitz sued for libel. He said, "I have learned a very bitter lesson, and that is if you permit them to make these allegations and then do nothing about it, years later you are confronted, 'Well, if it wasn't true, why didn't you take action?' " *

At the start of the campaign, Spitz received a $500 check from Molony; on December 28, Tom Murray, treasurer of the Abel-Burke-Molony campaign committee, sent a $1,000 check. Raising funds for the New England campaign became largely a local responsibility. Spitz used $1,600 of his own money and borrowed $3,500. About $2,600 was raised through a raffle for a color TV set. All together, he estimated that $7,000 was collected. The largest single outlay, about $3,700, went for advertising, especially for three meetings that Abel, Molony, and Spitz addressed in the first two weeks in January, in the New Haven area, Boston, and Worcester.

But aside from advertised meetings, there was the problem of the distribution of literature at the plants to catch the workers as they moved on and off shifts. Here Stevens had the obvious advantage through his control of staff representatives in the district and their close relations with the majority of the locals, making for maximum distribution with little trouble. In several areas Spitz could count on similar support, but in others he lacked "forces." "We had to depend upon rank-and-file people who hauled themselves into Boston from Providence every morning, on some bitter cold mornings, and then come back to their plant to go to work. We had three people who worked in a plant that hadn't yet been brought into the union and who were on a night shift besides. After working their shift, these unpaid volunteers would sleep a few hours, travel to a plant for leaflet distribution—for them it was like getting up in the middle of the night—and then get back home from Boston about ten o'clock. They'd catch a few more hours of sleep, and then go back to whatever shift they were on."

In addition to charges of subversion and fiscal irresponsibility, Stevens now raised a dues scare. If Spitz succeeded, he said, an increase in dues would result. By building a dues-increase scare, Stevens hoped to stir up residual suspicions of the rank and file that their pay checks were going to be cut down while the union treasuries waxed fat.

One Stevens leaflet, headed "$7 Dues Spitz," reported: "Spitz is running scared. Spitz has been running around the District making crazy promises he knows he can't keep: 1. More staffmen; 2. More office girls; 3. More lawyers; 4. More technicians. Do you realize that if his promises

* Appendix 3.

are kept, the cost would not be $7 dues, but $10 or $15 dues? Do you want to pay for these jobs he is creating (and are not needed)?"

"All I have said," Spitz replied, "was that I intended to put the staff to work. We have enough staff men. We don't need more technicians. What we need are staff people who are willing to work. This caused shudders to run down the backs of some of the staff people."

In reply to Stevens on the dues-increase issue, Frederick P. Macary, local union president of the Waterbury-Farrel Division of Textron, recalled, in a mimeographed letter, the 1962 convention in Miami "when McDonald tried to ram a $5 dues assessment down our throats. You members were at our last union meeting when I asked Roy Stevens about his position [on] this unfair dues assessment. His answer, if you remember, was that he supported McDonald. I am proud to say that I was one of the leaders on the convention floor, with the help of Larry Spitz and many other rank-and-file leaders, who helped defeat this unfair dues increase by the slim margin of 76 votes. With many of the staff voting with McDonald (including the New Haven staff) we still beat the motion down. How would you like to be paying $10 a month instead of the $5 a month you pay now?"

In angry rejection of Stevens's Communist charges against Spitz, his committee in the Boston area pointed out that he "has had to comply with Article 3, Section 4, Page 6 of the International Constitution. This states that 'no person shall be eligible for membership, or for nomination or election or appointment to, or to hold any office, or position, or to serve on any committee in the International union or a local union or to serve as a delegate therefrom who is a member, consistent supporter, or who actively participates in the activities of the Communist Party, Ku Klux Klan, or of any fascist, totalitarian, or other subversive organization which oppose the democratic principles to which the United States and Canada and our Union are dedicated.'" The leaflet proclaimed in bold type: "The Landrum-Griffin Act says the same thing. Since this is all known to Absentee Director, Roy Stevens, why is he participating in a campaign of filth and deliberate misinformation?"

Spitz supporters in various locals backed up their charges of neglect and absenteeism against Stevens in considerable detail. For instance, in Claremont, New Hampshire, members of the Joy Manufacturing local claimed that Stevens in the four years of his directorship had not once shown up in their neighborhood until the active weeks of the campaign, when he appeared four times.

The Spitz committee contrasted Stevens's inactivity with the aggressive program to which Spitz had pledged himself: (1) To improve working conditions; (2) To provide leadership and assistance to locals on strike, in negotiations and in arbitration; (3) To establish area-wide pension and

SUB funds; (4) To convene periodically district-wide conferences of local union leaders in various fabricating plants under Steelworkers jurisdiction.

Despite all refutations, the charges that Abel was strike-happy and that dues would be increased, as well as the Joe McCarthy–type smears against Spitz and the implication "Abe is a Jew" did cut deep. But the attempt to pin a segregationist tag on Abel was largely unsuccessful. Spitz's close relationship with the Negro membership and his own participation in civil rights activities was widely known.

As part of the attack against Molony, the Stevens supporters also distributed a circular entitled "Joe Feathers His Nest." This implied skulduggery and a "warm embrace" with employers because he had bought a house previously owned by a minor Bethlehem official. This counterthrust to the attack on McDonald's *dolce vita* proclivities, Spitz asserted, was meant to imply that "while Dave McDonald was valiantly fighting the battle in negotiations for the rank and file, Molony was negotiating with a Bethlehem Steel executive for his own benefit."

Election Proceedings in New England

Toward the end of the campaign, Spitz and his associates became increasingly concerned with the technical aspects of the election on which its integrity depended. The difficulty in gaining adequate communication with the widely dispersed locals as well as the need to counter Stevens's activities made it necessary to set up emergency *ad hoc* machinery for dealing with the actual election proceedings.

On January 26, by registered letter Spitz formally requested local unions to supply exact information with regard to the location of the polling places, the times set aside for voting, and the time and place for the ballot count.* As district director, Stevens already possessed this information. As a candidate, Spitz was entitled to this information under the provisions of the Landrum-Griffin Act and the union constitution. He requested the local union officers to inform him where accredited observers could identify themselves to the local tellers' committee. Each observer would carry a formal communication from his local union attesting his membership in good standing and a letter of authorization from Spitz in behalf of the three candidates for international office.

Covering all angles, Spitz also dispatched registered letters to the general superintendents of plants on whose premises the election was to be held. He formally identified himself as representative of the "opposition slate" of Abel, Molony, Burke and himself. He reminded them that,

* Two months before, he had sought similar information in his drive to win local union nominations.

under the Landrum-Griffin Act, all candidates were entitled to assign observers at designated polling places and ballot-counting areas. To avoid misunderstanding, their names would be sent to the plant superintendents, their number to depend on the number and location of polling places set up in the plant.

There was no uniform pattern for the location of polling places. Under the union constitution, each local could determine whether the voting would take place in the union hall or at the plant. Where a local union and its officers clearly favored a particular candidate, there was usually a distinct advantage in holding the election at booths located in the plant: members could vote on the way in or out of work. However, if the leadership sensed that the vote would run counter to its wishes, the union hall or some other place outside the plant was usually designated. The more trouble it took to vote, the smaller the turnout; to that extent, the opposition would register something less than the fuller strength it could expect when ballots were cast in the plant.

Just how this worked out was to be seen in New Hampshire, at the large Scott & Williams Local 4524 and the smaller Needle Local 5332 in Laconia and the Joy Manufacturing Company Local 2944 in Claremont, where elections were traditionally held on the premises. At these plants, Thomas Breslin, the subdistrict director, had prevailed upon the managements to forbid the pro-Spitz, pro-Abel local leadership to establish polling booths. The intention was to reduce the vote, which was clearly anti-Stevens. Since the managements were concerned with retaining the good will of the incumbent district leadership, they acquiesced.

Later on, Goyette brought out some of the detail: "There's an awful lot of ways for an incumbent to control an election. If we in my local could have voted in the plant, if my brother's local union at Laconia Needle, and if Joy Manufacturing at Claremont had permission to vote in the plant, the district director today would be Larry Spitz. The management, to our surprise, told us at a very late date before the election that we could not vote in the plants, although that's where we traditionally voted. So we really had to hustle. We found we could rent some trailers—and this was an expenditure Roy Stevens couldn't complain about—this was just supplying places for people to vote. We got four trailers, and after the second shift, we moved them directly opposite the plant at two and three o'clock in the morning, heated them up. We got a great vote—461 for Spitz, 83 for Stevens. But if we could have voted in the plant, we could have got at least 300 more votes. That could have made a difference, probably enough to put Spitz over as director. Remember Stevens won by a few more than 500 votes out of more than 20,500 votes."

The night before the election, Breslin informed Goyette that the executive board of the Joy local had switched its support from Spitz to Stevens. Al Revisio, the local chairman at Joy and until just before the election a cochairman with Goyette of the Spitz campaign in the North Country, later explained: "I decided to put it up to the Executive Board. We always were 10 to 2 for Spitz. But the pressure was getting hot. So to take it off, I threw it back at the Executive Board and they went 6 to 5 for Stevens. So I had to go along with the Executive Board."

"You see," said Goyette, "it isn't the employees the management has to deal with directly. If the management doesn't like the local officer's position on a plant problem, it's very easy for them to refer it to the step in the grievance procedure where the staff representative comes in. So, when the company manager revokes the permission to vote in the plant, he is looking for a favor at some future date. The staff representative and the director then owe the company something."

At Joy Manufacturing, where in-plant voting had also been banned by the management, slightly more than 40 per cent of the 750 eligible voters participated—the smallest percentage of any of the New England locals with 500 or more members.

Looking back a year after the election, Goyette said:

If we had it all to do over again, I can assure you we would not regret supporting a candidate as worthy as Larry Spitz. I would probably work much harder the next time knowing that while we worked hard it just wasn't hard enough. This man is to me far superior to anyone I've ever met in the Steelworkers union and I've met an awful lot of people. Larry's not only got the ability and experience, he's a helluva worker, someone who seems to start in the morning and at night he's still as strong. All he asked of the people was to work and service the members to the best of their ability, not like some who go to a race track, or a bar, and come back at 5 o'clock and say "Whew, what a helluva day I put in today." You ask them where they've been and they're very disturbed. Sometimes you may get a snide remark, like it's none of your business. Then you really have to fight and say, "Look, as long as I'm paying my dues and you're my staff representative, it is my business." Then they cool off a little bit and say, "Well, I don't have to report to you. All I have to do is report to my boss and that's it." These are the kind of remarks that make it hard for rank-and-file members and some staff to work together.

CHAPTER 16

Contest in the West

The people of the earth go down,
Each with his wealth of dream.

ARCHIBALD MACLEISH

In California and the Far West, the drive to evict the McDonald leadership found its warmest welcome among the rank and file.

Sierras and the Rank and File

Manuel Sierras, a Mexican-American born in Arizona, became the chairman of the Abel-Burke-Molony campaign in southern California. Then forty years old, a stocky five foot four or so, he had been a member of the Steelworkers since 1946. For three years before that he was a member of the Boilermakers Union. A welder by trade at the time of the election campaign, he had not been an officer of the local union for three years. Before that he had held the presidency of the American Bridge U.S. Steel Local Union 2058 for two terms, after filling just about every position in the local union: shop steward, department grievance man, general grievance man, financial secretary. He was, in the full meaning of the word, a rank-and-file leader.

For Sierras the international union was both as distant as Pittsburgh and as close at hand as the staff representative. Sierras's fight against the union hierarchy began in 1956, because of his dissatisfaction with the contract settlement that year: "There was quite a gap between the actual wages in basic steel and in fabrication. Our productivity is high, our security is low. New machinery replaces men: in ten years, the local's membership dropped from 2,400 to almost 1,200."

When the dues revolt of 1956 came out of the East, Sierras and his associates supported Rarick. Following the campaign, the group maintained an anti-establishment identity. In the course of events, the local union critics built a common ground from which to survey the "hierarchy" as personified in Charlie Smith, the district director, and a subdistrict director, Bill Brunton. "The people in charge of District 38 were our targets," said Sierras flatly.

Brunton came out of the United Mine Workers, carrying the aura of the old-timer, the arrogant bearer of an unexamined tradition. Whatever glamour had once shone from such a heritage had been tarnished by Brunton's personal behavior. Part of Brunton's subdistrict was the local of Kaiser Steel's Fontana works, which after the 1959 strike had become the model of "mature" labor-management relationships. Among the local union hierarchy, it was McDonald country. Sierras summed it up:

"When Brother Abel first announced he was a candidate," Sierras said, "I frankly didn't think he was serious, because out here in District 38, from the district director all the way down to the last shop steward, they were pretty well lined up in favor of McDonald, and I knew that Brother Abel would have a hard time trying to overcome this situation. Through the years, when we in my local union talked about Abel, we were talking about a union man. This wasn't so when the conversation came around to Brother McDonald. To us, he was a distorted image of a union man.

"It's true we had a tradition of dissent in our local criticism. I would like to think constructive criticism. It's also true it's not characteristic of many locals. In my local the membership is highly educated on union issues. You have to produce for them.

"In our local the Anglo membership runs about 60 per cent and the minority members—Negroes and Mexican-Americans—40 per cent, not over 15 per cent Negroes. We have cooperation between the minority groups. But it's not the minority versus the Anglos. When it comes to voting on union issues, voting for local union officers, this is not the problem. We have some Negro officers; we've had them through the years. We've had Mexican-American officers, but I was the first Mexican-American elected to the presidency of my local union."

In Sierras's local, plant-gate elections were the rule, by a permanent decision of the local. Nominations were made at the local's business meeting at the union hall. The time for nominations came just before Thanksgiving, and Sierras called Joseph Molony, whom he had supported against Hague in 1955:

"I told him who I was and what I wanted to do. He was very glad, he said, that he had a supporter out here. He told me to go ahead. I asked him for any instructions as to what I should do, as far as the press release was concerned. He said there was no need for him to interfere, that he knew I knew what I was doing.

"Before that call to Molony, I had held a meeting of seven union brothers from my own and other locals at a private home and discussed the whole situation, for three or four hours. Some of them thought I was crazy. They thought that Molony, Abel, and Burke didn't have a chance out here with the Smith machine that was already in motion. Their argument was that Charlie Smith and the subdistrict directors out here had everything pretty well sewed up. They were saying that the machine would be able to deliver 10,000 votes majority for Brother McDonald. It was all settled!

"Right after Brother Abel announced he was going to be a candidate, two officers in my local union came to me and said they were for Abel. A couple of weeks later, they had changed their minds! Somebody from Billy Brunton's subdistrict office had talked to them. So the only support I could get for Brother Abel and the slate was from the rank and file. Well, I understood this from the beginning. This is the reason I called that meeting. I invited thirty-two people; seven came.

"But I knew that the only thing we had to do to overcome the machine was to mobilize the rank and file. The only reason that they were going to vote for McDonald was because there was nobody here actually agitating for Brother Abel. I pointed out that as soon as we could get started, and rank-and-file people could see that people out here were actually campaigning for Abel, I was sure we would be successful.

"We appointed a press agent from another local union. Two or three days after the first publicity, we got an answer. It came from Brother Cass Alvin—a staff representative and assistant to Smith. In essence he said my committee was a bunch of nuts. All we were trying to do was stir up murky water. This got to the rank and file! They figured 'Who is Cass Alvin to make a statement such as this? Now I'm for Abel; if I'm for Abel, then I'm crazy too.' It disturbed them that a man like Cass Alvin, assistant to Smith, would come out with a release blasting rank-and-file people that were trying to campaign for Brother Abel."

The real test of Sierras's leadership came at the local nominating meeting:

"Three staff representatives were present—Brothers Edmond Tanski, Del Coffee, and John Despol—which was quite unusual. Generally we're lucky if we have a single staff representative there for one of our meetings. I was fifteen or twenty minutes late. McDonald people saw I was late and they took advantage of it. Right at the start of the meeting, they opened up for nominations. I was late because I had to pick up my wife at work. She didn't have a ride that day so that meant she would have to walk about three or four miles home—no bus service, no streetcar. I ran on down and took her home, not thinking they were going to call for the nominations right at the start.

"The meeting starts at 4:30 in the afternoon, right after the shift breaks. There must have been about sixty or seventy brothers there at the meeting. Out of a membership of 1,400. This is the usual attendance. Sometimes lower. It takes at least twenty-one members to make a quorum. So when I arrived, right away I asked the $64 question, 'What happened?' When they saw me come in, one of the brothers jumped up, met me at the door and said, 'Well, you're too late, Brother McDonald has been nominated, the whole slate, and Abel and Molony and Burke were left out.' So I asked him, 'How come you didn't take the floor?' He said, 'Well, when we didn't see you we figured you'd chickened out.' They ramrodded right on through. Nobody got up to nominate Brother Abel.

"I asked for a vote to reopen. The staff representatives began to move up and down the aisles, talking hard, trying to discredit Abel, Burke, and Molony. They said, 'You guys are doing something wrong here. Why rock the boat? Everything's going to be all right. You're going to be sorry.' But we won the vote to reopen, and nominated the full slate of Abel, Burke, and Molony.

"The staff representatives were highly disturbed by the nominations. Brother Despol made a big show of taking down notes of everything I was saying, making all kinds of faces. They had me ticketed as the leader of the opposition."

For the next month, Sierras and his associates got their political bearings: "They took up a collection from the rank and file to recompense a member for 'time' lost to enable him to work in the campaign, and to pay for printing leaflets: a lot of committee people made telephone calls from their own homes and paid for them. My telephone bills—I did keep track—came close to $300. Long-distance calls all up and down the state of California, to Oregon, to the state of Washington. I got in touch with people in Colorado, in Utah, in Arizona—people I had known through the years.

"The response was very, very good. As for the rank-and-file people, they weren't actually voting for Brother Abel—it was a protest vote against Charlie Smith as well as against Brother McDonald, and this included anybody that had anything to do with the administration.

"I began getting calls from various local unions, rank-and-file people. We needed people to handle our literature, in and outside plants. By mid-January, we began receiving literature and buttons from the Abel headquarters back in Chicago.

"One red-baiting leaflet the McDonald people put out had this paragraph: 'Why hasn't the leadership of the opposition group repudiated the open support of the *People's World*? Why is the leadership of the opposition group accepting the active support of every left-wing extremist in the Los Angeles area without repudiation?' The decision was made to ignore the smear and continue to campaign on a clean basis. Like I told them, why start a pissing match with a skunk at this point?"

Sierras was clearly a union-intoxicated man, and whether president of his local or not—he was defeated for a third term in 1960—he went back to the ranks at the plant, and remained a regular attendant of the monthly local meetings.

For several years prior to the Abel-McDonald campaign, a series of incidents shaped the attitudes of the local membership and provided fuel for Sierras's watchful stoking. During his presidency came the 116-day strike of 1959, a "really hard and bitter strike." For the average rank-and-filer, it was costly. Members suffered personal hardship, and finally, according to Sierras, the "contract itself really demoralized the membership."

Telling It to Ike

In the course of that strike, Sierras brought the whole matter forcefully to the attention of President Eisenhower himself. During the eighty-day period of the Taft-Hartley injunction invoked after the strike had been going on for months, "I decided that being that President Eisenhower was down here playing golf at Palm Springs and being that we were going through a hard and bitter strike here, the least that he could do was to listen to a personal plea by the steel strikers in the Greater Los Angeles area."

Sierras began to carry out the logistics and requirements of protocol for a President-picketing motorcade. He sent a telegram to President Eisenhower notifying him of the impending visitation. At the same time, he wired McDonald and Smith, informing them of the action. Sierras was not surprised when he received telegrams from both men advising him against going to Ike. But plans were already set:

"We were gassing up the cars, the families were notified, and the membership was ready to leave the next morning at nine o'clock. . . . I pointed out to the members and their families that we wanted an orderly caravan, no drinking, nobody getting out of line, no fighting, no violence. We started out with about fifty cars and 250 people. When we got on the freeway, we had our cars decorated with different signs, against the Taft-Hartley injunction, picket signs and 'On to Palm Springs' placards hanging from the sides of the cars. We attracted quite a bit of attention. . . . People driving toward us made U-turns and joined the caravan to Palm Springs.

"A little later, on the way, we arrived at Fontana. The people from the Kaiser works were ready with their cars, their families, and some of the local union officers. We regrouped. Must have been about one hundred cars, about five hundred people. We caravanned through Palm Springs. I had announced the time of our arrival at 1:30. When we arrived at the President's country club I was informed that I wouldn't be able to talk to President Eisenhower. . . . Instead it was agreed that his press secretary, Jim Hagerty, would come out and talk to me provided that I told the pickets to stay at least fifty yards away, which I did. He came out in an automobile, with Secret Service people. By this time, there were the TV cameras and newspaper reporters. We had a discussion that lasted about ten minutes. Hagerty tried to tell me that we shouldn't have done this, that President Eisenhower was looking after the best interests of the American people."

Sierras replied that he and his fellow workers were American citizens and had a right to present their ideas to the President. This response did not calm Hagerty.

"At first," said Sierras, "Hagerty got real personal. When I walked up to him with all the respect in the world, I addressed him as Mr. Hagerty, and this was on the level. But then he got a little excited. He berated me and the pickets; they were hollering and chanting 'We want Ike, we want Ike.' Then he got down to using my first name, so I decided to address him as Jim. I informed him that as far as I was concerned he was just a messenger boy for President Eisenhower and the person I came out to talk to was President Eisenhower. He didn't appreciate that." Sierras added that the pickets and he were prepared to stay there and picket until such time as "we would get an answer from President Eisenhower on this resolution we had drafted."

Hagerty proposed that if Sierras would pull the pickets and start back on the freeway, he would hold a news conference immediately and Sierras would get an answer to the resolution by radio.

"Sure enough, we drove for about twenty minutes, and we got an official acknowledgment of the resolution on the car radio. Our mission was accomplished. To be real honest, the reply didn't amount to anything. It didn't affect the Taft-Hartley injunction. But it was an acknowledgment that we were alive and kicking."

This incident marked Sierras further as a man to be watched by international union headquarters. With the aid of the top leadership, opposition to him was built up. A few months later, running for a third term, he was defeated in a bitter election. After the election, a hassle over the local union's finances was followed by the appointment of an international union "commission" to investigate the local's books. John Despol, the staff representative, appointed administrator of the union's affairs, began a series of hearings into the patriotism of Sierras and some of his associates. Following these sessions, Sierras said, Despol removed him and other grievance committeemen from office for failure to pass the test of patriotism according to his standards.

Subsequently the House Un-American Activities Committee also got into the act. Sierras and his fellow members appealed to James M. Bassett, the executive secretary of the Los Angeles Central Trades Council and an important political figure in the state. Bassett said he could intervene to ward off the committee hearing and its witch-hunt possibilities if Charlie Smith, the district director, as the responsible leader of the Steelworkers District, would request him to do so. But, said Sierras, Smith "didn't see fit to do this for us." After Despol removed him as grievance committeeman, Sierras went back to the ranks:

"Well, after that, during the years '62, '63, '64, all I was doing was punching my time card, doing my work, minding my own business, going to union meetings and sitting there, listening to what was going on, and very seldom taking the floor," Sierras said. "The rest of my friends quit going to the union meetings, they gave up because they saw that what happened to me could very well happen to them, too. They became afraid and then they got apathetic."

Thus, Despol's intense personal opposition kept Sierras and others out of office. But according to Sierras, his sense of commitment, his concern for the union, and his pride kept him functioning. He remained part of the local's political life.

During the campaign, Sierras found himself spending what was for him large sums of money. He would take off a few hours from work, although he tried not to do this too much. His wife worked as a seamstress in a garment factory and helped make up for the "gouges" in his pay.

Late in January, when Walter Burke came to the Los Angeles area, the Sierras committee was already back in business. Now enlarged, it carried the names of local unions from American Can, Bethlehem, and other plants. Then, in the last ten days of the campaign, Chris Gellepis, a staff representative in the subdistrict, declared himself publicly for Abel. "That was a shot in the arm," said Sierras. "We all felt that he had been under pressure and this was one of the reasons why he hadn't declared himself sooner. We all understand what he was up against. If Brother Abel didn't get elected the chances were that he would be minus a job."

Bellying Up

Even the simple distribution of literature had become hazardous. About this time, a district-wide conference was called, ostensibly to discuss the Legislative and Educational activities of the union. Such a gathering, made up of representatives of all local unions in the area, is an important cross-section of the membership. Since Tom Consiglio, the staff representative in charge of L&E, was strongly pro-McDonald, Sierras and another Abel supporter undertook to counteract the establishment pressure by passing out leaflets to the delegates as they entered the hall.

"While I was doing this, Brother G. J. Conway, a subdistrict director, showed up and started to holler at me. We just stood our ground and passed out literature. Delegates would glance at it and throw it on the sidewalk, and some of them tramped all over it. Some of them even made some gestures, you know, that are not proper. But me and this brother took all this."

When Conway finally stopped yelling, Sierras said: "You ought to start campaigning for Brother McDonald because from what I can see, you people are losing ground." Swearing, Conway ran into the hall.

"By this time quite a number of delegates surrounded me and this other brother and kept asking questions about Abel, Molony, and Burke, and we were trying to answer them. Actually, what they were trying to do was to stir up some kind of a fight. In the meantime, another brother, an enormous fat guy, tried to push me around. He walks up to me and bounces me around a couple of times with his belly. . . . Anyway we waited around until the meeting was over and the delegates began pouring out. I got hold of three of them and explained Abel's program. Later on, one of them came around to see me. He told me he couldn't actually come out in the open but that he would do it under cover and tell certain people to vote for Abel."

The Mexican-Americans had become impressed with the importance of achieving and maintaining their identity within the union context. Sierras felt increasingly that the Mexican-Americans were "short-changed by their own people"—the people they had voted for. What was true in the community in general was true inside the union organization. In this subdistrict, the so-called "minority groups" were rapidly approaching fifty per cent of the union membership and still had perhaps only one Negro and two Mexican-American representatives on the international staff in the area.

For men like Sierras, the transition from dissatisfaction at the workplace or inside the union to the community at large was natural. Sierras saw a great need for somebody to "step out in the Mexican-American community and try to lead a program that would benefit the community— in other words, genuine leadership."

For years, the Mexican-American Chamber of Commerce had been the political arm of the Mexican community. "Just because they are the richer businessmen, just because they're the professional people, they think they know what *we* need," said Sierras. "Consequently, they're the ones that have been running the show, and the Mexican community has had sad experiences in electing people to represent them properly. The only way the Mexican-American community can come out of the apathy is to introduce leaders that are going to do something for the community. This was where the labor movement—the Steelworkers—came in, especially in the Los Angeles area. We had something coming. We didn't get much leadership under McDonald. We were putting lots of hope in the new leadership. That's why we pushed so hard for Abel."

Fontana, the Crowning Jewel

So far as the world outside was concerned, Kaiser's Fontana mill, Local 2869, was the gem of McDonald's achievement in labor-management cooperation. But in addition to membership distrust of the subdistrict director, Billy Brunton, the Kaiser long-range profit-sharing plan had fallen short of its promise. When the Kaiser plan was first launched, it aroused considerable interest and enthusiasm. But Sierras and others decided that it had turned out to be "another device to speed up the work and to compete with your fellow workers. In order to make the money the plan calls for, you actually have to push the brother that's working with you to make him do more work. Instead of the company doing the pushing, you're doing it."

By many, Fontana was heralded as the prototype for union-employer relationships in and outside the steel industry. Locally, however, Fontana frequently became the arena of dispute between various groups in the local and the international union as well as between the local union and the Kaiser management. For example, three months after the Dues Protesters in the Fontana local had elected a president in 1957, it was placed under an "administratorship" imposed by the international union. Two wildcat strikes had broken out, as Lloyd Ulman points out, "after a friendly employer had insistently demanded that the International intervene and discharge its contractual obligations." * In the minds of many members, the removal of the local's anti-McDonald president was regarded as punishment for his support of Rarick. Moreover, the report that the employer had urged such intervention seemed to them an example of collusion between the international union and employer against the rank and file. Under such conditions administratorships often become police actions, restoring a semblance of order without necessarily eliminating the causes of the discontent. Moreover, Brunton's outside "business" activities, which had come under government scrutiny, increased the hostility between the international union and the membership.

* Lloyd Ulman, *The Government of the Steelworkers Union*, p. 172.

After Kaiser broke the united front of basic steel in the 1959 strike and signed a separate contract with the Steelworkers Union in October of that year, both sides agreed that a special board of three leading arbitrators—George W. Taylor, David Cole, and John T. Dunlop—was to lay out a plan to make the enterprise more productive and the wage structure more satisfactory, and to replace rancor with amity. The Kaiser plan was introduced early in 1963. It was both innovative and optimistic, and carried with it an immense fund of good will in most areas. An intensive campaign of education and persuasion was led by Marvin Miller, McDonald's assistant in the field of human relations. To the outside world, Fontana's tripartite long-range sharing plan was considered the single spot to which the McDonald administration could point with confident pride for a vote of resounding support. But in the shakedown cruise, the Fontana plan failed to land the workers on an island of security.

Miller, as the chief union evangelist for the plan after General Counsel Arthur Goldberg became Secretary of Labor, had replaced him on the tripartite committee. "It's been three years," Miller told the workers in January 1963. "There has been some criticism, I know, of inadequate reporting back to the membership whom we represent, and that criticism is valid, except for one thing. We have not been working on the usual type of problem. We had to be inventive . . . and we—the union, the management, the public members—had to adopt a rather important ground rule. We said no negotiator was to be held to any position he might take. Until everything was agreed to, nothing was agreed to. In that framework, you can see our hesitancy in coming back and saying, 'Well, this is where we are now.' "

The plan went into effect March 1, 1963. Hence by the time of the international union election of 1965, the "long-range sharing plan" had been in force for just under two years.

Ronald Bitonti, a trustee of the local, became a spokesman for the opposition. His objection, he said, was not to the idea of the "fruits of progress" plan but to the procedures, the method of adoption and application of the plan, which had resulted in a cleavage between workers who participated in the "fruits of progress" and those who worked on an incentive basis. Individuals doing the same job would take home wages as much as $40 a week apart. A few years before, he had been chairman of the plant grievance committee and made an unsuccessful run for the local union presidency. When the news came that an anti-McDonald candidate was in the running, he phoned John Rooney, Abel's assistant, offering to help. Within a few days Abel wrote Bitonti and impressed him with the importance he attached to receiving the Fontana nomination. For Abel to win the nomination at Fontana, the public-relations pivot of the McDonald administration, would be a definite psychological victory.

Since Bitonti had insisted on maintaining his opposition to the local leadership, he found himself caught in combat with the whole district apparatus of the establishment. He had been barred from holding the post of grievance committeeman. Bitonti was convinced "they" were trying to remove him as a "troublemaker." "I had the choice of either giving in to them or fighting for principle. Anyway they filed new charges and I got an injunction to prevent them from removing me. Well, I was successful, for a while."

Then the local union leadership, on the grounds that he had appealed to an "outside" agency, the California State Labor Commission, suspended him for three years. This took place after he had announced his support of Abel. He was barred from running for local office until 1970.

Having made a commitment to Abel, however, Bitonti worked to keep it. When the Fontana local nominated McDonald only by a slim margin, Bitonti redoubled his efforts. He called Phoenix, Arizona, where John Dean, president of the Reynolds Aluminum plant, got his local to nominate Abel. In this area, Abel had been favorably regarded; the local union hall was named after him. But other Bitonti calls revealed that "lots of people were afraid to buck the machine."

Even more offensive than Smith, the district director, was Brunton, the subdirector. His extracurricular financial activities involving vending-machine operations had come under investigation by state and federal government agencies. While the charges of corruption against Brunton were the most obvious, by the time of the election many members were convinced that company officials had found some local officials, not all in the Steelworkers union, highly amenable to company favors. Thus the local union was kept in a continuous uproar, with suspicion directed against both management of the plant and the administration of the union.

This pile-up of discontent—capped by disaffection with the working out of the "long-range" plan—convinced Bitonti that a strong campaign could be built up for the Abel ticket. He joined forces with Terry Fernandez, a Mexican-American who once worked with Abel in Ohio, and arranged to meet with Walter Burke on his western swing in late January.

Inside Fontana, there were at least two main groups. One wanted nothing to do with McDonald; the other was Rarick's old group, which never had liked what was going on. Both groups were for Abel but against each other. As Bitonti put the question: "How were you going to get everybody together? We decided to stay anonymous—not form a committee in Fontana. All individuals active in the local decided to stay apart from a formal relation to the campaign. Instead, I kept in touch with the international headquarters in Chicago, and with other groups. From time to time, I held meetings with Manuel Sierras and some of his people to see how things were going in that area. . . . But so far as a committee at Fontana was concerned—no. Their strategy—the other side—was always to attack the individuals who would be backing Abel— not attack Abel but his backers."

As the campaign developed, Bitonti and his allies began to receive literature from the campaign headquarters. A distribution committee was appointed to hand out leaflets at plant gates, for which permission had to be obtained from Kaiser's labor relations department. The man who arranged for the clearance was Lee Troupe, the only elected local officer who went on record as supporting Abel. Like his brother-in-law, Terry Fernandez, Troupe also had worked with Abel in the Ohio days.

Important to the "underground" Abel organization in Fontana, Bitonti said, were some of the older Rarick backers, including a couple named Joe and Minnie Luksich. In the 1958 local union campaign, Minnie Luksich was thrown out of local office along with President Thomas Flaherty because they charged Brunton with a variety of improper practices. "The Luksich couple brought suit and got paid all their salaries. . . . If they'd had a Landrum-Griffin Law at the time, I don't think they could have kicked them out in the first place. . . . Brunton had dictatorial powers. It was either his way or no way at all. . . . Over the years Brunton got in deeper and deeper. His defense in the vending-machine deal was that they were just a client and he introduced them to the company. But I dug it up in the Federal Building in Los Angeles when I started going through the Department of Labor files."

With the backing of three of his brothers, the thirty-three-year-old Bitonti proceeded confidently, although his older brother was on the McDonald side.

The Landrum-Griffin Act, bitterly fought by the trade-union movement as a method of hobbling labor's self-government, actually afforded Bitonti and others like him a fallback means of protecting their franchise inside the union. "There's one part of the Landrum-Griffin Law that proved effective for the rank and file—the right to vote and to know that your vote is going to be counted. As far as giving a member the right to get up at a membership meeting and speak, there are points of the Landrum-Griffin Law I like. Also the election part, and the part about where an individual has the right to find out where the money is going, how it's spent. If I want to, I can write to the Labor Department, which I have done, and find out all the financial information on my local union and the international union. Those points I like. The secondary-boycott provisions and things like that I don't like. But the part where my union rights are protected—that I like."

But Steve Lakich, a McDonald supporter, was able to view Fontana from a different angle. A graduate of California State Polytechnic, he got his degree while working in the Fontana plant, where he started in 1959. He came from a Steelworkers family. When he was twenty-three, just ready to graduate from Cal Poly, he ran for local vice-president. Denied access to trade-union rolls, he grubbed through the city directory, and wherever it said "steelworker," he underlined the name. He threw a little working party with his college buddies and typed up labels for three thousand names out of the nearly seven thousand in the plant. When the mail was delivered, his angry opponents charged that he must have sneaked into the union hall to get those names. Under the Landrum-Griffin Act, he had been permitted only to *see* the list! "They'd say 'Here it is, but don't take it out of the union hall because we need these lists right now in the office.' "

Lakich began to learn about politics in earnest. The 1962 campaign was a rough baptism. Some of the members, he said, couldn't understand why a college graduate would want to get involved in the labor movement. They recognized the union's need for well-educated technicians, but running for office was different. The opposition also identified him with student demonstrations at various colleges, including Cal Poly. Then he was charged with being the leader of a Communist organization. This rumor was spread in the open-hearth area of the plant, where he was not known. The rumor had its effect at the time.

Running independently, he was "nicked out" by twenty-one votes out of six thousand cast. But the exposure did him no harm. The following year, when the vice-presidency became vacant, Lakich was nominated by Bitonti, then a trustee, to fill the vacancy, and he became vice-president in August 1963.

As vice-president, he became chairman of the Fontana Incentive Committee, a full-time job, handling the administration of the wage incentive plans. He was also appointed a member of the local's Sharing Plan Committee. In 1964 Lakich's prestige grew: he came out third among the twenty-five candidates for nine delegates' places to the international union convention.

In May 1964, the Fontana local's officers received the Canton, Ohio, newspaper—the Golden Lodge issue—running "I. W. Abel for President." Clayton Neff, a grievance committeeman, told Lakich he wanted to set up campaign headquarters right out on the main street for Abel, but Lakich, politically more cautious, told him not to get involved: "You don't know he's going to run. These people are probably radicals just trying to promote something. I can't see Abel running against McDonald."

When the Fontana local met, McDonald won the endorsement over

Abel, 98 to 60. Many of the Dues Protesters of 1958 supported Abel. These people, Lakich said later, had been charged in the past with being Communists, just as he had been: "I don't think they are. They are protesters. No matter who's on top, they're going to be against the establishment. But the Dues Protesters played it real smart. They did not want to stir up old opposition. They did not openly support I. W. Abel."

While Lakich openly supported McDonald, he understood the reasons for the discontent with the McDonald regime: "We have a lot of problems with the sharing plan. The sharing plan is why, I think, he lost the local! Yet of all the locals in the international, this was the one everybody expected him to carry. The McDonald approach made me mad. It made the president, Jim Vezie, mad. They used to have these nine-man committee meetings of the three international officials and three company brass and the three arbitrators. They never would meet right at Fontana. They'd meet at Palm Springs. They wouldn't invite us local leaders to their sessions.

"They once had a meeting in Upland, which is about ten miles from Fontana, and they didn't invite us. Then one day the three public members, David Cole, John Dunlop, and Dr. Taylor, said they wanted to come down to the tin mill. This time they asked staff man George Sirolli, Jim Vezie, and me to come down to the mill. This made it look nice, made it appear to the workers as if we had been meeting with them all day. They were going to tour the mill to make it look as if we were trying to resolve the workers' problems. The three union men of the nine were McDonald, Charlie Smith, and Marvin Miller. The three public members were there for prestige. They never had made a decision. You know, they were supposed to be part of our grievance procedure. If we can't resolve a sharing plan dispute, they arbitrate. They've never arbitrated; they've always referred it back to the local committee or the parties to resolve. They're for show. It helped the plan, you know, gave it the right appearance when they first kicked it off. But as I say, they would have their meetings in Palm Springs—all over—in New York. But they'd never invite us local people. We used to get so mad."

Why, then, did Lakich support McDonald? If the Steelworkers needed a change, said Lakich, he did not think it should be I. W. Abel: "If he was so great and he had been the second man for twelve years, then the problem with the sharing plan—and other problems—was also his problem, not just David McDonald's. Every basic steel agreement we have is signed by David McDonald, the second man is I. W. Abel, and the third man was Howard Hague. Maybe I liked McDonald for what he did over the years and I couldn't see him retired in this way."

During the first year of the Kaiser sharing plan, Lakich confirmed, on the basis of his own knowledge, the fruits of progress were found to be good. In 1964, the second year, they dropped; in 1965 they went lower. The lower they dropped, the larger became the discrepancy between the "fruits of progress" sharers and those who remained on incentive pay. They did the same work. The situation deteriorated so badly in the summer of 1964 that the members picketed the union hall. Their signs read: "USWA Unfair to Organized Labor" and "Equal Pay for Equal Work." Several members of the Fontana local wrote to President Johnson to complain that they could not gain a hearing in their union. McDonald was furious.

Lakich summed up the mood at Fontana this way: "Dissatisfaction developed because of the wage discrepancy between those who were paid under the sharing plan and those under the incentive plan. Added to this, the Committee of Nine had not consulted the local union leadership. A main psychological ingredient in the plan was that this was to be a mutual-aid program between union and management. All the local leadership got was a decision handed down to them by the big boys on top."

To cap it all, when Burke appeared in Los Angeles, company officials at Kaiser Aluminum refused to let him campaign on company grounds. Word of this discrimination got around. "The most effective factor operating for Abel," said Lakich, "was that he had good people backing him. They not only passed out leaflets, but people would take them. You began to sense something big was happening. The rank and file were sure going to speak on election day."

CHAPTER 17

Canadian Role

This is the charge I keep as mine . . .
to cancel the dividing line.

LESLIE PINCKNEY HILL

For Canada, the start of the campaign was a time of hesitation. William Mahoney, the Canadian national director, held publicly to the belief, as did Director Larry Sefton of District 6, covering all of Canada west of Toronto, that there would be no contest. On November 2, nine days before the start of the nominating period, Mike Fenwick, Sefton's assistant, wrote to the officers of more than three hundred local unions in District 6. Obviously at Sefton's behest, he proposed that the locals nominate the three incumbent international officers, along with the incumbent district directors, Sefton and Mahoney. In a similar message on November 6 to the three district directors and staff representatives in Canada, Mahoney held off from a commitment to an alternative course.

Mahoney's November 6 memorandum was being delivered in about the same mail that brought him the formal announcement by Abel, Burke, and Molony. Five days later, on November 11, Mahoney abandoned his hands-off position. In a formal letter to the Canadian locals, he acknowledged that "a contest has developed for the three top International Officers of our union." His tone was that of a leader of a small nation being drawn unwillingly into an orbit of conflict for which there seemed little enthusiasm. Sloughing off embarrassment, Mahoney pointed out that the "Abel-Molony-Burke team is supported by a large majority of the International Executive Board. [This was somewhat exaggerated.] It is the unanimous recommendation of your Directors in Canada that

213

we support Abel, Burke and Molony." He was on the side of the greater battalions. The day before this letter went out, Mahoney and Sefton had attended the meeting of the executive board in Pittsburgh, when the first test votes taken by the board revealed that Abel's supporters were in the majority.

Aside from the political practicalities, the Canadians did not find this a difficult decision to make. The memory of McDonald's inept handling of the Canadian issue and the consequent revolt of the delegates in the 1956 Los Angeles convention remained vivid. In addition, McDonald's attacks on the political program of the Canadian locals, with their participation in the creation of an independent political party with a trade-union base, continued to rankle. But Mahoney played it low key. In fact, he implied that with the opposition so strong, McDonald and Hague might think better of running for re-election. "As of now, they have decided to contest the election although both are over 60 years of age— the normal retirement age under our union's pension plan—and are entitled to adequate pensions." The choice, said Mahoney, was "between a younger and an older team."

The same day, Larry Sefton wrote to the key people in his district, the largest geographically, that after "a hard look at the developing events and in the belief that Brother Abel and his associate candidates will make the best team in advancing the interests of the union and assuring its stable continuity, the Canadian directors are agreed that we advocate their support in nomination and election by our locals." In words that hardly signaled an all-out crusade, Sefton urged that "due recognition would be paid to the part hitherto played" by the McDonald-Hague leadership.

Sefton's union life was classic in its directness. He began his working life at seventeen as a hard-rock miner. He toiled in the mines at night and attended school during the day. After seven and a half years, the miners, then under the jurisdiction of the Mine, Mill and Smelter Workers, struck for recognition in the winter of 1941–42. The strike was lost. Young Sefton was blacklisted, got a job in a fabricating shop, and became a member of the Steelworkers Union.

After several years, he was appointed a staff representative. He became director of District 6 in 1953, after defeating William Mahoney, who had been the preferred candidate of the established leadership. As head of a huge geographical area stretching from the province of Ontario west to the Pacific and north to the Alaskan border, Sefton came to administer about thirty regional offices throughout the district to cover far and lonely places. About half of the Canadian Steelworkers are in iron ore and other base metals. Within two years Sefton established himself as a man who would not hesitate to buck McDonald.

He advocated the election of Molony over Hague for vice-president. In the ensuing years, Sefton's prestige in the international union grew.

When late in October 1964 Sefton, along with Molony and Griffin, attended the wedding of Walter Burke's daughter in Milwaukee, the four were no longer the politically closely knit group they had become during and after the 1955 vice-presidential election. In the preceding two years, Griffin had indicated a change of head if not of heart toward McDonald. His own ambition led him to support McDonald and hope to win Sefton over to his side, despite Sefton's known contempt for McDonald. He understood the strategic importance of Sefton's support and the latter became the object of an intensive pursuit by Griffin. Griffin phoned him early and late; once at 3 A.M. he informed him that "Dave wants to see you." Then McDonald called Sefton to Pittsburgh and offered him the choice of the candidacies for vice-president or secretary-treasurer. Sefton knew that both Burke and Molony were biding their time and he had no intention of opposing either one. The combined efforts of McDonald and Griffin proved unavailing.

The three Canadian district directors—Sefton in Toronto, Pat Burke in District 5, with headquarters in Montreal, and James Nicholson of District 2, the Atlantic Provinces—and Mahoney, the Canadian national director, all now presented an impressive united front in support of the team of Abel, Burke, and Molony, which received the nomination of practically every Canadian local. In early February, Abel sent letters to the Canadian membership. But the campaign itself was not carried on with bonfire enthusiasm. To be sure, the essentials were observed: letters were sent out to locals, some campaign material was distributed, but basically there seemed no inclination to get steamed up.

As is generally true in bilingual Canada, the campaign material was in both English and French. The majority of the membership in District 5 was French-speaking, and the province of Quebec, churning with separatist agitation, was a matter of special concern to the trade-union movement. For that persuasive reason Pat Burke, the incumbent director of District 5, had agreed to step down, enabling two French-Canadians to wage a contest for the vacancy. Subsequently, the heat of battle in Quebec stimulated greater participation and brought out a vote that was larger than usual in District 5.

In the last week of the drive, Mahoney, Sefton, Pat Burke, and James Nicholson stressed the importance of voting but placed the responsibility for the contest on their comrades below the border: "There is a strong feeling among our American brothers that rank-and-file participation in union affairs has given way to personality to the detriment of the union's vitality; that we have tended to become a sleeping giant; that division in the leadership of our union must be ended." In French, the urgency of this paragraph was somewhat reduced. But the Canadian directors emphasized their conviction that Abel, Burke, and Molony "see the role of the union clearly—and as Canadian unionists see it."

To indicate the extent of support that Abel had already received, the district directors noted that he had received nominations from 1,310 locals to 904 for McDonald. Apparently they believed that local leaders in remote constituencies had to be reassured that they were not going it alone; a whiff of the band-wagon atmosphere would not hurt. Canadian steelworkers were made to feel that they ought not to stand aloof while their top officers' support of the Abel team placed them in the mainstream of opinion in the international union that spanned both nations.

Moreover the Canadian directors emphasized that the Canadian vote could prove decisive. There was also a special reason for building up a large vote in Canada: one of the candidates for the three international tellerships, John Shipperbottom, was a Canadian. Named to run on the Abel ticket, this veteran financial secretary of Local 1005 (Stelco in Hamilton, Ontario) was Canada's sole representative on the ballot; the McDonald slate did not include a Canadian. The Canadian directors hoped that this appeal to national pride would provide additional stimulus in their get-out-the-vote argument.

With one minor exception, all the campaign material was carefully designated as paid for by voluntary contributions. Sefton had been deeply involved in difficult negotiations with the Steel Company of Canada (Stelco) in a local distinguished by a recalcitrant rank-and-file leadership. For that reason, not until literally the last hours of the campaign did he permit himself to steam with anger at McDonald, and then only in reaction to the president's last-minute tactics. The day before the elections McDonald flew into Hamilton to appear on TV and conduct an open-line radio program, in which he sharply attacked both Mahoney and Sefton. McDonald's specific target was the recent contract between the union and the Steel Company of Canada, with about eleven thousand workers, who had ratified the agreement by only a narrow margin. At the Stelco plant and in the Algoma Steel Corporation a considerable group of workers, some under Communist influence, were especially hostile to Sefton, whose activity in the socialist-oriented New Democratic Party of Canada increased their normal animosity against him. Taking full advantage of their discontent, McDonald, who was pushing for votes where he could find them, charged that Sefton had neglected his negotiating responsibilities by politicking for Abel and Molony. At no time, said McDonald sorrowfully, had the Canadian directors asked for assistance from the international president. "If they had asked me," he said, "I probably could have helped the workers with some of the things they wanted to see in the new contracts."

This reflection on their union integrity brought an angry retort from both Sefton and Mahoney. In his labor column in the Hamilton *Spectator,* Bas Korstanje noted: "The foes of the United Steelworkers of America had a field day. . . . Two Canadian directors of the union were tongue-lashed in public by their International president, who hinted they were not doing their job. In returning the compliment, the Canadians called their International leader a fake and a ham actor. All this happened on the eve of the union's International elections. And it must have left the Steelworkers' foes in stitches.

"What Mr. McDonald's visit to Hamilton accomplished is another open question. There was not enough time for him to meet with any large number of union members here. He had not officially been invited by any local union. Arrangements for his trip were made by a 'rank-and-file committee' which in the past was never pro-McDonald. On the contrary, members of this committee have usually been anti-administration, especially anti-Canadian administration."

At the Stelco local, McDonald received 1,610 votes to Abel's 1,023. He carried his ticket with him by somewhat smaller margins. In contrast, the pro-Abel Shipperbottom received 2,081 votes for international teller in the same local. On the basis of the Stelco count, there seems little doubt that if McDonald had come up to Canada and campaigned earlier and harder, he would have done better throughout Canada, especially since Sefton was too deeply involved in negotiations—the same ones that McDonald charged him with neglecting—to devote much time to campaigning.

From the start, the Abel team had placed major reliance on the Canadian sector of their campaign. But in general, Sefton acknowledged that his friendship for Burke and Molony, rather than his concern for Abel, had determined his position in the campaign. Nevertheless if McDonald had arrived in Canada earlier and had delivered the same sort of attack on Sefton as he had in his blitz the last day of the campaign, a Sefton counterattack would undoubtedly have aroused greater participation in District 6 for the Abel ticket. "The Communists in Hamilton went for him only because they opposed me," observed Sefton. "They had fought me for my support of the New Party. I had a Socialist orientation, but to McDonald this was all one and the same thing with Communism. He was ready to go for Communist votes. McDonald simply had no understanding of politics in the world. He simply refused to accept the distinction between Socialists and Communists. In fact," said Sefton broadening his political brush, "I think nowhere in the world is there such a lack of political sophistication as in certain sections of the labor movement of the United States."

At any rate, despite their supposed political awareness, the Canadian steelworkers did not seem caught up in the election campaign of their own international union. They considered the international election essentially a fight between Americans. The average union member, observed Murray Cotterill, the public-relations director for the Canadian Steelworkers, is primarily interested in his union at the local level. His major concern is with his local union officers. His next level of interest would be in his district officers.

As staff public-relations man, Cotterill not only concerned himself with the chores of publicity, but over the years—especially since his association with the union was based on commitment rather than merely on technical competence—he played the role of the staff intellectual and "candid friend."

"I've always tried to follow one rule," said Cotterill. "I've always tried to follow the ancient Roman policy with our directors. In ancient times, I am told, a member of the Praetorian Guard, placed beside the emperor especially during a victory parade, was instructed to repeat to him at frequent intervals: 'Remember, O Caesar, thou art not a god.' In all events, the truth happens to be that the vast majority of our members in Canada aren't quite sure whether the USWA is a national or an international union. Their local union fights mean much more to them than the great high-level contests the newspapers play up. That's why the Canadian participation, though important to the outcome of the international election, was comparatively meager."

CHAPTER 18

Negro Workers in the Election

Lift your hidden faces
Ye who wept and prayed,
Leave your covert places
Ye who were afraid.

FRENCH CAROL

From its start, the United Steelworkers had placed considerable emphasis on the importance of civil rights in and outside the labor movement. Aside from the question of public policy, the practical fact facing an industrial union like the Steelworkers was the heavy proportion of Negro membership, perhaps about 16 per cent of the total. The union kept no breakdown of workers by color or nationality. Black workers were concentrated at higher percentages in the South, the Chicago-Gary area, Youngstown, Buffalo, and Baltimore. Almost as a matter of course, strong civil rights resolutions were passed unanimously at conventions and conferences. But now black workers had become restive with what they regarded as merely verbal recognition.

Despite the push for integrated seniority lines in the plants, few Negroes had yet won their way into the higher-paying brackets. Over the years, to be sure, the union had brought about an appreciable difference to the lives of Negro workers. In the Lackawanna, New York, plant of Bethlehem Steel, a Negro open-hearth worker one day recalled the years he had waited before being advanced from the semiskilled sector to a better-paid skilled job for which he had long been qualified. Only, he said, when the union had applied pressure had he been given the job and the pay his skill entitled him to: "For a long time around here management pissed in our ear and told us it was raining—until the union came along." He was unusually fortunate. The average black worker was still kept well down on the ladder.

Equally lacking was adequate representation of Negroes at various levels of union government. Of the approximately eight hundred staff representatives in 1964–65, only about twenty-three or twenty-four were Negroes. Over the years, whites had accepted Negroes as fellow members, but because of application of the Wagner and Taft-Hartley laws rather than the growth of genuine understanding and mutual regard. Now, when the election campaign began, the managers in both the McDonald and Abel headquarters became keenly aware of the strategic importance the nonwhite union members could play.

Months before, the competition for Negro support had become an essential part of the campaign, and a sizable group of Negro delegates to the 1964 convention had gathered to discuss more effective approaches to problems facing the Negro membership. Earlier, at the Democratic convention in August 1964, Alex Fuller, a Negro leader in District 29 (Detroit) and a vice-president of the Wayne County AFL-CIO Council, and Director Charles Younglove of District 29 met with McDonald. They told him he was "in trouble." McDonald replied reassuringly: "When you're president of a large union like ours, you're bound to have some problems." McDonald, preoccupied with national politics, refused to pursue the matter.

At the Steelworkers convention in Atlantic City a few weeks later, Fuller and some of his fellow Negro delegates convened an Ad Hoc Committee to draft some proposals to McDonald "indicating some concerns of the Negro membership." * McDonald met with the group's representatives and promised to call a meeting "before long" of the union's Civil Rights Committee. Such a meeting was not called.

In November, the Ad Hoc Committee had met in Detroit. Their stated purpose was to win for Negro steelworkers "more consideration": advancement to the international executive board, full integration within the districts, reorganization of the union's Civil Rights Committee.

The group endorsed Abel by a substantial margin. Following adjournment, "certain McDonald people," said Fuller, "began to 'work out' on members of the Ad Hoc Committee." Since Pittsburgh was the center of precontract discussions, many of those who had attended the Ad Hoc Committee meeting were now invited to "face President McDonald to convince them to 'stick with McDonald.'" The chief escort of the erring brethren into the presidential presence was Ernest Clifford, a strong McDonald advocate and a Negro, who had been made a full-time staff

---

* Among the delegates were W. A. Davis of Buffalo as temporary chairman, Aaron Jackson as temporary secretary, Tom Johnson from Alabama, Rayfield Mooty from Chicago, Curtis Strong from Gary, and Hughes Anderson from Youngstown, Griffin's district.

member of the union's Civil Rights Committee, and then, in the campaign's closing days, "Assistant to the President."

The Steelworkers Union was especially sensitive to the race issue because of the entrance by Governor George C. Wallace of Alabama in the spring Democratic primaries in 1964. Wallace scored heavily in various steel centers in the North, such as Gary and Baltimore. This development clearly indicated that division between Negroes and whites was serious enough to promise trouble in the union as in the nation. Negroes would obviously react sharply against any candidate suspected of racial discrimination. A rumor or a hint was quite enough. At the same time the issue could cut the other way: a candidate's preoccupation with civil rights could be used against him among the white workers. An adroit campaigner could make it appear that he was unenthusiastic about civil rights in one district and a dedicated advocate in another. Officially, the union's commitment against racial discrimination was clear. But the rhetoric of racial justice, a staple of convention reports and oratory, was a considerable distance from the reality of broadening the participation of minority groups—not only Negroes but also Mexican-Americans—in the life of the union and its decision-making process.

In 1960 the pressure of the Negro workers had clearly expressed itself in the first convention of the Negro American Labor Council, headed by A. Philip Randolph, president of the Sleeping Car Porters and a vice-president of the AFL-CIO. Prominent at that 1960 meeting were Walter P. Reuther and I. W. Abel. McDonald had turned down an invitation to attend. Thus long before his campaign for the union presidency, Abel had identified himself with the Negro demands for wider recognition in the labor movement.

But during the election campaign, Abel found himself tagged with the charge of racial discrimination. Furious that he should have to prove his consistency in the field of racial attitudes, Abel sent Joe Germano a memorandum specifying his personal position over the years:

When I was made director in February 1942, the first individual I put on my staff was Jim Mason . . . one of the Republic Steel strikers in Canton in 1937. . . . He served the district in the capacity of organizer, negotiator, administrator, and for many years up to his retirement served as District treasurer of our District COPE. . . . I had another Negro staff representative, Ellison Jeffries, in the Columbus sub-region. Later I persuaded Director Albert Whitehouse to give Sam Stokes an opportunity on his staff in Cincinnati. . . . In 1962 Dorothy Grant, who had worked in the Canton district office for years, was brought to the union's Pittsburgh office.

But Abel's denial not only failed to win over Negro support but also alienated some white supporters who had hoped to identify him with their own racist attitudes.

As the campaign got under way, Jim Griffin as McDonald's manager added a number of Negroes to his district staff. At the start, the Negro membership had reacted no differently from white steelworkers; they were for Abel or for McDonald, or indifferent to both. But as the campaign grew hot, overt racial propaganda began to take effect. Abel people, such as Nick Zonarich, found that many of the McDonald people were operating under few if any inhibitions in raising the race issue, with Vice-President Howard Hague in charge of its exploitation.

Word of the use of racial issues came from Alabama and Tennessee. One staff representative, Horace Brock, from the large aluminum local in Tennessee, and Cecil Robertson from Gadsden, Alabama, raised the alarm that the racial issue was hurting Abel in areas where he normally expected considerable strength. Because of Zonarich's close relations with the aluminum locals, he went on his own to see his friend Eugene Calhoun, a Negro staff representative in Birmingham. Years before, Zonarich had been instrumental in having him appointed staff representative. Calhoun, wearing a McDonald button in his lapel, greeted Zonarich cordially.

"I understand," said Zonarich, "they're swinging with Dave McDonald." Calhoun said: "That's right. I've made a lot of meetings. I have been going night and day for the last few weeks, telling my friends to vote for McDonald. I'm told this fellow Abel is anti-Negro. I've got my people believing it." How did Calhoun come to this belief? Calhoun told of a staff meeting in the office of the district director, then R. E. Farr. "We were told that Abel was anti-Negro and a Ku Kluxer. And you know how my people feel when you tell them he's a Wallace supporter."

By this time, the civil rights agitation in Alabama and the South generally had been reaching new degrees of tension. The rumbles of January and February 1965 were a prelude to the march on Selma. Governor Wallace was challenging Dr. Martin Luther King, Jr. The Negro steelworker's sense of identity was involved and it was not difficult for him to accept what was so easy to believe. What lent further credence to the charge against Abel was the announcement by John Nichols, a steelworker appointed by Wallace as an assistant to the state Secretary of Labor, that he was supporting Abel. When Nichols announced his support, the McDonald campaigners quickly made banner-headline use of his Wallace connection, in the North.

To counteract McDonald's cultivation of the Negro membership through a mixture of racial suspicion and diverse entertainments, the Abel supporters had early given high visibility to Negro leaders. Alex Fuller was advertised as the No. 2 man in the management of the Abel campaign, Germano being No. 1. In addition, James (Jimmy) Jones, an international representative of Philadelphia, widely known in liberal circles and in Americans for Democratic Action, came out in support of the Abel ticket. For years, Jones had been associated with McDonald but had become increasingly disaffected. Aware of Jones's attitude, Zonarich had told Calhoun: "I don't want you to believe me. I'm going to have Jimmy Jones call you." But reassurance from Jones in Abel's behalf came too late. Calhoun said helplessly, "How could I, after campaigning for McDonald among my people, go back to tell 'em that I did the wrong thing? They'd cut my throat." In remorse, Calhoun told Jones: "They've made me call meetings of the Negro people—the director and the staff, they made me call meetings. We accused Secretary-Treasurer Abel of being anti-Negro and that he's George Wallace's man . . . and that the Ku Kluxers down here are supporting him. [The Negroes] are going to vote 100 per cent against Mr. Abel." Continuing his soundings, Jones called Joe Neal, a Negro staff representative in District 8 in Baltimore, and found the same situation developing there.

Now Jones decided to come on strong for Abel. At Coatesville, Pennsylvania, he found Ernest Clifford, McDonald's Negro "assistant," busily occupied among black voters. "He was sent in," said Jones, "by Howard Hague to Philadelphia while I was still neutral. . . . He carried money with him to various meetings to talk to people and buy these people off in one way or another and spread this hate business. And this man was a member of the union's Civil Rights Committee!

"I blame a lot of this on me. If I had come out campaigning openly early for Abel it could have been different. . . . But I was a so-called loyal guy. . . . Hugh Carcella, the district director, practically double-crossed me. That guy used to sit and talk with tears in his eyes and tell me that he knew Abel was the best man and he would say, 'God only knows what would happen to this union if it wasn't for a guy in headquarters like Abel that we could depend on.' Then Carcella went to Pittsburgh and saw Hague, not Abel. Then he came back and put the pressure on me to go for McDonald. I said to him: 'No I won't do it.' The guy then began to pull some of the dirtiest campaign tricks. Had I come out early in the campaign, the vote of District 7 would have been completely different."

Under normal conditions, Jones did not believe that the McDonald people would have bothered to cultivate Nathaniel Lee, the Negro nominated for international teller on the McDonald slate, or Hershel Donald, who was in charge of "Negro affairs" for the campaign committee. Over the years, Lee had been anti-McDonald, like Griffin, his district director. Lee and Donald were used in areas of heavy Negro concentration, like Molony's Buffalo district and Germano's Gary-Chicago district.

Lee's presence on the ticket was the first time, Jones said, that Negro steelworkers had a real chance to "vote for one of their own."

Clear evidence of Abel's public and private attitudes was not sufficient to refute racist attacks against him. In District 26, no Negro staff man had been appointed for six years prior to the campaign. Griffin now appointed Negro staff men, one from Republic Steel, another from Youngstown Sheet & Tube, and a Negro secretary was added to the Warren subdistrict office.

In District 29, covering the Detroit area, a strong committee of more than fifty of Abel's Negro supporters was headed by Floyd Chambers. Key people were assigned to nearly every sizable department in the big mills. Others were given jobs of persuasion in their home locals; to get out the vote and to see that literature, buttons, and printed slates were distributed in and around locals and in plants where the voting was conducted on the premises.

Alex Fuller explained the process of persuasion. Staff representatives would call on members they had served, confident that they would be listened to with respect: "Down through the years you help a lot of people, so you ask if they will give a few hours toward the campaign. We just asked them. We had some chaps who asked what we were paying— the Jimmy Higgins type of volunteer for the cause is dead!—but our position was that we had no money. If we caught Negroes who seemed as if they wanted to be bought, we shamed them. We said the work they would be doing would help them for a long time to come. The response turned out good in our district. Of course, a staff representative has a special relation to people. He gets involved in grievance procedure. Many times when they win grievances, people get reinstated. This is appreciated. Their contact is close."

Moreover, in Fuller's opinion, "Dave did it to himself. On the Negro issue, Dave was always difficult to get to—until the campaign began and the Negro votes were needed." Through tradition, the union had built up a hierarchy of leadership dominated for a long time largely by Irish Roman Catholics. While Philip Murray was often heard to say that he would not let the Church "meddle" in his union, many of his associates often made use of the religious factor whenever it was politically expedient. In short, the feeling had grown that the leadership elite was largely confined to a single religious and ethnic sector of the union.

On one visit to Alabama, Joe Molony discovered that something new was being added. He was asked, "Is it true that you're going to let this fellow Abel, who is Jewish, head up the union?" Molony patiently pointed out that Abel was not Jewish; that he was of part Welsh and part German descent. But Hague's political brew had become more potent. In his speeches in Birmingham and Gadsden, Alabama, only a handful of Negroes attended his meetings. Molony had begun a routine campaign speech designed frankly, as he said, to win votes rather than fight causes:

"You know, we have a wonderful vocabulary of accommodation, compromise, and all that. But there are certain things, God damn it, we must draw the line at. So I'm standing on the platform bellowing away at the troops. I'm talking to an exclusively white audience. A few Negroes were sitting on the curb, just out of curiosity, I guess. In the midst of uttering a whole string of clichés, I said to myself: 'What the hell am I doing? I'm down here in Alabama and I'm addressing what obviously is a Goddamn Ku Klux audience. This is not the kind of speech I deliver to steelworkers in Pittsburgh or in Buffalo. I'll make a civil-rights speech.' I then told them that we looked to them perhaps to give us leadership in the North and I prayed that they would find a solution to the race problem even before we did in the North. I said: 'I know that you are the victims of your culture and your background and your history. Well, you've got to change. You're members of the United Steelworkers. You address each other as brothers; we're the only institution—the trade unions—that call each other brother. Oh, the Communists call each other comrade, but we call each other brother and sister. And you'd better start calling these good people, your brother members of this union, you've got to start calling them brother after you leave this hall.' And they sat there stony, stolid, and silent. After the meeting, three or four of the local leaders, obviously shocked, said to me: 'Joe, you're not going to get no God-damn votes down here speaking out for Nigras.' I told him: 'Look, I want to be elected vice-president of this international union very badly. I don't want to do anything to hurt my friend Abel and my friend Burke, but I just have to be true to myself. I cannot avoid mentioning the race situation whether I'm in Pennsylvania or in Alabama. If this is going to beat us, so be it; I don't give a good God damn.' I'm afraid I cost Abel and Burke some votes down there, but I'm glad I did it."

Abel was thus caught in a two-way squeeze: to some whites in the South he was viewed as pro-Negro as well as anti-establishment; for the Negro he had been tabbed a Ku Kluxer. Alex Fuller said: "The McDonald supporters used a two-edged sword. This is a vicious game. This was an exercise in democracy I shan't forget for my lifetime. But it takes a lot out of you. Abe didn't get shaken until the last few days. He became upset when he saw Dave pulling every trick in the bag. Aside from the visits to officials in Washington, they sought to get the NAACP involved. I talked to Herbert Hill, the NAACP's Labor Secretary, and told him to stay out of this. Hill told Roy Wilkins, NAACP's General Secretary, 'We've been approached by a Congressman wanting you to say something to the right people on behalf of McDonald, we have friends in both camps plus the fact that McDonald forces have really done nothing for us in this area.' "

On the McDonald side, Griffin found himself in a tough fight to retain his directorship in the Youngstown district against Russell Thomas, the

Abel-backed contender, a subdistrict director of no particular distinction.

Here the racial issue was clearly in the open. Oliver Montgomery, president of the area chapter of the Negro American Labor Council, charged Griffin with being anti-Negro and with failure to hire a regular Negro staff member since he was elected director in 1947. To this charge, Nathaniel Lee, the McDonald candidate for international teller and long a leader of the state NAACP, issued an indignant denial. Griffin, he said, was a proved friend of the Negro whereas Thomas had never belonged to the NAACP. Disregarding Lee's response, the Negro American Labor Council group in Ohio urged the election of Thomas. In evaluating the situation later on, Griffin said that Abel benefited by a white backlash. Griffin believed that when he hired two Negro staff people during the campaign, he lost more white votes than he gained black ones. Political bookkeeping of that sort is hard to audit.

In Canton, Ohio, one local McDonald leader, Al Lebbano, described how "volunteers" were working inside District 27, headed by Johnny Johns, a strong pro-Abel man. He reported that John Green, the president of the Ohio NAACP, "is using his committee plus contacting NAACP chapters throughout the state in various locals with Negroes. He and Nathaniel Lee are working on them locals down there, in Abe's old district. I'd like to get Dave here if only for one hour." Lebbano informed Griffin that he would be "the Charlie McCarthy so as to keep Dave in the clear as he is staying away from dirty campaigning. I'll bring out the dirt on Abe. *Compre?* . . . Some rumors are really getting around (I don't know how they started): Abe is strike-happy, living in the past, and he will keep men out in the streets all the time. . . . We are also pounding the fact that Abe praised Dave all these years while working shoulder to shoulder with Dave, and now he says he is all wrong."

More comprehensively, the McDonald campaign among the Negro membership was analyzed by Hershel Donald, a member of the staff of Eugene Maurice, director of District 13:

The first broad examination of Negro attitudes and reactions to the McDonald versus Abel contest revealed the following: More than 90 per cent of all Negro employees of the International and district staff favored Abel and had already made their commitments. Percentage of local union officers was equally high.

The job was therefore to overcome the tremendous influence of these people who represented the major power structure in the United Steelworkers of America among the Negroes and significantly the interested public that believed them—not an easy task.

My plan was to completely remove civil rights from the campaign as a major issue and reintroduce it in selective areas where it could have its most effective impact. For example, in the heavily industrial area of Gary and East Chicago, Indiana, where George Wallace had unbelievable success with the white and Spanish steelworkers in the 1964 Democratic primary, and where McDonald's strongest support was coming from some of the same people because of their anti-Germano feelings. Bread-and-butter issues produced the best results.

By way of contrast, Buffalo had a more militant, progressive and progress-conscious Negro Steelworkers representative with a less militant-type white steelworker. We therefore flooded this area with both types of literature, with a full-page ad covering civil rights and two appearances by Nathaniel Lee. The results in both areas were better than expected, using this same basis in providing an incentive and motive for our ticket.

Donald's plan of operation among Negroes had been promptly approved by Stephen Wexler and Ross Thomas of McDonald's publicity bureau. But after the first three weeks of the campaign, Donald was "completely out of touch with any overall strategy." With the arrival of Joe Angelo, the subdistrict director from California, at the Pittsburgh headquarters, Donald still claimed that he was able "to eliminate or neutralize all known opposition" to McDonald among the black steelworkers in the five districts clustered in the Pittsburgh area. But he was worried that money was becoming a status symbol and who got how much became a problem. In the later weeks of the campaign, Angelo directed Donald and Lee to concentrate their resources on districts headed by anti-McDonald directors—in Buffalo (District 4), in Chicago (District 31), in Cleveland (District 28), in Detroit (District 29), and in western Canada (District 6).

On his return to headquarters, Donald found that Angelo was overburdened with responsibilities. Negro affairs were "of no particular concern to anyone in the office." This attitude was, he was certain, not one of "disrespect or deliberate indifference." Some time, money, and attention, he said, and a "few common courtesies" might have avoided several difficult situations. Donald did not elaborate, but later sent out a private letter to Negro coworkers deploring the lack of Negro "growth" in the Steelworkers Union. He addressed himself to a consideration of the reasons.

"The greatest single enemy to equal distribution of job opportunities for Negroes is his indifference to the affairs of his local union," Donald noted. He acknowledged that the Negro's minority position accounts, in part, for his indifference. But this lack of interest, he said, makes the black worker "a target for collusion between the local union officers and management." Tied to this condition is the fact that the local union's power structure was, with token exceptions, white. This combination of white local leadership and white management limits the "growth potential" of the often unsuspecting Negro workers. As a consequence, white local union officers were regularly re-elected. On the district level, Donald deplored the reluctance of directors to hire Negro staff people who might stimulate greater Negro motivation and as a consequence might even evoke hostile reaction from whites.

Baltimore provided an example of how McDonald's supporters had, in Donald's words, reintroduced civil rights in selective areas. In late January, McDonald and Abel spoke in the same union hall a week apart. Whereas between 450 and 500 Negroes appeared at McDonald's meeting, a week later fewer than fifty showed up for Abel's meeting. Half the Negro community leaders who originally had accepted an invitation to lunch with Abel the day of the meeting failed to appear. A Negro leader whose organization sometimes received financial contributions from the district organization later explained that Albert Atallah, the district director, had "advised" him not to.

At about the same time, Abel and McDonald moved into the Southern district. Accompanied by Zonarich, once chairman of the aluminum workers' negotiating committee, Abel made a series of speeches in the aluminum area of eastern Tennessee. Alcoa Local 309, at Maryville, near Knoxville, had nominated Abel by three to one, so this was considered Abel territory. But between the time of the nomination and the vote, two months of speechifying, campaign activity, infighting, and intensive entertaining by McDonald representatives served to alter attitudes of the membership.

In Alabama, the Abel and McDonald appearances overlapped. "With jutting jaw and confident smile," reported the Birmingham News, McDonald announced, "I shall be elected." Essaying the role of the betrayed and disillusioned man, McDonald said, "There is no bitterness on my part. I'm hurt that a man whom I considered a friend would do this to me." McDonald scoffed at Abel's accusations that he was a "tuxedo president" out of touch with the rank and file ("Would you wear a pair of overalls to the White House?" he asked) and that he was not sufficiently active in unionizing nonunion fabricating plants in the South. "I've passed plenty of handbills down here," McDonald claimed. "Why doesn't Abel come down here and do it too?" At that point, he glowingly described the "breakthrough" in the Alan Wood Steel agreement, which he reported had been approved by employer and union "except for some technical details." "How does that sound to you fellows?" cried McDonald. "You can't beat it, Daddy," came the happy response.

Abel, McDonald said, "had Pearl Harbored me. . . . He loved me in September and hated me in December." To counteract the "tuxedo" charge, some of McDonald's associates now distributed handbills with the picture of Abel himself wearing a tuxedo! Ross Thomas, McDonald's public-relations man, had unearthed a photo taken in 1958 at a party given by the union at the Touchdown Club in Washington, at which McDonald's close associate Frank N. (Nordy) Hoffmann, the Steel-workers legislative and political director, was host. The original photo shows a group of about thirty men dressed in dinner jackets, government labor-relations men, Congressmen, the then Senator Hubert Humphrey, and McDonald and Abel. McDonald and Humphrey were cropped from the photo, and the part with Abel in it appeared in the photo reproduced in the McDonald campaign literature.

This "cropping job" was one of a series of misrepresentations to come out of the McDonald camp. It certainly revealed, however, that Abel on occasion also wore a tuxedo! Trading blows, Abel said: "My worthy opponent says he feels he has been 'Pearl-Harbored' by me and my fellow candidates. The only way this could have happened is that he and his associates were goofing off and not doing their job."

CHAPTER 19

Two Weeks to Go

Now is the time approaching,
By prophets long foretold.

JANE LAURIE BORTHWICK

Aliquippa, northwest of Pittsburgh, was hard-core country for the Abel forces. This was the domain of the Jones & Laughlin Steel Company and the union's historic cradle—the Valley Forge of the union's bitter struggle for recognition in the late 1930s. The district was now headed by Kay Kluz, a McDonald director under great obligation to the chief who had approved him as acting director and seen him through several legal challenges. The Abel team was therefore bucking the district organization and the majority of its staff representatives. Nevertheless, the district had nursed strong islands of dissent, skepticism, and dues protest. Many of the local leaders, veterans of union struggles, often acted as if they had the right to ask questions of those they chose and paid to lead them. When Walter Burke arrived, he fully expected to be greeted with sharp if not entirely hostile questions. They came at once. How was it that Abel, Molony, and Germano, who had quite recently said such flattering things about "the leader," were now seeking to throw him out?

It was a question that deserved and required a careful answer: "This campaign, this crusade, has been brewing for some time. We had to be sure that we had a candidate in whom we could repose great trust and confidence, with whom we, directors and staff, could go to the membership and win. . . . When you involve any of the elected officers or board members in such a contest, you have a very agonizing decision to make. They have to lay their jobs on the line. You cannot run for the job you hold and for the one you'd like to have. So you have a decision to make. I. W. Abel made that decision. . . .

"This has turned out to be a rather nasty campaign. Had it not been for stabilizing and dedicated efforts of I. W. Abel in recent years, meeting with local people and discussing their problems with them, this union would be further along the road to pot than it is today. While McDonald was resting at his golf course home in Palm Springs and celebrating in posh nightclubs in New York and San Francisco and elsewhere, I. W. Abel was out attending district conferences and discussing our members' problems with them. . . .

"This is the first time in the history of this union you dues-paying members have had the chance to vote for a slate of officers who come from the ranks of the Steelworkers—no clerks, no errand boys, no henchmen, but people who know what it is to work with their hands, who contributed on the picket line, not in an office somewhere to the early successful struggles of this union. With all respect to the late Phil Murray, he and his associates who founded this union came from the Mine Workers . . . but they were mineworkers, not steelworkers.

"It's ridiculous for McDonald to say that up until this campaign all members of the Executive Board agreed implicitly with him and a voice was never raised against any of his plans and policies. This is not true. We argued and fought our case and our cause. When the decisions were made, true, we went along with the majority. The time has arrived when we can no longer go along."

Replying to McDonald's charge that the election of Abel would inevitably mean a strike, Burke called it a "damnable shame for the union president running around the country, in the press and on radio and TV, assuring the corporations that 'there won't be a strike if you elect McDonald.' The fact is that nobody at this stage knows whether there is going to be a strike or not. I. W. Abel and Dave McDonald are not going to decide this alone. We're going to let the membership through their chosen representatives decide it. Like anyone else with common sense, we will do every possible thing to avoid a strike and at the same time negotiate an equitable and decent agreement that you can live with. For a change, the contract will be signed by all the local union representatives and all the staff members responsible for negotiating that contract. It will not be foisted on you."

Tom Murray, the bald, round-faced assistant secretary-treasurer accompanied Burke to Aliquippa. A man of wide-reaching and intellectual curiosity, he had hovered over the details of the union's financial organization almost from its formation. He was the prototype of the union civil servant, a permanent undersecretary. His background in internal matters, his flair for language, and his inscrutability won him a special place inside the union. With the launching of the Abel-Burke-Molony campaign, Murray became its treasurer. Although McDonald's original prospectus held out the possibility of a certain modernizing of the union's organization, Murray was one of those who measured the vast distance that remained between flackery and actuality. He had fretted but remained loyal. He had been concerned about the expenditure of huge sums without commensurate return to the union and the membership. When the decision was made to mount a campaign against McDonald, Tom Murray's support was considered a resource of considerable importance. As Abel's assistant, he understood, better than almost anyone else, the fantastic war of nerves that McDonald and Hague had been carrying on against Abel.

Often Murray suspected that McDonald was pleased to see him "get the hell out" of the way for a period of weeks. As long as the diligent Murray remained at headquarters, he stood like a permanent, immovable, usually silent rebuke.

When Murray spoke for the Abel ticket, his opposition to McDonald provided the staff with reassurance of continuity. For them, Murray was "Pittsburgh." When Murray accompanied Burke into District 20, "enemy" territory, he found the text for his speech in the threat McDonald had made in Baltimore to fire Abel and all those supporting him, after his re-election.

"I would like to feel," Murray told the Aliquippa audience, "that I am very high on Mr. McDonald's list. He should know, however, that the union's Constitution would prevent him from doing that. This talk of 'firing' is familiar talk to people who have lived for years in these valleys around the Ohio River. McDonald talks like a boss. When he gets irritated or frustrated, he doesn't think, act, or talk like a union man. He's always going to fire somebody."

McDonald did not attempt to create trepidation among the companies he dealt with, Murray said, "but he uses fear against everybody else." Murray pointed out that the staff men who in recent months had organized a union had initially favored McDonald and feared for their jobs if Abel should be elected. "It's hard to believe that our whole staff could have been mistaken about whom they should fear. But they were made fearful and that's what started the staff men's organization going."

Now some of the district talent arose. Tony Rinaldi, head of the Armco Steel Local 1360, identified himself as one of "those frustrated local presidents that have gone home from negotiations a couple of times with our tails between our legs, in 1962 and 1963." As a member of the international's Wage Policy Committee, he said he was wise to the ways of the union. "McDonald was going to make the committee 'well traveled.' That means he'll spend all the God-damn money he can on our expenses. Well, we'll take it, but that doesn't mean he is going to get our vote." Another president, Scotty McGarry of the large U.S. Steel-American Bridge local, then cheerfully saluted all those in attendance as "fellow rebels and disloyal people. . . . I have been castigated up and down the district because I had the temerity to go to my district director and tell him that I personally was for Mr. Abel. So, I'm called a traitor, a Judas, and many other things."

The acrimonious atmosphere in the plants was described by Jerry Beck, a staff representative in District 20, who bucked Director Kluz by supporting Abel: "Active people like Abel are facing all kinds of arguments in the plants. In some local unions, pro-McDonald officers are throwing money around like it was going out of style." "Those of you who have come here tonight are not to be questioned as to where you stand," declared Michael Zahorsky, the grizzled organizer of the meeting. "I was at the mill gates yesterday and this morning. . . . One fellow said: 'God damn it, Mike, I never voted for anybody, but God damn you, I like your position. You let us know where you stand. And we love you.' " Confidence in Zahorsky, the local leader, became a vote for Abel.

From Chicago headquarters, Joe Germano now issued a warning letter: "The McDonald-Griffin team are getting increasingly dirty. In the next two weeks, they will be throwing the book at us. They have a lot of money and will be financing committees in local unions throughout our union. That makes it imperative that you have your people active and that you see to it that your handbills be at plant gates at least as often as the McDonald forces, preferably more frequently. . . . If you find foremen in your plant who are cooperating in a whispering campaign against Abel, trace it back to the source and call the companies involved."

Just at this stage, new tensions arose when the can manufacturing negotiations broke off. Management spokesmen for Continental Can and American Can blamed the union's "internal situation" for complicating the contract discussions. McDonald had hoped to exploit the news of a "record contract" to be reached before the election as further evidence of his ability to deliver. And James Robb and Al Whitehouse, the directors in charge of the negotiations, angry and frustrated—the latter especially, because of his need to establish himself as a visible candidate—heaped the blame for the recess on Abel. "Forces supporting Mr. Abel have deliberately attempted to prevent an agreement from being reached," they said. "They have gone so far as to threaten company representatives with reprisals at the local level if the companies should go forward in a good-faith effort to conclude a prompt, peaceful agreement." At a news conference, a pro-Abel leader, Ray Blasky, president of American Can Local 4453 in Milwaukee and a member of the negotiating committee, promptly challenged the Whitehouse-Robb allegations (the *Wall Street*

Journal, January 27, 1965). "Why didn't you tell the bargaining committee about those threats, if there were any?" he shouted. Whitehouse made no reply. Blasky's outburst set off a shouting match between Abel and McDonald committeemen.

"Supporters of ours have been excluded from the can negotiations," Abel said. "None of them has been in touch with representatives of the can companies. Therefore, they could not have resorted to threats of any kind as alleged by Mr. Robb and Mr. Whitehouse. Let me say further that if company representatives stooped to such tactics as the McDonald forces have resorted to, our union would be quick to bring unfair labor practice charges against them."

Abel nevertheless saw an advantage in the postponement of the can negotiations: "Ramrodding through a settlement which would not be acceptable to the rank-and-file members of our union could have led to local-level turbulence, and this the more responsible representatives of both union and management always want to avoid. The situation parallels that in steel. Negotiations have been recessed while members of our union are about to exercise their democratic privilege of choosing international leaders they feel more nearly represent their views and desires. This is a family matter and should be of no concern outside of our union."

In both basic steel and the can industry, therefore, where multi-employer bargaining was involved, the employers were now feeling the pressures of the campaign. Thus McDonald was unable to benefit from negotiations that, if concluded before the election, might have redounded to his political advantage. In contrast, the Alan Wood Steel agreement affecting a single company, though still "tentative," could be claimed as a positive accomplishment in the field of "total job security."

Abel's continued effort to maintain the position that the election was a "family affair" seemed unrealistic and rigid even to some of his advisers. His rejection of various invitations to debate with McDonald had only resulted in increased radio and TV exposure for the incumbent.

The orchestration of the McDonald public-relations campaign was now in full crescendo. At this time the North American Newspaper Alliance distributed two long Sunday-feature pieces by Vera Glaser on David and Rosemary McDonald. Picking up a McDonald theme, the Glaser piece reported that the "cries of possible fraud have set the White House, Labor and Justice Departments to mulling over the advisability of detaching personnel from the Office of Labor-Management Reports and the Federal Bureau of Investigation to polling places to insure an honest count." Since the "cries" of fraud had been raised only by the McDonald side—as early as December 19, shortly after the results of the local nominations showed him trailing Abel—the finger of suspicion was pointed at Abel and his associates.

In interviews with the "stockily built, friendly" Abel and the "white-haired, handsome McDonald, youthful, articulate, flamboyant," Mrs. Glaser attributed Abel's confident bearing to his superior standing in the local nominations. Abel had enumerated to her the districts he would carry and whose directors had announced their support for him. McDonald snorted at Abel's claims: "The only way district directors could possibly deliver the votes of the local would be by stealing," he told Mrs. Glaser. Abel's comment was: "There is always a chance of fraud and we will be on the lookout for it," adding that the "Landrum-Griffin Law carries stiff penalties for union voting irregularities."

The possibility of voting frauds was very much on the mind of Monsignor Charles Owen Rice, who described in the Pittsburgh *Catholic* how voting frauds might be perpetrated:

A printing firm [the Cornelius Printing Company, the official union printer] will send each local enough USWA ballots to cover its membership, together with an extra supply. Ballots are not numbered, making it relatively easy to sweeten the count with unused ballots. As each union member enters the polling place, identifies himself and shows his badge, he is given a ballot and his name is checked off the membership list. At the end of the day the ballots are counted and totals for each candidate entered on a tally sheet which is mailed to Pittsburgh. It is simple to doctor the final figure. Merely adding a "1" after 324 would lift the vote to 3,241. The entire membership of a local rarely turns out to vote. What becomes of the unused ballots? A few people working quietly . . . in a back room can and have marked them for members who didn't show up. On election day, district directors are in constant touch with their locals. Excess votes can be shifted from one local to another if needed to swing the vote. An official can "forget" to sign the tally sheet, seal it properly, or mail it by the required deadline.

Such a blueprint for electoral skulduggery, which Monsignor Rice described to Mrs. Glaser, was not an act of pure imagination. It had its roots in observation of the Steelworkers elections of 1955 and 1957. The reporter, however, seemed unaware of the charges of election fraud that had been raised when Howard Hague, and then McDonald himself, in full control of the election machinery, had been declared the winners in those other elections.

At this time, McDonald was working over District 38, headed by Charles Smith, while Abel, Burke, and Molony were back in Buffalo, Molony's home district. Despite considerable publicity, there was no crowd in the ballroom of the Buffalo Statler. Directing himself to the "younger union members," Molony scoffed at charges of a power struggle. In June 1964, he noted, more than three thousand Steelworkers local unions had held their triennial elections of officers. McDonald, he said, had cheered the "wonderful demonstration to see thousands of locals conducting elections." Thirty per cent of the local officers were replaced by new officers. But, said Molony, "McDonald's view now is: 'When somebody runs against an incumbent in a local union, that's democracy, but when someone runs against McDonald, this is a power struggle and will ruin the union.' Well, we don't believe you have to wait for someone to retire or die to run for international office in the United Steelworkers."

Germano, when he rose to speak, revealed the rash of irritation with McDonald from which had spread a whole series of decisions. He recalled when the first decision about McDonald was made. Early in 1964 at a nonferrous industry meeting in Pueblo, Colorado, he and Molony had determined that the time was ripe to enact a retirement provision in the constitution. Then he recalled how McDonald, displeased with "retirement" talk coming out of Districts 4 and 31, took steps to keep their delegations far apart at the September 1964 convention, by seating them against opposite walls of the huge Atlantic City Auditorium: "It would take Molony and his delegates and Germano and his delegates at least a half an hour before they'd get over there to contact one another. Then, of course, there was intimidation, coercion and the harassment down on the Boardwalk," during the convention.

"Now I am told: 'All these years you were a friend of McDonald and now you are supporting Abel.' Yes, I've been a friend of McDonald and a friend of Abel too. But my first obligation is not to any friend but to the 115,000 members I have the privilege to represent in District 31. . . . We are not supporting Abel, Molony, and Burke just because we want opposition to McDonald; we're supporting them because we think the membership of this great organization is entitled to something different."

Abel's own tone had become sharper: "Drift and destruction have been growing with this union of ours. . . . We need to restore collective bargaining to its rightful place—the collective bargaining table—and take it out of the plush hotel suites, the country clubs, and the businessmen's clubs and place it back in the hands of elected representatives of the membership. . . . We'll take it away from this palace guard that has surrounded the 'crown prince' and have been making decisions as to what's good, bad, or indifferent."

He bore down hard on "the great conspiracy, joined by the representatives of the steel industry and spokesmen and associates of the McDonald team—a conspiracy of pure propaganda. It was designed to make the membership and the general public believe that if I should be elected, then the union membership and the basic steel communities will be plagued with great unrest and strikes and hardship."

Abel cited evidence of management interference in Baltimore: at least six steelworkers had informed him that their superintendent at a Bethlehem Steel plant had called them in because they were wearing Abel buttons.

Once again Abel contrasted the difference between the background of McDonald and Hague and that of Molony, Burke and himself. "We three," he said, "as steelworkers have engaged in strikes. We have gone without pay. We have walked the picket lines. We've got involved in some of the scuffles. We know something about it. Mr. McDonald never has. Neither has Mr. Hague. They never worked in the plants or the mills. They never had to engage in this kind of struggle. This is the first time the membership of this union can vote for men who came out of the steel plants and the mills."

The Lackawanna meeting at night was well attended. It also included a considerable group of Mexican-Americans. All the top speakers, without much skill in Spanish, welcomed them and a special Mexican band with a *"muchas gracias, señores."*

Molony described McDonald's behavior pattern at negotiations— "flashy with no substance." Then he recalled an incident several months before in Pittsburgh, at an executive board meeting, to "give you an idea of why we're trying to heave him out." Here is Molony's editorialized version of McDonald in full cry:

"Gentlemen, we must quickly negotiate a contract. We should have it all signed by the end of November but certainly not later than Christmas. (*Then in sad and melancholy tones, he repeated these extraordinary words*:) As we cannot wait until the time comes to reopen the contract, we cannot and must not reopen the contract. This will cause stockpiling and stockpiling is bad. (*Now nobody had ever proved to me why stockpiling is bad, but McDonald says it's bad, so it must be bad.*) The idea of strike is out of the question. President Johnson would never permit it. (*I'm breaking my back at this time trying to elect Johnson. We're all working for him, but Mr. McDonald says President Johnson will not allow a strike.*) There's another thing. Think of the foreign competition. It will ruin us and another thing, we don't want to get into the mess that Reuther is in. (*I sat there stunned. I jumped to my feet and I said: McDonald, would to God that we were in the mess that Reuther is in.*) The steel industry is not in the best of financial condition. (*The thought occurs to me that it's a damn good thing we didn't know all of these expressions 25 years ago or we never would have joined the union. We'd be afraid. We sure as hell would never have gone out on strike.*)"

McDonald's negotiating style, Molony said, must now go out of fashion. "We're going to negotiate at arm's length with the companies, respecting the management as they return the respect: no clandestine meetings, no meetings at the summit, no stage business of McDonald and R. Conrad Cooper of U.S. Steel, intimately known to McDonald as Coop.

"You should see the Coop and David Show on television over in Pittsburgh. *Olé!* Yeah. McDonald's puffing away at the pipe. Cooper's got the cigar going. One fellow speaks for a million people. The other fellow, a top vice-president of U.S. Steel. Dave turns to Coop and says, 'Well, what do you think would be good for the boys today, Coop?' Coop takes a couple of puffs. He says, 'They really don't need anything, Dave.' Dave says, 'Well, we ought to give them something. They are paying $5 a month in dues, you know.' Then they sit down and figure what the hell is left over after they've built a couple of basic-oxygen plants. You give your votes to Abel and you're not going to get an Abe and Coop show."

Here Molony abandoned the jesting tone and talked of what had led him to join the union years ago: "I joined the CIO because I wanted to feel like a man for once. I was tired of being shoved around by pushers and foremen. It was a matter of the spirit. When I joined, nothing happened right away, but I felt different. When we had to go on strike, we did something that I don't see done any more. We sang songs and they came from our heart, that 'we shall not be moved.' There we were, a Gideon's band—just a few without resources, without real guidance and with the leadership of only one man, Phil Murray—aye, and John Lewis, give him credit. We faced the richest and most ruthless and most arrogant industry in the world. And we beat them to their knees. We did it singing on the picket line. When you stop singing, the revolution has ended and so has the progress of the union. I have witnessed two great social revolutions in my day—because the CIO was more than a union, it was a great revolution. I have also witnessed the great social revolution as the Negro seeks to capture and obtain the rights which are given to all other citizens. And they too sing, that 'we shall overcome.'

"If Abel and Burke and I assume the leadership of the United Steelworkers, we shall literally in our hearts sing again and take on this stale and arrogant industry and let them know who the hell is master. . . ."

The purpose in scheduling all three candidates on the Abel team at one time, as at Chicago and Buffalo, was to bring out the troops and to achieve the maximum impression that only the presence of the entire team could create. That was the hope, but it succeeded only occasionally.

In speaking and delivery, Abel was no virtuoso of the impromptu. What he lacked in flair he made up in presence—the epitome of the rugged soldier of labor's crusade. He projected integrity, and a rough good nature that was the secret of his popularity with the local union officers and grievance committeemen across the country. He made a deep impression on steelworkers without trying to sweep them off their feet: "This crusade is necessary. . . . Not only would the steelworkers be better off because of it, but the entire labor movement and all the workers of the country will be better off because Burke, Molony, and Abel and our colleagues have dared to shock the world with this contest. . . . We're proving to the country that the United Steelworkers is a democratic institution."

Only in the comparative intimacy of such meetings was dirty linen exposed. In the last week Abel began to slash out against the McDonald charges that he and his colleagues were racists. He recalled how he and Walter Reuther had attended the founding convention of the Negro American Labor Council, to which McDonald refused to go, and how A. Philip Randolph "waged his unsuccessful battle for the umpteenth time to enlist the support of the AFL-CIO in this great crusade for human dignity." He warned that McDonald had been resorting to "very low tactics" in Tennessee, Alabama, Gary, and Baltimore, charging the Abel team with being racists. To his great distress, this attack, said Abel, was meeting with a "measure of success." He described one of McDonald's associates, "John Pastin, a staff member, as the lead-pipe agent who slugged $400 contributions for McDonald's campaign from every male representative they could browbeat and $100 from each of the office girls they might scare."

To the rugged iron-range country in Michigan, Burke had come late in January at twenty-two degrees below zero, rough even for that region. Consequently the meeting in Negounee was attended by no more than a hundred members. The Iron Mountain local sent word that it couldn't send a full delegation to the meeting, held on a week night, because of "the difference in time and the swing shift." Three or four hardy souls from the Ironwood local nevertheless did make it, traveling 140 miles over glare ice. To the faithful gathered there, Burke brought optimistic reports of his Western trip.

He deplored McDonald's description of the Abel team's eight-point program, announced in mid-December, as a "blueprint for disaster." What was this disastrous program? Burke spelled it out: restoration of rank-and-file control over union policy, re-establishment of the collective-bargaining table as the focal point, and the return of the Human Relations Committee to its proper function of fact-finding.

Up there in remote Negounee, far from the centers of leadership and decision, the members unburdened themselves to a man who might become secretary-treasurer. Suppose, they asked, if McDonald was defeated and continued to hold office until June 1, as he might do under the constitution, wouldn't the negotiations be affected adversely? Burke thought that if McDonald did not voluntarily step aside as head of the Steelworkers negotiating team, the executive board might help him make up his mind. For the first time in the union's history, the majority of the board was recorded in opposition to the international president, and with the roll-call strength to defeat him on any significant issue. It would be Abel's responsibility as the president-elect to conclude the negotiations, rather than McDonald's.

What about McDonald's warning that if the facilities of the American Arbitration Association were not used to supervise the election, the union might find itself tied up in litigation? Burke explained:

> The trouble could take on a variety of forms. McDonald might allege that fraud had been committed in the casting or counting of ballots. But, the Landrum-Griffin Act imposes very severe penalties on those who are guilty of fraud, ballot-box stuffing or mismarking of ballots, or deliberate loading the vote in one direction. It's no longer a matter of having your wrist slapped under our union constitution. People guilty of election fraud can go to jail and pay substantial fines. We feel this is going to be a strong deterrent to monkey business.

Burke said McDonald's proposal to employ the American Arbitration Association was an insult to the union, and it was unworkable besides. With more than three thousand far-flung local unions, many of them having five, six, or even ten or more polling places, "nearly eight or ten thousand outside watchers would be needed to supervise the elections."

Watching at the polls on election day was only one aspect of the problem. An observer would have to appear at least a day or two beforehand to check on the arrangements made by the local union; he would have to stay for the count, which could take additional days. There was also the added cost for expenses and transportation and recruitment of almost ten thousand watchers. McDonald had told the executive board that the total charge would run to about $250,000. "Actually," Burke said, "the total cost would mount to more than $2 million, money to be paid out of the international treasury. The AAA proposal is another gimmick. McDonald expected it would be turned down. He hoped our refusal would make us look bad to the outside world. We think we're going to have an honest election. We have great confidence in our local union officers and tellers, and we won't need 8,000 or 9,000 snoopers looking over your shoulders."

Dialogue with the Membership—An Exploratory Operation

The question-and-answer period became a significant feature of many Abel-Molony-Burke meetings. Only an open international election could have provided the unprecedented opportunity for ordinary members to question the union's top leaders. Seldom if ever would McDonald wait for questions: he would deliver his speech and leave, shaking hands as he strode out of the hall. He was perhaps more confident than his opponents of the efficacy of the afterglow of a personal appearance. In contrast, the Abel team had to face up to sharp, discerning, often antagonistic questions. In Akron, for example, a part of District 28, Burke found himself involved in strenuous probing by members of fabricating locals that predominated in this area.

As director of District 32, also chiefly a fabricating district, he was especially sensitive to the grievances among fabricating members everywhere. A man recognized by the chairman as Red asked why the executive board had agreed to McDonald's large and wasteful expenditures, which Burke now so bitterly criticized. District 28 Director Paul Schremp, presiding, turned to Burke and said, "Do you want to answer that, Walter?"

Burke replied: "Of course. I would say, very frankly, that the board— I've been a member of it and so has Paul—has to take some responsibility for the things that have been going on. But, in some justification . . . I, for one, always wanted to feel you could rely upon our president and that you could trust him to use his discretion and judgment in a way which could conserve the resources of this union. . . . Now these Phil Regan shows, the TV Meetings of the Month, were proposed to the board as a public-relations program which shouldn't cost too much money. So, out of respect for the president and the office, the board gave him a number of blank checks. But not in recent years. The brakes have been put on."

Moreover, the campaign has made the board bolder. "In the last couple of months, we have actually resorted to roll-call votes to beat back some of his ideas and programs. Happily, at long last, we're in a position to carry these roll-call votes. The roll calls will continue. . . .

"The general assumption that every check has to be signed by I. W. Abel as secretary-treasurer is not so. The signatures of McDonald and Abel are printed on the checks and are countersigned by somebody in either the secretary-treasurer's office or the president's office, who is authorized to fix an actual handwritten countersignature on that check. . . . Great sums of money have been spent which wouldn't have been spent if the board had recognized earlier what was going on. But we are now being vigilant. When we are elected, this kind of monkey business isn't going to happen."

Inspired by the mood of confession engendered by Burke, Director Schremp now provided additional details: "McDonald has employed detective agencies. He has hired bodyguards. I asked somebody, 'What the hell do they do—this detective agency?' 'Well,' this fellow explained, 'the only thing I ever saw them do is they walk into Dave's hotel suite before he walks in at night, look under the bed, look in the closets, walk out—and then tell him he can go in now, it's safe.' [Laughter.] He does this by virtue of his own authority; these ridiculous things were not cleared with the executive board."

In further revelation, Schremp traced the growth of opposition: "Five years ago, a group of directors got together and talked of fielding a candidate against McDonald. Some of the directors felt that if they were to talk to Dave they could get him straightened out. Well, Brother McDonald didn't change. He went from bad to worse. In the last year or so, it became quite evident that something had to be done and people like Burke, Molony, and Abel just couldn't sit still to see this union continue to go downhill. . . . They elected to do it this time because four years from now, it might be too late. We have to change the leadership. Nothing wrong with this union—only something wrong with the top leadership."

Burke's candor, his willingness to respond calmly and fully to the sharp prod of a rank-and-file member, expanded that day in Akron into a statement of his own past accountability and that of his running mates for what had gone on under McDonald. Even Schremp, a complaisant type for many years, caught the contagion of Burke's frankness. Burke conveyed the strength and purpose of the entire Abel team. They were staunch in defense of their union but no longer of its inadequate leadership.

Quayle's Final Wave

Quayle's Wave III was conducted on January 25 and 26, 1965, just two weeks prior to the February 9 election. The poll now gave 56 per cent of the vote to McDonald, 44 per cent to Abel, a gain for Abel of 2 points between December 30 and January 25. The analysts attributed the gain to the "observation" that McDonald had been less successful than Abel in reaching union members. Should this trend continue, said Quayle, McDonald "should still win, but it could be by an extremely small margin. If it should accelerate, Abel can score a come-from-behind victory. However, if President McDonald and his supporters can improve and increase their efforts in the last week of the campaign, the trend can be broken and reversed. McDonald could then win by a large margin."

According to Quayle, McDonald had slipped in those areas which he had earlier identified as his major strengths—younger union members, members having the least seniority, the least affluent members, members working in nonbasic steel plants, and workers not under incentive pay. Geographically, Quayle found that the sources of major support for McDonald were in the Southern states, Canada, and the Far West. The incumbent had gained substantially in the South, in the East, western Pennsylvania, and western New York. He had slipped but did not fall behind Abel in Canada, on the West Coast, and in the Midwest.

Where, then, should McDonald go during the last ten days of the campaign? In Quayle's opinion, the South—solid for McDonald—could be eliminated and the Midwest could be considered "Abel country." Quayle urged McDonald to concentrate his campaigning as follows: two days each in Canada and western Pennsylvania and New York and three days in the Eastern region and again on the West Coast.

At this juncture, Quayle found that the strike issue was beginning to take hold: "McDonald can now get more mileage out of the fear of a strike as long as he makes the issue in moderate phrases and terms."

Quayle once again stressed his finding that McDonald could win the election only through personal contact and direct communication. This, he said, was more important for McDonald than for Abel because "McDonald's support comes mainly from the less interested, less articulate, less active union member."

He sharply criticized some of McDonald's statements, as reported in the press, as being too diffuse: "We doubt if many members could tell us the main reason why McDonald seeks re-election. In Abel's case, it would be to secure better local representation and return to trade union fundamentals. From now on in, we urge David McDonald to hammer away at the essentials." He urged saturation visits and mailings that would include three to ten copies of flyers stating the basic themes. Quayle urged McDonald to "run scared." McDonald could still win and "even win big. Without Quayle's program, he risks allowing Abel to quicken the pace and come from behind."

According to Ross Thomas, the McDonald publicity man, the Quayle reports provided some sound political advice. But:

The poll was presumed spread out over the entire country and Canada and tried to indicate the sentiment toward McDonald. . . . I regarded it quite cynically . . . especially one that involved such a wide range of people. . . . Canadians, Southerners, Westerners, the Pittsburgh area, Chicago. . . . I was thinking when these polls came through that if they were true (with their wide margins for McDonald), then McDonald should conduct a rocking-chair campaign because he didn't have to do anything. . . . [Quayle] couldn't compare it to a political campaign because there he would take a cross-section of American society. Here he took persons who worked in a specific industry who happened to belong to a labor union. In such a poll, his sample would have to be extremely broad (or carefully structured) in order to get a true cross-section. . . .

It was a very iffy report. *If* McDonald goes out and campaigns, *if* the issues are brought home to them, *if* the propaganda is presented in simple, readable form. It was political common sense which we tried to carry out. . . .

After the election, President Johnson wanted to know: what happened. Quayle replied: "I told them that if they didn't get out and work, they were going to lose. Well, they lost."

CHAPTER 20

Last Week of the Campaign

No longer forward nor behind
I look in hope or fear.

JOHN GREENLEAF WHITTIER

In the final days of the campaign, both sides desperately attempted to outmaneuver each other, seeking to add to the suspense the element of surprise. The McDonald managers decided to supplement the bang of big-name dropping with the subliminal use of photographs to link connections of their candidates with the greats of the land. Relying on leaks from McDonald headquarters, the Abel strategists warned of a McDonald blitz by TV and radio, which would bracket a "strike-happy" Abel with movie reels of violence that characterized union organization drives and corporate resistance of the 1930s.

Since the candidacy of Al Whitehouse for secretary-treasurer remained practically invisible if not inaudible, the McDonald campaign handlers decided to beef it up through saturation distribution of the second and final issue of *Unity News,* the McDonald campaign publication, by direct mail to the home of every member. This issue featured a photo of Vice President Humphrey shaking hands with Whitehouse, captioned *"Best Wishes from HHH.*—Vice President Humphrey extends good wishes to Al Whitehouse, candidate for secretary-treasurer." The appearance of this photo brought particular distress to the already jumpy Abel headquarters. Word of mouth among steelworkers, who held Humphrey in considerable esteem, indicated that the Humphrey-Whitehouse picture was proving a shot in the arm for McDonald forces in what were considered safe Abel areas.

Over the years, Abel and Humphrey had developed a warm friend-

244

ship, based on shared experience and mutual regard. While McDonald always let it be known that his friends were Presidents—Eisenhower, Kennedy, Johnson—Abel was securely happy in his relations with Humphrey, who for him was the embodiment of aggressive liberal and labor advocacy. During the 1964 campaign just a few months before, Abel had traveled on the Humphrey campaign plane to provide advice on labor matters where necessary and to identify local union stalwarts who came to shake Humphrey's hand. Humphrey's own knowledge of the Steelworkers Union was rooted in his Minnesota experience, where the District 33 organization was headed by Earl Bester, now an Abel supporter.

Obviously, Abel could not remonstrate directly with the Vice-President for what appeared to be intervention in the internal union struggle. But Smaile (pronounced Smiley) Chatak, a legendary union character, had no inhibition in the matter. Chatak's close association with Phil Murray had placed him in the union's pantheon of folk heroes. The approbation of Chatak, a man of relentless, single-minded purpose, was sought by the most powerful. His disdain, which he could chop out in unadorned and fragmented prose, made men quiver. An old coal miner of Yugoslavian descent, he was the prototype of the rank-and-filer: for him the sun of trade-union loyalty could shine only on the worthy. Chatak wrote Humphrey how upset he and his friends were that Humphrey should now seem to lend himself to the McDonald campaign, especially when the Abel supporters, out of consideration for him and his high office, had carefully avoided involving him in the union's political battle.

At the same time, thirteen district directors telegraphed Humphrey expressing disbelief that he or President Johnson would "directly or indirectly become involved in our union election." A similar wire went to President Johnson.

Vice-President Humphrey, clearly upset, wrote to Chatak:

DEAR FRIEND:

I would never knowingly do anything to hurt either you or I.W. I greatly respect I.W. He is one of the finest men I know and, as for you, there just isn't anyone who has been better or more kind to me.

I spoke at the AFL-CIO legislative conference [held earlier that month in Washington]. Before and after the conference, dozens of pictures were taken with different labor leaders. This picture with Al Whitehouse is one of about 100 taken on that occasion.

I hadn't the slightest idea of who Al Whitehouse was for or against. In fact I wasn't even thinking about the struggle in the Steelworkers Union. I was there to speak of the President's program and to thank you good friends in the labor movement for all your help in the recent campaign.

I deeply regret the picture was used. It was done without my authorization. I am sorry if I have caused you any concern or worry. Please believe me when I tell you that I had no such intention.

Your Friend,
HUBERT H. HUMPHREY

That same day Humphrey wrote to Abel, enclosing his reply to Chatak:

DEAR I.W.:

Please note the attached copy of a letter to our mutual friend, Smaile.

Apparently I have been "used." I regret this and I trust that this photo has not done you any damage.

I have not been involved in matters relating to the officers of the Steelworkers Union. You have never asked me to take a position and for this I respect you.

On February 4, the Abel-Burke-Molony campaign headquarters made public both Humphrey letters. The McDonald roorback turned into a boomerang.

In a surprise switch, Abel now announced that he would appear with McDonald on *Meet the Press* the next Sunday afternoon, February 7. The McDonald people were flabbergasted: they had built up considerable publicity on Abel's refusal to "meet the champ." On the West Coast, where McDonald supporters in Fontana were gleefully making the point that Abel was "too chicken" to face McDonald, silence fell. Manuel Sierras reported that the announcement was good for the morale of the Abel supporters in strong McDonald territory. "Those other guys looked like damn fools," he said. The practical advantage of a debate had finally become clear. An election of this magnitude was not the "family affair" Abel had described it and sought to keep it. Moreover much of the younger membership, new to the life of the union, would not consider the use of TV a defilement of the trade-union temple. The final practical consideration: if Abel did not appear on *Meet the Press,* McDonald would have a full half-hour all to himself with the possibility that he could launch a last-minute attack that would be too late for Abel to answer. By appearing on the program, on the other hand, Abel would have fifteen minutes of network time, questioned by the same group of reporters. So Abel accepted.

As prelude, Abel issued a "major policy statement" at a news conference in Washington. New procedures, developed the weekend before in Buffalo by his supporting directors, were announced to eliminate the deficiencies that they charged had characterized the conduct of contract negotiations under McDonald:

(1) The union's elected 163-man Wage Policy Committee must be kept duly informed on major negotiations "with settlement terms being

worked on at the bargaining table instead of in 'summit meetings' by one or two men from the union and one or two from management."

(2) In the event of a deadlock, the Wage Policy Committee should authorize a referendum among the workers who would be directly involved in strike action. This rank-and-file expression should serve as a guide to the Wage Policy Committee.

Abel stated: "These policy changes will make both management and union negotiators more keenly aware of the rank-and-file needs and desires. . . . The present incumbent has virtually excluded the membership from the bargaining process in major negotiations. The McDonald approach has produced neither industrial peace nor a fast enough rate of progress. . . . By bringing rank-and-file sentiment more directly to bear at the bargaining table, we can avoid the kind of communications breakdown which, under McDonald, produced two of the three longest strikes in the history of our union."

In this way, Abel hoped to undermine the effectiveness of McDonald's recurring theme of "Abel, the strike-happy." By advocating a new union structure, Abel hoped also to allay the fears of his reputed "tough line" if he became president. As to the union's no-contract, no-work tradition, he said, "Our policy has been one of not calling strikes, but of just letting them happen." He advocated a policy that would permit the extension of the basic steel contract past its expiration date if it appeared likely that an agreement could be "worked out peacefully in one week, two weeks, or a month."

Abel also sought to cope with the issue that was doing him great damage—the race issue. Jimmy Jones, the black international representative, had determined to counteract what he called the "racial issue smear" against Abel, at least in his own district. At the plant gates of the Lukens Steel Company in Coatesville, southeastern Pennsylvania, Abel spent the afternoon after his departure from Washington distributing leaflets and introducing himself to the men coming on and off shifts. Jones's considerable prestige in the area was recognized through his various posts: chairman of the Human Relations Committee of the Philadelphia AFL-CIO Council, president of the Negro Trade Union Leadership of Southern Pennsylvania, and a leader in the Philadelphia Americans for Democratic Action. His joint appearance with Abel was meant to reassure black workers who had been canvassed by McDonald's personal representatives such as Ernest Clifford, the black member of the union's Civil Rights Committee.

Until the last week, the racist attack on Abel was carried mainly by word of mouth. As the campaign came to its climax, McDonald himself decided to carry the ball. At meetings in Pittsburgh and Braddock, Pennsylvania, McDonald now directly accused Abel of using an appointee of Governor George Wallace of Alabama as his "contact man" in the Southern states. In the Pittsburgh *Press,* reporter Edward Verlich wrote that McDonald charged Abel with "sending campaign materials to a man named Nichols, who is assistant Secretary of Labor to Governor Wallace." The story was headed "McDonald Links Abel, Dixie Racist."

Reporters interviewed John Nichols in Alabama. "No, sir, I'm not campaigning for anybody," he said. "I started out talking for Abel at the beginning but three weeks ago I stopped . . . having anything to do with the campaign because some of the boys said it might look as though I was speaking as a state official. But I was speaking as a member of the Steelworkers Union. I have never sent out any letters or anything. I was just talking about how I felt. I'm still a member of Local 1013," which embraces the Tennessee Coal & Iron Division in Birmingham.

In Detroit, Abel charged that McDonald, "desperately trying to reverse the tide, has stooped to guilt by association technique." His coordinator in Alabama, he said, was in fact Cecil Robertson of Gadsden, a union staff representative. McDonald headquarters, however, persisted in describing Nichols as a key figure in the Alabama campaign, and immediately distributed part of the Verlich story among black workers. They used the headline and the lead paragraphs which played up McDonald's charge but cropped Abel's indignant denial. Both Wexler and Thomas said defensively, "We're not responsible for how a story is used." Three days after McDonald's open "racist" attack on Abel, the widely circulated black newspaper Pittsburgh *Courier* published a page-size pro-Abel ad, signed by Alex Fuller, with a "Message to All Steelworkers," recapitulating Abel's long association with black causes.

McDonald now counterattacked: Abel's proposal for a ratification referendum for basic steel contracts, he said, was a desperate effort "to grab the spotlight." He once more announced his intention to call a meeting in mid-March of two thousand local union presidents in the fabricating field, mining operations, and independent basic steel companies. At this stage, to call what might have been almost a rump convention, however, could be only an empty gesture. It would not provide him the kind of practical support that Griffin had envisaged in urging such a conference well before the election. In contrast, the Abel campaign strategy in some districts had already focused on the problems of fabricating locals. In New England, with a large membership in fabricating plants, Lawrence Spitz was banging away on McDonald's past neglect of the fabricating locals. On a nationwide basis, Burke was doing the same.

Along with the promise of a conference of fabricating locals in March, McDonald also proposed the creation of a new department at international union headquarters to concentrate on their particular requirements. He said he would propose to the executive board "an all-out campaign to coordinate negotiating policies within various fabricating industries."

In the last days before election, McDonald charged that he had "caught" the Abel campaign headquarters tampering with the election procedures. Samuel E. Perish, the union's subdistrict director in District 31, at Harvey, Illinois, had sent a letter to recording secretaries of locals under his jurisdiction asking them to send election return sheets to him. Under the constitution, McDonald pointed out, locals are required to send such returns directly to the international tellers. Since Perish worked under Joe Germano, McDonald insinuated that something evil was afoot. The next day, Germano issued a hot denial. Mr. Perish, he said, was merely following instructions Mr. McDonald had issued in past elections to all members of the executive board in which he urged staff representatives to "assist local unions" in complying with election rules. "McDonald now finds fault with staff men who are following his own past advice," said Germano. This incident became a prelude to McDonald's later accusations of corrupt election practices in Germano's district.

Campaign Finances

The question of how the campaigns were financed and where the money came from soon arose. Late in January, Murray Seeger reported in the *New York Times* that on the basis of internal evidence the cost of the contest would range between $500,000 and $750,000. This total included contributions from union staff members who continued to draw their pay while taking sides in the campaign. Ross Thomas, McDonald's publicity director, estimated the total direct costs at about $225,000 for printing, mailing, and public relations. Since the campaign was without precedent, there was no comparable pattern for expenditures with past elections. Moreover, neither the union nor the government required reports of money received or spent.

The McDonald side was generally acknowledged as the better-financed group. At one stage Thomas said his office would spend "at least $100,000 and another $25,000 or $50,000 if it is available." The Abel committee, with headquarters in Chicago, modestly claimed that it expected to spend about $90,000 through its main campaign headquarters. Tom Murray, the Abel committee treasurer, said that since at least $50,000 was needed to open his committee's office, he scoffed at the total of campaign expenses the McDonald office at first was willing to acknowledge.

As to the sources of the Abel committee's funds, Murray emphasized that it had collected only from "interested friends." "We will take nothing from companies and nothing from the 'elite,' " whom Murray identified as "lawyers and businessmen who might have a special interest in the outcome or control of the organization." Most of the money for Abel's campaign chest was coming from the professional staff men, who split roughly three to two in favor of Abel. District directors on each side made individual contributions of several thousand dollars. McDonald with a $50,000 salary, and Abel with $35,000, presumably contributed their proportionate shares to the campaigns. There was comparatively little direct cash contribution from the rank and file. *Unity News,* in its two issues, ran contribution coupons. According to later reports, a total of only $800 came in from individuals—members and pensioners —from this solicitation for McDonald support.

By the time the campaign was over, however, Jim Griffin estimated that a combined total of at least a million dollars was spent, with about $500,000 to $600,000 spent by his side. He said he would not be surprised if "roughly" the same amount was spent for Abel. Griffin was worried (as was General Counsel David Feller earlier) about raising such large sums because, he said darkly, they were bound to expose the union to the danger of outside corrupting influences. For that reason alone, Griffin thought that perhaps the time was ripe for a change in the constitution to permit the union's international officers to be elected by convention rather than by national referendum.

The strategy of fund raising in the McDonald camp had first been spelled out in the latter part of December. At that time Frederick H. Sontag, the "mysterious stranger" described by Steve Wexler, sent a flurry of memos to Griffin, including one entitled "Fund-Raising Suggestions Among Friends of Mrs. McDonald, Mrs. Hague and Mrs. Whitehouse." The internal character of the memorandum indicates that Sontag was planning to use the names of the candidates' wives as a cover, leaving their husbands clear of any direct or legally awkward involvements.

Toward the end of the campaign, the McDonald camp required a fresh supply of money in a hurry. Thousands of dollars in unpaid debts had piled up, including those owed to Robert A. Maheu Associates, the detective and general service agency that handled a variety of undetermined errands for McDonald before and during the campaign. The man who came to the rescue was Ernest Nassar, a lawyer who over the years handled McDonald's personal affairs and sometimes those for the union, although he himself was not among the union's counsel in Washington or in Pittsburgh. His brother, on McDonald's staff, handled some of the administrative details for the union. Nassar now came forward with $100,000 in the form of a loan. He and his backers were betting on a

McDonald victory. When, subsequently, Nassar was informed that no money was available for its repayment, according to Griffin, he tore up the note "like a gentleman."

In the closing days of the campaign, Walter Burke estimated that McDonald backers were spending at least $75,000 on the radio spots alone: "These slick Madison Avenue type commercials . . . are trying to sell McDonald like a brand of male deodorant." The cost of the two complete mailings to the million members plus the great variety of brochures and leaflets, according to Burke, ran the McDonald printing bill up to $300,000. "We will be outspent at least six to one." He implied that McDonald's campaign had been heavily supported by funds raised outside the union. Neither McDonald, Hague, nor Griffin denied the charge.

BOOK **III**

THE ELECTION

_____

CHAPTER **21**

"Meet the Press"

. . . His answer trickled through my head,
Like water through a sieve.

LEWIS CARROLL,
THROUGH THE LOOKING-GLASS

On Sunday, February 7, both McDonald and Abel appeared on *Meet the Press*. The attention of the Steelworkers Union and a considerable part of the labor movement was focused on the program, originating in Washington. The handlers of both candidates had briefed, curried, and groomed them for the questioning.

For McDonald especially, this was to be the day! Ross Thomas said later: "We of course had challenged Abel to debate. Regardless of 'Honest Abe's' reputation as a near-saint, I think McDonald could have cut him apart in a debate. Inside our campaign headquarters, the mysterious Freddy Sontag had been horrified at McDonald's accepting the *Meet the Press* invitation so readily—especially since [producer Lawrence] Spivak was having a difficult time getting Abel to agree to come. Freddy Sontag said . . . we should bargain for the reporters . . . to make sure that our friends were there. Well, about this time I got a call from Victor Riesel, the syndicated columnist, who wanted to know if there was anything I could do to get him on the show. I said: 'Not a thing; I could call up Spivak and tell him you'd like to be on if you'd like me to . . . but I don't think Spivak is going to take my recommendations. Write him, or call him up yourself.' "

In preparation, Ross Thomas hurled questions at McDonald. Answers in rehearsal came out strong and satisfactory. McDonald was seemingly a relaxed professional, familiar with TV lights and cameras. At one point during the rehearsal, he suggested that he might introduce a "light touch" to convey his sense of ease in such an environment. "I'll say to Spivak when he introduces me as 'Mr. McDonald,' that 'If I knew that we were going to be formal, Larry (I'll call him Larry), I would have worn my tuxedo.' " Thomas promptly said, "That stinks, don't do it." Elliot Bredhoff, David Feller's partner, also disapproved; the audience would not be sophisticated enough to catch any "in" jokes.

Spivak greeted Abel and McDonald. He informed McDonald that past acquaintance made no difference on this program and that protocol did not permit first-name familiarity. Through the toss of a coin, McDonald was to appear first before the panel, consisting of Vera Glaser (North American Newspaper Alliance), Herbert Kaplow (NBC News), Hobart Rowen (then of *Newsweek*), and Spivak.

Ned Brooks, the moderator, explained that the thirty-minute program was split between the two candidates. Spivak started off:

"Mr. McDonald, you have charged your opponent Mr. Abel with being strike-happy. Since 1952, during the term of your presidency, you have had two strikes. Why do you think he is more likely to start a strike than you are?

MCDONALD: You know, you kind of amuse me, calling me Mr. McDonald, Larry, because if I knew you were going to be so formal, I would have worn my tux.

SPIVAK (evenly): Do you mind answering the question now?

(Inside the control booth, Thomas almost collapsed when he heard McDonald use "that smart-ass crack." Steve Wexler groaned.)

(In Youngstown, Ohio, James Griffin was watching the program in his living room. He was surrounded by family and friends. His own reelection as district director was at stake the following Tuesday. Here now was his candidate for president, to whom he had tied his own political future. When he heard McDonald's reference to the "tux" and Spivak's frigid reply, he was almost mad enough, he said, to put his foot through the TV screen. Recalling the episode two years later, Griffin still was furious at McDonald's "God-damn ineptitude.")

MCDONALD: Of course not . . . As you mentioned, there have been two shutdowns forced upon us by the industry against our will in both of those years.

SPIVAK: The question is why do you think, or why do you say that he is more likely to have a strike if he is elected president than if you are reelected president?

MCDONALD: Oh, I think that is just because of the nature of the speeches which he has been making.

SPIVAK: Since when do speeches make strikes, Mr. McDonald?

MCDONALD: Speeches can incite people to get into the mood that they will be forced into a strike.

SPIVAK: Would you hesitate to strike if you thought it was in the interest of the union?

MCDONALD: I have never had a strike; I have never called a strike. I suppose if the situation were such that we had no choice, we would have to call one, but I am not strike-happy. I don't want to strike; the people don't want to strike. I repeat we have been forced into several shutdowns which haven't been strikes as such.

SPIVAK: You say that that 116-day strike was not a strike, was just a shutdown? Aren't you just playing a game of semantics there, Mr. McDonald?

MCDONALD: No, this is no game of semantics at all; I never called a strike.

ROWEN: Mr. McDonald, a good deal of Mr. Abel's campaign centers around the accusation that you have been too close to steel management. Walter Burke, who is on his team, said in Chicago the other day that he and Abel and Joe Germano "are damned sick and tired of cooling our heels in the hotel lobby while these guys"—meaning you—"are wheeling and dealing up in [R. Conrad] Cooper's room." What is your answer to that charge?

MCDONALD: The answer is that this is an absolute falsehood. There is not a thing that goes on in negotiations that our whole team isn't informed about. If you will just look at that officers' report which is lying on the desk in front of you, you will see the whole story of all of our negotiations since our last convention.

ROWEN: Mr. McDonald, how do you explain the fact then that Mr. Abel was nominated by some 1,310 locals to 904 for you and that your own executive board is so completely split that on a weighted basis you are in a minority today?

MCDONALD: I can explain that very simply. While I was tending to my union business, Mr. Abel and his cohorts were out politicking. They were building a political machine.

MRS. GLASER: Mr. McDonald, there are some pretty emotional charges flying back and forth in this election. If you should not win, do you expect to contest the results?

MCDONALD: Of course, I expect to win so overwhelmingly that I don't think there will be any need of anybody even thinking about contesting results. . . .

SPIVAK: Mr. McDonald, one of the criticisms that has been made about you in this campaign is that you have lost touch with the rank and file of your union. What is your answer to that criticism?

MCDONALD: Oh, this is so much hogwash. I have already answered that one, I think. While I have been working, my opponents have been simply politicking. I have been in collective bargaining conferences while my opponents have been running around the country building up a political machine. I haven't lost touch. How do you lose touch whenever you make the sort of agreements that I have made? That my team has made, I should say.

SPIVAK: Once before someone comparatively unknown by the name of Rarick ran against you, and he was able to get over 200,000 votes against you.

MCDONALD: That is right. That is right.

SPIVAK: If there isn't opposition to your presidency, how do you explain that?

MCDONALD: Of course there was opposition then. They had a good program. They wanted to reduce the dues. Our convention had raised the dues by $2 a month, and they formed a dues protest committee. They wanted to reduce the dues. But we won that election rather handily.

ROWEN: Mr. McDonald, what kind of a wage settlement are you going to try to get if you are re-elected?

MCDONALD: Oh, I won't negotiate with you. I am awfully sorry. We do our collective bargaining across the bargaining table, not through the public news media.

ROWEN: One of the points that Mr. Abel has made is that you haven't won a general wage increase in money terms, that is, since October 1961.

MCDONALD: That happens to be true.

ROWEN: Are you going to try to get a . . .

MCDONALD: Let me put it this way: We didn't go after wage increases. We took a survey of the membership, in many ways. We had teams out in the field, and we had people coming in, we had talked to the Wage Policy Committee, we talked to thousands of people. They wanted income and job security and this is what we strove for—income and job security—like we are now striving for total job security.

MRS. GLASER: Mr. McDonald, why is it that we can't seem to get an answer to how much this very ambitious campaign of yours and Mr. Abel's is costing? Can you tell me what you are spending in your campaign?

MCDONALD: No, I don't know.

MRS. GLASER: Where are your funds coming from, sir?

MCDONALD: From voluntary contributions.

MRS. GLASER: Are they all coming from the rank and file, or do you have some outside sources?

MCDONALD: Oh, there are a lot of people who are friends, who have made contributions.

MRS. GLASER: Can you be more specific than that?

MCDONALD: No, I can not. They send money. They send money in to the treasurer of our campaign. He isn't here. I can't ask him.

MRS. GLASER: Would I have access to your treasurer and be able to ask him?

MCDONALD: I suppose you could.

MRS. GLASER: Now, Mr. McDonald, you are 62 years old and I understand that you could retire on full pension of $25,000 a year if you chose.

MCDONALD: That is right.

MRS. GLASER: Why do you want this job again?

MCDONALD: Because I love the Steelworkers so much, and I want a chance to do a good job for them. I have been in this labor union business since I was a kid, and I want to get some more good, sound labor agreements for our people, without shutdowns, incidentally, without shutdowns.

KAPLOW: Mr. McDonald, would you be amenable to extending the negotiating talks if you don't reach agreement by May 1?

MCDONALD: Now, Mr. Kaplow, I am not going to answer that question. We will talk about that at the bargaining table, if it becomes necessary. Undoubtedly we have been slowed down. If this campaign hadn't taken up so much of my time, perhaps we would have been further along in our negotiations. We still have an awful lot of local issues which must be discussed.

KAPLOW: Can you say what will determine whether or not you would go along with it?

MCDONALD: The International Wage Policy [Committee] will make that determination . . .

SPIVAK: Mr. McDonald, you said, "My opponent wants to go back to the good old days. I want to move ahead." What specifically does he want to do that would take you back to the good old days in your union?

MCDONALD: Well, all his speeches are about "the good old days" . . . He is talking about the '30s, not the '60s. We want to go ahead into the '60s. We want to do something constructive. We don't want to return back to things which are nonexistent, which never were "good old days."

SPIVAK: Those are pretty vague generalities, though. What specifically—

MCDONALD: Of course they are vague generalities.

SPIVAK: What specifically has he suggested in his campaign that would take you back rather than forward?

MCDONALD: His general speeches have just been that. He doesn't have a program; he has never enunciated a program. . . .

ROWEN: Mr. McDonald, is there any chance this election might be crooked or stolen?

MCDONALD: I would hope not, I would hope not.

ROWEN: You have made certain suggestions about further monitoring of the election that have been turned down.

MCDONALD: Yes, that is right.

ROWEN: Did you make those suggestions because you fear that the present machinery isn't adequate?

MCDONALD: I made those suggestions because of what has just happened in the International Union of Electrical Workers, and I didn't want this thing to get all fouled up like they are fouled up. That is why we asked the American Arbitration Association simply to oversee this election.

Now, it was Abel's turn.

SPIVAK: Mr. Abel, at a recent Washington press conference you said a strike would be less likely if you were elected president than if Mr. McDonald was. Upon what do you base that conclusion?

ABEL: We base that conclusion on the fact that we would present on a more factual basis the aspirations and the aims of the membership and convey to the management representatives more emphatically the determination on the part of the membership.

SPIVAK: Mr. Abel, do you think it is going to be possible to give the rank and file of the union a more direct voice in national negotiations, as you have proposed, without increasing the probability of strike?

ABEL: Yes, we certainly do believe there is a possibility of giving them a more direct voice in it. After all we do have a democratic labor union, and it does provide for the membership to have a voice in the policy-making and the direction of this union.

SPIVAK: Are you familiar with what has happened in the United Auto Workers Union, the strikes that have been caused there, and the strike in the International Longshoremen's [Association] that is going on now, because of direct intervention of the rank and file itself?

ABEL: I don't think that is necessarily the result of the direct intervention of the rank and file. It is because there have been problems in those industries that haven't been met.

SPIVAK: One more question: Do you think if you were president you could negotiate a decent agreement for your own union without running into the strike probability?

ABEL: I have in my years in this union, as a director, a staff representative and a local union officer, negotiated many agreements, hundreds of them, and we haven't had the necessity of strikes constantly. We have had some strikes, yes, but by and large we negotiate our agreements without them.

ROWEN: Mr. Abel, you have worked side by side with Mr. McDonald in this union now for 12 or 13 years, and I believe you have said that you have been urged before to run against him. My question to you, sir, is, if Mr. McDonald is such a threat to the welfare of the average steelworker, why haven't you made this move before?

ABEL: For several reasons. We have, as we have said during the course of this campaign, made efforts to convey our position and our differences within the family of the Steelworkers. We endeavored—we hoped that we would be able to do it in that way. But we have finally determined, as we have engaged in this campaign, to make the contest that we are in now.

ROWEN: Doesn't it seem a little bit unreasonable to rise up suddenly and suggest that everything that has gone before is not good and ought to be changed, dramatically?

ABEL: It isn't the case of suddenly rising up. Certainly there can be dissatisfactions and disagreements over a period of time with respect to policies and determinations, and you finally reach the point that tolerance ceases to be a virtue. . . .

MRS. GLASER: Mr. Abel, recently you and the directors of your union's executive board who support you voted down a proposal to bring in outside neutral monitors to observe this election. Wouldn't it have been preferable, sir, for the Steelworkers and for the man who is going to be elected president to have that extra assurance of a clean, honest election?

ABEL: Of course you are assuming that by bringing in an outside agency you would have that assurance. Quite frankly the reason for our position is simply this: We are a democratic labor union. Our constitution is quite clear in spelling out the provisions for the providing of membership the right to vote in an election and elect their officers, and of course it places the responsibility for the conduct of these elections on certain officers and elected tellers of the local union membership. The constitution is quite elaborate. It takes 15 pages to spell out the conduct of this method, and we certainly feel that the officers of our local unions and the tellers who will be elected to assist them are competent people, they are honest people, and we certainly do not question their integrity. We think they should provide the services for which they are responsible.

MRS. GLASER: Sir, what is your reaction to a letter that one of these union officials sent out? This is on the letterhead of the United Steelworkers of America, District 31, the district of your campaign manager, Mr. Joseph Germano. I understand you know about this letter. It . . . instructs local union officials to send their vote tally sheets not to the International Headquarters in Pittsburgh as the Steelworkers Constitution specifically requires, but . . . to hold their tally sheets so that they can be mailed out of an office in Harvey, Illinois, which is in Mr. Germano's district.

What reasons, sir, would your campaign manager have for attempting to bypass this procedure and have the ballots mailed from an office in his district?

ABEL: I haven't seen the letter. All I know is what I have read in the press. I am not sure that the letter does say that they should be mailed in to the Chicago office. It probably says that they should be brought in there for mailing. That is a procedure that has been followed down through the years, a system of assisting these local union officers in seeing that the local union's returns are filed properly and on time. . . .

MRS. GLASER: Do you support this letter or do you repudiate it?

ABEL: This is something that has been done down through the years. It is something you might call "past practice," and it is a step that has been taken to assure that some local union's vote is not disregarded because of failure on the part of the Recording Secretary, either intentionally or otherwise, to file the return to the Pittsburgh office and the tellers. . . .

MRS. GLASER: So you support this letter?

ABEL: I have no quarrel with that letter, no.

KAPLOW: Mr. Abel, where and when, before you became an announced candidate, did you express disagreement with McDonald's policies?

ABEL: Oh, we have had disagreements on a number of occasions, within the international executive board and in meetings of groups of us.

KAPLOW: And you never felt called upon before this time to actually make it a fight?

ABEL: That is right. . . .

KAPLOW: Mr. Abel, when you opened your campaign you charged that Mr. McDonald had showed—and these are your words—"utter contempt for the ability and integrity of union officials and of the members themselves."

Will you tell us specifically how he did that?

ABEL: "Utter contempt for the officials and the members." Are you referring to the American Arbitration Association suggestion or in general?

KAPLOW: I don't know. You made the statement, so I ask you. Where did he show utter contempt for the ability and integrity of union officials and of the members themselves?

ABEL: The contempt was of course with respect to the local union officers conducting the election. We have said that on previous occasions, during the course of this campaign, certainly with respect to the local union officers and committeemen, wage-policy committeemen, in exercising their responsibilities, that in many respects these have been disregarded, yes.

KAPLOW: Why, then, did you sign the 12th Constitutional Convention report in September of last year, where it said, "Throughout the past two years our formula of teamwork in the leadership and unity in the ranks has proved its worth over and over again. We must see to it that the leadership team continues to function as well and that our ranks are strong."

Why would you sign a report like that if you thought he was as bad as you think he is?

ABEL: Well, you sign a report like that and—as a matter of fact, I would point out to you that our conventions are always policy conventions. There is nothing political, of a political nature in them, and, of course, this is a report compiled of all of the operations and functions over a two-year period. There are many things in there.

After the broadcast, neither Abel nor McDonald wasted time on an exchange of amenities. Abel's supporters, Nicholas Zonarich and Charles Baker, considered that their candidate came out of it on the plus side; the McDonald advisers, still upset by McDonald's *gaffe* at the opening of the program, considered the match at least even, but they had hoped for a knockout.

In Los Angeles, Manuel Sierras told how workers in his plant reacted:

"The next morning, when I hit the plant, the membership was talking about the debate and . . . right away they knew they had a winner in Brother Abel. The way Brother McDonald answered the questions, they figured he was hiding something. Whereas what Brother Abel had to say was strictly along the lines of a unionist. Certain mannerisms that Brother McDonald used didn't quite go with the rank-and-file people . . . like trying to comb his eyebrows and things like that. Some of them said, 'Well, we finally got a chance to see a real phony.' Before this, you know, the opposition was going around saying that Abel had chickened out as far as the television interview. Well, for a while, this demoralized the Abel supporters and demoralized me to a certain extent. Let's face it. Brother McDonald's had a lot of experience with make-up, so what we were worried about was that Brother Abel would get up there, you know, and get a little nervous, and have Brother McDonald more or less overcome him. But then when Brother Abel agreed to the television debate, we made sure our supporters would tune into the television channel. The outcome was very good."

Back in Washington, McDonald and his publicity man, Ross Thomas, left for the National Airport. Thomas recalled the next twenty-four hours:

"For the next day, we had arranged to have McDonald appear on important TV and radio programs around Hamilton, Canada, where we could exploit some discontent, and a press conference or two. So we went over to the National Airport where the private plane he used on occasion had come in from Pittsburgh to pick us up. The weather was a little overcast, so he announced he would not go. I told him, 'The prediction is that it's going to be clear. I'd not go if I thought we were going to crash but I think you'd better get up there.' He says, 'Let's get back to Pittsburgh.' I said, 'You've got TV, you've got radio, you've got a press conference, you haven't been to Canada in this campaign. It will take about six hours of your young life, and you'll never know the difference; let's go.' Jack McKenna and Asa Atwater of the staff backed me up. He didn't want to go through. . . . After he got up there and carried through our program he turned to me and said, 'Wasn't this a splendid idea I had to come up here?' I said, 'It was a dandy.' See? After he got up there, it was all his idea. On the way back, with all done that could be done, no more votes to get, just before we left Canada, he picked up a couple of imperial quarts of Canadian whiskey. He proceeded to sip that on the plane coming back. 'Mother's milk,' as Bernard Shaw described it. Now he could drink all he wanted to. It was all done.

"On election day McKenna drove him out to the polls. Wexler and I were out there, met him, rode back with him, through his old neighborhood. The old neighborhood, that old gang of mine; here he used to walk to school, there he used to play handball. . . . But he lacked the common touch, whatever that is. He could turn on a certain charm if he wanted to. It depended on who was around and how much they'd do for him.

"I thought six weeks of working with him was about enough, although I came away with a liking for the guy. He did work hard during that time. (Was he approaching humility?) He was damn near there at the last. . . . I kept him worried, so that if he did lose he wouldn't collapse completely. . . . It wasn't such a letdown as it might have been because all of us tried to tell him he was in trouble. . . .

"If I were running the opposition, I think the margin would have been much larger—with emphasis on, perhaps not the exact words, but 'time-for-a-change.' I think I would have let up on the personal attacks a little and tried to ridicule him because of his inadequacy as a labor leader. . . . With a little digging I would have brought up the personal glorification campaign that he had going for himself over the years. I would have brought in Regan, the singing cop, and his associates more, and some of his friends. I would have used a lot of things that would have convinced a lot more people that it would have been time for a change. . . .

"It was an interesting six weeks. When it was all over, I was thinking, well, if this is the way the big boys do it, I feel sorry for the small ones. They struck me as so ill-prepared. He had so little internal help, so little loyalty after ten or fifteen years. The loyal ones were the ones who used to drink with him and tell him what a great guy he was. When it came to an election, they were of absolutely no use."

CHAPTER **22**

Election Day and After

Lo, the day of days is here.

FREDERICK LUCIAN HOSMER

By Tuesday, February 9, the campaign headquarters of both candidates
—the Penn-Sheraton in Pittsburgh for McDonald and a Chicago office
building for Abel—had set up receiving centers to collate the returns
quickly. Banks of telephones were installed to receive reports from the
friendly district directors and from cooperative elements in the hostile
areas behind enemy lines.

A critical question was how many members would vote. Speculation
ran to about 70 per cent of the total eligible compared with the putative
50 per cent in the 1957 Rarick-McDonald contest, the only previous
union-wide presidential campaign. Privately, some of the realists in the
Abel camp were not sanguine about an automatic advantage flowing
from his large majority of local union nominations. Such nominations
reflected the opinion of the small active core in a local—usually made up
of local union officers and the presence and pressure of staff men assigned to the local unions. In the election itself, the response depended
on a variety of factors: the relationship of members to the local leadership; the attitude of the local leadership toward the staff representatives
and of the latter to the district director; and the effectiveness and reputation of the candidates.

Both headquarters had sent out separate instructions to implement the
new official regulations governing the use of observers, the product of
the Landrum-Griffin Act. In districts where the local machinery was controlled completely by partisans of one candidate, the mechanics were

264

handled with considerable dispatch. Since the use of certified watchers was a new procedure, meticulous care was exercised to avoid violating the exact letter of the regulation.

The companies and government circles were worried that the margin of victory might be so close that doubt would hang over the negotiations when they were resumed. On the other hand, a decisive victory by either candidate, if immediately established, would restore negotiations to a more realistic basis. It could reduce the ambivalence of management and the ambiguity of the union leadership.

On election day, Abel voted in Canton, Ohio, at the union hall of his home precinct, Golden Lodge, Local 1123. Although this was friendly ground, opposition observers assigned to the polling place charged that while Abel appeared to be greeting old friends, he was actually election-eering at the polls. Abel left quickly.

McDonald went back to his "home local," No. 1272, the South Side Pittsburgh plant of Jones & Laughlin, where he was cheered by a crowd of supporters. An enthusiastic Abel supporter who shouted "All the Way with I.W.A." was knocked down. The NBC cameras were whirring and Herb Kaplow managed to record the comment of a McDonald supporter: "That guy always falls down." In the meantime, the photographers took a shot of a weeping McDonald being embraced by a rank-and-file steel-worker. Ross Thomas denied that he had planted the scene: "I wouldn't have had the nerve."

In California, the Fontana vote attracted special attention. Never before at Fontana had an international election received such intensive scrutiny by the rank and file. All the local officers except one were for McDonald; both Fontana locals—the plant workers and clerical workers —had nominated McDonald. On form, Fontana was emphatically McDonald country.

Before the election, the sealed ballots consigned to the local had been placed under security in a bank vault, then transferred the afternoon be-fore election day to the Fontana police station. On election day the packet of ballots was unsealed by nine tellers elected by the local, one teller to supervise the voting at each polling place. The nine elected tellers were assigned twenty-four assistants. At the same time, Ken Whitaker of the Fontana *Sun Telegram* noted that ballots were unnumbered, a fact which some observers thought could lead to "complications."

The count took place in public view on the stage of the W. P. Brunton Auditorium. Only the elected tellers were permitted to handle the ballots. The certified Abel watchers were told sternly by the local officers that they could look, not touch. Counting was slow, with the tellers working in shifts of twenty hours, followed by four hours off. Two groups of three men worked steadily. Official observers were permitted on stage, with one man representing each side at the table. Members seated in the audience held a tense vigil. Results were posted at periodic intervals.

The tellers completed the tabulation twenty-seven hours after the polls were closed, just past midnight Thursday. Then the official report, signed by the McDonald-supporting local president, H. James Vezie, and the recording secretary, George R. Mitchell, was sent off to international headquarters by registered mail at 1:30 P.M. Thursday. Abel's thirty-seven Fontana observers constituted themselves an honor guard and escorted Mitchell in an informal victory march. They were determined to permit no technical or mechanical mishaps or any funny thing to happen on the way to the post office. At Fontana, Abel had received 2,767 votes to 1,965 for McDonald!

The fact that Fontana voted to oust McDonald caused general surprise. Harry Bernstein, the respected labor editor for the Los Angeles *Times,* reported that the "Kaiser Steel Company workers, said to be the highest paid steelworkers in the world, have voted to oust the man credited with the unique contract which brought about top wages. The upset at Fontana is having wide reverberations because of its possible effect on the long-range 'fruits of progress' contract now in effect between the United Steelworkers of America and the company."

In the Los Angeles area, Manuel Sierras, carrying the memory of past elections, had kept in constant contact with the Chicago campaign headquarters: "From past experience in the Molony campaign in 1955 and in the Rarick campaign, we knew that our job was to make sure that Brother Abel got a true count. . . . In our area, election night was hectic. The count started coming in about 7:30, and by 9 o'clock we were pretty confident that Brother Abel was the winner in this subdistrict."

After the election, the Sierras committee sat down to "more or less review" how people voted. "We found that the Mexican-Americans and the Negroes in six locals voted for Brother Abel with the exception of one local at Bethlehem." The majority of the members of that local were Negroes. In the weeks before the election, they had become a special target of a task force of pro-McDonald staff representatives, one of whom was a Negro assigned to the local.

In general, the returns were reported in spasms. Counting paper ballots was long, slow, wearing work. By Thursday the Associated Press began to report returns from 2,473 out of 3,092 locals, giving Abel 219,089 and McDonald 210,659. Steel company officials, publicly silent but not indifferent, kept in hourly touch with returns. "An Abel victory would be counted the greatest upset in union history," one company official declared. Joe Germano claimed firm victories only for both Burke and Molony over Hague and Whitehouse. This claim led the Chicago *Tribune,* in its predictive role, to speculate that the election might result in the unusual situation of McDonald's alone being re-elected, with the two other officers and a solid majority of the executive board arrayed against him.

With the returns from the big locals coming in slowly and the result in doubt, court actions already had begun. In Indiana, McDonald supporters sought to hold up the counting of ballots in the Gary local through a court order, but the federal judge refused to grant the request. For its part, Abel headquarters was considering court action in the Philadelphia district, where discrepancies in the vote were being charged. Several McDonald supporters then announced that they were going to Canada to see what was holding up the report of the vote there.

At this point, Germano charged that local McDonald people in his District 31 were sitting on the vote in locals they controlled, thus countering the McDonald accusation that Germano was withholding the tally in Abel locals in the same district. With February 19 the deadline for the submission of local tallies, some newspapers began to report dolefully that because of reported discrepancies in various vote counts the final results might not be known "for months." On Saturday, February 13, Germano closed the Abel headquarters. This act of finality was as much a gesture of confidence in the outcome as it was of furious disgust that several of the largest locals in his district had given a majority to McDonald. With an air of achievement, Germano announced that in his district Abel had defeated McDonald by a margin of 5,500 to 6,000 votes. This was something less than the makings of the famous victory he had predicted.

A storm boiled around the Gary local. Its ballots were impounded by a court order issued after McDonald's local attorney charged vote fraud. But the judge subsequently found no evidence of irregularities and ordered the clerk of court to retain custody of the ballot boxes. The judge did not rule specifically on the charges. He doubted, he said, that he had jurisdiction, which he believed belonged under the law to the Labor Department.

Typical of stories at the time, the Chicago *Daily News* pounced upon the union, characterizing the contest as "a disgraceful exhibition of irresponsibility on the part of union officials. Both sides have protested counting procedures, and the issue seems sure to land later in the courts. Counting alone may take weeks, court determination months. . . . This breakdown in the internal self-government of the Steelworkers suggests a need for public regulation over union elections, which are not the private business of unions but public concern of greater consequence than many elections officially public. And perhaps the protective measures that the Landrum-Griffin Act is supposed to provide union members and the public need strengthening."

Abel remained cautious about final results: "Our initial optimism was well founded. While it is not my intention to claim victory until the final votes are in and the official count certified by the international tellers, all the evidence gives us grounds for believing we have won by at least 10,000 votes."

Such a close vote could only mean that the winner would not be determined until the international tellers had officially tabulated the tally sheets. Meanwhile the McDonald headquarters saw their hopes go glimmering as the estimates continued to report a narrow but consistent lead for Abel. Steve Wexler charged irregularities. "It all comes down to the question of who stole what," a McDonald spokesman said bitterly, reminding the media of McDonald's proposal to have the American Arbitration Association supervise the election.

Considerable impatience was expressed over the sluggish rate of the tabulation. Damon Stetson observed in the *New York Times* that "supporters of Mr. Abel, who perhaps had less cause to complain because their candidate was ahead, expressed dissatisfaction nevertheless, and talked of possible changes in voting and counting procedures that would make future elections less cumbersome, easier to report and better protected against fraud of any kind." At the same time, Wexler said wryly, "If you analyze what's happening, you can see that the procedure was written in the constitution so that those in power could stay in power. That's what it's doing here, but ironically, this time McDonald's not in power. As secretary-treasurer, Abel controlled the mailing of the ballots, the election machinery, the international tellers (incumbents who ran on the Abel slate), and has a majority of the executive board." The McDonald supporters began laying the groundwork, through publicity and other methods of persuasion, for a possible appeal for governmental intervention.

Both sides were amassing as many protests as possible to offset each other. They were following traditional political practice: "When in doubt, challenge!"

CHAPTER **23**

The Government Observes:
Confrontation and Scrutiny

God makes a path, provides a guide.

ROGER WILLIAMS

This was the first contested national election held by the union since the passage of the Landrum-Griffin Act in September 1959. That law was considered by most union officers as a massive intrusion into the internal government of labor organizations; the range and nature of its intervention was unprecedented. Perhaps its most intimate application to union governance was spelled out in Titles IV and VI, which cover the conduct of union elections.

In November 1964, during the nominating period, the Labor Department found itself involved in Steelworkers election problems. Complaints from scattered districts came to the agency protesting various nominating procedures. Under the law, the Labor Department ruled that it could not entertain those protests because the complainants had not exhausted the remedies available under the union constitution. Only when a member has "invoked such available remedies without obtaining a final decision within three calendar months after their invocation," is he entitled, under the law, to file a complaint with the Secretary, not later than one calendar month after that. The frustration in such a protracted period, a maximum of four months, lay in the fact that it would take the grieving candidate well past the election.

But officials in the Labor Department did not completely seal themselves off from reality. There was the case of Joseph Kender, president of the Republic Steel Local 2265 in the Cleveland area, who charged that he had been denied reasonable opportunity under the law to become a candidate for director in District 28. His appeal to the union's executive board was turned down. Thereupon, on January 27, 1965, he sued the union and moved to enjoin the election, but was denied by the court. Prior to the February 9 election, he filed a complaint with the Secretary of Labor to obtain a place on the ballot. But the Labor Department, through its Office of Labor-Management and Welfare Pension Reports, was not in an eager-beaver interventionist frame of mind. Under the law, it was a matter of proper timing. Frank Kleiler, the conscientious and judicious bureau head, and his associates concluded that the statute did not "contemplate" the involvement of the Labor Department in the electoral process until *after* an election. Only in the postelection period could a formal complaint be properly brought to the Secretary of Labor. "It seems almost absurd," a Labor Department official admitted, "that we should have to tell the complainant you can't complain about the nominating procedure in time to do you any good, that you must wait until the whole election is over. But this seems to be the statutory scheme we have to live with. By putting this limitation in Section 402, Congress made it quite clear that it didn't want to get the Department of Labor involved in elections prematurely and that it wanted to provide for ample opportunity to resolve all protests inside the labor organization before the Labor Department entertained a complaint." Kender's lawyer argued that a literal following of the procedures, even if successful, would be to close the barn after the horse was stolen. But the Labor Department could only shrug a reply: it is so written in the book of laws.

Government's Cautious Entrance

As February 9 approached, tensions mounted. Both sides were jumpy. Before Landrum-Griffin, the election machinery was firmly in the grip of the international union. There was no official outside scrutiny. But the old order was dramatically transformed by the case of the bitterly fought election of the International Union of Electrical Workers (IUE).

Despite its initial reluctance, the Labor Department was finally constrained to intervene in the election contest between James B. Carey, incumbent president, and the challenger, Paul Jennings. The "practicalities" of the situation as they evolved led Secretary W. Willard Wirtz to conclude that the case had become exceptional and required his intervention. It is doubtful whether the department would have moved as it did without the assent, indeed the urging, of AFL-CIO President George Meany, no admirer of Carey's, who normally would not have encouraged government intervention. The government acted under the authority granted the Secretary of Labor by Section 601 of the Landrum-Griffin Act "to investigate without a complaint and to make a report to interested parties, when he believes it necessary . . . to determine whether any person has violated or is about to violate any provision" of the act. For the first time, the Labor Department had taken over the ballots in an international election and was ready to conduct a recount.

Government Intervention: First Phase

Against the background of the developing IUE election case, the Steelworkers election was watched with concentrated interest. After a flurry of charges and countercharges, both campaign managers agreed to extend an unprecedented invitation to the Secretary of Labor to send government representatives to the union headquarters to observe the opening and tabulation of the return sheets from the more than three thousand locals.

Why did the Labor Department acquiesce, despite its past reluctance, to this limited form of "pre-complaint" participation? For that matter, why was the department invited? The reason must be found in the structure and personnel of the union's election machinery. The three international tellers were, first, charged with responsibility to open, count, and tabulate returns and, second, to hear and rule on protests arising from the elections. Since, as candidates for re-election on the Abel slate, they were interested parties, the McDonald forces feared that the incumbent tellers, against whom they had entered their own candidates, would invariably resolve doubts about irregularities in favor of Abel. On the other hand, the Abel campaign managers considered it likely that the international tellers might be suspected of tilting their decisions toward Abel. The timely presence of impartial government representatives as observers might at least inhibit any tendency toward improper activities or lessen the propensity to charge that they were indulged in.

This unprecedented type of participation by government was agreed to just twelve hours before the deadline. To ensure the observance of all the proprieties, the government representatives would have to be present at union headquarters before midnight on February 19, the cutoff time for the receipt of return sheets from the local unions. Kleiler and Charles Donahue, the Labor Department's solicitor, flew to Pittsburgh, where shortly before midnight they met at the union headquarters with the three international tellers, headed by Wayne Antrim, and the two lawyers, John Pastin and Harry Guenther, representing respectively the McDonald and Abel camps. With other department representatives present, two of whom, George Avery and William Kane, were to become the permanent government observers for the next two months, they again emphasized that the presence of Labor Department representatives did not constitute supervision and was not intended to subtract from the constitutional responsibilities of the tellers.

By this time, ten days after election day, an estimated 150 protests from all over the country had been submitted to the tellers. In past elections, the tellers had held closed hearings on protests at locations convenient for the interested parties and the witnesses. Should the Labor Department representatives also attend those hearings? Kleiler believed it necessary, but this extension of function was a decision that belonged to the union alone.

Present at the opening on February 22 were the three tellers; Avery and Kane of the Labor Department; and Benjamin B. Naumoff, regional director of the Bureau of Labor-Management and Welfare Pension Reports, who was an expert in representative elections from his years at the National Labor Relations Board; John McCaulley, adviser for Abel; John Pastin, for McDonald; two international union clerks; and George Abrams, the director of the Honest Ballot Association, whose services were retained, under the constitution, by the tellers for the tabulation.

Late or "untimely" returns were placed to one side, not to be counted. So were sheets lacking local union seals. The advisers for both presidential candidates watched each other like hawks. The mechanics of the count were under way. It was to go on for days with the tellers making it clear that constitutionally they were in charge.

Outside the Steelworkers headquarters, tension was mounting. Dope stories in newspapers began cropping up. Rumors were circulated diligently. In Bal Harbour, Florida, where the AFL-CIO Executive Council was meeting, newspapermen began to write speculative stories casting doubt on the election procedures themselves. David Feller, doubling in brass as special counsel of the AFL-CIO Industrial Union Department as well as the Steelworkers Union general counsel, made himself available to reporters, who naturally considered him a good source for a lively story on dull days. In the *Wall Street Journal* and over the wire services, radio, and TV, a statement was attributed to Secretary Wirtz that if the results of the election were close, the Labor Department would conduct a recount, perhaps a rerun, of the election. Antrim and his associates were furious. According to the department, the secretary had issued no such statement. Trial balloons along these "general lines" had been wafted in Miami by a "union spokesman." With a sharp nose for the uses of publicity, Feller had provided newsmen covering the Executive Council meeting with "background" information on McDonald's plans. Speculation on a "recount" resulted. Several reporters refused to accept the "inspired" stories. For example, Damon Stetson of the *New York Times* refused to use the planted story on the grounds that both origin and responsibility for it seemed rather obscure, and he warned his desk against using the wire story.

Pressure for an extension of the basic steel contract began to rise. President Johnson wanted the steel contract extended beyond May 1. Over the telephone, he expressed his concern about the possibility of a strike to AFL-CIO President George Meany at the Executive Council winter meeting in Florida. In reply to a convenient question at his news conference in Bal Harbour, Meany said that since "they lost time under their election procedure . . . they should try to make it up and extend the negotiations." Meany's statement on the bargaining posture of an affiliated union caused eyebrows to rise. Fully aware of the limits of his power and responsibility as federation president, Meany would normally avoid even an "advisory" opinion in matters of this sort, but this time, he said, he made the remark "on his own."

With the Steelworkers leadership in uncertain transition, Meany also expressed his disapproval with the referendum method of electing international officers. "Now, if the Steelworkers elected their President through the delegated convention method, they'd have done it last September in Atlantic City and it would have been over with. . . . The Steelworkers difficulties came about due to a clash of personalities. . . . This got into their Executive Board and they chose sides, and went to it. But I don't think it represents dissatisfaction on the part of the membership with the leadership. McDonald has done a very good job. Unfortunately his personal publicity was not too good. He was pictured as somewhat of a playboy, and I don't think he is as much of a playboy as the image would indicate. . . . He was providing the union with good sound leadership."

In the meantime, back in Pittsburgh, Chairman Antrim, after consulting the two camps, formally invited the government advisers to attend the protest hearings, which were then being scheduled.

In the presence of the parties, the government maintained a discreet reticence. They requested information only where it pertained to their special function as observers. Present only by consent of the parties, without statutory authority to intervene, they did not in any way abuse the terms of their invitation. Nevertheless both sides competed for their attention and good will. Each side sought to make points against the other, obviously seeking to lay the groundwork for possible legal appeals and formal government intervention at a later stage.

On March 2, for internal consumption, the tellers announced the unofficial tabulation of the unchallenged returns:

Abel	306,801
McDonald	298,949
Burke	311,949
Whitehouse	266,762
Molony	298,468
Hague	279,066

Tellers:

Shipperbottom	246,517	Palumbo	239,188
Antrim	240,825	Gurovich	195,569
Caruso	268,881	Lee	275,843

The closeness of the preliminary total—a margin of 8,000 votes for Abel—indicated that the internal fight was still on. Antrim had now been compelled to face his own grim moment of truth: he had presided over his own defeat, losing re-election as international teller by a narrow margin. Both his colleagues on the Abel slate, John Shipperbottom and Steve Caruso, were re-elected, while the leading vote-getter among the teller candidates was Nathaniel Lee, the only Negro candidate, who ran on the McDonald slate. Lee's fellow-candidates, Guido Palumbo and John Gurovich trailed.

Although Abel's margin over McDonald was narrow, his teammates, Burke and Molony, ran ahead of their opponents with considerably larger pluralities. The figures were leaked to the press and became front page news. McDonald refused to admit defeat. Abel was prepared to accept the results.

In the meantime, McDonald had called a meeting for Monday, March 8, of the union negotiating committees of the eleven companies for pre-bargaining discussions. The election returns, though unofficial, had an obvious effect on the meeting. The company negotiators seemed now to be adjusting their thinking to a take-over by a new administration, while the union itself faced a dilemma. The international tellers had until May 1 to announce the official results. McDonald's term did not officially expire until June 1. Might Abel replace McDonald as chief negotiator before that? Abel, however, discounted the likelihood of this happening. He was sure that McDonald would not consent to abdicate until his time ran out.

On March 12, more than a month after election day and twenty days after the closing day for returns, Abrams of the Honest Ballot Association, having completed the arithmetic of the recheck, furnished slightly changed figures: Abel 306,805; McDonald 299,143.

Antrim stressed that only interim decisions had thus far been made. Ahead were weeks of protest hearings in all parts of the country, to start March 15 in Philadelphia.

Diary of Election Protests

Intensive hearings were held throughout the country, including Puerto Rico. Charges of lies, fraud, and intimidation were made. Sharp arguments accompanied complaints of technical violations. This exploration of the inner workings of the electoral life of the union was recorded by government observers in daily dispatches to the Bureau of Labor-Management and Welfare Pension Reports in Washington, where they were analyzed daily by Kleiler and his staff. The field reports cover well over a thousand single-spaced pages, from which a selection has been made. These reports remained confidential and were not seen by the parties directly involved in the election.

With the presidential vote so close, it was to the advantage of the partisans to be sticklers on every point. The final decision could conceivably rest on the accumulation of votes in small locals as well as in large. Experience in previous elections led both sides to expect skulduggery, and each side sought to convince the government observers that the other side was guilty of it. Where a district was controlled by a McDonald director, protests usually came from Abel supporters, and vice versa. In divided districts, protests crisscrossed. In locals, often the scene of competing ambitions, rival local officers collided. In certain areas the voting had taken place in turmoil, with the police called in and courts sometimes invoked. In large locals where the vote ran potentially in the thousands, both sides had assigned their full quota of watchers, but in smaller locals, unmanned by watchers of the opposition, balloting was carried on with slight regard for the interests of the opposition.

The hearings followed this format: The three international tellers sat as judges. All witnesses were sworn. The two Labor Department representatives, present strictly as observers, did not forsake that role even when invited to do so occasionally by one side or the other. The McDonald and the Abel slates each had their representatives to "protect" the interests of their candidates. Under strict constitutional construction, only a member of a local whose votes were in dispute could make a legal complaint.

Despite precise regulations in some respects, the election procedure did not provide adequate controls to make certain that the votes of a local recorded on the return sheets corresponded to the votes counted. Where the reports were entered by local officers, there was the possibility —in the absence of adequate watching by the other side—that they might rig the entry.

At this time George Avery, one of the two Labor Department observers, informed Antrim that Washington was concerned about the possibility that the tellers, all Abel men, were giving unequal treatment to the protests. For example, they had decided that the comprehensive protest submitted by McDonald was to be handled as a single protest for hearings in Pittsburgh. Since McDonald's protest involved locals scattered over the United States and Canada, difficulties might occur in assembling persons from distant locals into Pittsburgh. Antrim replied that since it was the practice for the complainant to make his protest and then transfer the burden to the locals whose elections were being protested, he considered that a greater hardship had been placed on Abel, whose complaints were in fact submitted and processed on a local-by-local basis. He would not concede that there was a need for changing the established procedure.

As was expected, the hotly contested New England district—Lawrence Spitz, the challenger, against the incumbent, Roy Stevens—produced a wide range of protests from 19 local unions out of the 152 local unions in the district. Battling for every vote, Spitz in the unofficial vote was running behind Stevens, 10,059 to 10,576, although much to his satisfaction, Abel, whom he supported, had squeezed out a victory in the district over McDonald, 10,566 to 10,365.

Spitz charged that threats had been used against complainants and that at least one complaining member had been pressured into dropping the complaint. Seeking to overturn the vote in some locals to which he had been denied access, Spitz emphasized Stevens's failure to provide him with the list of addresses of locals to which he planned to assign observers. Stevens replied that under the constitution he was barred from giving membership lists to anyone. In support of Stevens's technical defense, the McDonald adviser, a member of the international union's legal staff, triumphantly produced a telegram from Abel in response to a complaint by James Griffin; the latter had charged that Directors Paul Rusen and Paul Schremp of District 23 and 28—strong Abel supporters—had refused to provide him with a list of addresses of the voting places in their districts. To give out such information, Abel had said, was contrary to the "strict policy" of the international union. If Griffin, however, wished to pursue the matter, Abel went on, he could consult the files of the Office of Labor-Management and Welfare Pension Reports, to which all unions are required to report under the Landrum-Griffin Law. In his rejection of Griffin's request, Abel had therefore provided Stevens with a defense against Spitz's charge.

At the Pittsburgh hearing, an employer was shown to have played a role at the polling place. The top executive of the Jessup Steel Company, charged with openly favoring McDonald, had entered the polling area on the plant premises and signed his name in the voters' registration book. To add to the gaiety, the company's personnel manager later came to the doorway of the polling place and jokingly asked members to vote for him. Then the plant superintendent, with one of the local union office girls seated in his lap, spent a considerable time in the polling area.

In addition to all this, the Abel election watchers thought it peculiar that the election was conducted in the company conference room, whereas all previous local union elections for this plant had been held in the local union hall, some distance from the plant. The tally at Jessup gave McDonald 671 to Abel's 164, with an unusually high voter participation of 90 per cent. Nevertheless, according to the government representatives, insufficient "hard evidence" was adduced to indicate that the reported misconduct had affected the outcome of the election in this local, since the vote margin for McDonald was so wide. This conclusion would seem to be a *non sequitur*.

The Sensitive Matter of Ballot Distribution

Because of an accumulation of complaints regarding the distribution and receipt of ballots, Chairman Wayne Antrim held a special session on March 29 for an appearance by George Cornelius, the president of the privately-owned Cornelius Printing Company of Indianapolis. This company was the official printer of the Steelworkers Union, as it had been for other unions, notably for the United Mine Workers. A respected figure, Cornelius was the Nestor of union printers, a friend of international union officers. Over the years his company has functioned practically as an auxiliary arm of the Steelworkers and other unions. Responsible for the printing and distribution of *Steel Labor,* the monthly union publication, Cornelius was the custodian of the only full membership list of the international union as well as of the roster of the officers of each of the more than 3,200 local unions. Thus Cornelius was a *de facto* part of the union apparatus.

At this time, protests had been submitted to the tellers that ballot shipments to Puerto Rico had been delayed, misdirected, or otherwise gone astray. Cornelius explained his relationship to the union. In this election, he said, the printing firm sent out the ballots as instructed by the international secretary-treasurer. His records showed that thirty-nine Steelworkers local unions were located in Puerto Rico, and to each of them, he said, ballots had been shipped from Indianapolis on January 19, 1965, via air mail, first class, registered, return receipt requested. From these thirty-nine shipments, only twelve locals received ballots prior to election day, February 9, 1965. On February 5, he received a request from the international office for reshipment of ballots for five local unions. Ballots were thereupon sent that same day to the international's staff representative in Ponce for distribution to these five complaining locals, which, said Cornelius, had received their ballots in time to vote.

With regard to the lost shipments of ballots, Cornelius had asked the Post Office Department to investigate. It was his understanding, however, that several Puerto Rican locals had finally voted with ballots they had borrowed from other local unions in Puerto Rico! Some communities on the island, Cornelius said, did not have house-to-house mail delivery but operated on a drop-point system whereby a postman leaves mail at a nearby gas station or store, to be picked up by the person to whom the mail is addressed. Such a procedure, familiar in poor neighborhoods, obviously did not make for careful handling of ballots. While this explanation would seem to exculpate Cornelius, the sloppy procedure was a clear responsibility of the international union.

In Cleveland the hearings affecting District 26 were bitter. This district was headed by Griffin, who as McDonald's campaign manager was indispensable. If Griffin, a capable and complex man, had not agreed to manage McDonald's campaign, McDonald would most likely not have run for re-election. But at the same time, Griffin had to fight for his own political life. The strategy of the Abel forces to throw Griffin off base worked. In this district Griffin—the incumbent since 1946—had received 16,230 votes to Russell Thomas's 14,722; Griffin's narrow margin of 1,459 was a severe blow to his pride and prestige.

Thomas protested that Griffin had brought suit against several of his supporters on charges of libel. He contended that Griffin's court action, a few days before the election, constituted "threats, intimidations and coercion" that adversely affected the vote for Thomas. This Griffin denied. He argued that the vote in the district was largely a slate vote; there was usually a direct relationship between votes cast for district director and for international officers. McDonald had also carried the district.

In their report to Washington, the Labor Department observers remarked that despite Thomas's objection, Griffin was entirely within his constitutional right as a citizen to take necessary action to protect himself against published statements he considered "false, malicious and libelous." Despite this judgment, his resort to litigation on a matter affecting an internal union situation—especially before internal union remedies were exhausted—was construed by some as a violation of the union constitution. At any rate, this issue was one that would have to be resolved finally by the international executive board.

Protests from District 36-G, the Florida-Puerto Rico Division of District 36, were heard by the flying tellers and their troupe on one day in Tampa and Miami, the next in San Juan. To many in the union, 36-G was considered the "oddball district"—where people were "taken care of" by McDonald, or for one reason or another kept out of sight or placed in a limbo where they would be in the union but not of it. It had become a reservoir of sinecures. Meyer Bernstein, a veteran staff man, called it an organizational cesspool. Its expenditures heavily outweighed income from dues and assessments. Personnel of 36-G were usually assigned to provide McDonald with prompt attention on his Florida trips.

At the Miami hearing, Lucille Van Pelt, president of Local 6343, which covered Sunray Chairs, Inc., protested the reported vote: out of 121 eligible, 2 went for Abel and 114 for McDonald. Yet, she swore, only nine members actually voted. The nine ballots that had been cast were picked up by Carlos Sugerez, a staff representative, who carried them out of the hall. During the balloting, she said, he had handed her a piece of paper that had McDonald's name and others already provided with crosses. She had meant to vote for McDonald anyway, but, outraged by this open flouting of the rules she went ahead to protest, despite a telephoned warning that this action could make trouble for her and the local she represented. The tellers decided to void the vote in this local.

From Miami, the tellers' entourage flew to Puerto Rico, where seventeen locals were involved in special protests. Lack of facility in English made the geographically isolated membership dependent upon the Spanish-speaking staff representatives. The difficulty was heightened by evidence of the members' lack of basic understanding of their rights as members and the responsibilities of the union leaders to them. Eight locals had received no ballots; of the nine locals that received their ballots on time, all reported overwhelming majorities for McDonald; not a single local came anywhere near reporting a credible vote for Abel. Lopsided results could mean overwhelming enthusiasm for McDonald, an enormous diligence on the part of the staff representatives or of their local union officers, or hanky-panky. No Abel observers were present at these polling places.

The Puerto Rican protests also revolved about the failure to receive ballots in time for the election. Where voting took place, staff representatives had provided a batch of ballots from locals that had received them by air. One staff representative, testifying before the international tellers seven weeks after the election, brought in six packages of ballots still unopened. These envelopes were postmarked on January 18, 1965, and had been sent by regular surface mail, not by air mail, special delivery, as required. They had arrived in Puerto Rico by ship, not by plane, and apparently were held up because of a dock strike. Antrim expressed perplexity since Cornelius, the printer responsible for distribution, had earlier testified that all ballots had been sent by air mail. As it turned out, the tellers voided the vote of only one of these locals, on the technical ground that its returns lacked the required union seal!

Local 6455, Puerto Rico, representing the Presbyterian Hospital employees, had simply not been sent ballots, because their dues, though checked off, had not been forwarded to the international union. Only after the election did they discover that the employer, though deducting the dues regularly for the five previous months, had failed to remit them. Sticking to a literal interpretation of the union law, Antrim ruled that despite the circumstances members of the local union were not in good standing and therefore not eligible to vote. The Labor Department representatives considered the chairman clearly in the wrong. Under the Landrum-Griffin Act, the members of this local union were eligible to vote and should not have been penalized by the union for the employer's dereliction. The whole matter ought to have been brought earlier to the attention of the union headquarters by the staff representative, to avoid such a serious discrepancy and the resulting disfranchisement. A picture of administrative neglect clearly emerged.

RIGHT TO CHALLENGE | 280

The California sessions—at San Francisco and Los Angeles—heard a variety of charges. In one local that McDonald carried, checkoff lists were not used to verify the voters' eligibility. The local union officials rejected a proposal by an Abel representative for checkoff controls as a reflection on their honesty; instead, voters were required to sign a book. In contrast, at other locals complaints were made that members were not required to sign their names and that only a check list was used. Standards were not uniform.

In defense of his local's relaxed election procedures, one officer testified that checkoff lists had never before been used to identify voters at elections. Moreover, since the local tellers would have had to check a long line of voters, he said, members would likely be discouraged and walk away without voting. Aside from that, he added, only three people of the more than 2,800 in the plant did not belong to the union and they would be easily identified as ineligible to vote.

The chief target on the West Coast was the Fontana Local 3869, with more than 6,300 eligible members. Yet Abel had carried this Kaiser Steel local by 2,782 to 1,965. In this local, families like the Bitontis were split. Obviously, the need to protest the Fontana result was inspired as much by a desire of the McDonald supporters to save face—to attempt to prove that the local had gone to Abel by fraud— as by the practical objective of having the vote thrown out. With the margin of victory comparatively narrow, every vote denied Abel became a vote for McDonald. But the tellers and the government observers found the procedures at Fontana entirely proper.

Complaints seesawed. From the Abel side, a protest was directed at Local 1981 (the Pacific Iron & Steel Company and other firms), where McDonald received 1,304 votes to Abel's 376, out of 2,241 eligible. Here, Abel watchers were not permitted to examine the ballots and ballot boxes before the voting began; sealed packages of ballots were opened before election day in the absence of Abel-Burke-Molony observers; ballots and boxes were distributed to persons in fifty-one units improperly designated as tellers; ballot boxes were returned prior to closing time; and practically all the unit ballot boxes, unsealed and unsigned, were carried into the local union office by individuals, many of whom were active campaigners for the McDonald slate; unused ballots were returned, in most instances, in the envelopes that had contained McDonald sample ballots. A vote of 81.2 per cent of those eligible was recorded—which the Abel complainants considered so high as to lead them to suspect ballot-box stuffing.

In response, the McDonald supporters explained that membership of this amalgamated, or catch-all, local was scattered over fifty-one plants within a twenty-five-mile radius, with plant units ranging from five to three hundred members, with an average of sixty. The local's two business representatives defensively argued that the constitution contained no election provisions to cope with the special conditions of an amalgamated local union. So they improvised. The large turnout, according to one business agent, arose from the fact that it was easier to bring out a heavy vote in an amalgamated local where the smaller units made it possible to generate more interest.

The Labor Department observers reported to Washington that the testimony of accumulated violations was convincing enough to justify a rerun of the election in this local. (They did not convey this judgment to the international tellers; to have done so would be a violation of their observer status.) Nevertheless, this local's vote, which ran heavily against Abel, was finally accepted by the international tellers, whose fairness had been questioned by McDonald supporters on grounds of alleged partiality to Abel. In making this decision, the tellers were apparently determined to balance off the protests of one side against the other by a rough sort of distributive justice.

After California, the push was on for winding up the hearings. The McDonald forces now moved in with a blanket appeal to cast doubt upon the integrity of the entire election.

First, McDonald charged that the AFL-CIO Industrial Union Department, then headed by Walter Reuther, had actively campaigned for the Abel slate.

"The turmoil of this election," said McDonald, "has not only pervaded the rank and file, it has also brought into sharp focus a pattern of active campaigning for my opponent's slate by employees of another labor organization, namely the Industrial Union Department [IUD] of the AFL-CIO: Nicholas Zonarich [IUD's director of organization], who campaigned throughout the country, especially in the aluminum locals; and Elmer Chatak, the IUD coordinator for eastern Pennsylvania. Another IUD employee was Estes Riffe, who concentrated on the locals in the can industry."

There was no doubt that the three men, members of the Steelworkers, had campaigned for the Abel slate. But the Labor Department representatives found no merit in the charge because there was no showing that union funds were illegally expended in these campaign activities.

McDonald's prime target, however, was Director Joe Germano of District 31, the union's largest. Said McDonald: "The Steelworkers have suffered nothing but ill repute from the election in Chicago." He charged that two of Germano's subdirectors had instructed recording secretaries to bring the locals' return sheets into the subdistrict office for mailing to the international tellers. Both subdistrict directors, Samuel E. Perish and George E. Green, testified that when McDonald had blasted them in the press for this instruction a few days before election, they specifically instructed the local recording secretaries to prepare the returns themselves and to send them directly to the international tellers. Nevertheless, Perish caustically observed that in sending his first letter to the recording secretaries, he had repeated the instruction sent to the locals when Rarick ran against McDonald in 1957.

But the international tellers were reminded that the charge cut both ways. They had already heard protests that the return sheets of four locals in Hugh Carcella's Philadelphia District 7, which McDonald had carried by lopsided majorities, had actually been submitted to a staff representative, who then sent them on to the international tellers. Thus the past practice in Germano's district was identical with current practice in Carcella's.

McDonald also charged that a "blackout" of election results from District 31 had occurred when "it looked as if my opponent was not winning. . . . The democratic process in District 31 has degenerated into a reign of terror. Steelworkers are afraid to talk to steelworkers and local union officers are fearful that reprisals will be taken against them if they do not follow orders from the District Director. I have personally spoken to many individuals who have knowledge of irregularities. Some were asked to stuff ballot boxes, others were ordered to request extra ballots, and turn them over to staff representatives, and still others were asked to adjust the final tally in favor of my opponent and his slate."

But the Labor Department observers found no evidence of unjustified delay or irregularities.

Considerable stress was then placed on an alleged "pattern of voting" developed in District 31, which cast doubt on the honesty of certain local union returns. According to this "pattern," where McDonald observers were present, the vote was generally close, and ranged from 55 to 65 per cent of the total eligible. But where McDonald observers were not present in a local union, the results were quite different. For example, at the Calumet Steel Division of Borg-Warner Corporation (Local 1027), "out of 627 eligible voters, 606 voted (96.6 per cent) and the presidential vote was 562 to 44 in favor of my opponent. At a U.S. Steel local, out of approximately 340 eligible voters, 329 voted (96.5) and the vote was 10 to 1 against my candidacy. . . . Similar voting patterns have been noted in Districts 4, 27, 29 and 32."

According to the government representatives, allegations and evidence alike were vague and general, and so lacked a basis for intelligent evaluation.

In fact, the vote in District 31, which Germano had proclaimed would be a runaway for Abel, gave him only a narrow margin, with participation several percentage points below the national average. Why hadn't the much-touted Germano "machine" delivered as expected? Summed up, the answer given by sources friendly to Germano was that over the years of his incumbency, grievances had piled up against the district leader. Leaders of large locals developed separate interests and ambitions. While Germano's support on the executive board was indispensable in Abel's decision to run, the votes of the members in his district were not deliverable, any more than Director Charlie Smith could deliver his district intact to McDonald in the fourteen states comprising District 38.

In a furious twenty-eight-page reply to McDonald's charges, Germano flayed him for a "vicious, scurrilous, and intemperate indictment of District 31 and of the staff representatives, local union officers, and members. . . . In making the general accusations, McDonald has blithely and contemptuously branded well over one-quarter of a million members of this union and their representatives as cheats, thieves, terrorists, incompetents, and/or frightened dupes." He deplored McDonald's failure to present his charges in person. If he had, Germano said he too would have appeared.

Germano charged that two lawsuits filed by McDonald's supporters, with the attendant publicity, were "terribly disruptive and seriously damaged the reputation of the union. . . . The real purpose of these lawsuits was to provide a beachhead from which to launch an election challenge."

McDonald's accusation that a "pattern of voting" indicated dishonesty of certain returns in the district impelled Germano to say, "I cannot stress enough the revulsion with which I view such charges by a man who has headed this union." McDonald contended that he scored higher at local unions where his observers were present than at locals where he lacked observers, but, said Germano, this assertion was "belied" by a tabulation of results in locals at which both McDonald and Abel observers were present.

According to this tabulation—not rebutted by McDonald supporters at the hearings in District 31—McDonald was victorious in 57 out of 223 locals, and tied at one other. This percentage figured out to victories for McDonald in about 26 per cent. McDonald had stationed observers in at least 49 locals; he won in only 15 of them, or 30 per cent. The difference between McDonald's overall winning percentage and his average of locals where his observers were present was therefore 4 per cent. As an essential part of his strategy, McDonald had concentrated his observers in District 31 at the basic steel plants. He actually carried subdistricts 1, 2, and 3 of District 31, where large basic steel plants are concentrated. He did this while losing more locals than he won in each of these subdistricts, which was evidence of the fact that the big local unions favored McDonald while the smaller locals, even in these areas, were carried for Abel. (This was a blow to Abel's expectations that he would score especially heavily in large basic steel plants.)

At 42 of the 57 local unions that McDonald won, he had *no* observers. At 34 of the 49 local unions at which McDonald observers were present, McDonald *lost*. His share of victories at locals where he had no observer was 24 per cent, not appreciably lower than his winning percentage at locals where his observers were present.

Continuing to play his own numbers game, Germano confessed that although a little more than 60 per cent of the members voted nationally, in District 31 "we were below this figure, only 59 per cent of our eligible members having voted. In general, in the Abel districts only 57 per cent of the eligible voters voted, while in McDonald districts a whopping voter turnout of 67 per cent was recorded. In many of the McDonald districts where Abel could produce few if any observers, the voter percentage exceeded 70 per cent and in one case exceeded 80 per cent. My point quite simply is that anyone can play the numbers game. In the final analysis, however, the question is who received the greater number of votes."

The charges of a "blackout" of election returns in District 31 was rejected by Germano as "false and baseless," an opinion that the government observers shared.

McDonald charged, finally, that union funds were illegally used in Canada in Abel's behalf. There the three districts had given Abel a majority of about 9,600—Abel 24,749, McDonald 15,157. By casting doubt on the validity of the Canadian vote, McDonald hoped to establish a legal basis for a recount, if not a rerun, of the election. While it was questionable that Canadian members of the Steelworkers Union fell directly within the purview of the U.S. Landrum-Griffin Act, in order to avoid possible litigation on that point a representative of William Mahoney, the union's Canadian director, entered a reply to McDonald's charge before the tellers, whose jurisdiction over the international union's election procedures was unquestioned. What made the point of Canadian sovereignty largely irrelevant in this instance was that the union's international constitution had been made to conform with the provisions of the Landrum-Griffin Act.

At any rate, the Canadian representative admitted that on November 11, 1964—two days after the nomination period began—Mahoney had indeed sent a letter to the 450 Canadian locals, by cheap-rate mail, recommending the nomination of the Abel team. The total cost of postage on the letters, prepared in the union office at Toronto, came to about $13.50 (Canadian) for which Mahoney was ready to reimburse the union. Nevertheless, insisting on maintaining his national identity, Armond Park, the Canadian representative, pointed out that the distribution of such a recommendation was not prohibited by Canadian law.

The Labor Department representatives reported that while the use of union funds was clearly in violation of the Landrum-Griffin Act, the amount of money involved was negligible; its use, therefore, did not seem to have been a factor in the decision to send the letter at union expense. Furthermore, since the letter was sent out almost three months prior to the election, "an effect on the election could not be shown."

McDonald's complaint about Canada was hardly substantive, but he never ceased to hint darkly that had it not been for the districts north of the U.S. border, he might have made it.

Confrontation and Scrutiny

On April 20, as the tellers were completing their report confirming a clear though narrow victory for Abel, McDonald proposed to Secretary of Labor Willard Wirtz a course of action by which the "current election situation . . . can be quickly clarified." Of such a proposal Abel knew nothing. Then in an appeal to Abel's spirit of unionism, McDonald proposed to Abel and the international tellers that the official election report be held up until the last possible date, on the ground that the contract negotiations, moving toward a May 1 deadline, might be disturbed by such a political announcement. Abel agreed. Thus, while McDonald placed his request for delay on lofty ground, he had begun a desperate maneuver to place the election result under a cloud. Just a few days before, the recount of the election of the International Union of Electrical Workers, conducted by the Secretary of Labor under Section 601 of the Labor-Management Report Act, had resulted in the reversal of the first result: Paul Jennings was declared the winner over the incumbent president, James B. Carey, originally certified the victor by his union's election board. If sufficient doubt could also be cast on the Steelworkers Union election, perhaps the Secretary of Labor would be induced to find a basis for full intervention. Accordingly, McDonald wrote Wirtz that he was "advised" that a substantial number of irregularities and the closeness of the vote would be sufficient to call for a new election under the provisions of the Landrum-Griffin Act: "If a majority of the members of the United Steelworkers of America who actually voted in the election actually cast their ballots for me, as I believe they did, it would be no service to them if I were to fail to pursue every avenue to establish that fact. If fraud exists and remains undetected, it will constitute an invitation to more widespread fraud in future elections in this and other unions. . . ."

Then McDonald proposed that since the Secretary of Labor had the power under Title VI of the Labor-Management Reporting and Disclosure Act to institute a complete investigation, as he did in the IUE election, he might, at least, first initiate a limited investigation, in a small number of selected locals throughout the country. If a quick investigation disclosed evidence of fraud, McDonald said, the Secretary would then be justified in mounting a full-scale investigation. If, on the other hand, fraud should not be disclosed, McDonald would be "happy" to accept the results as announced by the tellers as final.

Haste, McDonald warned, was the order of the day: "The longer the uncertainty the greater the damage to the Steelworkers Union, the labor movement, and the country as a whole. My own personal interest would best be served by graceful and honorable retirement. But I cannot abandon my responsibilities or sacrifice the long-run interests of my union and its membership."

Within a day or two, the resumed negotiations with the steel companies were scheduled to reach a crisis. With the expiration of the contract on the midnight of April 30, would a strike be called, in the "no contract, no work" tradition? Patient and effective work by William E. Simkin, the director of the Federal Mediation Service, resulted in an agreement of an extension of the contract for four months, until September 1. Negotiations were to resume May 18. On the money side, the agreement required that starting May 1, the companies place in an escrow fund 11.5 cents an hour for each working hour, for the 425,000 union members then employed in the basic steel industry. It was agreed that the union could reopen the contract after August 1 and be free to strike thirty days after that if no agreement had been reached. Similarly, the companies had the right to serve a thirty-day notice of expiration of agreement. Under this "floating" or "open-end" agreement, neither side was compelled to follow such a time schedule.

The leaders of the Steelworkers Union closed ranks. Fears that McDonald and Abel would "outmilitant" and "outdemagogue" each other at the bargaining table were now shown to be unfounded. When McDonald brought the proposed agreement before the Wage Policy Committee for approval, he was given a hard time by more than a dozen highly aggressive committeemen. As a lame-duck president, McDonald needed help and sweated for it. Abel spoke strongly in support of the interim agreement and the four-month extension. So far as he was concerned, he said, the fact that the union held an election was strictly none of the companies' business. To some extent management was using the union elections for slowing down negotiations; it should not be permitted to get away with it. After Abel spoke, the tide of argument turned, and the Wage Policy Committee ratified the interim agreement.

In the meantime, McDonald and his associates, with their minds on election results not yet officially announced, had been in touch with his confidential agents, Robert A. Maheu Associates, to formulate a separate line of attack. On April 28 Maheu's Washington man, Walter L. Fitzpatrick, informed McDonald that he had presented a program of investigation based on McDonald's talks with Maheu, which was already in Vice-President Howard Hague's hands. Their investigation "should carry the stamp of former FBI agents." Maheu himself was a former FBI agent.

The details of the program were not spelled out, but obviously it would require the outlay of a large sum of fresh money, of which none was in sight. George M. Harrison, a leading AFL-CIO vice-president and chairman of the Ethical Practices Committee, reported that McDonald had come to AFL-CIO President Meany to ask him for a sum of money to enable him to finance "a survey of Steelworkers' attitudes" in connection with the election. Meany had consulted Harrison, on whom the significance of McDonald's euphemistic request was not lost. He said to Meany: "George, I wouldn't give him a dime. That guy is two ounces lighter than a cork."

From Pennsylvania, David L. Lawrence, former governor of the state and a power in the Democratic Party, had let it be known he was interested in McDonald's fate. Edward J. Hickey, a prominent Washington attorney with wide relations in the political and labor field who had reportedly been retained as a special adviser by the McDonald committee, also transmitted word of concern; Hickey's close relationship to AFL-CIO President Meany was meant to impress some people. In addition, the ineffable Phil Regan, whose far-flung "human relations practice" brought him into personal relationship with a variety of politicians of high and low degree, apparently busied himself in McDonald's behalf. A stream of agony messages and telephone calls to Capitol Hill and the White House took shape. The gist was that McDonald felt he had been let down politically, and this "after all I've done for the Administration." Word was steered to the White House, to Bill Moyers, the President's news secretary, and to Joseph Califano, the President's assistant in charge of labor-management relations. While Moyers later acknowledged that Abel and his associates thought that the President was "soft" on McDonald, Abel stayed clear of any pressure. "We appreciated that," Moyers said.

Desperate, McDonald now sought a meeting with Labor Secretary Wirtz, which was arranged for April 29, the day before the international tellers were to announce their final report. Originally the McDonald-Wirtz meeting was to have taken place in the Secretary's office. Then rumors of the meeting began to circulate, and Wirtz, disgusted with the leaking of what was to have been a confidential conversation with McDonald at the latter's request, and also determined to avoid publicity, changed the venue to McDonald's year-round Madison Hotel suite in Washington. McDonald was accompanied by General Counsel David Feller and several others.

For nearly two hours McDonald stormed around the suite, claiming that the government had not done what it should have in his behalf. Was he going to get a break from the administration or wasn't he? "They owe me something, they owe me something!" was McDonald's refrain. His facial tic became more active. The hotel apartment turned into a weird theater of exhortation, anger, pleading, reproof, and recrimination as McDonald hurled charges of base ingratitude at the administration. Wirtz calmly kept assuring him that he would receive fair treatment: "If the facts are there to justify action, we'll proceed on the basis of those facts." The facts had already been gathered in the reports and analysis made by the Labor Department's observers and technicians. (See Appendix 4, "The Government's Scrutiny of the Steelworkers Election.")

Actually Wirtz's primary concern ever since November had been the eventual outcome of the collective bargaining in steel. While a union election of this magnitude was obviously important, Wirtz regarded the "group dynamics" in Pittsburgh as a subordinate factor in the larger national picture. The relation of all this to bargaining and its impact on the economy was at the top rung of Wirtz's hierarchy of worries.

Mindful of McDonald's support in the past, President Johnson, himself a veteran of close elections, had expressed privately his solicitude for McDonald's political fortunes. He let his friends—and subordinates —know he cared. He had cultivated McDonald's support as he had that of other key union leaders. It was unlikely that the President had met Abel, except perhaps to shake hands on the platform of the Steelworkers convention. Vice-President Humphrey, however, knew Abel well. While Abel's friendship with the Vice-President hardly constituted a countervailing force to McDonald's with the President, we have seen how it had already proved useful largely as a result of McDonald's campaign ineptitude in implying Humphrey's backing. This episode rankled in McDonald's bosom.*

At any rate, in a letter dated April 29, the day of his emotional confrontation with Wirtz, McDonald withdrew his April 20 request for an investigation of the election. Without referring to their meeting, he noted bitterly that as a result of his willingness to defer action until after "the collective bargaining situation was resolved," he had diminished his chances to prove his charges of fraud. Wirtz could only repeat

---

* Nearly four years later, in October 1968 on a TV panel show, McDonald, though describing himself as a lifelong Democrat, announced his support of Richard Nixon and bitterly assailed Hubert Humphrey, the Democratic candidate for President, for "lack of integrity" and "reliability." When Irv Kupcinet, the conductor of the program, pressed him to explain his reasons, McDonald refused. In the intermission, Labor Secretary Wirtz, on the panel in behalf of Humphrey, asked McDonald what accounted for his bitter personal attack on Humphrey. McDonald replied, "You should know. You know what happened in the Steelworkers election."

that the administration would act if facts could be presented to justify action.

The following morning, April 30, high up in the Penn-Sheraton, before a crowd of newspapermen, photographers, and banks of TV cameras, the international tellers at last made public the official election results. Abel received 308,910 to McDonald's 298,768—a margin of 10,142. For vice-president, Joseph Molony received 300,414 to Howard Hague's 278,786—a margin of 21,628; Walter Burke received 313,229 to 266,381 for Al Whitehouse, or a majority of 46,848. Wayne Antrim had also to announce that he himself had been defeated, while his two teller associates of the Abel team had been re-elected. Nathaniel Lee, the Negro candidate on McDonald's ticket, had run first.

After the tellers had gone, Abel and Germano entered the room. Abel answered questions, some friendly, some hostile. Weeks of campaigning had taught him how to handle the media with equanimity. Then the president-elect and his campaign manager left.

An hour later, as the reporters had been forewarned, McDonald and Hague swept into the room, accompanied by an entourage. McDonald was grim as he strode to the stage. Suddenly his face turned a deeper red and he let out a bellow which startled the crowded room. Pointing his arm dramatically at Joe Murray, Phil Murray's adopted son and a bitter foe of McDonald's, McDonald yelled, "You, out!" Then gesturing with his thumb to Charlie Barranco, his chief bodyguard, he said, "Charlie—out!" Barranco pushed Murray. Murray pushed back and challenged Barranco to do something about it. All this took place in the eye of the cameras. Then McDonald switched signals. If Barranco had indeed tried to strong-arm Murray out of the room, the ensuing fight would get bigger headlines than McDonald and the election returns. McDonald now said: "All right, Charlie, forget it." Turning to the newsmen, McDonald sought to explain his rage: "I didn't want him here. He's no press man." Having disposed of this embarrassment to his satisfaction, McDonald smiled at the cameramen: "Ready to roll?" Then he chanted, with professional aplomb: "One, two, three," right up to ten.

He then read a declaration of intention to press the matter further. The next step, he said, was an appeal to the international executive board. He was not ready to concede defeat.

CHAPTER **24**

McDonald Maneuvers and Caves In

It is something to have wept.

G. K. CHESTERTON

McDonald thus gave every appearance of preparing to carry his appeal to the executive board, the union's court of last resort. He could not, he said, "abandon my responsibilities to the members . . . to contest the Tellers' Report to the fullest extent." Leaving the details of responsibility to others, he flew from the scene of frustration and disappointment to his home in Palm Springs. There he stayed for more than two weeks, until May 16, the eve of the executive board meeting.

In the interval, McDonald sought to give friends and enemies something to chew on. He told District 20 Director Kay Kluz, according to Kluz, that R. Conrad Cooper of U.S. Steel had been approached by "certain Abel associates" to convey the following offer to McDonald: If McDonald would agree to forego the election protests, he would be given the title of "president emeritus" with a salary of $50,000 and an unlimited expense account. But, said Kluz, McDonald told him that he rejected the proposition.

This story was greeted by some of Abel's friends as incredibly silly. Abel himself was furious. He and his associates saw in this "weird concoction" an attempt to picture Abel as so shaky in victory that he was prepared to buy his way out of further investigation. Some of them cynically concluded that in purveying the story to a district director, he was signaling that at a proper time he would accept such a "compromise formula."

Instead, Abel and his associates now moved more confidently. The

McDonald contingent in the executive board was wavering, with several of his supporters indicating that they were not disposed to go along with his election appeal. For example, Director Roy Stevens of District 1, who had squeaked through in the bruising struggle with Lawrence Spitz, was anxious not to upset the applecart. Bill Moran of District 9 was outspoken in his belief that it was time to call a halt. To have held an election at all was burden enough; the board, he felt, should accept the tellers' report as final and binding.

Word came that Hague was canvassing alternatives: if he gave up his protest, would a government job be available to him? And to McDonald?

He sought the help of James Cuff O'Brien, the union's director of retired members' activities, who also acted as the union's liaison with the Democratic National Committee and with the office of Vice-President Humphrey. Both Secretary Wirtz and Assistant Secretary James J. Reynolds, Jr., were kept informed of the feelers. When Abel was told that Hague was bargaining for a government job, he suggested caustically, "Why not get him a job on the House Un-American Activities Committee?" But neither O'Brien nor Meyer Bernstein, the union's representative for international affairs, found Abel's black humor helpful. They were concerned with hastening Hague's exit from the union.

With the approval of Abel, Humphrey had begun to arrange for a spot for Hague in one of the government agencies. On May 8 Hague delivered a slashing attack on Abel at a conference in Cincinnati—Al Whitehouse's home district. He charged that McDonald "may have been cheated out of his office." This speech angered those who were trying to provide him with a job. Called down for rocking the boat, Hague explained lamely that it was camouflage: it might look better if he maintained the appearance of continued opposition.

The fallout from Hague's efforts was not without effect. The Scripps-Howard papers in the industrial centers of Pittsburgh and Birmingham, and in Washington, urged editorially that Wirtz conduct an investigation into the election. A long story by Scripps-Howard's chief Washington correspondent, Jack Steele, recapitulated the Hague charges and concluded that Wirtz would be required to carry on an investigation, if McDonald simply asked for it. Other newspapermen pursued another tack: William Eaton in the Chicago *Daily News* and John Pomfret in the *New York Times* reported that pressures were mounting on McDonald to accept the official results of the election. Pomfret found that "sources close to McDonald" believed that he would be less inclined to protest the election to the Labor Department if he received assurances that no retaliatory action would be taken by the Abel forces. At the same time, *Business Week* for May 15, 1965, referred to Hague's "strongly worded speech" in which he charged that Canadian union officials, to whom Landrum-Griffin restrictions did not apply, had used "union money freely" to elect Abel.

To follow through on McDonald's intention to challenge the tellers' report, on May 12 his faction submitted to the international executive board and to Abel as secretary-treasurer a list of nine "contests" in behalf of McDonald, Whitehouse, Hague, Guido Palumbo, and John Gurovich, the latter two being the defeated teller candidates on the Mc-Donald slate. McDonald was thereby following the only course open to him under the union's constitution, which provided (Article V, Section 19) that an appeal from the tellers' report may be made through the international executive board. Only after he exhausted this final internal remedy could he carry his appeal to the Secretary of Labor under Title 401 of the Landrum-Griffin Act.

By this time, McDonald and his legal advisers—David Feller, Elliott Bredhoff, and Stephen Wexler—knew that the federal law would provide at best a rocky road for him to travel. If, as was likely, his appeal was rejected by the executive board, he would have to convince the Secretary of Labor that the election had been fraudulent or irregular. Within sixty days of the filing of a valid complaint, the Secretary, if convinced, could then bring a civil action in a U.S. District Court. By this time, of course, Abel would have assumed office. If, perhaps a year or two later as the litigation ran its course, the court found that the violations had indeed affected the election, it could then order a new election under the supervision of the Labor Secretary. Obviously, appeals could follow to the Court of Appeals and then, conceivably, to the Supreme Court. During this period of several years, Abel would occupy the presidency, with the majority of the executive board and staff representatives presumably on his side. Under such conditions, as one observer noted, it would take a miracle for McDonald to win an election the second time around. As a practical matter, therefore, McDonald's appeal to the outgoing executive board, over which he formally presided, though without a majority since January 4, was now only a forlorn hope.

The day before the executive board met, the Abel caucus of district directors assembled to consider the nine contests listed in McDonald's complaint. Bernard Kleiman, then attorney for District 31, concluded that none of them possessed merit except that which related to the ballot mixup in Puerto Rico. The Abel forces, Kleiman advised, should welcome a full investigation of the allegations of the voting irregularities. He felt that the testimony taken before the tellers would sustain this position.

The Abel caucus now produced a retaliatory weapon against the McDonald camp. This had to do with an alleged violation of the union constitution by Jimmy Griffin * when he filed a libel suit of $550,000 against Russell Thomas, his opponent.

Joe Germano seemed not inclined to move for strict construction of the union constitution in the Griffin case. Several board members, however, contended that Griffin should be judged by the same strict standards he had applied to others.† As of the moment, however, a majority of the directors in the Abel caucus voted not to press the legal point. The dissenting directors insisted they were not going to let the Griffin case drop. In subsequent developments, the case became an important bargaining point in the settlement of the election controversy.

Another court case involved Walter Bachowski, who had opposed Paul Normile, the incumbent director of District 16. Bachowski had filed a libel action in Common Pleas Court in Allegheny County against four steelworkers in whose names a "false, scurrilous, libelous and malicious" handbill had been issued. Bachowski charged that Normile knew or should have known about the handbills and was responsible for their distribution and publication.

At this point Abel reported that he had news that seven directors, or nearly half of McDonald's supporters on the board, were now prepared to accept the tellers' report—and to reject McDonald's protest.

The self-interest of at least one director was clear: Roy Stevens, the New England district director, who now was not inclined to reject the tellers' report, which, after all, had pronounced him a narrow victor over Lawrence Spitz. Moreover, during the course of his campaign, Stevens's attacks on Spitz had resulted in the latter's filing of a libel suit against him. Thus Stevens was interested in two things: the confirmation of his election and getting Spitz to drop the libel suit. In effect, if Griffin was in violation for moving to the courts against his opponent, Spitz was equally in violation of the union constitution in bringing suit against Stevens. There was one practical difference: Griffin, elected, ran the danger of being punished, whereas Spitz had already been declared defeated and was not readily subject to a drastic penalty.

---

* According to Article XII, entitled "Discipline," "Any member may be penalized for . . . (c) instituting, or urging, or advocating that any member of any Local Union institute action *outside the Union* against the International Union, Local Union, or any of their officers without first exhausting all remedies through the forms of appeal of the International Union . . .; (g) slandering or wilfully wronging a member of the International Union." A member convicted by the International Board of such offenses might be fined, suspended, or expelled, following which he could be removed from his office or position.

† See p. 67. As a member of the executive board, Griffin had sat in judgment on Mamula and confirmed the penalty. Now, four local unions in District 26 had brought similar charges against Griffin. Procedurally, their charges were to be processed for hearing before the executive board at the same session that would hear McDonald's appeal.

If the Abel nose count was correct, the tellers' report would probably be approved by about a three-to-one majority of the executive board. Confident that McDonald's complaints would be rejected, the caucus broke up at about 11 P.M.

Meeting in a parallel caucus, the McDonald directors had also been considering the next steps. Several directors, already in touch with Abel, were now ready to concede McDonald's defeat. Kluz explained solemnly, "I owed political debts to McDonald—and I've paid them."

When Abel reached home late that night, he found a message from Director Bill Moran, requesting a meeting for the following day at 9 A.M., an hour before the executive board meeting at the Penn-Sheraton. The next morning Abel, Burke, Molony, and Germano met with Moran, Stevens, Hugh Carcella, and Eugene Maurice, director of District 13. Maurice, a dedicated McDonald supporter, had already decided to support the tellers' report. Griffin, a key figure in the controversy, preferred to remain aloof from the parley.

The negotiations were tight. Talk focused on the three lawsuits that had been brought up in the course of the campaign. If Spitz would drop his suit against Stevens, the McDonald directors would recommend that Griffin drop his suit against Thomas. They urged that the charges hanging over Griffin for violation of the union constitution by his premature use of the courts should also be killed. Would the Abel majority wash out the charges against Griffin?

As a candidate for secretary-treasurer, Al Whitehouse had had to retire as district director, and so now, in defeat, he would no longer be on the union payroll. Would Abel, as president, agree to retain Whitehouse on the payroll for a few months until his 60th birthday in November, to enable him to qualify for a full pension? Without hesitation, Abel said "yes."

After further bargaining, those Abel directors who had argued the night before for pushing the case against Griffin now assented to a formula of settlement. But Larry Spitz as a complainant before the board was adamant. He would not "barter" on the subject of his suit against Stevens, who, he said, had impugned his integrity, charged him falsely with being a Communist, and injected into the campaign the issue of anti-Semitism.

But what about McDonald himself? In his behalf a proposal was brought forward, naming the price of peace: he would withdraw his "contests" of the election if given the title of president emeritus, with full salary, an unlimited expense account and an automobile. This was identical with Kluz's oblique "report" of two weeks before. Abel replied firmly: "Nothing doing"; the pension of $25,000 provided under the constitution for retiring presidents was ample. He would not consent to additional perquisites. McDonald had reached the dead end in his bargaining.*

The preliminary terms of the understanding included: no retaliatory discharges of staff representatives and no merger of districts, which might eliminate certain district directors friendly to McDonald.

In return, McDonald was to agree not only to withdraw his "contest" but also to congratulate Abel, Molony, and Burke on their victory. Abel would respond in an appreciative manner. The scenario was laid out. Now McDonald and his supporters on the board made their entrance; several minutes later, Abel, Molony, and Burke and their fellow district directors entered. The doors closed behind them. McDonald read a seven-and-a-half-page statement explaining his decision not to proceed with the appeal before the board or follow through with an appeal to the government under Landrum-Griffin.

McDonald stressed his right, along with that of his running mates, "to ask the Secretary of Labor to investigate this election to determine whether it was conducted fairly and in accordance with the laws governing union elections." But, he said, he had decided not to pursue that course.

"I have also urged Howard Hague and Al Whitehouse not to request the Secretary of Labor to conduct any inquiry into the election and they have agreed." The assembled board members applauded. Abel expressed his appreciation. The uncertainty was ended. Then the two men moved two flights below to repeat their statements for the reporters.

A wet-eyed McDonald's voice quavered: "On June 1, 1965, I will begin the first period in my adult life in which I have not been engaged full-time in the work of the labor movement. As I look back over these years, I can truthfully say that the labor movement, and in particular the United Steelworkers of America, has been good to me."

With the withdrawal of McDonald's "contests," the board moved steadily. It set aside all other protests, with one exception. Director Hugh

---

* McDonald's hopes for important recognition from the Johnson administration were far from realized. His associate Howard Hague had, in accordance with the agreement, been made a consultant to the Office of Economic Opportunity; later on he was assigned to another job in the Department of Health, Education and Welfare. Whitehouse was kept on the union payroll until his retirement in November 1965, when he qualified for a union pension. He subsequently found a job as a state director for Kentucky of the OEO. As for McDonald, he was tapped for what he later called an insignificant appointment as an adviser on the U.S. delegation to the Intergovernmental Committee of the World Food Program which met October 11–15, 1965, in Rome. He remarked bitterly that he deserved better than that of the Johnson administration. His trips abroad as union president had supplied handsomer perquisites. Like exiled royalty, he went unattended by his erstwhile entourage. He spent considerable time seeking out influential churchmen at the Vatican, hoping to regain his full status as a Catholic which he had lost following his divorce and second marriage.

Carcella of District 7 argued for the admission of the vote of Local 1374 (a Bethlehem Steel unit), which McDonald had carried by 559 votes to Abel's 242. The international tellers had invalidated the tally of this local of more than 1,500 members on the ground that members from other locals had voted there in clear violation of the constitution (Article V, Section 13). But, argued Carcella, the tellers' action would impair his own effectiveness in the district because of the bad image that the implied fraud might project. While Carcella spoke, Abel's legal and administrative advisers, seated alongside the wall, caught Abel's eye and gestured negatively. But Abel failed to understand the signal, and acquiesced to the Carcella pleas. The board thereupon overrode the tellers' invalidation —the only reversal of the sort in the entire election. As a result, Abel's margin of victory was reduced from 10,142 to 9,825 in the United States and Canada, and served to cut his narrow U.S. majority from 550 to 233.*

The next day in Washington, McDonald sat at the head table for an AFL-CIO dinner at which retiring General of the Army Omar N. Bradley was presented the first Murray-Green Award for Public Service. AFL-CIO President Meany praised McDonald for dropping his challenge to Abel's election, "when he placed the welfare of his union and its membership above his personal interest." McDonald got a standing ovation. Relieved that future steel negotiations would not be hampered by union controversy, Secretary Wirtz coupled McDonald and General Bradley as "two great soldiers." McDonald's cup was now overflowing. When the banquet was over, he was "besieged . . . by dozens of admiring well-wishers and autograph-seekers . . . the handsome, white-haired, 62-year-old McDonald broke into tears. 'Say a prayer for me. Remember me in your prayers,' McDonald said over and over." Thus Neil Gilbride reported for the Associated Press.

When asked to comment on McDonald's throwing in the sponge, Meany said: "I think his decision was in the interest of his union—not to put it through the Labor Department and the courts. He might have been successful, perhaps. He made a good decision for the welfare of the union."

In New York, after several intensive days and nights of negotiation in which Vice-President-elect Joe Molony joined Al Whitehouse and James Robb, three-year contracts with the Aluminum Company of America, Reynolds, Olin Mathieson, Ormet, and Kaiser were signed, providing for slightly more than a fifty-cent package over a three-year period. These agreements were a triumphant prelude to the inauguration ceremonies on June 1 for the induction of Abel, Burke, and Molony. After an all-night vigil, Molony arrived at the ceremonies, tired but happy.

* See Appendix 5.

In Pittsburgh, the main ballroom of the Penn-Sheraton was packed. The platform was jammed. Among representatives of other unions were Vice-Presidents Leonard Woodcock and Pat Greathouse of the United Auto Workers. Vice-President Humphrey sent two of his aides. The advocates of the defeated McDonald sat with fixed smiles, while Abel supporters sat gleeful and expectant. McDonald, Abel and Meany entered through the side of the stage. McDonald and Meany were seated next to each other.

In the invocation, the Reverend Daniel Cantwell of Chicago talked of the generations of labor leaders: "It's good to have them alive and available for less strenuous service." McDonald lifted an eyebrow. "It was good," continued the implacable clergyman, to "understand that the officers of the organization are not the union, just as the bishops are not the church." Meany blinked an eye at the intrusive priest. The district directors sat unmoved.

Joe Germano, presiding, exuberant in victory, read a congratulatory telegram from President Johnson and proceeded to point the moral of the election campaign:

"The election proved that this union belongs to you, the membership. Through this election you restated the following things:

—The right to have adequate representation at meetings with your employers.

—The right to look at your union contract.

—The right to say something about that contract. . . .

—Above all, you have re-established your right to express yourself about your job, your work, your politics, or your leisure, and, if you wish, to talk about things you don't like.

"There were those who used our election to try to create confusion in our ranks. We all know how some on the outside tried to take comfort from the exercise of democracy in this union. . . . There's nothing more traditional about trade unionists than a good battle at election time. I. W. Abel is a trade unionist. Every bone in his body is union, every drop of his blood is dedicated to our cause. Abe's success will never be measured by the number of good stories he can get in the newspapers or the number of times he can appear on television."

Then Meany spoke, deliberately, in only general terms. He was ready to adjust to Abel. The swearing in of the new officers followed; each received the oath from the president of his home local union. Fittingly Leonard Kennedy, president of the Golden Lodge Local 1123, from which the first open call for Abel's candidacy came a year before, administered the installation pledge: "I do hereby sincerely pledge my honor to perform the duties of my office as prescribed by the laws of the organization, and to bear true allegiance to the United Steelworkers of

America . . . [to] deliver to my successor in office all books and other property of this Union that may be in my possession at the close of my official term. . . . To violate this pledge is to stamp me as a man devoid of principle and destitute of honor."

Now came the Gavel Ceremony. Germano as chairman extolled McDonald as a "big man. He has turned over emblems of office to successors and great new officers." McDonald rose. He was smiling hard. In the front row of the audience sat his pretty wife, Rosemary, whose eyes were wetly bright. The audience stood up. McDonald spoke. He recalled a quotation on his study wall which he attributed to Theodore Roosevelt: "It's not the critic who counts, not the man who points out how the strong man stumbled, or where the doer of the deeds could have done better. The credit belongs to the man who is actually in the arena. . . ." He urged his supporters to unite behind Abel, Burke, and Molony: "May I say [his voice broke] to my beloved Steelworkers good-bye and God bless you. I officially declare my term of office ended." He tapped the gavel once and turned to Abel: "Abe, here are the keys to the president's desk and office and the gavel." The two men sort of clutched at each other. "Wield it as a great president." And with that injunction, McDonald, made a last bow.

McDonald stood, *Newsweek* reported, "silver-haired, elegant" as contrasted with Abel "with the rockhewn look of one with whom steelworkers could identify." (Later Abel reported that the key McDonald handed him actually did not fit the desk; when they finally got the desk drawers open, they were empty. Hague's papers had also disappeared, but many of them were finally retrieved in a basement of the Commonwealth Building.)

Abel delivered his installation address to a cheering audience. "From this day we begin a new era in the history of the Steelworkers." Burke and Molony followed. The former delivered his text with the restraint of a prepared speech, while Molony, who seldom if ever speaks from a text, seemed to enthrall the audience for nearly an hour, while the platform dignitaries, after a while, began to indicate unmistakable signs of discomfort at his prolonged and witty eloquence.

"No other union," said Molony, "was so lucky as we as to have a duplicate of officers for the last six months. I only wish we could afford to continue in that great tradition. I salute McDonald—a great man in victory—even greater in defeat."

BOOK IV

THE ABEL ADMINISTRATION

CHAPTER **25**

New Beginning

Put down your foot and you shall feel
The steadfast and enduring earth.

JOHN HALL WHEELOCK

The three new leaders, somewhat self-consciously, walked tall in the land. Abel, Burke, and Molony had performed a deed generally looked upon with disfavor in the special world of union leadership. To challenge an entrenched union president had long been considered one of the more daring if not foolhardy exercises in labor politics. It was an act that bordered on *lèse-majesté*. But success in such an enterprise was so rare that the union establishment tended to shrug it off as usually a waste of time, money, and energy. When, however, the earth moves and the president of a large union suffers defeat, the resulting tremor loosens self-confidence and peace of mind in other places. More than one union leader, not normally given to introspection, begins to wonder whether the tolling of the bell in one union signals a message to another.

Now that Abel was elected, what sort of leadership would he provide? He was quite specific in reiterating his determination to restore decision-making to the properly constituted bodies, the district directors and the Wage Policy Committee. His particular target therefore was the Human Relations Committee which, he charged during the campaign, had far exceeded its original purpose as a "research" and "study" group through which union and management representatives could grapple with certain continuing problems at some distance from the crisis atmosphere that surrounds the expiration of a contract. This usurpation of functions by headquarters personnel, Abel said, could not have taken place without the permissiveness of an often absentee president. It resulted in technical

301

advisers doubling as courtiers. In defense, McDonald supporters in and out of the union had warned that under an Abel administration, the intellectuals and staff technicians would be reduced in number, function, and significance, all to the union's detriment.

But Abel sought to emphasize the opposite:

"That business about our being anti-intellectual is so much bosh. There is not going to be a forced flight of intellectuals out of this union. Of course, nobody who doesn't want to stay is compelled to stay. Far from narrowing the role of the staff, I plan to broaden it.

"The technical staff are important as advisers and experts. Their attitude is important. They must level with you and you with them. There must be a candid relationship, based on mutual respect. We don't want lackeys or ego polishers for the top brass. As to the place of the lawyers —well, we've got to have lawyers. But they should function in the legal field and not move into the administrative and political affairs of the organization. Labor history has shown that if union leadership abdicates, or slackens its attention to the job, a quick, bright and conscientious lawyer could persuade himself that he must, if only for the sake of the neglected rank and file, fill the vacuum. In the last decade or more, lawyers have taken such an administrative hand in our union."

The first significant change in the top personnel resulted with the departure of David Feller. Resigning, Feller explained that the "relationship between the president and the general counsel of the USWA has traditionally been and should continue to be an extremely close and personal one. . . . Such a relationship has worked well in the past and is, I believe, essential to the continued success of the union."

Shortly afterward, Abel appointed Bernard Kleiman, counsel to District 31, the union's general counsel. Elliot Bredhoff, Feller's law partner, was retained as Washington counsel. Bredhoff continued to serve with the union's top negotiating team, as did Marvin Miller, McDonald's chief assistant in contract matters and on the Human Relations Committee. Miller's retention was due as much to recognition of his ability as to emphasize that Abel's criticism of McDonald was based on the latter's improper use of the staff function, not of staff per se.

The Steelworkers were now expected to develop closer and more vigorous cooperation with other unions in the AFL-CIO. While Abel's general political and philosophic outlook resembled that of Auto Workers President Walter Reuther, it seemed clear that it would be a mistake to assume an automatic identity of interest between the two men and the two unions.

At this stage, Abel and his associates were clearly pleased with their electoral accomplishment. They believed that the national referendum had stimulated interest in the life of the union. "It shook us up, all the way down the line," Abel said with a grin. "It also shook up management. Basically, steel management doesn't have to worry. We seek mutual respect. I want neither a distorted Human Relations Committee as has existed here for several years, or codetermination of the steel industry such as unions and management in Germany have been trying to carry on. Neither Burke, Molony, or I will have any trouble communicating with our opposite numbers in management."

Resumption of Negotiations

Before the union house was fully in order, the resumption of contract negotiations in basic steel became the main item on the agenda. Thirty days before September 1, the expiration of the four-month extension agreed to in April, the union's executive board and the Wage Policy Committee announced that negotiations would not continue beyond that deadline. Both management and the union were dour and pessimistic, although Cooper for management and Abel for the union conceded that issues involving local plant conditions had apparently been largely resolved.

On August 24 Cooper made a "last ditch" offer. The union negotiators replied scornfully that it was "really the first offer made by management after eight months of negotiations." The next day Cooper announced to the news media that his offer was worth 40.6 cents over the ensuing three-year period. This, he said, was "as far as we can go. The burden of what follows falls on the union," which, he added sardonically, could now be "expected to indulge in its usual pea and shell game."

Before the same battery of TV cameras and newsmen, Abel replied that management's offer amounted, in fact, to only 37.1 cents. "If management is trying to exploit the fact that the union has new leadership, let it be reassured that while we have changed officers, we have not changed the objectives of this union. We have reached a point where tolerance is no longer a virtue."

Immediately after Abel's news conference, William E. Simkin, the determinedly optimistic director of the Federal Mediation Service, declared that there was still time to reach an agreement. At his White House news conference the same day, President Johnson stood on high ground: "We must never forget that our boys are still fighting in South Vietnam and that our economic strength is the keystone of free-world peace. The decision by steel management and by labor in the days ahead must certainly take into account the overall greater national interest. . . ."

The next morning Johnson phoned Abel and Cooper. Union and management met with Simkin. But movement was slight. The disappointed President started a series of maneuvers. On Saturday afternoon, August 28, he dispatched to Pittsburgh in the Presidential plane Wayne L. Morse (D., Oregon), who was the Senate's leading labor expert, and Under Secretary of Commerce LeRoy Collins. There was still no progress, and their failure gave the President "crisis" power. The Presidential plane was now returned to Pittsburgh to bring both sides to Washington. At 9 P.M. on August 30, President Johnson announced over TV that the strike deadline was postponed until midnight of September 8. This delay, of course, was a union concession. From that time on, the negotiations were constantly subjected to White House pressure. The parties no longer bargained alone; Johnson assigned Labor Secretary Wirtz and Commerce Secretary John T. Connor to "bear down." The President entreated both sides, "you fellers," to compromise. Alternating the pressures, he asked Secretary Wirtz, who had been dealing with the union negotiators, to take over conversations with management; he switched Connor, who had been concentrating on management, to take over as communicator with union spokesmen. He hoped thereby to obtain the maximum objectivity in gauging the attitude of both sides. Arthur Goldberg, recently appointed as ambassador to the United Nations, who had spent the previous weekend at the LBJ Ranch in Texas along with Secretary of State Dean Rusk, was believed to have played a role in advising the President.

On September 2, the parties took time out for sleep. The next day, the President publicly revealed his anxiety to negotiators and to the watching correspondents by pacing West Executive Avenue, the protected street running between the White House and the Executive Office Building. At one point, the union negotiators stood in the balcony of the Executive Office Building and exchanged salutes or signals—nobody could tell which—with the President. For hours the talks went on. Suddenly the press was alerted. At 6:35 P.M., Johnson, flanked by union and industry negotiators, announced that "an essential agreement" had been reached. He reported that both sides "bargained hard. They represented their interests with great skill and conviction but they always put the interests of the nation first." Abel then announced a meeting in Pittsburgh of the executive board for Sunday at 10 A.M., to be followed by the ratification meeting of the Wage Policy Committee at 2 P.M. Back in Pittsburgh via the Presidential jet, the weary union negotiators described to the committee in considerable detail how the "President and his aides kept reiterating the necessity for a strike-free agreement."

The essential point made by the union was that these were the first pay increases of any kind that were won by workers in basic steel since October 1961, and "without a strike." Secretary Wirtz reassured all concerned that, despite the impression the government's clear and present interest might have conveyed, both sides were "bargaining and bargaining hard. It was true collective bargaining."

The political importance of the *new* contract was obvious. This, the first contract negotiated under the leadership of the *new* union president, was regarded as a test of the skill and endurance and restraint of Abel and his *new* top team. Those who had considered him a permanent No. 2 man noted his self-possession under pressure, and the vigor and flexibility with which he pushed the union's position, without apparent loss of strength.

Then for no obvious reason, six weeks after the contract was signed, R. Conrad Cooper smashed the comfortable belief that calm would now prevail in the steel industry. In a speech to a large group of Pittsburgh businessmen, Cooper bitterly attacked what he called the "abuse of union power" and lamented the inability of Congress to "perform major surgery on the obese body of union power." He then heaped praise on McDonald as an example of true labor statesmanship. McDonald, he said, was defeated by a revolt of the "palace guard."

Abel jabbed back: "Mr. Cooper is the leader of the big steel companies which recently faced the union across the bargaining table. Their net worth is more than $9 billion; that of the Steelworkers Union is $21 million. If the Steelworkers Union can be characterized by Mr. Cooper as part of the 'obese body of union power,' what sort of bloated monster is the power of these companies 440 times as large as the union in their financial power? These ten companies, alone, exercise a power so great as to dwarf completely the small strength of a few hundred thousand men banded together in a union to better their wages, hours and working conditions." Then Abel commented on Cooper's praise of McDonald's "labor statesmanship": "Mr. Cooper's outburst candidly reveals that he attempted to involve himself in the democratic election of our union. . . . Obviously, Mr. Cooper was hurt in this encounter with the new leadership of the union. We do hope he ultimately receives and accepts fully the fact that our union has entered a new era; that it refuses to enter into private, cozy contract deals. . . . We choose to do our bargaining in an open, straightforward manner where there cannot be the slightest doubt about the function and responsibility of each of the parties."

Cleaning the Augean Stables

Just as Cooper launched his attack, the executive board met in New York to reorganize the union's civil rights structure, and to pave the way for eliminating discrimination within the industries under the union's jurisdiction. For the first time, an international officer—Vice-President Molony—was appointed to head the Civil Rights Committee, which had been a staff-level committee headed by staff men. Alex Fuller was made executive director; and Tom Murray, who had often taken initiatives in the civil rights field, became secretary. The campaign attacks on Abel alleging racial discrimination had remained a sore spot. Politically, the Negro steelworkers and the Mexican-American minority kept pushing for a more important role in the government and staffing of the union.

The revision of organizational values continued. Early in January 1966, Abel furnished the delegates of a District 15 convention with a report on the "state of the union," on the central theme that a union leader must not confuse the Great Society with café society. He did not believe, he said, in being an expense-account executive. He also made it clear that union staff members no longer could expect to live "high on the hog." As secretary-treasurer, Walter Burke had installed a stricter record of accountability.

"It may sound naïve," said Abel, "but I believe this union and its leaders should live by trade union principles. Those are our only status symbols." To explain what he meant, Abel told of some of the lush items he had cut out. Item: he dispensed with a $21,000-a-year suite in Washington's Madison Hotel that his predecessor had engaged. When he visited Washington, Abel said he would rent hotel space as he needed it. Item: the previous president sported two Cadillacs and a chauffeur— all out. Item: Abel dropped three or four bodyguards. "This president," he said, "no longer needs that kind of protective companionship." Item: he eliminated heavy spenders on the staff of the union subdistrict of Florida and Puerto Rico. Item: Three secretaries were trimmed from the president's staff.

Two cases involving personnel with close ties to McDonald illustrated the change in atmosphere in the new union administration.

The Barranco Case: Charles Barranco, McDonald's bodyguard, charged he had been unfairly treated by the new administration: his salary had been drastically cut when he was reassigned to other duties. For seven or eight years prior to the election, Barranco, fifty-two in 1965, had driven McDonald's cars, arranged meetings, attended all Executive Board meetings, "took care of the door," and even, he said, taken the "pulse of the rank and file prior to negotiations." His salary was $10,500 in 1962, $14,500 in 1963, and $15,797.85 in 1964. That year his reported expenses came to $15,310, giving him one of the highest incomes in the union.

After Abel's inauguration in June 1965, O. L. Garrison, director of District 36-G and an old friend of McDonald's, wired Abel requesting that Barranco be assigned to his Florida district with headquarters in Tampa. Promptly acceding to Garrison's request, Abel instructed Barranco to report to Garrison as a staff representative at a salary of

$9,750 a year, with a special $15 per diem for the first thirty days, after which he was to receive the regular per diem of $6 per day.

This unexpected financial rearrangement hit Barranco hard; a sharp drop of almost $6,000 a year in salary alone, not counting the loss of the heavy expense account. This meant a drastic adjustment in his life style; his lower salary would also affect the size of his pension and life insurance. He protested through the local of the union's headquarters employees. Following a series of grievance meetings spread over a year, both sides agreed to submit the dispute to arbitration. Professor John A. Hogan of the University of New Hampshire heard the case.

After two days of hearings, supplementary briefs, and four hundred pages of testimony, Hogan decided that Barranco's grievance, under the terms of the contract, was unjustified. While he conceded that the "cut of almost $6,000 a year in pay and the impact on his pension are undoubtedly severe jolts, Charles Barranco is still ahead of the game. He was lifted quickly by President McDonald from an organizer's rate to a rate more than 60 per cent above it. He enjoyed one of the top salaries in the union for a number of years. Retention of this rate upon his return to organizing work . . . would create a gross inequity between Barranco's rate, that of his fellow organizers and that of 'key personnel' in the field." On the basis of the evidence, he rejected as unjustified the charge of "political reprisal" made against the new officers.

The Agnes Vaughn Case: Agnes K. Vaughn, at the time of the 1965 election, held a secretarial job in Local 4380 in Tampa, part of District 36-G. In closing out superfluous offices, the new international officers unexpectedly found themselves sued by Mrs. Vaughn on the ground that in discharging her they had violated a personal agreement—a copy of which she produced—signed by David McDonald and countersigned by Mrs. Vaughn. This "agreement," dated June 3, 1963, assured her that she would be paid the top salary assigned to district secretaries plus any increases granted to other secretaries in that category; that she was to be granted two first-class round trips a year from Florida to Pittsburgh at Christmas and any other time she chose; that if her present job was abolished, she would be ensured a post in the Pittsburgh office or some other area of her choice.

The explanation for this agreement was that Mrs. Vaughn was being compensated for "her hard work and loyalty . . . to the United Steelworkers . . . and its predecessor, the Steel Workers Organizing Committee, from the time of its inception when she gave freely of her time and efforts, at a time when the Organization had little money to pay help."

Upon her discharge in January 1966, Mrs. Vaughn charged the international union with a breach of "contract" on the ground that its provisions required that she be retained as an employee until 1973. When the Abel administration rejected her contention, she picketed the union offices in Tampa. In his column Drew Pearson alleged that her discharge was an example of political retaliation by Abel against a McDonald supporter. When it seemed clear that McDonald would avoid an appearance in an open proceeding, Mrs. Vaughn finally abandoned her suit, accepting the union's offer to pay her airplane fare and to ship her belongings back to Pittsburgh. Whatever the reason for McDonald's largesse to Mrs. Vaughn, favoritism—not always revealed in personal contracts—had often characterized the McDonald regime in providing "tender, loving care" for a variety of people in and outside the union.

Two district directors caused the new administration considerable distress. One was William J. Hart, of Pennsylvania, who supported Abel in the 1965 campaign. The other was Charles J. Smith of California who did not.

Hart's extracurricular activities had attracted considerable attention. An active figure in Pennsylvania Republican politics, he sought also to exercise influence through his presidency of the AFL-CIO Allegheny County Labor Council. Late in 1966, he was charged with trying to "steal" his election to a third two-year term as council president. His opponent filed formal charges with AFL-CIO President George Meany. The latter sent Lane Kirkland, then his administrative assistant, to investigate. While Meany was pondering a recommendation to set aside Hart's election, Hart was named state Secretary of Labor and Industry by Pennsylvania's Republican Governor-elect Raymond P. Shafer. Earlier that year, William Scranton, also a Republican, had named Hart to an $11,000-a-year state labor job.

Despite hints from his colleagues in the Steelworkers Union, Hart did not resign his membership from its executive board, or even take a leave of absence. He was reported collecting both state and union salaries. There was no constitutional provision to cover such a situation. The constitution did require that each district director administer his district full time, thus raising the question whether Hart could hold both his jobs. Since the situation was unprecedented, the officers and the executive board were not inclined to make him quit. After several months, the matter resolved itself when Hart resigned his state post following a dispute with the governor.

Smith, director of District 38, was indicted in February 1967 for misuse of union funds. He had been under grand-jury investigation for many months. The year before the Steelworkers Union executive board had appointed a "commission" of executive board members, headed by Director John Johns, to investigate similar charges brought against Smith by members in his district. The commission reported that the charges were not proved so far as the union was concerned. Smith stood exonerated. In September 1967, Smith was scheduled to go on trial as a result of the grand jury's findings. As of September 1, Smith was granted a leave of absence by the union on the ground of chronic illness. To replace Smith, a district director since 1946, the executive board named Lester Thornton, a subdistrict director under Joe Germano. Several weeks later, Smith finally pleaded guilty to two felony charges, but avoided a prison sentence; he was placed on probation. Under the Landrum-Griffin Act, he was barred from holding office for five years after expiration of his probation.

The Union's External Relations

While Abel gave primary attention to the union's internal business, he took time to express his views on the social issues agitating large sections of the country, and to relate them to his union. To a convocation at St. Vincent College in Latrobe, Pennsylvania, located in the steel community, where he received an honorary degree, he observed in March 1966 that the "demonstrations and the strikes and the protests have a common element: People are looking for a new set of values or a rearrangement of old values. . . ." This same need for a change, he said, made manifest in the Steelworkers election, required the union to be "responsive to the needs of the membership." Since then, he found that "encouraging progress" had been made in broadening the participation of union representatives in the last negotiations. In gaining "the best wage and benefit package in the basic steel industry since 1956," which included a historic breakthrough on the pension front, allowing workers to retire after thirty years of service regardless of age, the methods used in this accomplishment were especially significant: "More local bargaining committees, staff members and persons were involved in the negotiations and more local plant issues were resolved than ever before." It was not enough to rest on these laurels; the international union had begun, he said, to review the "entire collective bargaining approach for discussion and decision" in preparation for the Steelworkers convention in September 1966.

After enumerating the various changes in the operational services at headquarters, Abel referred to one of the basic themes of his campaign— to move the Steelworkers Union back into the mainstream of the labor movement. At the November 1965 convention of the AFL-CIO Industrial Union Department, the Steelworkers Union was represented, for the first time in many years, by a full contingent of delegates. Local USW unions that had remained aloof were being urged to join and participate in local and state AFL-CIO labor councils. At the same time, Abel established closer relationship with the national AFL-CIO under President Meany. In December 1965, he had been elected an AFL-CIO vice-president, replacing McDonald on the AFL-CIO Executive Council. In contrast to past practice, the executive board of the Steelworkers Union was holding more meetings "to provide the widest latitude for discussion of policy and programs."

The entire union, he said, is "recharging its batteries": "We don't want Steelworkers to be surface citizens or surface union members. We want them to get involved. . . . When they see a wrong, we want them to speak up. Unions like ours came into being because workers needed them. The labor movement must never permit itself to become captive of the 'establishment' no matter how comfortable the accommodations may seem."

In April 1966, exactly a year after he and his fellow officers appeared in Washington at the convention dinner of Americans for Democratic Action, Abel delivered the main address at the League for Industrial Democracy in New York, to present the LID's annual award to A. Philip Randolph, a colleague on the AFL-CIO Executive Council. The occasion afforded Abel a fresh opportunity to state his position, and organized labor's position, in eliminating discrimination: "By its very nature, a trade union has the means by which it can help eliminate discriminatory practices, whether they be industry-inspired or inherited." At the same time, he warned that "contract clauses, in themselves, would not do the job of eliminating discrimination. They only affirm the union's moral and legal obligation to bargain fairly and equitably for every member, regardless of race, creed or color. We will not tolerate any device that sets aside certain jobs for members of a particular race or religious group."

Thus Abel cultivated his union's image in academic and liberal communities. As guest of honor at a huge labor dinner in Pittsburgh, attended by a cross-section of national labor leadership numbering more than two thousand, he was hailed by Auto Workers President Reuther as a "symbol of the highest tradition as exemplified by our great founder, Philip Murray. . . . I. W. Abel represents the best in the labor movement." Then addressing Abel directly, Reuther said: "With your leadership as head of the United Steelworkers, we can forge solidarity between our two great unions. . . . No force on earth can halt the march of the U.S. labor movement. There is much unfinished work on the agenda." Abel replied in kind.

Thus, in 1966, Abel and Reuther seemed to synchronize their thinking and their approach to trade-union problems as well as the more comprehensive national issues. "We supped," Abel said, "at the same ideological table." The long estrangement between the UAW and the

Steelworkers during the McDonald presidency was at an end. A few weeks later, Abel addressed the Auto Workers convention at Long Beach, California. This was the first time since 1946 that a Steelworkers president—then Philip Murray—had appeared at such a convention. This sign of cooperation between the AFL-CIO's two largest unions indicated, said Abel, that "we won't be going off in different directions, just because the other fellow thought of an idea first."

On another level, that of the techniques of collective bargaining, questions were being asked and to some degree answered. Had the Steelworkers leadership in fact made any decisions or recommendations on changes in collective bargaining procedures, as promised in the campaign? The answer was both "no" and "not yet." To cope with this problem, a committee of the executive board had been appointed to study the diversity of collective bargaining approaches. One result of its efforts was to cause internal controversy a year later.

For the first time, a Steelworkers executive board met in Canada. After all, the Steelworkers were an international union, a fact which was often forgotten in the United States, and often resented by some Canadians. More than 10 per cent of the union's membership was Canadian, yet this large segment of the union still maintained an arm's-length posture toward the government of the international union itself. The events of the dramatic 1956 convention had shown how the Canadians, when aroused, could battle on an issue that affected their national identity, and the election of 1965 revealed how apathetic the Canadian membership still remained with regard to even the most significant of elections.

At this time, also, the Steelworkers became engaged in twin enterprises: the development of a structure for coordinated bargaining in the copper industry, and of discussions for merger with the Mine, Mill and Smelter Workers (expelled from the CIO in 1949–50 on charges of Communist domination). The general pattern of coordinated collective bargaining, already launched by a dozen unions with members in General Electric and Westinghouse, was now to be staked out for the copper and brass industry. This bargaining technique, initiated by the AFL-CIO Industrial Union Department for its affiliates, was to be extended to include other unions.

CHAPTER **26**

The First Abel Convention

We cannot kindle when we will
The fire which in the heart resides.
MATTHEW ARNOLD

Fifteen months after his inauguration, Abel stepped to the front of the stage at Convention Hall in Atlantic City, to the welcoming roar of the 3,500 delegates at the thirteenth constitutional convention. Smiling faintly, he gazed at the sea of faces. More than most, Abel was sensitive to the importance of recognizing those who had been neglected or mortified by McDonald. He was not going to run a bulldozer over the delegates. He did not forget, for example, how his friend Nick Zonarich, the director of organization for the Industrial Union Department, had been humiliated by McDonald as he attempted to deliver his speech on "organizing the unorganized." At this convention, Zonarich was to speak twice.

Abel addressed the delegates sincerely and directly, reviewing the months since he and his associates had assumed office. The luster of the occasion was dimmed when President Johnson canceled a planned appearance at the last moment. But later in the week, Hubert Humphrey delivered a "homecoming" speech of spectacular length and fervor. He reviewed past relations with the Steelworkers, at local, district, and international levels, and wound up with the pledge of allegiance to the flag. (Two years later, when Johnson withdrew from the Presidency, the Steelworkers leadership became the vanguard of the Humphrey for President movement.)

But the internal politics of their own union promptly absorbed the new officers' energies. Following a policy of "no recriminations, no retalia-

312

tion," they determined to avoid the "cult of personality" resolution, a ritual that had characterized past conventions.* Replacing it was a comprehensive resolution, recounting the organization's achievements since its founding, and listing all past leaders, including McDonald. But no sooner had the resolution been presented than Buena Parker, a grievance committeeman from Local 2869 (Fontana, California), which had voted for Rarick in 1957 and for Abel in 1965, moved that McDonald be invited to address the convention. The convention was thrown into an uproar, and the surprised leaders on the platform could not conceal their dismay. Abel put the motion to a standing vote. From the front of the hall, it seemed as if the motion had been narrowly defeated. After a momentary appraisal of the situation and the mood of the convention, Abel suggested that those opposed to inviting McDonald withdraw their objection and proposed, instead, the unanimous passage of the motion. The delegates thunderously applauded Abel's adroit generosity.

That night the wires were hot from Palm Springs, where McDonald heard the heady news. Perhaps this could be his return from Elba. He telephoned his campaign strategists, Directors Jim Griffin and Hugh Carcella, as well as several newsmen covering the convention. It was clear that with even slight encouragement, he was prepared to fly to Atlantic City. But Griffin, no romantic, told him flatly that he had better stay away. Carcella also warned him that he ought to quit while he was ahead. The next day McDonald's telegram of regrets to the convention was read off routinely by Secretary-Treasurer Walter Burke, along with other messages. There was no movement in the hall.

The convention turned to pressing problems. The heat of the race issue was mounting. The union's reorganized Civil Rights Committee had understood the difficulty of eliminating discrimination in the plants, where many whites resented the new competition from black workers for the better jobs. Race discrimination was placed in clear trade-union terms by A. Philip Randolph, a guest speaker. He expressed fear of the "growing white backlash," the strong possibility of confrontation of blacks and whites, a collision that could destroy such progress as had been achieved only after the greatest sacrifice. He told the more than three thousand local union leaders in the Steelworkers convention—of Polish, Czech, Slav, and Irish origin and many Negroes—how strongly he opposed the use of violence:

"I looked upon the faces of white citizens . . . when Negroes were

* Instead of the customary outsize portrait of the incumbent president against the back curtain of the stage, only the photograph of Philip Murray, the founder, was given this place of honor. This caused Monsignor George Higgins to exclaim in humorous disbelief that it seemed to him "metaphysically impossible to have a labor convention without having the pictures of all the top officers blown up at the back of the podium."

marching in Chicago for the right of open occupancy in housing, and the faces were ugly with rage and resentment. . . . Negroes threw bottles and Molotov cocktails, turning over automobiles, throwing rocks, looting stores. . . . I want to see the civil rights leaders take great care against overheating the black ghettoes with the racial and social chemistry full of explosive ingredients. This could escalate into a race war which could become catastrophic to the Negro and America. . . .

"I believe the strategy now in order is to shift from the streets to the conference room to discuss problems and find answers. I don't mean that all demonstrations should be eliminated immediately, all boycotts, all picketing now carried on by Negroes—any more than labor, as a whole, can eliminate strikes or picketing." What he looked forward to was the development of an economic and social program—a freedom budget of $10 billion a year for ten years—that would have the goal of benefiting all of America's thirty-five million "working poor." He reminded the Steelworkers delegates that 25 per cent of the "working poor" were non-white and about 75 per cent white. The convention delegates cheered his conclusion: "The black working poor and the white working poor must unite in order to create full employment under the leadership of organized labor. Only full employment can be the basis of fair employment."

The significance of the convention was made even clearer by its fervent reception of Auto Workers President Walter Reuther. During the twelve years of his presidency, McDonald had refused to invite Reuther to a convention. Most of the 3,500 delegates had therefore never heard Reuther address their meetings. In the tumultuous reception given Reuther by the assembled local leadership, Abel, Molony, and Burke found support and vindication of their broadened approach to the labor movement.

The new leadership had promises to keep in the revision of the union's political structure, and the delegates showed they would not let the new team forget it. Politics of two kinds was involved: a new election procedure that would require changes in the union constitution; and broader participation by the membership in the union's decision-making and contract-ratification processes.

In the area of constitutional change, a retirement age for international officers was settled without debate. The Constitution Committee, now headed by Vice-President Molony with Lawrence Sefton of Canada as secretary, recommended that a member be disqualified for nomination to international union office if he had attained the age of sixty-five before the end of the nominating period. The new provision permitted, for example, Director Joseph Germano to be eligible to serve an additional term after the expiration of his current one, since his sixty-fifth birthday would fall in December 1968, during the next nominating period. On the other hand, if a member's eligibility to run for office were based on the date of the "assumption of office," Germano would have been ineligible to serve an additional term beyond 1969, since he would have reached his sixty-fifth birthday six months before the date of installation in office, namely June 1, 1969.

The Constitution Committee also proposed to restore to the secretary-treasurer the powers which had been taken from that office, at the behest of Philip Murray, in May 1952 and transferred to the office of the president. Voicing his confidence in Abel, Burke as secretary-treasurer made it clear that he felt there was no practical need specifically to restore certain powers to the secretary-treasurer. While Abel appreciated this expression of confidence in him as a person, he insisted that as a matter of principle the full powers of secretary-treasurer be spelled out. So the constitution was changed.

Then came disagreement. With the last election on its mind, the convention reviewed the method of "nomination and election of international officers." As in the past, various proposals were made to change the nomination procedure—mainly to reduce the number of local union endorsements necessary for a place on the international union ballot. Abel called for a standing vote. The vote seemed close. He pronounced the motion lost. A delegate's demand for a roll call was followed by shouts of support from various sections of the convention hall. Abel responded: "You want a roll call? Do you want to spend the afternoon on this question? I don't think the delegates want to go through a roll call on this question." There was no roll call. In the history of the Steelworkers, a roll call had never been held—not under the presidencies of Murray, McDonald, and now not under Abel. The prospect of a roll call—long, time-consuming, and uncertain—remained unlikely, without effective sponsorship and the necessary psychological and physical preparation for such an event.

Proposals for numbering election ballots in international elections and the installation of voting machines came up again. Charges and dark suspicions of ballot stuffing that surrounded the past elections—the 1955 special vice-presidential election, the 1957 McDonald-Rarick contest, and even that of 1965—sustained interest in this proposal as a possible deterrent to improper practices. When Abel sought to reassure the convention that the matter would be studied by the executive board, a delegate from District 13 refused to let go. He had not yet heard, he said sharply, an "honest answer as to why it is beneficial to the rank and file not to have numbered ballots. As a teller in our local union, I must say that a steelworker who travels far out of his way to cast a vote for a man of his choice and finds only an unnumbered ballot awaiting him tears up his ballot in disgust and tells us and the international union to go to hell, because his intelligence is being insulted."

A little later, the committee recommended rejection of a proposal by Joseph Kender, president of Local 2265, District 28, to punish recording secretaries who failed to comply with the constitutional procedures in filling out returns. Smarting from his failure to win a place on the ballot in the 1965 directorship election, Kender had by this time succeeded in getting the Labor Department to start litigation against the international union for alleged violations of election provisions of the Landrum-Griffin Act. In 1964, he argued, hundreds of local unions had been disqualified in the nominations procedures as a result of willful neglect or ignorance on the part of the recording secretaries.

Kender's arguments aroused the interest of many delegates but not enough to win the 30 per cent needed for a roll call. "Everyone here wants to see election machinery that is as nearly perfect as is possible," Abel said. "We all recognize that the conduct of a democratic election, whether it be within the union or within our political subdivisions, does create some inequities, apparently; at times, some errors. Above all, however, they all provide for people to register protests. . . . We are all aware of the interest of the government—under the Taft-Hartley Act and the Landrum-Griffin Act—to protect and safeguard the rights of the individual in the conduct of elections, whether they be by referendum or by convention."

There arose the recurring convention issue of the place of staff representatives in the life of the union and of the convention in particular. Since the last convention, the Staffman's Organizing Committee had become an independent union. For that reason some locals proposed that staff men should not be permitted to act as delegates for local unions unless they were duly elected at a membership meeting. Often staff representatives, it was charged, "pick up credentials" from small unions that could not afford to send a delegate to the convention. Thus, said delegate Archie Broadfoot, "When we have a voice vote, 600 or more staff representatives—some of whom might have been duly elected, but many may not—can get up on the floor."

In response, a staff man and subdistrict director, Joseph LaMorte of District 31, charged the delegate with bad faith in thus setting local union members against staff men. "Some of the delegates want the staff to be nice boys. They want us to be politicians so that we run and hide when some member hollers. . . . Now look, if we are going to be running around like whipped dogs every time a member yells, then we are going to be the same whipped dogs when management yells. . . . I ask the delegation here to allow the staff to have their rights as first-class dues-paying members of this union and not attempt to shame them."

Emotions on this issue ran deep. Lines of delegates, waiting at the various floor microphones, were shouting for recognition. Despite Vice-President Molony's assurance that staff representatives were properly elected as delegates, "particularly now because of the Landrum-Griffin Law," he noted, delegates persisted in their contention that the influence of staff men as delegates at a convention was topheavy. But, Frank Mirocha of Local 65 considered Molony's observation irrelevant: "I don't think that 500 or 600 international staff representatives—all members of the Staffman's Organizing Committee, the SOC—should be allowed to come as a body before this convention and set policy for us. It is tantamount to saying, 'Speak, but I have got you by the throat.' How can you speak? The convention is stacked when you have 600 such people here who are of one mind, who have been 'communicated' with." The convention nevertheless voted down change in the procedure for the election of delegates.

Next arose another sensitive issue: redistricting the international union through a change in the internal administrative boundaries. The union was long recognized as "overdistricted," carrying an unnecessary bureaucratic load with heavy expense. Despite the objections raised in the 1964 convention, the union's latest Audit Report showed that some of the questionable districts still existed, completely staffed with directors and office and administrative personnel—the whole panoply of political machinery and pork barrel. Some districts had a smaller membership than many local unions in other districts. "If we are going to practice austerity, we are going to have to start from the top down," a delegate said sharply. To such charges of inaction, Abel reported that the weird and expensive District 36-G—covering Florida, Puerto Rico, and the Virgin Islands—had already been abolished, its locals apportioned between two neighboring districts. Looking toward further action, a study of the entire union structure was under way: "These things that grow up over the years certainly can't be wiped out overnight," he observed. The Steelworkers Union was as much a victim of the workings of Parkinson's Law as other institutions.

The perennial subject of the union's dues and fee structure, perhaps the most sensitive of union issues, drew resolutions from 248 locals. It included a proposal to establish a strike fund to be financed by increased dues. Proceeding with great circumspection on this matter, the international leadership opposed a dues increase, but they encouraged full discussion of the idea.

Over the years, the concept of a strike fund was regularly rejected by the Steelworkers Union, following closely the pattern of the United Mine Workers. The traditional opposition was rooted in the belief that an international strike fund would tend to encourage workers to strike;

hence·strike relief had become a responsibility of locals or districts rather than of the international union. The argument was now advanced that proper distribution of strike relief "would give incentive to man the picket lines and stick it out until the battle was won."

Murray Cotterill, the Canadian staff representative, arguing for a dues allocation for an international union strike fund, pointed out that the costs of collective bargaining and the administering of contracts were on the rise, so that even the most carefully run local treasuries had little money left for relief. Lines of delegates again lengthened before the various microphones on the floor. Rather than terminate the debate, the leadership felt that the delegates should have the completest sense of participation.

When late in the day the calls for "question" began to be raised, Walter Burke, presiding, refused to curtail discussion. He preferred to "make the rounds" across the convention floor to recognize those still wishing to be heard. When Vice-President Molony described the day-long debate as "inspiring," illustrative of the "democracy which exists in our union," the delegates clapped enthusiastically. The dues issue itself Molony found to be "a topsy-turvy situation. . . . My memory of conventions of the United Steelworkers is that the officers are constantly presenting a plea to raise the dues and initiation fees, and the delegates spend all their time knocking down every effort to raise them." Nevertheless he saw at this convention no real consensus for a dues increase. In the event of a strike in the basic steel industry, he argued, "We can't tax our members enough to build up the kind of a strike fund that we would need." Then he echoed arguments often made by delegates on the floor of other conventions: "God help us, in our ranks there are many thousands of members who are paid low wages, and do not enjoy the benefits that so many of you do enjoy, and can ill afford to pay any more in dues. They should not be asked to do it."

The range and intensity of this debate on dues and initiation fees proved a useful exercise for the new administration. The opposition of the union's officers to an increase in dues at this time was not without guile. Strategically, it would have been an unfortunate error in judgment for them to have sponsored such an increase at their first convention. Having demonstrated its reluctance to raise dues, the leadership paved the way for a time when, with proper preparation, it might persuasively ask for a change in the dues structure.

The interior life of the union inevitably affected its outward behavior in dealing with employers. The delegates had long been deeply concerned with how the contract decisions were made. The way in which contracts were negotiated and concluded had created such discontent over the years that it had swelled into the single most important issue in the

1964–65 campaign. Promise of change was a promise the new officers knew they would have to keep. A special committee of the executive board, under Vice-President Molony, had therefore been at work since October 1965 in preparing for the restructuring of the union's bargaining procedures, especially in basic steel, to reflect the change in the character and attitude of the membership.

Molony's committee now urged changes to "bring about greater involvement and participation by the membership." First, the international Wage Policy Committee would continue to initiate and formulate wage policy for the entire union's membership, but it was no longer to be the union's ultimate, although often *pro forma,* instrument of contract ratification. As a response to the new demands, industry conferences were to be created for basic steel, nonferrous industry, the aluminum industry, and can manufacturing. Made up of representatives of local unions within each industrial sector, together with district directors and presiding officers designated by the international union president, these industry conferences would have the responsibility for implementing the union's national wage policy. Industry conferences would possess the authority to reject or ratify contracts, and in the event of strikes they would have the authority to approve the contract settlement that emerged. Moreover, authority to recommend strikes would reside in the industry conference, subject to the approval of the membership. "The wishes of the membership before a strike is fundamental to a democratic union," the committee said. Once the membership authorized a strike, the international executive board could, as the strategy indicated, set the date.

As chairman of the restructuring committee, Molony reminded the delegates that past dissatisfaction with the Wage Policy Committee frequently arose because, once broad agreement on wages and pensions was reached, the local issues, often the most sensitive, were submerged by vote of the committee. Molony's ability to slide along a tangent between old troubles and new was never more apparent than in this discussion. He now raised the possibility of abandoning industry-wide bargaining and reverting to company-by-company bargaining, although the Steelworkers tradition for at least fifteen years had been to bargain industry-wide. He was determined, however, to keep local issues from being neglected. While the impression generally persisted that basic steel was the pacesetter for the union's negotiations in other sectors, new patterns were in fact often set elsewhere: the extended-vacation plan had first been negotiated in can manufacturing in 1962, the year before basic steel; supplemental unemployment benefits were negotiated with the can manufacturers in 1955, in basic steel not before 1956; and the provision for retirement after thirty years of service regardless of age was developed in the aluminum industry in May 1965, several months before the union won it in basic steel.

In light of the changes in the union's pattern of membership, therefore, the operative functions previously held by the Wage Policy Committee would now belong to the industry conferences. This transfer of powers, which Molony saw as "fundamental to any democratic union," at first threw a scare in the business community. According to *Business Week* for September 24, 1966: "Contracts could be more costly for an industry that's the keystone of the national economy. Settlements could be much harder to sell to the rank and file." The fact is that up to then, as *Business Week* acknowledged, the Steelworkers Union "had lacked a channel through which the rank and file could make its wishes known and pressures felt."

The fears of management were premature. After examining the changes in the bargaining structure, observers from the management of basic steel at the convention concluded that the changes were not so drastic as they had anticipated. The rank and file had not taken over, after all. Contracts would not ultimately have to be ratified by referendum.

The Racial Issue at the Convention

For months before the convention, the union leadership sought ways to make clear its concern for effective implementation in the field of civil rights. With new authority as president, Abel had addressed the Baltimore convention of the Negro American Labor Council in May 1966 pledging support to an alliance of mutual assistance, a "coalition of conscience" of black and white workers. The following month, Negroes demonstrated outside the Pittsburgh headquarters of the U.S. Steel Corporation to protest continuing discrimination in plants and offices. While they had also picketed the company's Southern operations in Birmingham, the National Association for the Advancement of Colored People declared that the problem was not just a Southern one. In Pittsburgh the demonstrators charged that the steel company was guilty of "tokenism": out of a total employment roll of 4,500, only a hundred Negroes were working in the company's offices. To this charge, U.S. Steel's R. Conrad Cooper replied that in Birmingham a thousand Negroes had been promoted to jobs not previously accessible to them. He countercharged that the NAACP was pressing for "preferential hiring and promotion practices, which would be discriminatory to non-Negro employees." Along with management, the union found itself placed on the defensive by the NAACP in Alabama, and blamed for "lack of real progress." The stubborn facts of persistent racial discrimination in Birmingham surfaced. Not long before, several locals led by white leaders had threatened to pull out of the Steelworkers Union because of the AFL-CIO's strong position against segregation. Groups of other union leaders—in rubber in Gadsden, Alabama, and automobiles in Tennessee—had also been identified with the Ku Klux Klan and White Citizens Councils. Evidently a deprecatory sigh by the union hierarchy was no substitute for action. Despite the touted "steady advance," therefore, Molony refused to dismiss the delegates' charges of failure directed at the union as a whole: "We have found enough merit in NAACP charges to cause our union distress—even though great progress has been made by our organization in the effort to eliminate such practice."

Speaking on the last day of the convention, Monsignor George Higgins emphasized organized labor's moral responsibility for the achievement of racial justice. That issue, he told the delegates, would be the historic test for American society: "Ten or twenty years from now, the American people and history itself are going to judge the labor movement, the Church, American industry, almost exclusively on one criterion —what did the labor movement, what did the Church, what did the business world do to advance the cause of civil rights in this decade? Some segments of the labor movement are not going to look very good when that history is written."

After the civil rights resolution was read, delegates from Districts 31 (Chicago-Gary) and 27 (Canton, Ohio) urged the incorporation of a new civil rights component in basic steel contract negotiations. In the opinion of Al Lebbano (Local 1200, District 27), the steel employer was "the guy causing all the trouble in our plants [the Republic Steel Works in Canton]. For years he has been telling our people that management is not discriminating, that it is the union that is discriminating." He demanded to know why a resolution to put "civil rights language in the contract has been dropped in the Resolutions Committee," and "whether Vice-President Molony, chairman of the union's Civil Rights Committee, is behind us" and whether he would help out on the executive board. "I will," said Molony from the platform.

At this point, Nathaniel Lee interposed his concern about another matter closer to home: "token employment" of Negroes by the international union. He found little change, he said, in the number of Negroes employed by the union in the past fifteen years. Lee's observation carried special cutting power because he was one of three international tellers, and the only black man ever elected in an international union referendum. From a small Inland Steel local in Texas a Mexican-American delegate, Paul Montemayor, identified himself as a member of an "invisible minority." "The struggles and the needs of our Negro brothers," he said, "the shadow of their purpose is so great, they kinda left us in the background." Now, because of the increased activity of the international union, he was sure "the Mexican minority of the Southwest will no longer be invisible."

But Samuel Stokes of District 27—the Canton area—was not so appreciative of the union's accomplishments. "Who are we talking to?" he demanded. Three quarters of the delegates had already gone home. So, said Stokes, "most of them who ought to have heard the 'beautiful things' are out of earshot." To him, this seemed in line with the traditional spot for civil rights: "low place on the totem pole." The black delegates laughed and applauded.

Now the leadership opened its defense against the critics. Molony indignantly denied that civil rights was at the bottom of the totem pole. This convention, he said, had devoted more attention to the "pressing problems of civil rights than any previous convention." "Maybe so," said delegate Joe Pickens, an officer of Republic Steel Local 1098, in the Cleveland district, No. 28. He observed flatly that in his local "99½ per cent of the craft workers and maintenance men are white. We cannot get colored people even into helper jobs."

At this point, David Chappell, a Negro delegate from District 23, provided a psychological analysis for the leadership: "We have made up our minds a long time ago that we can never let you think that we are satisfied. We might appreciate what you have done, but satisfaction is a long ways off, because we have learned that you either go up or go down. We cannot say 'We are satisfied,' because when we do, it goes down." To this Molony replied: "I fully understand the motivation of the speakers because I too was brought up in the philosophy that it's the squeaking wheel that gets the grease."

But Archie Broadfoot from Ohio (Local 1104, District 28), a delegate since the 1942 convention, said that as a black he had never seen "human rights, civil rights and civil liberties respected by the Chair as at this convention. There were no stooges at the mikes. This has been a Steelworkers convention all the way through. Never, never as long as I can recall have you been treated like Steelworkers the way you have been now. You have been treated with utmost respect. Patience is a virtue, and brother, they have it up there on the platform." Broadfoot had expressed directly what the leadership had hoped to communicate by its actions: the contrast between its tolerance of dissent and McDonald's impatience with criticism.

Now Jimmy Jones, the veteran black international representative, gathered the strings of discussion together. "I love what is happening here on the convention floor. When my white brothers take the floor and my Mexican-American brothers take the floor and express their concern about what is happening to our black brothers in this union, that goes all over the nation today."

Jones did not have the last word. A white delegate, Al Unger of Bethlehem Steel's Local 2599, District 9, refused to let the convention quit without giving it a particular piece of his mind. The civil rights discussion was not for him. This convention, he impatiently declared, was not assembled "to discuss race, creed or religion, but to back up the United Steelworkers. We are here as a body. I am not here to discuss or learn anything about somebody else's problems." It was a simplistic statement of "business unionism," with racist overtones. Satisfied that he had told "them" off, he sat down. The mood of the Negro delegates turned blue. Molony, refusing to let the discussion end on such a note, took over the platform mike. "I am afraid I must disagree with the previous delegate. We *are* here to discuss race, creed and color, and any discrimination that may exist, whatever it is." The applause indicated that some semblance of good will had been restored. Molony now put the appropriate question to the delegates: "Is it the judgment of the convention that the chairman has been sufficiently goosed this afternoon?" Amid the laughter of the delegates remaining in the hall, the civil rights program was passed without objection.

Politics After the Convention

Following adjournment, the Steelworkers Union had its work cut out for it in the 1966 Congressional political campaign. As in other unions, considerable sections of the white community—including many union members—began whipping up resentment against candidates who had favored civil rights legislation. In many areas, union members and their families were clearly breaking away from their traditional support of such liberal and prolabor candidates as the brilliant and dedicated Paul H. Douglas, the three-term Senator from Illinois. The prounion mayor of Waukegan, who in 1965 had presided over a Steelworkers meeting in support of Abel, now attacked Douglas. He announced his intention to run against Douglas, and finally diverted support to Douglas's Republican opponent.

A backlash developed among many categories of workers who feared a too rapid expansion of Negroes into their districts. At the same time, the increase of "black power" activities had caused whites—among them rank-and-file union workers—to respond with almost eager hostility to the outbreak of violence in civil rights demonstrations. Negro leaders such as A. Philip Randolph, Roy Wilkins, Whitney Young, Jr., and Martin Luther King, Jr., issued emphatic statements hoping to blunt the effect of Negro extremism. But a pervasive irrationality, fed by tensions and prejudice, began to pervade larger sections of the white union community. The AFL-CIO Committee on Political Education tried to introduce a strong jet of reason to cool the rage on both sides. Through a leaflet entitled "Can You Talk About Race . . . Without Losing Your Temper," it sought to appeal to reason. The United Auto Workers' *Washington Report* sent out a special issue entitled "Paul Douglas Battles for His Political Life." In many strong steel union centers—Chicago, Gary, Baltimore, the districts of Pennsylvania, and in Ohio—the feeling against civil rights had developed especial virulence. The international officers of the Steelworkers Union now addressed its members through a letter mailed directly to a million homes in the United States: "Many of our good union members have deserted labor's proven friends and embraced the candidacies of sworn enemies of the union. . . . Apparently they have permitted their justifiable concern over recent racial rioting to affect their judgment in choosing candidates.

"No one in his right mind, of course, approves of riots or wanton destruction of property as a means of protest. But we must not kid ourselves: electing labor's enemies in November will not cause these problems to disappear. . . . Many of the traditional enemies of labor—from the far left and the far right—are today actively agitating and exploiting the unrest that exists among Negroes and other minority groups. These forces are not trying to solve our racial problems; they are trying to magnify them. . . ."

Despite extraordinary effort to stem the tide, the labor movement failed to overcome completely the effects of the backlash. Actually, labor could check off only one real victory—the defeat of George P. Mahoney, the Democratic candidate for governor of Maryland. Although Mahoney had won the nomination in the Democratic primary through a racist appeal, in the election he was defeated by a combination of normally Democratic, labor, and liberal forces that supported a then inconspicuous Republican named Spiro T. Agnew.

In the months following the convention and the disappointing midterm national elections, the issue of hiring and promoting black workers again came up strongly in the steel areas, especially in Pennsylvania, right at the door of the international union. Criticism of the industry's lack of adequate progress was aimed at the union by James McCoy, a black staff representative who was also chairman of the Pennsylvania NAACP Labor and Industry Committee. Alex Fuller, director of the USW's Civil Rights Committee, responded that the union had already committed itself to work with state civil rights commissions on the widening of job opportunities. But he wondered out loud that all this special attention was being directed at the Steelworkers Union when "unorganized plants are not coming under civil rights fire, not to mention some other segments of labor that have not moved as strongly as we have and yet aren't being attacked." To Fuller, the character of the complaints was stained by the obvious playing of internal union politics.

The pressure on the international union's civil rights structure, therefore, came from two directions—from the dissatisfaction with the companies' policy of "deliberate speed" in correcting past inequities and from organizations like the NAACP. With aseptic objectivity, U.S. Steel declared that Negro workers with sufficient seniority for higher-level jobs lacked educational qualifications. At the same time, the company reiterated its opposition to any "recourse of preferential hiring, promotion, or treatment of any one race at the expense of other employees with equal qualifications and equal rights." This company position gratified many white workers who felt their tenure threatened by the push of black workers for jobs that had been denied them.

Putting it another way, Fuller found the main problem to be that while Negroes in the past suffered because of "dual" or segregated lines of promotion, the company would only go just so far in righting past wrongs without doing harm to the hard-won union rights of white workers. To be sure, the company's primary interest was in avoiding conflict rather than in supporting union rights. By now the pressure against union and company began to be applied by the federal Equal Employment Opportunity Commission (EEOC), which refused to take a partial "yes" from union and company as a satisfactory answer to the problem. But the leadership in the EEOC, at this time, was intermittent and wavering. President Johnson was tardy in appointing even an interim successor to its departing head, Franklin D. Roosevelt, Jr. While the NAACP maintained steady pressure against the companies, Molony promised it that the Steelworkers Union would "help in every way we can." With the support of the union, the NAACP continued to push the steel and aluminum companies, especially in the Pittsburgh area, to hire and promote Negroes. The international union could urge local union officials to inform plant managements that white union members would not refuse to work side by side with Negroes. The NAACP believed that the union could also insist more aggressively that apprenticeship training be opened to Negroes to qualify them for the more skilled jobs.

Over the next two years, the demands for more effective implementation of the union's civil rights policy in plant and union grew stronger. In fact, the charge that Negroes were not sufficiently represented in the union's staff and among the elected district officers swelled into a major theme that could not be disregarded.

Educational Component

When the role of the staff representative was cussed and discussed at conventions and other occasions, the leadership, for its part, directed itself to the necessity for the general improvement of these key union employees. As a group, the staff men were now organized into the SOC —Staffman's Organizing Committee—which gave them status and job security. But their individual quality and the scale of performance to the international union and to the locals in the districts were uneven— not surprisingly in view of the hit-and-miss way in which they were chosen for their jobs and the fact that under McDonald many of them were drained of a sense of commitment. They often constituted a corps of political outriders who felt little need to prove themselves through service to the members. Competent staff men therefore necessarily carried a double load: their own responsibilities and sometimes those of others. Under these conditions, the international union was overstaffed and overstuffed. Union members, whose problems and grievances were being neglected, were convinced that they were not getting their dues' worth. Moreover, the incompetence of certain directors was attributed to the low performance of men who would have done better if they had been held to standards of accountability by the directors and international officers. This pervasive condition underlay a constant theme of the Abel campaign: a new emphasis on education and the re-education of staff men. Education was to vitalize the new beginning. The educational principle now had to become the concern of the international union, not merely the often uncoordinated efforts of district and local unions in developing institutes and programs with some of the state universities. Many of the latter were worthwhile, but too often they took on the aspect of a week's vacation or a respite from the plant. In addition, the new international officers hoped to establish a policy of open publicity, in contrast to the former secretive approach except where McDonald's image-building was concerned; to make *Steel Labor,* the monthly publication, more attractive, readable, and relevant to the union's membership; to keep its officers and the executive board current on national and international development. But a development program for staff representatives held high priority.

The key to this program was the appointment of Professor Fred K. Hoehler, Jr., of Michigan State. A leading administrator in labor education and a sophisticated practitioner, Hoehler had long recognized the psychological pitfalls which beset the educational process inside the union movement. For many leaders, never too secure, education signaled trouble: rank-and-file leaders with "labor education" under their belts might develop political ambitions of their own. Areas of dissent and discontent might develop direction and leadership. One local leader listened to the educational prospectus and said: "Great stuff, but no thanks. I'm not going to have you train a guy to take my place." He had no intention of creating his own opposition. But far-reaching events had begun to change the attitudes of leadership. The vast enterprise of the Steelworkers Union, with its system of directors, subdistrict directors, and nearly seven hundred staff representatives, required more than the practical wisdom that a director might incidentally impart to his staff, or that a perceptive staff representative might acquire through experience. It demanded a new strategy. "To expand and integrate the educational function within the total union structure" became the responsibility of the executive board and its Advisory Committee on Education.

Under Hoehler, the Education Department inaugurated a series of conferences for the executive board itself. The purpose was to bring together the officers and district directors every six months for an intensive week-long seminar at a distance from international headquarters. Starting in March 1966, several seminars were held at Colonial Williamsburg, Virginia. For the executive board seminars, an *ad hoc* faculty was made up of outstanding academicians and experts.*

In addition, each district director was asked to appoint an education coordinator from among his staff to "implement a program of continuing education" and to keep after local unions, which were often slow in starting education programs of their own.

The international union's Staff Training Institute opened in mid-April 1966, and extended for nine sessions through June 1967. The faculty was made up mainly of the officers, several directors, the general counsel, and other department heads.†

Courses were held in a well-equipped lecture room and library in the Sherwyn Hotel, across the street from the international union headquarters. These made up the Clinton S. Golden Center. The name carried special meaning. Golden's enthusiasm for workers' education had always set him somewhat apart, even from Phil Murray, whose background in

---

* These included John R. Coleman, then associate director of Economic and Development Administration of the Ford Foundation (now president of Haverford College), Leon Keyserling, former chairman of the Council of Economic Advisers; Charles L. Schultze, then Director of the Bureau of the Budget; and Stanley Ruttenberg, then Assistant Secretary of Labor for Manpower Administration. At the second session, on "The Labor Movement—Where It Is and Where It Is Going," the faculty included Professor John T. Dunlop of Harvard, Gus Tyler of the International Ladies Garment Workers Union, and Dr. Ross Stagner, chairman of the Department of Psychology, Wayne State University. At the third conference, on "Behavior in Complex Organizations," the speakers were Professors Amitai Etzioni of Columbia, Eugene Jacobson of Michigan, and Harold Leavitt of Stanford.

† There were sessions in economics, in communications, and in public relations and labor law; specific classes were held on the union's constitution, policy and election procedures, labor history, industrial engineering, collective bargaining, fiscal policy and finances, insurance, pensions, and grievances and arbitration. In addition, the role of the staff representatives was examined. Intensive sessions were devoted to civil rights and the social role of the union. The importance of the white-collar workers in the universe of labor organization was discussed; there were seminars on the international labor movements and international economics.

the United Mine Workers convinced him that labor education was nothing to monkey around with.* Golden's career included a formative period on the faculty of Brookwood Labor College in Katonah, New York, the nation's only resident labor college in the 1920s and 1930s. Brookwood produced alumni who were to play a creative part in the development of the labor movement. Abel was not a product of Brookwood, but for him the 1930s had been a period of intensive self-education and his admiration for Golden as a man helped shape Abel's attitudes. Thus personal sentiment and historical continuity impelled Abel to revive the name of the man who had viewed the union's role in its larger social context. To many, Golden was the personification of confident integrity. At a large Eastern university, Golden was once sharply questioned by a member of the audience: "How can anyone believe that there is such a thing as an honest labor leader?" Pointing his finger at the heckler, Golden replied instantly, "Brother, you're looking at one now." †

Under Hoehler, the institute started off with a considerable display of enthusiasm. But participation was spotty: good from some districts, meager from others. By the end of the first cycle of nine institutes, Abel reported that the response from the participating staff representatives justified the expenditure of the union's time and money.

One staff man found that the institute made him "realize that most of us really had a desire to learn more . . . and rekindled the spark of idealism that has been buried too long. . . . The Staff Institute was just 25 years late in coming." Another staff man found the course inadequate for the purpose: he contrasted his 3½ month break-in training as a crane operator at Inland Steel with three weeks training provided by the union for a staff man. "Now I ask—who needs more training—a craneman or a staff representative?" He urged a year's course to develop a staff representative equal to the performance of his many tasks. But another staff man saw a drawback in the institute: three weeks' absence from his office results in a "formidable build-up of work when he returns." When another returned some veteran staff men pooh-poohed the institute as "old hat, not for them." But another veteran found "the things I was taught will help me in my work. With my age and educa-

---

* Murray reflected the belief long prevalent among unions in the AFL, which continued into the CIO period, that "there was a difference in purpose between the advocates of workers' education . . . and the leaders of the official trade union movement. The leaders of the majority of the unions felt that experience was the best teacher for day-to-day trade union tasks and that classes for workers might well become an avenue for the support of policies contrary to those favored" by the established labor organizations. *Labor Education in the United States*, Lawrence Rogin and Marjorie Rachlin (September 1968), p. 16 (for the National Institute of Labor Education at the American University).

† *As Steel Goes*, R. R. R. Brooks, Yale University Press, 1940, p. 183.

tion, there were some things I could not pick up, but over all, I think it was great." Another pointedly remarked that he could not think of a "more worthwhile way to employ union funds."

But there was a wide gap between high hopes and actual achievement. Not many district directors had bothered to work out a schedule of attendance at the institute for their staff representatives. Although a budget had been prepared for an average attendance of twenty staff men at each institute, participation fluctuated from a low of nine to a high of twenty-one.

Perhaps the staff development program would have been continued at high pitch under the sustained guidance of Hoehler and his assistant, John Powderly, a grandson of the founder of the Knights of Labor. Unfortunately, Hoehler found it necessary to resume his obligations to Michigan State.* For a while he continued as a consultant for the program. But such a center could succeed only under sustained direction. His departure was a blow to the program, inasmuch as the union leadership had hoped for a continuation of his guidance. As his successor, Abel named Bruce Alexander, an experienced and dedicated staff man from District 15. But at this stage, the Steelworkers Union had not been able to maintain what was expected to be a new level of union education. Alexander pushed for stronger support.

In 1967 there were summer institutes at seventeen universities in the United States and Canada, with about 1,500 Steelworkers attending. The general theme that year was "The Young Unionist." In 1968, twelve institutes were held in the United States and one in Canada. The drop was attributed to the increased work load on all local union officers, staff men, directors, and international officers arising out of the long copper strike, the special dues convention, negotiations in the can, aluminum and basic steel contracts, the regular convention, and the 1968 national Presidential campaign.

In all, eleven three-week sessions of the staff institute were held between April 1966 and May 1968, with a total of 171 staff representatives, about one out of every four, attending.

Early in 1966, the union had introduced the concept of "educational coordinators" for each district, as an adjunct to the Education Department of the international union. In addition to the founding meeting in January 1966, two full-scale coordinators' meetings were held, one in December 1966, the other in January 1968.

* Late in 1969, Hoehler became executive director of the newly established AFL-CIO Center for Labor Studies in Washington, D.C.

CHAPTER **27**

Abel's Other Life

Consider well your ways and lives.
RIDGELY TORRENCE

As 1967 moved on, the Steelworkers leadership prepared to face management in the next year's negotiations in basic steel. In completing the negotiations of the 1965 contract, Abel and his fellow officers had disproved the charge that they were "strike-happy." As to the Human Relations Committee, now abandoned, Abel had always made the point that the purpose of the original committee, under McDonald, had deteriorated into phony "summitry." Agreements were made, he said, without proper participation of the elected responsible union representatives.

Despite earlier attempts to distort his position in labor-management relations, Abel sought to establish ground rules for a continuing dialogue on industry problems between union representatives and management. In a 1967 Labor Day speech he attracted attention by proposing that unions and management explore the "causes of industrial peace" as guidance for future labor-management behavior. Abel's speech stimulated a spate of dope stories. The *New York Times,* formerly a critic of Abel for what it regarded as an advocate of "old-fashioned trade unionism," now saw in Abel's remarks the signs of a resurrection of a McDonald-type Human Relations Committee. Union circles promptly termed this judgment wide of the mark.

But prior to his speech, representatives of management had in fact approached Abel to inquire whether the union would agree in advance of the 1968 negotiations to submit unresolved issues to arbitration. This proposal was debated for hours behind the closed doors of the union's executive board in Washington in mid-October 1967. Several directors who were strong Abel supporters in the campaign of 1965 vehemently disagreed. The management proposition, they suspected, would abort the whole collective bargaining procedure; open-ended arbitration, agreed to even prior to the start of negotiations, was a device that could create more problems than solutions. They did not believe that the union leaders, on various levels, would agree to yield their role in collective bargaining to outside arbitrators. It was quite another matter, they said, to maintain the arbitration system, built up over many years, for the interpretation of grievances arising out of contracts already negotiated. In many parts of the union, dismay was expressed that Abel should have considered the management proposal seriously enough to present it as he did to the board. In Toronto, Lawrence Sefton was impelled to hold a long explanatory session at a conference of his Canadian associates, where he expressed his strong dissent.

At the same time, the union leadership anticipated that the following year would be one of concentrated pressures. Since the contract then in effect terminated on August 1, 1968, negotiations would be taking place in a Presidential election year and with the nation caught up in the continuing Vietnam War. These combined circumstances could result in governmental intervention in steel negotiations, with the national administration itself determined to find an ironclad guarantee of peace in the steel industry. Moreover, the Johnson administration was convinced that the union would wish to avoid embarrassing a friendly White House.

For their part, the steel companies were determined not to permit their proposal to be shunted aside even by the union's executive board. They turned the pressure up. A few weeks later, R. Conrad Cooper, chairman of the steel management's bargaining team, delivered a speech in which he again opened up the possibility of a "no strike" agreement in steel. An Associated Press dispatch from Pittsburgh reported inaccurately that the "basic steel industry announced tentative agreement with the United Steelworkers on a plan . . . for submitting unresolved issues" in the bargaining sessions the following year to "binding arbitration." In a later story, the wire service reported that "the leadership of the Steelworkers is considering a plan to surrender its right to strike in the 1968 contract talks. . . . I. W. Abel is pictured as the chief architect of the plan." This story gained credence when it was followed by an AP interview with Abel in New York in which he was quoted as saying that "strikes are losing their force as a weapon in labor contract negotiations." Abel, then in attendance at the United Nations as an alternate delegate of the United States delegation, hotly denied he had ever made such a "ridiculous" statement. On the financial pages of the *New York Times,* a writer saw "irony" in the situation, asserting that Abel, who had campaigned against McDonald's "labor statesmanship," was now moving into a McDonald pattern. This latest interpretation reinforced the editorial of several weeks before. In view of all this speculation, Abel saw possible danger to his position inside the union. Clarification became imperative.

Suspicious union leaders saw in this drumfire of publicity the making of a management maneuver to stir trouble inside the union. Through a combination of pressures from the companies and misrepresentation in the press, the average steelworker and his local union leadership might have understandably felt somewhat bewildered. Even if Cooper had not deliberately planned to create union turmoil, the result would prove a dividend for the employers.

That was how the situation stood when the Steelworkers executive board met again on December 2, 1967, in Bal Harbour, Florida, a few days before the AFL-CIO convention. Despite Abel's previous assurances to the local unions that all discussions on "arbitration" with the companies were only "exploratory," rumors of impending change persisted. The union leadership was confronted with a credibility gap that could widen.

The exploratory talks with the companies' representatives, the officers now stated in a sort of "white paper," were not a furtive exercise of a small group of union and company leaders. Rather they were an outgrowth of certain informal discussions, agreed to in the 1965 basic steel agreement, for the study of issues not resolved at that time, such as apprenticeship, testing, training, and job classifications. The proposal to hold such discussions was not widely noted. To some district leaders and particularly officers of large local unions in basic steel, these unpublicized conversations conveyed the unmistakable echo of the time when the Human Relations Research Committee was transformed without effective notice by McDonald and his associates into the Human Relations Committee. Was the new leadership in fact going to take the union down the McDonald path?

Not so, replied the officers. The concept of "arbitrating any issue which could not be resolved in the forthcoming negotiations" was only "experimental" and would not, in any event, have prevented the union from resuming the traditional format of bargaining or from considering alternatives. Indeed, when the "conditional" arbitration proposal was presented to the executive board by the international officers and General Counsel Bernard Kleiman—the union group that had met with the industry's coordinating committee—it was heavily stressed that "no agreement of this type could possibly be reached, under any circumstances, without prior approval from all policy-making bodies within our union, including the international Wage Policy Committee, the newly established Basic Steel Industry Conference of local unions and a poll of the membership involved."

But, in fact, Abel reported, out of the discussions with management no plan with sufficient merit had finally emerged "to warrant its presentation to the policy-making bodies of the union." His statement revealed a meticulous concern for union opinion, but its somewhat defensive tone also reflected the leadership's awareness of a restive, probing spirit inside the union. It had surfaced in the 1965 election, had become more articulate in the last convention, and had not submerged.

In dropping the proposal, however, the officers pledged "to our members, the labor movement at large and the general public that we will continue our search for new and better methods of bargaining . . . an unremitting responsibility of the leadership of this union." The issue had set in motion strong political currents inside the union. In 1968, the position of the union in the basic steel contract negotiations as well as the substance of the agreements was bound to affect the climate in which the new international union elections would be held.

By now Abel found himself concerned with the results of his promise to bring the union into the "mainstream of the labor movement." For him this had meant increased attention to interests of the Steelworkers Union beyond its immediate economic and structural concerns; cooperation with other unions in the AFL-CIO as well as with the national AFL-CIO itself; and diligent attention to his duties as a vice-president of AFL-CIO. In contrast with McDonald's lackadaisical attitude, Abel's interest in the activities of the AFL-CIO Industrial Union Department, headed by Reuther, had become evident.

To many observers it seemed clear that the combination of the two largest AFL-CIO unions—the Auto Workers and the Steelworkers—could result in a shift in power relations inside the AFL-CIO itself. These unions had a combined membership of about 2.5 million, making for considerable leverage both in per capita payments to the AFL-CIO and through a practical identity of trade-union philosophy. During the 1965 campaign and after, Abel's criticism of the AFL-CIO top leadership was as direct as Reuther's.

Nevertheless, as president of the Steelworkers Union, he would not, in fact could not, let it be assumed that he was automatically allied with Reuther in the councils of the AFL-CIO. He did not wish to be taken for granted. Just as significantly, Reuther did not seem to apply himself to the necessary business of consulting with his "natural" allies—officers of former CIO unions that make up the core of the Industrial Union Department. Some of his former CIO colleagues believed that Reuther expected them to share his growing indignation and dissatisfaction with George Meany's leadership without taking them into his confidence, often without informing them in advance of certain positions he had determined to take inside the AFL-CIO. Alternatively, Reuther rejected the fact or appearance of a caucus. Moreover, he believed that since they had as complete an understanding of the issues as he did, they ought not to require special briefing from him. But political understandings are seldom advanced by osmosis.

Sensing a shift in the climate of relationships, Meany saw the possibility of drawing Abel away from Reuther. He recognized that Abel was essentially a team player. He now began to make every effort to include Abel, as a member of the AFL-CIO Executive Council, in his more intimate conversations. Gradually he reached a point where he felt he could overcome Abel's remembrance of Meany's preference for McDonald. As AFL-CIO president, he took pains to explain his position to Abel (incidentally to deride Reuther's hortatory traits), and as time went on, to consult him in advance of Executive Council meetings.

The minutiae of such tactics of political seduction are not easily traced. Sometimes they are seen in a fleeting wink or a nod. Sometimes they are tangible testing points: for example, the subject of organizing farm workers, long a special concern of Reuther's. Especially dramatic was the emergence of the originally independent Delano, California, grape pickers' organization, under Cesar Chavez. Although the AFL-CIO had over the years invested considerable sums in the effort to organize the farm workers, the results were often disheartening and the question arose of justifying large expenditures of union money and manpower in an apparently unproductive endeavor. In December 1965, during a weekend of the AFL-CIO convention, Reuther flew down from San Francisco to lead a picket line in the Delano area. The resulting publicity in press and television helped make Chavez a national figure. Almost overnight, smoke had turned to fire: the Delano grape pickers caught on. A dusty little strike in California became a global epic. The effect on the AFL-CIO became equally clear in its heightened interests. Senator Robert F. Kennedy brought a Senate subcommittee to the Delano area and further illuminated the struggle. At a time when AFL-CIO leadership had been criticized for lack of social sensitivity, the struggle of the grape pickers became a rallying point for the labor movement.

In the ensuing months, Reuther urged the creation of a special committee of the Executive Council to provide fuller backing to the organizational drive of the now embattled farm workers. At the August 1966 meeting of the Executive Council in Chicago, a United Farm Workers Committee was chartered with Chavez as its director. In an accompanying action, Meany appointed a five-man Farm Workers Organizing Committee, with himself as chairman. He excluded Reuther, the sponsor of the idea, from the committee and named Abel. Despite

Meany's obvious snub to Reuther, Abel accepted membership—"You can't refuse the president of the AFL-CIO"—although he confessed at the time he knew little or nothing about farm workers' problems. This became the first of a series of Abel appointments by the AFL-CIO president at a time when the intensity of Reuther's differences with Meany was mounting. Several months later, in February 1967, Reuther resigned his post as vice-president of the AFL-CIO. Meany promptly appointed Abel to replace Reuther as chairman of the AFL-CIO Economic Policy Committee.

By now, Meany had made it clear that Abel would rise as Reuther's position receded. Rumors now began to circulate that Abel might be tapped as the successor to Meany in the event of his retirement. On numerous occasions, Meany, with easy access to the White House, had Abel accompany him to talks with President Johnson on federation problems. This was, of course, also a tribute to the political muscle that the Steelworkers had exerted in the 1966 Congressional campaign and would exert in the 1968 Presidential election campaign. As part of the labor and political establishments, Abel was invited to White House dinners. All the gratifying evidences of prestige and status were now his. Nor was this empty show. After all, the proximity of a Democratic President and White House influence could prove of immense value as the prospects of difficult basic steel negotiations in 1968 neared. By now, the Steelworkers were also deeply committed in the leadership of the copper strike, which, begun in July 1967, was destined to go on into the early spring of 1968. Meany's influence with President Johnson was a factor for Abel to reckon with as the time approached for some peacemaking formula in the bitter copper conflict. The influence of the AFL-CIO president with federation affiliates having members in the copper industry—some with old AFL backgrounds—made more feasible the establishment of a copper coordinating committee, headed by Steelworkers Vice-President Joseph Molony.

In the riotous summer of 1967, the racial violence in many cities led to the creation of the Presidential commission headed by Illinois Governor Otto Kerner and New York City's Mayor John V. Lindsay, a bipartisan body that also included a representative of organized labor. At Meany's suggestion, President Johnson named Abel, whose appointment to such a prestigious body highlighted the recognition of the problems facing his union, with its many thousands of black members.

Then, not many weeks later, again at Meany's suggestion, President Johnson appointed Abel a member of the United States delegation to the United Nations. For years, Meany had blocked Reuther's appointment under Presidents Kennedy and Johnson, to a similar U.N. post. Meany's satisfaction in Abel's appointment was spiced with the knowledge of Reuther's frustration. Abel himself was obviously not displeased with this wider recognition. He now attended U.N. sessions alongside an old associate, U.N. Ambassador Arthur Goldberg, once the Steelworkers general counsel.

Thus by late 1967, Abel became known as a man of rising consequence. Increasingly, however, his new duties called for extended absences from the international office. Unlike McDonald, Abel devoted his time away from union headquarters to serious matters. But many of Abel's union friends began to feel they did not see as much of him as they would have liked—and as some of them thought was necessary. His critics were less considerate in their remarks. All of which caused wide speculation on the difficult and varied tasks a labor leader of stature must perform. At various times, he might be agitator, organizer, negotiator, or administrator. He must often alternate between being radical and conservative, a direct actionist and a passive resister. What makes his job especially awkward is that he finds himself often having to play several of these parts at the same time.

As a political creature, he must be sensitive to demands of the rank and file, knocking at his door at union headquarters. And he must be there to open it. In his relations with employers he must establish confidence in his contractual responsibility and his responsiveness to new approaches without being susceptible to their blandishments. Nevertheless, because of the constant demands on his time, he must expend his energies carefully. When a comparatively new personality like Abel emerges from the mass of union leadership, he becomes a target of opportunity for those who wish to gain his good will and his support. Even the most modest of men finally assumes that he is being singled out mainly for innate talents and unique qualities, which he may or may not possess. When the request for "larger service" came from the President of the United States, especially an arm twister like Lyndon Johnson, it was difficult to resist. When it was reinforced by the urging of the president of the AFL-CIO, the answer could only be "yes."

But then came a time of diminishing returns. Anxieties began to follow in the wake of satisfactions. Grumbling began to be heard: "Where the hell is Abel?" While he was fortunate in the competence and loyalty of his associates, Vice-President Joseph Molony and Secretary-Treasurer Walter Burke, Abel himself had to be the outward and visible symbol of union leadership. Aside from the need to cultivate the vast interior of union relations, he now began to worry about the drain in the funds and energies of the Steelworkers Union, overtaxed in the long-drawn-out copper strike. He therefore had now to resume direct responsibility for superintending the revitalization of his union so as to fulfill the mandate of the 1966 convention. As 1968 began, he had also the task of preparing the groundwork for massive negotiations in can manufacturing, aluminum, and basic steel. The No. 1 man in the Steelworkers Union began to realize that public recognition could be overdone and that its temporary advantages and perquisites could actually turn into an organizational deficit for the union itself and for his own relations inside the union.

Comment on these developments began to appear in print, and Abel was disturbed. He fretted a little but never flared in anger. To one friendly reporter who had described the restless mood of his union, he said, "Well, I just want to tell you I've returned home."

That same week, early in 1968, Donald Rarick proved that there was no place like home; he announced his intention to run against Abel in the next international election a year hence.

CHAPTER **28**

Copper and the Dues Factor

O man, acclaim your heritage,
Your noble history of fire.

KENNETH L. PATTON

The Abel administration had succeeded in ending an ancient labor feud. After many months of negotiation, the Steelworkers and the Mine, Mill and Smelter Workers made peace through merger. In 1967, the USW absorbed the estimated 25,000-member Mine, Mill union in the United States, and shortly afterward the 15,000 members of the same union in Canada. The Steelworkers already had about 25,000 members in the copper industry.

Since 1949–50, when Mine, Mill had been expelled from the CIO on charges of Communist domination, the life of the Steelworkers and the Mine, Mill unions was scarred by hand-to-hand encounters, ideological and physical. Both sides had spent millions of dollars and uncountable man-days to protect themselves or raid each other. Now, as a result of an agreement effective July 1, 1967, 80 per cent of nonferrous metal workers, whether employed in mining or processing sectors of the industry, became members of a single union, a "solid front to negotiate with the 'Copper Kings.' "

Union battles in the copper industry had begun three-quarters of a century before, when copper workers were first organized as the Western Federation of Miners. The copper-producing states later became known as "Joe Hill" country, the terrain traversed by the martyred organizer and songwriter of the Industrial Workers of the World. Identifying their common interests,* the Steelworkers officers noted in the announcement

* Semi-annual Audit Report, October 23, 1967.

338

of the merger that Mine, Mill "has had a violent but rich history in American labor, and its growth and history in many respects parallel that of the Steelworkers and its predecessors."

Signaling another change in the union's political climate, *Steel Labor* launched a series of "Heroes of Labor." A biography of Joe Hill was followed by one of Eugene V. Debs, the Socialist candidate in five Presidential elections. The Steelworkers publication also played up the story of six-time candidate Norman Thomas, the Socialist leader who had been a mainstay of labor's struggles, especially in its days of trial and organization in the 1930s, through the Emergency Committee for Strikers Relief. Names such as Joe Hill, Debs, or Thomas had been anathema to McDonald, whose disdain for radicals or socialists of any sort had bordered on a "Know-Nothing" position.

Merger to Strike

The addition of new membership brought responsibility for conducting the negotiations with the copper and brass firms. The merger of the two unions meant the possibility of a union-employer confrontation that had been absent from the copper industry for many years. It was accomplished through coordination with a dozen or more other unions with smaller memberships that also had bargaining units in the industry.*

In previous years, the various permutations and combinations of unions within one company and among companies had created a comfortable chaos for the employers. With comparative ease they had picked off the smaller, often mutually hostile unions, one by one. As price of survival, the weakened and outcast Mine, Mill union would often hasten to agree to a contract, inferior in many respects to those in comparable industries. This capitulation, in turn, undermined the bargaining position of the Steelworkers. With the merger, and in concert with the other unions, the Steelworkers could now bargain more effectively with the Big Four: American Smelting and Refining Company (8,000 workers), Anaconda (10,000 workers), Kennecott (8,000), and Phelps-Dodge (5,000).

So the Steelworkers, its numbers augmented, the drain on its treasury and manpower now stoppered, was prepared to do battle. The union's declared objective was to modernize labor-management relations in the copper industry. With the breakdown of negotiations, however, the copper strike began on July 15, 1967. Neither the union leaders nor, for that matter, the management anticipated that the strike would turn into

* These were: Operating Engineers, Teamsters, Mine Workers, Auto Workers, Machinists, Potters, Aluminum Workers, International Brotherhood of Electrical Workers, International Union of Electrical Workers, and several Metal Trades Councils and locals in the Canadian Labour Congress, plus a few independents.

an endurance contest in which nearly 50,000 strikers and their employers were locked for more than nine months, principally in seven states: Arizona, Montana, California, Nevada, Utah, New Jersey, and New York.

In addition to wage and pension demands, the union fought to develop a pattern of company-wide bargaining; this the companies resisted. As a result of the merger, the union's strategy had been transformed. "The merger has had a hell of an effect because now we can negotiate for the whole plant," one Utah striker observed. "Now for the first time the companies are faced with a coalition of unions. They're determined to break the back of the unity movement. . . . They won't get to meaningful negotiations until the copper supply is used up." But the companies, forearmed, had stockpiled copper to withstand the siege. Fully loaded hundred-ton copper cars squatted on railroad sidings ready for shipment.

The months wore on. The financial strain of the strike was felt especially inside the Steelworkers Union, which had to carry the burden of strike relief for tens of thousands of member families. From mid-July to mid-December 1967, the union spent $200,000 to $400,000 a week for strike relief. About half the recipients of strike benefits were the recently added membership from the Mine, Mill and Smelter Workers. Staggering under the financial load, the Steelworkers executive board at its December 1967 meeting announced a special convention for no later than March 31, 1968, "to review the financial status of the union." Through directors and staff representatives, preparations were made to prepare local union sentiment for the likelihood of the first dues increase since the brawling convention of 1956.

In the meantime, the copper strike held. It became a dramatic order of business for the AFL-CIO convention in December 1967 at Bal Harbour. Steelworkers Vice-President Molony announced that "for the first time in the history of the copper industry we have unity, we have friendship and trust between all of the unions of the AFL-CIO. Yes, and also the Teamsters stand with us in this battle." This all-embracing description—including the Teamsters, who were ten years gone from the AFL-CIO—was greeted with tumultuous applause. The conjunction of the occasion and the cause stimulated Molony to greater efforts:

"The companies are hell-bent to preserve the old ways of bargaining —mine by mine, plant by plant, state by state, union by union. All you have to do is look at the record: wage rates are a hodgepodge; expiration dates in this industry are all over the calendar; local union pitted against local union, worker against worker, rivalry and distrust between international unions. Is it any wonder that wages are low and working conditions are bad?"

He recounted the story of efforts made to settle; how Senators Mike Mansfield and Lee Metcalf of Montana had urged President Johnson to appoint a fact-finding board; how the President referred the proposal to Defense Secretary Robert S. McNamara, Labor Secretary W. Willard Wirtz, and Commerce Secretary Alexander B. Trowbridge; how the co-ordinating committee of the striking unions had agreed, while the companies continued to reject the proposal. He demanded that Attorney General Ramsey Clark "investigate these bandits . . . who hope that frustration and despair will weaken our unity and determination . . . through the classic maneuver of divide and conquer."

To Molony's passionate urgency, the AFL-CIO unions—including the absent Auto Workers and the disaffiliated Teamsters—responded with an outpouring of financial support that ultimately came to about $800,000. The convention vibrated with unaccustomed emotion. One union president after another pledged financial support, and, in their fashion, played variations on the theme that Joe Hill never died. Joe Keenan, secretary of the International Brotherhood of Electrical Workers, not usually given to convention speeches, talked of the copper strikers "in the desolate areas far away from the swing of things . . . who must feel they are all alone. . . . We have to do the job for them, the job we are destined to do, to organize the downtrodden of this country."

In this unexpected way, therefore, the Steelworkers Union was indeed stirring the often sluggish mainstream of the labor movement; their officers were being heard with respect; their energies were directed to leadership in a great struggle. And the new copper members of the Steelworkers—those who had come in from the cold—now felt a kinship with the larger union, without which the former Mine, Mill would have had to settle for the same bare minimums of the past, without a struggle.

Late in January 1968, Labor Secretary Wirtz and Commerce Secretary Trowbridge named a copper fact-finding panel: Professor George W. Taylor of the University of Pennsylvania, Monsignor George Higgins of the National Catholic Welfare Conference; and George Reedy, President Johnson's former news secretary. After weeks of hearings, the panel's findings and proposals failed to provide an acceptable formula from the union's point of view.

To nudge the situation along, the International Longshoremen's Association now announced that their members would not handle copper going in or out of the United States and Canada; its members would not cross the lines of striking workers who began to picket "copper-carrying" ships. Under this additional pressure, the White House called a meeting of Wirtz and Trowbridge and members of Congress from the copper states to discuss "the serious situation existing in the copper producing states."

Shortly after, the National Labor Relations Board's General Counsel Arnold Ordman issued a complaint—requested by Kennecott more than four months before—charging the Steelworkers and associated unions with unfair labor practices by refusing to bargain. This NLRB action increased the squeeze on the union to acquiesce to the bargaining formula proposed by the Taylor panel. Negotiations were resumed.

After eight and a half months and three weeks of negotiation, the strike was ended by late March. The first break came in mid-March when the Phelps-Dodge Corporation, which had no foreign copper holdings, settled with the Steelworkers; Kennecott Copper followed with agreements covering its Western copper mines and lead operations; on the weekend of March 23–24, settlements were concluded for American Smelting & Refining and for Anaconda. Negotiations continued separately for the employees at Anaconda and Kennecott's brass, wire, and cable facilities. The settlements generally followed a three-tier contract structure: (1) one contract for the mining, smelting, and refining of copper; (2) another for other nonferrous metals such as lead and zinc; and (3) a third for the fabrication of copper wire, cable, and brass. Two major union goals were not won: a common expiration date for contracts and uniform economic terms for all workers. At considerable cost to both workers and companies, the Big Four copper companies had reached a settlement with the twenty-six-union coalition, headed by a determined Steelworkers Union, with a depleted treasury.

The Dues Factor

With considerable uncertainty if not trepidation, the Steelworkers leadership approached the special "dues" convention of March 20, 1968, in Atlantic City. Not since January 1952, in Murray's last year, had a special convention been held. Nor could the union leadership forget the roaring 1956 convention, when embittered delegates returned to their home locals to organize the first presidential election contest in the union's history. Ever since that year, the idea of a dues increase was considered dirty, dangerous, and repellent, no matter how great the union's need to cover its rising costs—more than doubled in twelve years—or how dire the need for building a strike fund for the union's collective bargaining arsenal. At the 1962 convention, an oblique formula for replenishing the treasury was beaten by the mistrustful delegates, much to McDonald's furious disgust. As recently as 1966, the newly elected leadership thought it wise to turn off what appeared to be considerable convention sentiment for an increase in dues. But by 1968, the reality was grim: the union's finances were run down; costs of administration, on the international as on the local levels, had more than doubled since 1956; the copper strike had taken about a million dollars a month for relief; and the new leadership faced negotiations with the basic steel corporations. However great the objective justification for a dues increase, the leadership found itself on a tough spot: having made a virtue of refusal to raise the dues in September 1966, it was making an awkward 180-degree shift just eighteen months later.

Moreover, in advocating also the establishment of a "strike and defense fund," Abel moved to new ground. The Steelworkers Union, continuing to follow the pattern of the United Mine Workers in this respect, had regularly rejected proposals to establish a clearly identified strike fund as distinct from the general treasury. In recent years, belief in the efficacy of strike funds had grown rapidly; forty-seven other international unions now had strike and defense funds. In preparation for the special convention, the USW had consulted officials of the UAW and other unions on the best procedures for building such a fund.

As the union's top financial officer, Secretary-Treasurer Walter J. Burke now proceeded to present the rationale for a dues increase on the basis of a new formula. Instead of the current $5 a month, members were asked to pay a flat $10 a month for the succeeding five months to accelerate the build-up of a strike fund of $25 million. After the expiration of the five-month period, monthly dues would be established at an amount equal to two hours' base pay, with a ceiling of $10 a month; no dues, in any case, would fall below the current $5 a month. He pointed out that a form of graduated dues payment had been recently adopted by several other unions, including the Auto Workers, that were comparable to the Steelworkers Union in size and diversity.

Since by this time the basic steel companies had already begun to stockpile their product in anticipation of a strike, Burke believed that the immediate increase in dues to cover the five-month period before contract termination had become an obvious, necessary defense measure. The prevailing period of full employment, said Burke, was a time when the members—certainly in basic steel—could pay the assessment with a minimum of injury. Aside from anticipating future needs, the millions of dollars spent for copper-strike relief out of the general treasury had to be replaced. Although he acknowledged that some in the union looked upon the merger of Mine, Mill with the Steelworkers, which brought added financial responsibilities, as a "mixed blessing," Burke defended the merger as "one of the most significant, progressive and fortunate events which has occurred in our union in many years."

Just as the needs of the international union had grown, argued Burke, many local unions faced problems equaling or exceeding those of the international. He reminded the local leaders among the delegates that an increase in dues—part of which would be remitted to the local unions—would make the locals more viable. Burke's report was obviously geared to overcome the expected reluctance of local union leaders to do the politically unpopular thing of voting a dues increase.

Burke then contrasted the union's precarious financial condition with the size of the working capital of the eleven largest basic steel companies, three aluminum and four copper companies, which, he said, amounted to $4.8 billion: "You have only to compare approximately $5 billion of industrial financial muscle with our total net worth of $18 million (much of which is not fluid) to appreciate the difficulty we find ourselves in."

But the delegates were not easily persuaded. They subjected the dues proposal to an intensive and concentrated examination of union policy. Adhering to his role as the symbol of dues protest, Rarick, already an announced candidate for president, moved that the proposed dues changes be put to a roll-call vote, the ultimate weapon of the opposition. But fewer than 10 per cent of the 3,600 delegates supported Rarick. The motion for a roll-call vote was lost. Thus in this respect the historic continuity of Steelworkers conventions had not been broken: no roll call.

Early in the convention, a new delegate from Inland Steel No. 1010, the union's largest local, chided the leadership for failure to provide more information on matters before them: "Some of us haven't been coming to these things for 35 years. Some of us must run for local election. We are small people who do not get elected every time and are not sent down here free. . . . We have a right to know what's going on within our international union. . . . There is not a damn thing wrong with an international union acquainting the member at the bottom, the little guy like me that supports you, with what the hell I am going to pay you." Applause punctuated his repeated insistence for better internal "communication." This development—the presence of an articulate opposition, strongly supported—was not lost on the platform.

An attack on the dues increase came from James W. Sheppard, a delegate from a small Cleveland local (No. 4827, National Tool Division, National Cleveland Corp.), who said that he represented the "working poor," a designation that made some district directors wince. "I was sent here by my local union to express their feelings. Some locals are so small and so poor that the cost of sending a delegate to a convention is prohibitive. They are conned into giving their staff man their vote. This compares with a fox guarding the chicken coop. . . . I'm not a dues protester as such . . . [but] always placing the biggest burden on those least able to pay is what causes the great unrest and riots. . . . The hierarchy in the unions is becoming more and more business-minded, day by day, year by year. This is the main reason for the apathy from the rank and file in many of the local unions." Then Sheppard warned the platform and his fellow local union officers that the rank and file would "give them their answer" in the next local union elections in 1970. The warning was treated with respect.

From Canada's Ottawa Valley another first-time delegate, William Charbonneau, worried that a 100 per cent jump of $5 in dues might cause some small locals to drift away from the Steelworkers. In response, Albert Sisti, a New England delegate, argued that while the increase would hurt, "if we want strength in future bargaining sessions, we can't watch brother internationals in the AFL-CIO contribute to our strikers and not do something ourselves."

William Gailes, another Inland Steel delegate, complained that the Abel administration had not kept its promise in settling local grievances, which was why the people in Local 1010 were against a dues increase. His warning of a "credibility gap" between his local and the international was an uncomfortable echo of the charge directed against Mc-Donald a few years before.

Some heavy batteries now got into action: from the Irvin Works of U.S. Steel, Rarick's Local 2227, came a political attack on the Abel administration by a delegate who scoffed at the need for a strike fund, calling it "a slush fund for the executive board and the staff man to play peekaboo with." Out of Local 1211 of District 20, the Jones & Laughlin plant, rose Morros Brummitt in opposition to the proposed strike fund, on a legal ground: that the constitution already provided the executive board with power to assess the membership if, during the period of negotiations, it considered it necessary to raise additional funds. Brummitt, who was to run against Burke for international secretary-treasurer in the 1969 election, recalled that Lawrence Sefton and Vice-President Molony less than two years before, at the 1966 convention, had opposed the creation of a strike fund. Why this switch? Sefton explained: conditions had changed. Rather than have the executive board apply its constitutional power to assess and proceed to raise dues on a piecemeal basis, "we had enough confidence in you to call you here to lay our cards on the table, to come to you with the problems regardless of how damn painful they may be." His explanation was greeted with uncomplimentary noises.

At this point, Vice-President Molony, as chairman of the Constitution Committee, admitted cheerfully that he had opposed the creation of a strike fund in 1966. But if they sought to embarrass him with that reminder, they should have "gone back 25 or 30 years ago; I said even crazier things then." He made his pitch for the establishment of a strike fund in these words: "There would be no special convention here today were it not for the toughest and longest strike that you and I ever engaged in. We are here because 50,000 of our members—they are half and half, old Steelworkers and the new Mine, Mill Workers, whom we are glad to have in our company—have, with great courage and extraordinary endurance, survived a strike of eight months. We have spent great sums of money to help them just a little because these men live, for the most part, in mining camps—ghettoes, if you please—hundreds of miles from the nearest job opportunity. No matter whether you spoke for or against a strike fund, there is not a man or woman in this room who begrudges a single penny we have given to these good and brave people." What was done for the metal miners, said Molony, the executive board now urged the delegates to provide for all members of the union, through a strike fund; management, he said, was already flexing its muscles for a fight. The convention now rocked with applause. The genuine enthusiasm Molony turned on seemed to be welcomed even by those who worried about the effect of dues increase on their political position in their home locals.

Molony now matched the political concerns of the local leaders with his own: "There has been a lot of politicking around here. I think you should take careful note that the President of this union, the Secretary-Treasurer and myself too, will be seeking office in not too many months. Perhaps it is not the best way to win the affection and esteem and the votes of our constituents, by taxing them at such a critical time. But you don't see Abe flinching from this decision. He is putting his reputation, his leadership and his opportunity for re-election on the stake, the same as those of you who have the courage to vote your convictions. This goes beyond politics. This deals with the strength and the survival of the United Steelworkers. I ask you to accept your responsibility of leadership." Within a few minutes, for the first time in its history, the Steelworkers Union authorized the creation of a strike fund. It was a break with the old United Mine Workers tradition.

The convention now moved to consider the graduated dues proposal. There would be a three-way distribution of the increase above the current $5-a-month dues: to the strike fund, to the local, and to the international. Practical objections were raised. The lack of common expiration dates in fabricating and foundry contracts and the inroads on Steelworkers jobs by outside construction contractors would complicate a uniform collection of dues. There was also a psychological objection to overcome: since under the two-hour formula members would pay dues according to their hourly wages, the differential might create bad blood among them.

Another type of objection came from John Sargent, the highly articulate president of the Inland Steel Local 1010, the membership of which, he reminded the leaders, was only slightly smaller than that in twelve districts headed by directors and a full complement of staff representatives. At the 1964 convention, he recalled, a dues increase was considered unnecessary because the executive board intended to eliminate wasteful overhead by combining several smaller districts. But, said Sargent, the executive board pigeonholed the district merger proposal while the district directors were voted a $4,000-a-year increase. He now challenged the Abel leadership to do what the executive board under McDonald had failed to do: eliminate unnecessary district organizations. This struck home. But by this time, the practical details of merger of smaller districts were already under study in the executive board. Whether Sargent had wind of this or not was not generally known to the delegates. He could therefore score points against leadership, highly sensitive to the charge of unkept promises.

Though delegates began to call for the "question," Burke rejected the tactic of choking off debate. He was not, he said, going to have another 1956 bulldozer running over the delegates on the subject of a dues increase. But neither arguments nor the strategy of good will were always relevant. Frank Leseganich, president of the local at Youngstown Sheet & Tube (No. 1462 of District 26), informed the convention that his large local had instructed its delegates to oppose the dues increase, primarily, he said, because the international staff was excessively large. He himself was looking beyond his local presidency to higher office: an attack on the staff was as popular with some rank-and-file members as opposition to a dues increase. A few months later, he won enough local nominations for district director to run against the veteran incumbent, James P. Griffin, whom he narrowly defeated in the 1969 election.

Although the dues increase was declared adopted by a voice vote, another delegate insisted that only a roll call could adequately reflect the sentiment of the convention: "If you put it to a roll call, you would be disgraced by the vote you would get here today." His challenge was disregarded. "I got one question to ask you," said another delegate. "I walked into this hall with five votes, reflecting the number of members in my local union. On a voice vote I have got only one vote now, if I can holler loud enough. How can you determine whether you count delegates with five votes or one? How do you figure this in giving your decision?" To which Abel replied: "No, brother, nobody could tell that without a roll-call vote, whether one guy had five votes or one. You could only do that with a roll-call vote. . . ." Whereupon the delegate said: "What it boils down to is: everyone in here has one vote, and that is all." Abel reminded him, and other delegates joined in, that a general motion for a roll call on major issues had been voted down early in the convention. "We needn't," he said, "all be torn asunder. . . . All we are trying to do is leave the union in still better condition. We need not fight or fuss about it. . . . There is no need of going out of here with a public image of a divided organization."

Despite Abel's placatory remarks, the delegates continued restless. In lieu of a roll-call vote, he proposed a face-saving device: if delegates wished to place themselves unmistakably on record, they could, if they chose, send up a slip of paper to the convention's official reporter as proof of their compliance with the members' instructions to oppose a dues increase. About 10 per cent of the delegates submitted their "slips" to the official reporter of the convention to establish a record of their position, although not all delegates whose locals had mandated opposition presented slips. Nor did many of those who spoke against a dues increase trouble to submit slips. For them the record was clear. The slips count therefore signified nothing. As a symbolic roll call, it was not part of the regular order of business. Politically, it permitted delegates to get off the hook. If attacked at home, they could point to the record of convention proceedings, to be printed months hence, as proof that they had followed the instructions of the local to oppose a dues increase and that only over their objection had it been adopted.

With the enactment of the dues increase, the union's leadership could presumably look ahead to a period during which the bruised feelings of the latter-day Dues Protesters could be healed. The first meetings of the union's basic steel and aluminum industry conferences were held on the day after the adjournment of the special "dues" convention. Both the special convention and the basic steel conference provided unmistakable evidence of areas of rank-and-file dissatisfaction. Despite the clear need for stronger financing, the dues increase fueled discontent. Repeatedly, delegates had risen to say that they would not object to a dues increase if they had received more "service" from the union. Discontent over the handling of local issues in contract negotiations still persisted despite the greater attention paid by the Abel leadership to this locus of disaffection.

BOOK V

THE SHAKEN NATION

Suddenly, national trauma transcended everything.

On March 31, 1968, President Johnson astounded the country by announcing: "I shall not seek, and I will not accept, the nomination of my party for another term."

Allowing for the passage of a few days, AFL-CIO President Meany on April 3 "urged" Vice-President Humphrey to announce his candidacy. The next day, Humphrey flew to Pittsburgh to address the Pennsylvania AFL-CIO, in which the Steelworkers are heavily represented. The tumultuous convention became a Humphrey rally. Abel, exultant, saw personal and political satisfaction in the development.

As Abel shouted "Go, go, go, Hubert," the convention roared approval. Above all, Meany and Abel aimed to develop band-wagon momentum for Humphrey to deflect labor support from Robert F. Kennedy, who had announced his candidacy just two weeks before. For the Steelworkers leaders, the Humphrey cause took priority over all other considerations.

That same night, in Memphis, Martin Luther King, Jr., was assassinated. By this time, the country, already in a highly emotional state, approached hysteria. Riots broke out in scores of cities. The convulsive fury, punctuated by fire and looting, did not abate for days. The nation was almost torn apart.

In the middle of May, the United Automobile Workers, the AFL-CIO's largest affiliate, was suspended from the AFL-CIO for nonpayment of dues. Shortly after, the UAW formally disaffiliated itself from the AFL-CIO.

On June 4, Robert Kennedy was assassinated.

As a result of the UAW suspension, Walter Reuther was no longer eligible to serve as president of the AFL-CIO Industrial Union Department. At a special meeting of the IUD, which Meany addressed, Abel was chosen to head the IUD.

CHAPTER 29

Basic Steel Negotiations

> All things are doubly fair,
> If patience fashion them and care.
>
> THÉOPHILE GAUTIER

Abel needed time to concentrate on internal union affairs and on basic steel negotiations. But national politics had prematurely become uppermost. In Pennsylvania, the union's energies were diverted to the primary where the Steelworkers Union confirmed its political power by swinging a large majority of delegates to the Democratic convention for Humphrey.

The international union obviously had no choice but to operate on several levels. Local unions carried their bundles of unresolved grievances, "the local issues," to their negotiators. The joint negotiating calendar set a May 31 deadline for the clearance of local issues. After that, the union and company negotiators would turn to the big picture: the wage and fringe demands that cut across the eleven steel companies coordinating their bargaining efforts.

By June 1, 15,000 local issues in eleven companies had been reduced by agreement to 2,000. In U.S. Steel alone, 95 per cent of the 4,700 local issues had been settled, although the tough ones still remained for the top bargaining teams.

Industry-wide talks began on June 3 in New York in the ballroom of the Hotel Commodore, whose "golden decor seemed to mirror the wage aspirations of 640,000 steelworkers in the nation's basic steel mills." * Inasmuch as the USW negotiators, a few days before, had won from the

* *Business Week*, June 8, 1968.

can and aluminum industries wage and fringe packages that exceeded 6 per cent a year, the union target for basic steel could be no lower.

Both sides made their sales pitch. Industry representatives talked "poor mouth," of foreign competition and slim profit margins. The union's spokesmen cited the high cost of living. But on one subject there seemed to be agreement: neither side, they said, desired government intervention.

Headed by Abel, the union team consisted of Molony, Burke, Bernard Kleiman, the general counsel, and Elliot Bredhoff, the Washington counsel. Otis Brubaker, the union's top economist, was not included, an omission that some leaders considered a mistake. Despite the unpromising start, R. Conrad Cooper and his committee had by now developed a certain rapport with Abel and his fellow officers. For example, both teams were making common cause in a demand upon Congress to impose steel import quotas to counter the threat of foreign steel production.

June passed and no hard bargaining had taken place. The contract was to terminate August 1. The Steelworkers regular biennial convention was to open August 19, in Chicago. For that occasion the union leaders hoped to announce good news of a strong contract to counteract the continuing discontent. The copper strike had left everybody drained and shaken. Unless the basic steel contract came up to expectations, the convention could become an arena of discord.

Psychologically and financially, the union was now not without resources. With a $25-million strike fund building up since the special convention, Steelworkers would be less helpless in weathering a strike if it occurred. Also, for the first time, the majority of local issues had been bargained out, though some critical ones remained.

Under the union's new constitutional provisions, the basic steel contract would have to be approved by the newly instituted Basic Steel Industry Conference, made up of about five hundred presidents of local unions in the eleven large steel companies. In mid-July, the leadership of the basic steel conference proceeded to the local union membership for strike authorization, which it received by a 95 per cent vote. Late in July, the White House moved in to head off the crisis. The administration emphatically did not want a strike. The President's Cabinet Committee on Price Stability, set up a few months before, had opened a full-blast campaign for wage and price restraint, and the steel industry was the immediate target.

With only four days left before contract termination, union and management remained silent. The steel industry had insulated itself against pain: production was at a record high because of the stockpiling begun a few months before. If a strike did occur, the industry and its corporate customers could live on their accumulated industrial fat. On the other hand, if agreement was reached without a strike, the excessive production would inevitably lead to layoffs of steelworkers, who by producing too much in the preceding months had been made to contrive their own unemployment. Looking toward preventive action, Federal Mediation Director William E. Simkin, had already appeared discreetly in Pittsburgh to remind the negotiating parties that the family doctor was present, ready, and willing. But the gentle arts of mediation, at this stage, was not the particular form of technical assistance required. Only the White House could provide the ultimate pressure. The steel companies were informed point-blank that the administration would not tolerate a price increase; if they insisted on lifting prices, they must be prepared to receive unshirted hell from the government in ways they understood from earlier confrontations. At the same time, the stern warning against a price increase carried with it the admonition to the union negotiators that they would have to curb their wage demands.

To the labor men, this seemed like unrealistic rhetoric. The Steelworkers leaders could not agree to a contract that brought an increase lower than the range of 6 to 6½ per cent, which the Auto Workers had exceeded months before and which had already been won by Steelworkers who worked in can manufacturing and aluminum. Nevertheless a strong union deterrent to the calling of a strike would be its possible adverse effect on the prolabor administration and Humphrey's chances in the Presidential election. President Johnson continued to urge self-restraint. Finally, after some shadow boxing, a settlement was reached on July 30. The specter of a steel strike was exorcised. The union and the companies agreed to a contract without the open White House intervention so obviously applied in 1965. The total cost of the contract package to the industry was estimated at the predicted 6 per cent, including substantial increases in pension and supplementary unemployment benefits. But at least one important issue remained unresolved—the union's demand for increased pay for the more than 20 per cent of the workers not covered by incentive pay. This unresolved issue was submitted to a three-man arbitration panel for final decision. Recognizing that the USW was faced with a potential political revolt by black unionists, management negotiators also yielded to demands that special consideration be given to the job assignment of black workers.

But some of the provisions left areas of potential disaffection. For instance, the companies were given the power to make unilateral decisions in scheduling vacation periods throughout the year, instead of during the customary seasons. Older and higher-paid workers might afford and even prefer winter vacations; younger workers generally would not. Also, the contract did not include a cost-of-living clause; the

Steelworkers won such clauses only in the 1956–59 contract, after which it was phased out by agreement in 1960 and 1961. Wage gains were illusory: they were being eroded. The week after the terms of the contract were announced, some local strikes broke out and others were threatened. Steel management was resisting the extension of contract benefits to salaried workers who belonged to the USW, union spokesmen charged, because the benefits would then be automatically extended to other salaried employees not represented by the union. In an effort to abate the discontent, the union sought to work out that inequity with U.S. Steel, hoping that the other companies would follow the pattern for their salaried workers.

Shortly after the settlement, Bethlehem Steel announced across-the-board price increases and U.S. Steel cautiously went in for "selective" price rises. Inland and Pittsburgh Steel followed Bethlehem. President Johnson was furious. He called a news conference and attacked Bethlehem, specifically exempting U.S. Steel from his wrath. By order of the President, the Defense Department now announced that it would limit steel purchases to those companies which would not follow the Bethlehem price route; other government agencies were all primed to switch. By August 5, Republic and Armco Steel announced that their price increases would not apply to certain defense items. At the same time, the Federal Trade Commission hinted at an investigation and the House Small Business Committee began a staff probe of steel prices. Through a juncture of squeeze plays, reminiscent of President Kennedy's 1962 battle with the steel industry, Johnson turned back the recalcitrant steel companies. Bethlehem cut its price increase by half and the steel-price blitz of 1968 fizzled out. The companies bided their time in an election year.

Inside his union, Abel now could point with satisfaction to a contract achieved through steel negotiations entirely begun and completed under his leadership. He had won an agreement without a strike. Abel seemed to have proved his point: collective bargaining could take place under conditions of mutual respect without blurring the union's responsibility to its membership.

CHAPTER **30**

The Hot Chicago Convention

Obedient they but to a dream.

GEORGE DILLON

In the Steelworkers as in all other American unions, the "minorities" —black, Mexican-American, Puerto Rican—kept raising their demands for recognition.* At the 1966 Steelworkers convention, the Negro delegates, with some support from the whites, had made their dissatisfaction aggressively clear. In the Steelworkers Union, they were now talking tougher. They wanted more say and more jobs. At union headquarters, there was no disposition to take their demands lightly.

During basic steel negotiations in June 1968, forty-eight black staff representatives met with Vice-President Molony. Attacking USW's "lack of action" on Negro issues since 1965, they received a commitment for more effective moves to open up the higher-paid mill jobs to black workers and for a strong plant-wide seniority contract clause that would provide jobs heretofore closed to Negroes. They also argued, through their Ad Hoc Committee, for a black international vice-president. The group argued from precedent: since the USW had two vice-presidents until 1946, there was no reason why the August convention could not re-establish a second vice-presidency, presumably to be filled by a black member. An alternative method to achieve representation, the black group pointed out, would be to create four

* Of the 180 national and international unions—130 of them then AFL-CIO affiliates—at this time, only two had Negro presidents—the Brotherhood of Sleeping Car Porters and Actors Equity. Here and there were scattered Negro vice-presidents: in the Laborers, Packinghouse Workers, and Longshoremen. In most unions, Negroes were sometimes elected to local union offices or appointed to staff jobs—but not nearly in proportion to their numerical strength.

355

regional vice-presidencies, one of which would be filled by a black steelworker. In 1962, the United Auto Workers, for the first time, had elected a black member-at-large to its executive board. An important structural difference between the UAW and the USW, however, is that the elections of the former are held by convention, while the USW elects its international union officers by referendum. Since the total black Steelworkers membership was a minority, though a significant one of about 15 per cent, there could be no guarantee that a Negro would be elected by referendum.

How to meet the demands of the black spokesmen without alienating other sections of the membership was a question with no simple answer. The flick of the white backlash was already felt. The day before the union convention, Abel and his fellow officers held a press briefing. In response to a question, they declared that they would welcome the election of a black district director, which would mean membership on the executive board. But they opposed "discrimination in reverse" by creating board positions specifically designated for Negroes. Nevertheless, Abel and his associates believed that in Baltimore, District 8, with a black membership totaling 40 per cent, a black staff member would stand an excellent chance of succeeding Director Albert Atallah, who was retiring at the end of the current term. In fact, they had tried to persuade Atallah to resign prior to expiration of his term. As his replacement, Abel would have recommended Leander Simms, a black staff man. With the status of an acting director, it was thought that Simms would hold the inside track in a regular election. But Atallah stubbornly refused to quit; he had a white staff man in mind as his successor.

Members of the black Ad Hoc Committee, by now an identified national caucus, distributed "An Open Letter to President I. W. Abel from a Black Steelworker," pointing out that "Of more than 1,000 employees of the International, less than 100 are Negroes. Of 14 departments in the International, only two have Negro personnel. One of these two is the Civil Rights Department (obviously). Of more than 30 districts in the International, there are no Negro directors, and only one subdistrict director. Blacks were in the forefront during the formation of this union 24 years ago. Through the acceptance of crumbs down through the years, we now find ourselves hindmost. . . ."

What Abel enthusiastically described as the greatest basic steel contract in union history did not make the convention hall ring. The physical arrangements in the section of the Chicago Amphitheatre where the Steelworkers met were incredibly wretched: the heat was intense, the cooling system worked intermittently, the acoustics were erratic. Meeting at the same time, the Resolutions Committee of the Democratic Party as-

sembled nearby in critical sessions. Reports began to circulate that plans
had been made to prevent the Democratic convention by demonstrations
and physical assault. Mayor Richard J. Daley demanded that Governor
Otto Kerner call out the National Guard. The intermittent hours of calm
in the city seemed like omens of hurricane. During this week of foreboding, the Steelworkers convention met on August 19.

To meet objections, Abel emphasized that for the first time the basic
steel settlement, concluded a few weeks before, called for the insertion
in every contract of a provision for a joint union-management civil rights
committee; that two joint study committees had been set up to determine incentives in places where workers did not yet receive incentive
payments, with the stipulation that in cases of differences between union
and management, a three-man arbitration panel would make the final
determination; and that a joint study was to be made for the financing
of an "automation fund" to be built up in the next twelve months to protect the earnings of workers displaced by technological change. He reported an increase of 173,000 members during the previous four years,
bringing the total to around 1,200,000. The Steelworkers Union, he declared triumphantly, was "back in the mainstream of the labor movement . . . and making a few splashes, if you please." When AFL-CIO
President Meany addressed the delegates, he lauded Abel and then
recited his version of the facts in the dispute that led to the withdrawal
of the UAW from the AFL-CIO.

The Push for Black Representation

In a moving speech, Bayard Rustin, executive director of the A.
Philip Randolph Institute, described the character of social forces operating in the country, of the misunderstandings between whites and blacks,
Mexican-Americans, and Puerto Ricans. He frankly aimed to cool some
of the extremist demands made by certain black leaders on the outside.
"The black men," he said, "are tied in and cannot separate themselves
from white workers in this nation because the overwhelming majority of
black men are workers, and we are tied together in a single fate whether
we like it or not. [Applause.] Therefore, while every black brother must
fight discrimination in the trade union movement where it exists, he must
fight it as a family problem to be solved within the family among allies
and brothers." He expressed "absolute faith" in Abel's good will.

Shortly after, the convention took up the proposal to provide a second
vice-president to represent Negro membership. Urging rejection of the
idea, Lawrence Sefton, the Canadian, argued that the election of a black
to the executive board should be a part of "national development." But
several black delegates, claiming that about one-fifth of the membership

was black, observed angrily that no black was in a position to advance himself to election to a district directorship. Another black delegate argued that there "aren't enough black people in one district to elect a District Director. We are not begging . . . we need your help. We are here to say specifically, let one or two Negroes be placed on this Executive Board by appointment of the President of the United Steelworkers. . . ." Their language grew more vivid; they brushed aside the question of "constitutionality" as irrelevant, and called for "responsibility" of the executive board to "remedy" the situation of "an all-white Executive Board up there." Such "responsibility," one delegate observed, had been emphasized in the report of the Kerner Commission, on which Abel had been the labor member.

Vice-President Molony acknowledged the anxieties and the impatience of the Negro delegates, but he insisted that the union could properly be run only through democratic procedures. If a member is *denied* office *because* of race, he said, the union and its officers would "fight for his right, as a Steelworker, to exercise his democratic right to run for office. However, if a member says that he should be *provided* with an office *because* of his race, creed or color, that is another thing, and this union and its officers cannot and will not support such a plea. This would be a form of Jim Crowism in reverse. The claims that a Negro cannot be elected to high office do not hold water. Nathaniel Lee, a Negro, ran for International Teller in the 1965 election—the year in which Abel was elected—and he led the ticket for this office. . . . I would rejoice to be a part of a Board on which a Negro serves."

A black delegate from the Clairton Works of U.S. Steel in the Pittsburgh area replied to Molony's reference to Lee's election: "But you control the circle from which we have to run. In order to break this crust, there must be a place for us to run. We are asking you now to give us the second place on the ticket."

The pitch of the argument was heightened by a Negro shop steward, from Sparrows Point in the Baltimore area: "There is so much we want. We want to have someone up there. How about you listening to us today? Every people need a symbol. We need to look up there and know that our people are there in the policy-making framework. . . . This is the thing that hurts me so bad. We know it is utterly impossible to run a man for the top executive office unless he gets widespread publicity. A lot of money has to be behind him. He has to be known. It is time now that we put a black man up there so my daughters and the daughters of all these Steelworkers . . . can say: 'Yes, now we are part—we are a real part. We are in the policy-making part of this union.' "

A white delegate from Inland Steel pushed Abel to "do his homework" on the Kerner Report: "That Report talks about changing the system.

We have to give some serious consideration to changing the system of elections in our International. . . . The Negro brothers have raised serious questions."

The veteran Negro international representative, Jimmy Jones of the Philadelphia area, who served as Abel's aide on the Kerner Commission, asserted he felt a "wee bit ashamed" of this line of argument: "If a Negro gets on this Executive Board by appointment of President Abel or anybody else, he will be merely a figurehead for somebody else. And you will be the first ones along with me to call him an Uncle Tom. [Applause.] Don't tell me there isn't a possibility of getting a Negro elected, no matter how remote it may seem. But you will never get elected unless you have the guts to run for the damn job. . . . Fight like hell in this union against the evils that are there to make this a more democratic union. But you are not doing this when you say 'Throw the Constitution out of the window.' Once you do that, you are done."

Now Abel himself was impelled to participate, not only as president but also as one whose motives in the civil rights field had been questioned. Asking for "light and not so much damn heat," Abel's voice was heavy with feeling: "I was engaged in this fight before it became popular." He recalled in considerable detail how he had implemented his advocacy of civil rights over the previous twenty-five years by bringing in black staff and office employees. As to the argument for amending the constitution to designate a specific place for a Negro officer, he was certain, he said, that "our good Negro brothers don't want 'separate but equal' privileges in this union—but they want equal rights, equal opportunities, equal privileges." By an overwhelming voice vote, the convention rejected the proposed constitutional changes. At a midnight caucus, however, the black Ad Hoc Committee described the rejection as "explosive" and talked of future plans.

Later in the week, Richard Hatcher, the black mayor of Gary, Indiana, brought a glow to the convention, especially to the black delegates. While he praised Abel, Joseph Germano, and their associates for their great leadership and courage, and their support in his election to the mayoralty, "as a matter of conscience I cannot stop at the border of the internal union controversy: every group should be represented at every level of this organization."

Then the convention took up the matter of union election reform. At this point, Joseph J. Kender, President of Local 2265, District 28, who had been kept off the ballot in the 1965 district election, triumphantly called the convention's attention to the settlement made by the union's executive board with the Department of Labor and the Department of Justice with the consent of the Federal Court. That agreement, in effect, met Kender's contention that his rights under the Landrum-Griffin Act and under the union constitution had been violated. The case had hung fire for nearly three years, until October 1967, when to avoid a trial the union agreed to change the nominating procedure for candidates for international and district office.

Kender's remarks set off a heated discussion on the number of nominations required to run for international office or district director. Only six locals had proposed a change to reduce the number to its previous level, and the Constitution Committee recommended nonconcurrence. But the sentiment for change in the hall ran deep. Confrontation was in the air. When Abel finally asked for a standing vote on the committee's recommendation, the vote pro and con was almost even. The familiar cry for a roll call began to be heard. This time the requisite 30 per cent of the bodies seemed available. But the platform was reluctant. "I'm sure nobody wants a roll call," commented Abel. "Why doesn't the committee take another look at the section and come back with another recommendation?" This turndown of a committee recommendation was unusual. But the rejection was temporary. The next day, Vice-President Molony led the discussion. By now the leadership had lined up its supporters, and no longer were the delegates arrayed against the platform. By an uncontested voice vote, the nominations procedure was retained.

The question of revision of other election procedures came up, with resolutions from fifty-three locals urging that the elections be supervised by the American Arbitration Association. Sefton protested that "our elections are aboveboard and honest and we are quite capable of conducting our own elections . . . part of the whole life of our union . . . which we have been able to run for the last 30 years and will continue to do. . . ." In support of the proposal, Donald Rarick recalled, as he never tired of doing, his famous run against McDonald. "Up until this time, even today, I hear people tell me in this hall that they helped steal the election of 1957. . . ." While Rarick gathered some support, the prevailing convention sentiment was clearly opposed to a "wholesale abdication" of the union's control of its own procedures.

Hostility toward field staff men was again expressed on the ground that from some districts they carried credentials as delegates "far outnumbering the weight of the ordinary grass root delegates." John Sargent of the Inland Steel local in District 31 said: "Over 700 staff members attend the convention, most of them as delegates. To make this convention a democratic expression of the elected delegates, it is very difficult to overcome a block of 700 staff members. . . . We believe every staff member should have a right to be elected from the locals he comes from. But they should not be able to pick up credentials from some obscure little local that often does not even hold elections for convention delegates. . . ."

At this juncture, Abel entered a defense in behalf of the embattled staff members, although many of them, McDonald appointees, were still not entirely attuned to him or to his administration. Only properly elected delegates could be seated at the convention, he said: if any staff members were not properly accredited, their seating should have been challenged before the Credentials Committee. "We ought not," he said, "to be carried away with the idea that any great number of staff people are here." He objected, moreover, to the proposal that a staff representative be required to represent only his own local because too often, he said, a staff man may be appointed to an area hundreds of miles from his home base. Sefton deplored the tendency to "distrust your staff . . . [who are] doing so much to promote the union welfare in their daily work. We can trust them to deal with the issues on an objective basis." He did not meet the point made by a delegate that a staff member often appears as a delegate for several unions, carrying multiple weight.

Actually, according to an analysis made for this study, four out of five of the staff representatives served as delegates. (See Appendix 6.) At this point, the convention was informed by Chairman Sefton that the executive board, under its constitutional power, had, two weeks before the convention, approved the consolidation of several districts, reducing the total from twenty-nine to twenty-four. With this change, a long overdue reform went into effect. The expected economies would presumably meet the objections of those who had resisted the dues increase as recently as the special convention of the previous March.

The convention delegates gradually surrendered to fatigue. The weather continued in the humid nineties. As the convention slogged on, the mood of the meeting caused great uneasiness among the leaders. By now demands for more rapid implementation of civil rights were counterbalanced by the unmistakable resentment displayed by considerable groups of white steelworkers in the lobby and in the aisles, if not on the record. Some of the union leaders themselves became restless. In the next few days, on August 26, the Democratic national convention was to open officially.

Moreover, the union's own political pot had begun to boil. Talk became louder about possible opposition to Abel. Rarick, for one, had already announced his intention to run. Now there appeared another with a rhyming name, Emil Narick. An assistant general counsel in the international headquarters, he was relatively unknown. The year before, he had been elected vice-president of the local of the union's office employees (Local 3657), separate from the more recently established Staffman's Organizing Committee (SOC). Even before the convention, word began to get around that Narick would run as an anti-establishment symbol. He was reported aggrieved at lack of recognition by the union's general counsel. When approached in the hotel lobby during the convention, he merely conceded that all this was "interesting speculation."

By the world outside, the Steelworkers Union was watched more closely for what light its behavior might shed on the Presidential campaign. This union was regarded as sure-fire Humphrey country. Its leadership had placed a considerable investment of men and money in his campaign. Yet despite his most vigorous efforts, his appearance at the Steelworkers convention had failed to whip up the crusading passion and exhilaration the leadership and most delegates had longed for.

While the entire top union leadership was whole-souled for Humphrey, there was considerable fragmentation in the rank and file. By this time, the polls estimated that Richard M. Nixon, already the Republican Presidential candidate, would achieve the normal minimal Republican response of perhaps 25 per cent among union members. But the union leaders were worried most about the inroads that former Governor George C. Wallace of Alabama was making. Strong Wallace sentiment had already registered on the political seismograph, not only in the South but also among white workers in certain industrial areas with large Negro populations and memberships. It was then luxuriating in the New England states, in the northern parts of Minnesota, Wisconsin, and Michigan, and in California. Union leaders recognized the depth of the sprawl. A choice between Nixon and Humphrey could be managed despite Humphrey's apparent lag as a candidate. If, however, in addition to Nixon's capture of 25 per cent of the labor vote, Wallace could garner an estimated 20 to 25 per cent, Humphrey would be unable to hold the great majority of labor votes, which was indispensable to his victory.

In the Steelworkers, the perplexities of labor leadership mounted. The convention had revealed large interior distances stretching between top leadership and a large body of rank-and-file leaders. A good contract was not considered good enough. Although outbreaks of dissent were finally diverted, modified, or subdued, Abel, Burke, and Molony understood that come November with the nominations for international office and for district directorships, the ensuing period might not be one of unruffled calm.

On the next to last day of the convention, a delegate from the Jones & Laughlin plant, a seeker after unity, suggested that the convention should hereafter open not only with the American and Canadian national anthems but also with the singing of "Solidarity Forever." Pleased with the idea, Abel thought it "might be well to sing together once in a while." If solidarity could be sung into his union, he was all for it. Certainly, at that stage, some form of organizational adrenaline seemed necessary. The mood of the leaders was earnest and dedicated, but somewhat less than triumphantly confident. They were pleased at least to have the convention end on a quiet note. Those who could, got out of town fast. With the adjournment, however, the energies of the majority were soon directed to the Humphrey-Nixon campaign.

CHAPTER 31

Unheroic Campaign:
Narick versus Abel

O come all ye faithful . . .

HYMN

In Pittsburgh, the fifty-two-year-old Narick now formally announced his candidacy. A former football star, Narick refereed weekend college and professional football games. As a staff lawyer, representing local unions before various government agencies, and with limited collective bargaining responsibilities, he had become known to some of the local leaders.

An opposition constituency, which Narick hoped to exploit, seemed to have developed out of a combination of factors, some of them conflicting. There was dissent: among the Negro delegates; with the 1968 contract; among the racially prejudiced. There was also the coalescence of antiheadquarters sentiment among the staff representatives, buttressed in part by the Staffman's Organizing Committee. In the 1969 international election, for the first time, the staff men would test and display their independence. On the level of local unions there were strong elements of alienation. In addition to all this, Abel fell short of being a charismatic figure and had in fact deliberately sought to avoid a personality build-up. He wanted respect, not adoration. He functioned in the calm assurance that the steelworkers he represented would give him an overwhelming majority.

Narick referred to the "discontent, despair, and utter helplessness that has developed on all levels of our union." Supporters of Abel, Burke, and Molony rejected as exaggerated Narick's characterization of the mood of the membership. But with the coincidence of Donald Rarick's sudden death from a heart attack just at this time, Narick believed he could win the support of old Dues Protesters and some members who had assembled behind a ticket called Rank-and-File Team (RAFT).

Implicit was the belief that Narick could gain adherents among the "white backlash" elements in the membership. By stringing together a series of discontents, the ganglia of an opposition could thus be constructed. Moreover, inside any organization there existed a residual opposition to incumbent leadership seeking an outlet. Narick became that conduit. He listened for every possible suggestion of support. The heady slogan "Return the Union to the Membership"—similar to Abel's in his 1965 campaign—could always be depended upon. "Abel didn't give the union back to us, so we're going to try and take it back," announced one Narick supporter. "We have arrived at a point in the history of our union where we can no longer drift along aimlessly on the path to nowhere," said Narick. "We must have new leadership identify not only with the older members but also with increasing numbers of the new generation."

If Abel could stage a successful revolt in 1965, why not Narick in 1969? The difference between the two men, their candidacies, and the years was considerable. First, when Abel finally announced his candidacy in 1964, he had carefully prepared the groundwork. He was the No. 2 man in the union; respected district directors were teamed with him, and he had the majority of the weighted vote of the executive board. The opposition to McDonald therefore had been managed by McDonald's peers. In contrast, Narick had to find supporters among local officers and rank-and-file members in whose behalf he criticized the Abel administration for "lack of democracy." He felt that he could count on at least the implicit support of staffers who were still residual McDonald men or who had become disaffected during the Abel administration. Employees of the international office had been in acrimonious negotiations with the union administration, and Narick, as the local's vice-president, headed the confrontation with the officers. The union management was determined to increase the efficiency of the employees, revise the job classification of the staff, and rectify an inequity in salaries growing out of the 1965 campaign. At that time several of the headquarters staff had their salaries secretly raised by McDonald in return for their support. Many of the staff were discontented as well as insecure because of persisting salary disparities.

A day after he announced his candidacy, Narick was transferred, with no reduction in salary, from his post as an "assistant general counsel" to a job in the Research Department. His new duties, vague as they were, confined him to the headquarters building and did not permit him to circulate among the locals. Immediately Narick cried "foul" and received valuable publicity. The transfer, clearly motivated by annoyance and political pique on Abel's part, was uncharacteristically vindictive. It stimulated a build-up for Narick among the rank and file, especially in the basic steel districts concentrated in the Pittsburgh area. Narick filed a grievance against the international union, as his employer.*

With Narick's emergence from the murk of opposition, Abel and his associates experienced a rising discomfort. They felt the irritation of established leaders against upstart opponents. In the meantime, David McDonald suddenly broke out of Palm Springs, California, into the news by announcing his support of Richard Nixon. He praised Nixon for his "indispensable aid" in settling the 116-day steel strike of 1959–60. He recited his own record of support for Democratic Presidents down through the years, but he denounced Humphrey for some undisclosed perfidy. He appeared in various places—including Pittsburgh, where he met with some of his old friends who were now backing Narick. He encouraged talk of himself as Secretary of Labor in a Nixon cabinet. As the only former prominent labor-union official supporting Nixon, this seemed a not impossible dream. The prospect stirred many of his former associates to greater efforts in behalf of Humphrey.

Abel himself had been named chairman of the AFL-CIO Committee for Humphrey. Its aim was not only to develop positive support for Humphrey but also to deflate the enthusiasm for George Wallace, which did not begin to abate until two or three weeks before Election Day.

After the Presidential election, in a subdued mood following the defeat of Humphrey, the leadership of the Steelworkers Union turned to

---

* The dispute was taken to arbitration. Harvard Professor John T. Dunlop was asked to determine whether Narick's rights under the contract had been violated. A hearing was held on November 17, 1969. Briefs were also submitted. The international union maintained that the local of its headquarters employees had entered a new contract with it on February 9, 1970, effective retroactively to January 1, 1970. This new agreement redefined the bargaining unit to exclude all attorneys assigned to the legal department (including Narick) and to limit its provisions to cover classifications well below the one to which Narick sought to be returned. Moreover, the new local was no longer an affiliate of the international but was now "independent." This development, said Dunlop, provided "perspective" to the arbitration proceedings.

Observing that "the issues of public policy and legal ethics can be reviewed in other forums," Dunlop then held that the long-term interests of the international union "justified" Narick's transfer from his legal post: "The sort of remarks which Mr. Narick made in the internal union election campaign and predictably would make and should have been entirely free to make, would have been most inimical for an international union lawyer to be quoted as having said in proceedings before various governmental agencies and the courts."

In a fourteen-page analysis, Dunlop concluded that Narick's transfer did not violate the collective bargaining agreement then in force between the local union and the international union as employer.

face its own internal struggle. In the meantime, Narick had appealed to "directors, staff and office personnel" for help in obtaining local nominations. "The torch," he said, "must be passed on to a new leadership." Narick's fifteen-point program included a "cost of living" clause in future contracts and "total job security and guaranteed annual wage," which in various forms had been called for by McDonald as well as Abel. Under the heading "No second-class Steelworkers," Narick made his pitch to the "majority of Steelworkers" who "do not participate in top benefits." To make "present wage conferences truly productive," he proposed "company-by-company bargaining." He aimed, he said, to end convention control by the "palace guard" through two immediate reforms: agenda to be supplied to all local unions at least thirty days prior to the convention, and the use of the roll call to tabulate all major issues as a substitute for "the steamroller tactics of a so-called 'voice vote.' " "The true voice of the membership," he said, could and should be recorded at conventions by automated equipment already in use elsewhere.

Just as Abel had charged that local issues were scanted by the McDonald leadership, so now Narick claimed that "pressure from the top caused local issues in basic steel, can, aluminum and office and technical units to be dropped from the last settlement." He, Narick, was "determined" that such issues be given their proper weight by reserving to the local plant level the right to strike on these issues—if necessary—after completion of negotiations on the economic package. The basic steel negotiations of 1968, he charged, had been conducted "behind a curtain of secrecy." As a result, "the present administration was able to ram the settlement through the Industry Conference with relative ease. Local officers, negotiating committees, members and staff were not allowed to make their opinions known to the leadership while there was still opportunity to act upon their objections."

On the subjects of the "strike and defense fund" and the "dues structure," Narick promised that the size and distribution of strike benefits would be determined by "trustees selected from the working members in each district," with benefits "a matter of right rather than of an unclear basis of necessity." On a dues increase, Narick proposed a "just and simplified dues structure based not on gross earnings, but on straight-time hourly earnings with a sensible formula for incentive workers." Bargain dues rates were always sure to attract support.

To elicit backing from local leadership, he proposed "to end the waste of the talent of our members which has resulted from the atmosphere of political intrigue prevailing during the last four years." This echoed a similar charge leveled against McDonald four years before. For better administration, he proposed the "selection of staff . . . on merit and ability and not on political considerations or advantage." He advocated a "membership contact" department to carry on a continuous survey of membership opinion on union problems and their solutions.

On another level, he called for the establishment of a "public review board" as an "impartial, internal mechanism for the redress of members' complaints against the International Union, its subordinate bodies or the officers of the union." He proposed to re-examine the USW's affiliations "including the AFL-CIO"; this proposal aroused considerable attention because it followed soon after the disaffiliation from the AFL-CIO of the United Auto Workers. Narick also exploited the criticism of Abel that was made the year before for his supposed over-involvement in activities outside the union. He himself, said Narick, would be a "full-time president . . . not become . . . preoccupied with assignments or projects that are unrelated directly or indirectly to the best interests of the membership."

At his news conference, reporters pointed out a public review board and the right to strike on local plant issues were concepts already in operation at the United Auto Workers. Narick replied that he "didn't care if an idea is mine or anybody else's . . . if it's a good one, I'll use it." Reporters pressed their inquiry harder: had he been in touch with the UAW? He had "no contact," he replied, with either the UAW or the Teamsters, which together had recently formed the Alliance for Labor Action. Not disowning the possibility of support from any quarter, he added that he had a "tremendous respect" for Reuther. When his references to Reuther were published, UAW officials assured the Steelworkers officers that they had nothing to do with Narick's candidacy or his campaign. Emil Mazey, UAW's secretary-treasurer, told Walter Burke, his USW counterpart, "We don't know this guy Narick from a hole in the ground."

Facing a full-fledged opposition complete with program, the Abel-Burke-Molony team addressed itself to "all recording secretaries of the local unions." Instead of a direct solicitation for nomination, the three announced that they intended "to stand (not run) for re-election." Therefore "respectfully, we ask that you bring this announcement of our candidacy to the attention of your Local Union members when nominations are under consideration."

They were playing it cool. As cochairmen, their committee now had both Joseph Germano, director of District 31, and James P. Griffin, director of District 26. Since 1965, Griffin, the mainspring of the McDonald campaign, had cooperated with the Abel team. They in turn, appreciative of his abilities, had given him an assured place in the leadership by naming him once again chairman of the U.S. Steel negotiating committee.

"We have tried," the three officers wrote to the local officers, "to work diligently and honestly in your behalf. We have tried to unify our membership and to encourage the leadership at all levels of our union to work as a team . . . we would like to keep our Union moving forward. We want to keep it united . . . responsive to the needs and wishes of the membership. . . . We hope you will vote to nominate us for re-election to our respective offices and then vote for us in the referendum next February. . . ." The words "nominate . . . and then vote" were a gentle reminder to local officers that they were not to rest on their laurels with the nomination process.

In an accompanying statement, the Abel team stressed that it had "kept every promise" of the previous campaign. Later in the campaign, they would release a broad new program "to protect, strengthen, and advance the interest of every Union member and his family under the challenging conditions which today threaten the jobs and incomes of all Steelworkers."

The RAFT group now named William Litch of Youngstown for president, to replace the deceased Donald Rarick; Morros Brummitt of Aliquippa for secretary-treasurer; and Frank T. Felix of Gary, for vice-president. In the battle for local union nominations, Narick concentrated on locals in the Pittsburgh area, and especially in those districts where contests for directorships had already been signaled. On the road weekends to referee football games, Narick often used such occasions to meet with local union leaders and rank-and-file dissidents. Before the Yale-Dartmouth game, Narick had sent word ahead to local union people in southern New England that he would hold a Steelworkers meeting in New Haven. This was clearly a first in Ivy League annals. Although the turnout was tiny, the Abel forces were soon dismayed to hear that in several of the largest locals in basic steel, Narick had won nominations over Abel by wide majorities. There was no longer doubt that Narick would obtain the estimated 126 nominations needed to win a place on the ballot.

Just at this time, steel production had dropped. About 65,000 steelworkers were laid off, and thousands compelled to work on short time. Thus while basic steel workers on the job were receiving an average increase of 31 cents in the hourly rate through the contract Abel had negotiated, their weekly take-home wage had dipped sharply. Narick placed the responsibility for the slowdown in the steel economy on Abel.

An even more disquieting factor was the hostility expressed in certain sections because of the union leadership's activity for Humphrey. Although more steelworkers and white union members in other industries had sympathized with the candidacy of George Wallace than finally voted for him, a considerable residue of Wallace sentiment remained.

Without explicitly exploiting such attitudes, Narick hoped to harvest a considerable number of votes on the theme that the Abel team had poured too much time and union money into Humphrey's campaign.

As the thirty-day nominating period wore on, political activity was unprecedented: contests for directorships were taking place in nineteen out of the twenty-four districts. In some districts, the contests resulted from vacancies created by the retirement of district directors; in others the target candidates were now strong Abel supporters such as Griffin (District 26, Youngstown), Paul Schremp (District 28, Cleveland), Kay Kluz (District 20, Aliquippa), Glenn Peterson (Minnesota Iron Range, District 33), Lester Thornton, acting director (District 38, Western states). In these and other districts, Narick sought to reinforce his political base by developing alliances with opponents of the incumbents.

For example, Joseph Odorcich, a staff representative in District 15, made common cause with Narick, as did Edward E. Plato in the Baltimore District and Joseph Kender in the Cleveland District. Odorcich, a veteran staff man, had been one of Abel's strongest supporters in the 1965 election, when Paul Hilbert, the director he now opposed, was hitched to McDonald. In developing the strategy for his election campaign, however, Abel had decided that his ticket would run as a team: that is, all incumbent district directors, including Hilbert, would have his support, in return for which, presumably, they and their district organizations would support the international officers. Thus Hilbert, to whom Abel owed nothing, now had Abel's support at the expense of an embittered Odorcich. Behind Abel's move to support all incumbents was the knowledge that district directors like Schremp, Griffin, and Kluz were facing strong opposition. Almost by reflex action, the Abel strategy in the districts generated support for Narick among the candidates who were bucking the establishment candidates, in effect creating Narick machinery in areas where he had been almost unknown.

The opposition to Abel now charged that they were being denied proper access to local union records. Suit was brought by the RAFT slate and came before Federal Judge Wallace S. Gourley, who directed all three international officers to appear before him. With considerable asperity, he declared that if the union officials did not "straighten up and fly right," he would bar the February elections. After three days of hearings, the judge acknowledged that under procedures of the Landrum-Griffin Act, the controversy belonged in the first instance with the Secretary of Labor. Aside from conceding his lack of jurisdiction, the judge declared that the union had "gone beyond" what was required of it in complying with union election procedures. This ruling, said Abel, absolved the international union of charges that it was playing favorites with the incumbent officers by providing them with the information denied their opponents. The union's "International Election Manual," now made available to the local unions in printed form for the first time as a result of the Kender suit, spelled out the procedures and requirements for election, and specified that declared candidates were entitled to receive the names and addresses of the recording secretaries of all local unions. The international officers invited the Labor Department to assign three representatives to observe the process of opening and tabulating the local nomination certificates for international office and district director. The international's request for the government presence, however, was limited to observation of the nomination procedure.* Narick secured more than enough nominations from local unions to assure his place on the ballot. Though his nominations showed a wide geographical pattern, the Pittsburgh area contained the highest concentration of Steelworker population in a relatively small area. Here Narick claimed practically a clean sweep of all locals' nominations, including the Jones & Laughlin Aliquippa local with 12,000. In California he won the nomination from the Kaiser Fontana Local 2689, the largest local on the West Coast; in the Baltimore area, the two Bethlehem locals, 2609 and 2610 in District 8, the largest locals on the East Coast, with a combined membership of more than 20,000, also nominated Narick. Such nominations usually reflected the support of local officers who could swing the majority of poorly attended membership meetings.

In the meantime, the Abel forces worked hard to win Negro support. Many black delegates had left the Chicago convention disgruntled because of the rejection of their demands for greater Negro representation among the "decision makers." In the Baltimore area, where Director Albert Atallah was retiring, the contest was being waged between two staff representatives. Edward E. Plato, white, and Leander Simms, black. The international officers had already made it clear that they would support Simms. Early in December, the thirty-man steering committee of the national Ad Hoc Committee of Negro Steelworkers, convened by

---

* Nevertheless, in the case of the nominating procedures for District 28, the international union had legally no alternative but to accept the supervisory scrutiny of the U.S. Department of Labor. Under the settlement agreement culminating the litigation initiated by Joseph Kender, following the district election in 1965, a precise method was stipulated by which nominations were to be conducted in District 28 in the 1968–69 election. Under the agreement, each announced candidate for the nomination in District 28 was entitled to report allegations of violations of the agreement directly to a designated representative of the Labor Department, without having to exhaust normal internal remedies. With the close of the nominating period, the supervisory role of the Secretary of Labor in District 28 was to be terminated. For Kender, at any rate, such a provision became a guarantee against repetition of the situation four years earlier, when he alleged he had been illegally deprived of his rights as a candidate for district director. Once again, Kender was running against the veteran incumbent, Paul Schremp; this time under the protective arm of the court.

Rayfield Mooty, Negro staff man, recommended that his group support the Abel-Burke-Molony ticket. Organized in 1964 to advance black representation in the Steelworkers Union, at the 1968 convention the AHC had fought aggressively and skillfully for the creation of a Negro vice-presidency. Despite the convention's rejection of the proposal, the Ad Hoc group now believed, as a practical political matter, that assurances given them by Abel and Molony warranted their backing the Abel team.

Ten days after the close of the nominations period, the tabulation showed that Abel had received 2,212 nominations to Narick's 326; Walter J. Burke 2,384, with his leading opponent, Morros Brummitt, just falling short of the 126 nominations needed to qualify for a place on the ballot; Joseph P. Molony received 2,372 nominations with no opponent qualifying. Contests for director were to be conducted in eleven districts, the largest number in the union's history. Four years before there had been only five such contests. This unusual number of contests promised that strongly waged district campaigns could affect the course of the union-wide election for international officers, and perhaps the heightened interest might raise the degree of participation by the membership in the February referendum elections.

Under the constitution, the nominations report of international tellers now went to the executive board, which had the responsibility of reviewing protests. As a consequence, the board ruled Morros Brummitt, Burke's challenger, eligible to appear on the ballot although he had apparently fallen two short of the necessary 126 nominations needed for a place on the ballot. After some discussion, the board, on Burke's urging, acceded to Brummitt's protests and certified two additional nominations to give him the required 126. In the District 15 contest, where the tellers had ruled that three candidates were eligible to appear on the ballot, a fourth candidate protested that he was entitled to an additional nomination that the tellers had denied him. The board again agreed, making it a four-way contest. In District 26, where Frank Leseganich and Robert Catlin were to oppose James P. Griffin, Catlin's name was dropped. Although the tellers had credited Catlin with exactly the minimum number of nominations, after evaluating the protests the board ruled that one nomination had been made at an improperly conducted meeting. This cleared the way for a confrontation between Griffin and Leseganich, the practically unknown local union officer. But Griffin's narrow margin of victory in 1965 indicated trouble ahead.

The evidence of support for Narick even in locals where he failed to win nominations, along with the almost studied indifference of many staff representatives toward the election, indicated to Abel and his associates that they had every reason to run scared. Four years before, the basic steel locals gave McDonald a greater part of their votes. After four years in office, and proud of achieving in 1968 the "best contract ever won in basic steel," the Abel team had not appreciably improved its political position among the basic steel locals.

Taking advantage of the facilities available to them as incumbents, the union officers announced that as of January 1, 1969, under the terms of the 1968 contract, "another round of benefits would become effective for some 400,000 members . . . in the Basic Steel Industry." This "strictly nonpolitical" release meticulously avoided mentioning Abel and his associates by name, thus avoiding the possibility of Narick's raising legal objection that Abel had used for political purposes organization channels that were not available to him.

At the close of the football season and the nomination period, Narick began to tour the steel districts intensively. To find himself the instant "leader" of an opposition that suddenly acquired shape and momentum was a heady experience for one hitherto unknown. Of Slavic origin, he actively cultivated the Slavic ethnic groups through their fraternal lodges and burial and insurance groups. For the first time in the memory of many veterans, such lodges were openly used in a Steelworkers political campaign.

Abel gave Narick the silent treatment. He devoted himself to local and district meetings, with an occasional "public affairs" speech to a nonunion audience. He was convinced that his performance would be recognized and appreciated by the membership. In the three and a half years since his election, he had acquired kudos for himself and his organization without being a Fancy Dan. He had emphatically disposed of the strike-happy charge. On the AFL-CIO Council, he had proved himself to be a team player, a role that came naturally to him. He appeared to work in close harness with Meany and had gained his confidence and the benefits that could be attributed to his good will. Meany privately and publicly pushed the point that Abel was "regular," while Reuther had been something else again. Nor was Abel insensible to recurrent rumors that he might some day succeed Meany as president of the AFL-CIO. The game of "possible successor" or "heir apparent" is an old political sport in the trade-union movement as elsewhere. It suspends criticism and encourages regularity.

But it was one thing to play "labor statesman," a term that Abel rejected, and another to carry on the arduous job of revitalizing a union. Abel was convinced that the Steelworkers Union was now moving along the right track. But the mere eviction of McDonald had not been enough to revitalize the union. Nor was it enough to evoke the nostalgia of the union's past as a supportive factor. The memory of a leader like Philip Murray, whose virtues appeared more shining with the passage of time, and Abel's own part in the union's epic struggles were not enough to inspire that large part of the membership too young to have known Murray. When Abel became president, he seemed to sense keenly the presence of forces of change at work inside the union movement. His response reflected his concern; but to implement that concern required more sustained initiative than he could successfully muster. By eliminating McDonald, however, Abel felt that he had earned the right of passage to unchallenged leadership. Now here was Narick, an unknown, attacking him on issues that often carried the ring of his own past criticisms of the McDonald leadership.

At last Abel and his supporters understood that this campaign had to be waged in earnest. While basic steel was important, about two-thirds of the union membership was not employed in the basic steel companies. The time was overripe for paying attention to the fabricating industries. The second week in January, the union officers undertook by administrative action to set up a Planning Committee "to explore the establishment of periodic Fabrication Conferences." This committee would cover about 500,000 union members not involved in the other industry conferences which had been set up by the 1966 convention for basic steel, nonferrous metals, aluminum, and can manufacturing. Narick promptly charged that this was another campaign gimmick trotted out right before the election.

Just at this time, Narick took a page out of the McDonald campaign and raised the suspicion of possible election skulduggery. Rather than have the American Arbitration Association supervise the elections, as McDonald had proposed in 1965, Narick wrote Abel that they jointly request the Secretary of Labor to "monitor and observe all aspects of our election . . . in a representative number of our locals and Districts throughout the United States." The Canadian districts, presumably, could not be included in such action.

With the installation of the Nixon administration on January 20, Narick sent George P. Shultz, the new Secretary of Labor, a copy of his letter to Abel, with a letter of explanation: "I have regrettably been distressed to hear too frequently expressions from many members of our union that I will not receive a fair and honest election. . . ." He complained to Shultz that Abel had ignored his request for a joint invitation to the Labor Department to intercede. On February 4, a week before the election, Shultz replied to Narick that in view of the safeguards provided by the union constitution and the procedures spelled out in the law, he would not intervene. The law's provisions and the legislative intent, he said, were meant to preserve a maximum amount of self-government by affording every labor organization the opportunity to investigate and consider allegations of election violations before bringing the matter to the Secretary of Labor.

In the meantime, the *Wall Street Journal* carried an item that Narick was receiving large sums of money from Republican politicians. Narick denied this and threatened suit. The reporter stuck to his guns.

The campaign attained a low-grade fever. Abel's first target was to hold Narick to about 10 per cent of the total. More realistic forecasters believed that Narick would receive double that. Actually, no one knew. Neither side had hired pollsters. At this time, however, considerable discomfort in and among Abel supporters pervaded the headquarters and the districts; the large number of district director contests caused considerable disarray in voting patterns. So great an upsurge of opposition in the districts was practically unknown. The *Wall Street Journal* quoted a union official as saying that through their 1965 campaign, Abel and his team had "opened up a Pandora's box. The whole thing's wide open now."

In Abel's camp, questions were again seriously raised as to whether the Steelworkers method of electing officers through referendum ought not to be scrapped. It was too late for this campaign, but what about the next? Why not elect officers by convention, as most international unions did? This was not a point they had cared to make in the 1965 election; in fact they had bitterly resented Meany's criticism of the union's referendum method of electing officers when in February 1965 he commented on the still uncertain outcome of the McDonald-Abel race.

Reports coming in from the field indicated, according to one local union officer—no supporter of Abel in the last campaign—that "the feeling here is that the men would support anyone against Abel. They still don't like the 1968 contract. There would be a heavy vote against Abel no matter who opposed him." With a fight on their hands, the Abel team began an active distribution of campaign material. In contrast to the campaign of 1965, when the Abel side relied largely on the ingenuity of a single publicity man, it now hired the Washington public-relations firm of Maurer, Fleischer & Zon, a group with considerable political savvy and union experience. It was the firm that had handled the labor segment of the Johnson and Humphrey campaigns in 1964 and 1968.

The material they prepared was designed for reproduction on a local or district basis. It undertook to make a point-by-point reply to the Narick program, the printed staple of his campaign. First they emphasized that Abel, Burke, and Molony were "tested men of the mills . . . the leaders came out of the plants, men of performance." "When I. W. Abel was elected President . . . in 1965, our union was in the midst of internal strife. The International Board was split down the middle. There was division among staff representatives. . . . Today all the top officers . . . pulling together . . . have brought unity to the ranks. They're making unity work in winning better contracts from united management." As to the strike issue, which Narick had raised in connection with the lengthy and costly copper strike, the Abel-Burke-Molony response was that as a matter of course they deplored striking: "Any loud mouth can call a strike. . . . It is a wasteful, non-productive thing . . . but the copper strike was a necessary strike. The Abel-Burke-Molony team is not strike-happy." Narick's demand that local unions be granted the right to strike over local issues was described as "falling for the company line. . . . One local union cannot take on an entire company—especially the large steel companies. . . . To change our present procedure would allow industry to use the old 'divide and conquer' system."

They recited the increased civil rights activity of the Abel team—an issue that Narick had found it useful not to cultivate. In this area, they emphasized Molony's leadership, the system of district civil rights co-ordinators, the creation of a civil rights manual, the union's structure for handling civil rights problems, and the publication of a union-wide *Civil Rights Newsletter*.

To those in the Narick camp who questioned the affiliation of the union with the AFL-CIO, they replied with a list of benefits flowing from "unity with the labor movement." "Some people may object to certain policies or practices of the AFL-CIO or some of its affiliates. The way to change those policies or practices is to work within the organization— not outside it. Affiliation with the AFL-CIO is as important to the United Steelworkers as inclusion in the United States is to any of the 50 states." This, then, was also the reply to those in the Steelworkers Union who sympathized with the United Auto Workers in disaffiliating from the AFL-CIO.

The fact sheet on metal fabricating, long an area of unrest, declared that "the Abel-Burke-Molony team is closing the gap between the membership and the leadership." It cited the union's new collective bargaining structure where members of the four major industries have the "widest possible latitude in the conduct of negotiations in their behalf; . . . direct representation in the adoption of collective bargaining programs; participation in strike votes and final fabrication of settlement terms." In connection with fabricators' conferences, members in two thousand smaller plants in scattered industries were to be brought together into a unified group for negotiating new collective programs on a more united basis. This would include movement toward "pooled pension plans, pooled supplemental unemployment benefits, joint medical and hospitalization coverage, and stepped-up efforts to organize low-wage competitors."

While the elevated slogan for the Abel-Burke-Molony team was "Roll the Union On," the business of shellacking Narick now also got under way. Narick was coming up strong. Looking into Narick's background, the Abel organization sought to refute Narick's claim to plant experience many years before at the Homestead and Wheeling Steel plants; Narick, they said, had never joined the union in those early struggling days. He, a "free rider who did not see fit to join the union that he now wants to lead," joined the Steelworkers Union only after he became a "payroller" at the union's international headquarters. Thus, the Abel people said, he then had no option but to join.

Narick, the Abel committee charged, had "never organized a member or a local union, never served on a plant grievance committee, never worked as a union field staffman, never led major contract negotiations, never walked a picket line." They belittled his outside activity in a wide variety of community organizations and his "moonlighting" as a football referee: he "never let his union duties interfere with his outside interests." By what right, therefore, the Abel committee indignantly asked, could Narick criticize Abel for work in the AFL-CIO, or in government, or in the United Nations?

Narick, they said, could not even make it in his own Local 3657; the employees of that local for international union headquarters had unanimously voted to nominate Abel and his ticket rather than Narick.

In the final stages of the campaign, Abel and his associates campaigned with increased intensity against Narick. For his part, Narick encouraged reports that Abel might become AFL-CIO president (Pittsburgh *Post-Gazette,* January 30, 1969) and leave the presidency of the United Steelworkers. In that event, he hinted, Abel would turn over the USW presidency to Molony, unopposed for the vice-presidency. Joe Germano issued a formal denial. "I would like to make it crystal clear, Abel will be re-elected . . . and, God willing . . . will serve our membership for the next four years. . . . President Abel has stated many times that he seeks no other office than the presidency of the Steelworkers. Our members, of course, are proud that some people are saying that President Abel might be offered higher responsibilities in the labor movement. . . . It strikes us as ironic that Abel's opponent on one hand thinks Abel does not merit re-election and yet on the other hand is on his way to the top position in the labor movement."

As election day approached, the district campaigns also intensified. Considerable time and attention were placed in the Baltimore district on the run being made by Leander Simms, the black candidate. Ten days before the election, Abel appeared there and put himself on the line so thoroughly in his support of Simms that some questioned the political wisdom of exposing himself to those who might resent his "intrusion" in a district election.

In the Cleveland area, District 28, Paul Schremp had run into serious trouble. Soundings in friendly sections of the district indicated strong

Kender sentiment. The key National Tube Local 1104, strongly pro-Abel in 1965, was now anti-Schremp and anti-Abel.

In Youngstown, Jim Griffin was hanging on the ropes. Abel's humiliation in having to suffer Narick as a rival was as nothing compared with Griffin's confrontation by Leseganich, who appeared to be one of the less distinguished local union leaders. A seasoned and sophisticated union leader, Griffin understood that under certain conditions in the district election, as in others, the comparative quality of candidates was almost irrelevant to a voter's decision or to a candidate's victory. He hoped, he said, it would make the difference, but for many he represented the establishment—in 1965, McDonald; in 1969, Abel. No matter which side he was on, he had become a target for opposition.

In District 38 on the West Coast, where Lester Thornton, the acting director, was being opposed by Joe Angelo, subdistrict director, who was once a close associate of Charles Smith and headquarters chief for the McDonald campaign, the currents were strong and crossed. To dispassionate observers, it seemed that Angelo, as more "native" than Thornton, a recent arrival from Germano's Chicago district, would be the likely winner, despite the burden of anti-Smith sentiment he had to carry. They were proved right.

By election day, February 11, Abel and his associates confidently asserted that they had turned off the Narick campaign. But they were no longer claiming a four-to-one margin. As the returns came in during the days after the election, the turnout of voters appeared distressingly low. About 450,000 out of the estimated total of 1,127,000 eligible members voted.

While it seemed clear that Abel was running well ahead of Narick, there was little to cheer about. Unofficial returns showed Abel had received about 260,000 votes to Narick's 180,000. More than 700,000 workers did not vote, as against 400,000 who stayed away from the polls in the previous contest. One pro-Abel director told of a young worker who wanted to know Abel's background. Told of Abel's trade-union record—organizer in the struggles of the 1930s, local union president, staff representative, district director, secretary-treasurer for a dozen years, and finally president of the international union—the young steelworker said: "To hell with him, then. He's been around long enough."

To the public, Abel kept a fairly cheerful face, but the results stunned him. He had received about 60 per cent of the votes cast, but no more than 35 per cent of the total membership of the union had voted. Narick's 40 per cent of the ballots represented far more than the normal "protest" vote. The small turnout signified pervasive apathy throughout the membership.

When the official returns were made public on April 18 by the international tellers, the proportion of the votes remained the same. In table form:

INTERNATIONAL PRESIDENT

I. W. Abel	257,651
Emil Narick	181,122

INTERNATIONAL SECRETARY-TREASURER

Walter J. Burke	285,923
Morros Brummitt	136,999

INTERNATIONAL VICE-PRESIDENT (UNOPPOSED)

Joseph P. Molony	349,336

As in the 1965 election, Nathaniel Lee ran ahead of his fellow tellers. Unlike in 1965, however, there was no contest in the election of tellers.

In the large basic steel locals, those with memberships of 500 or more—most of the largest locals in the union—Abel received only 43,749 votes as against Narick's 70,331, about 37 per cent of those voting in this industrial sector. Four years before, Abel received 99,020 votes against McDonald's 112,244, or 47 per cent of the vote in basic steel. At that time, Abel's disappointment in his failure to outvote McDonald in basic steel, the target area of the election, was somewhat mitigated by the realization that the incumbent could command traditional loyalties, especially in and around Pittsburgh. But for Narick to win about 63 per cent of the vote in basic steel—and against the incumbent—stirred misgivings among the union leadership. Only through the votes in the locals in fabrication, aluminum, and can manufacturing did Abel manage to bring up a margin of victory.

In one area—the locals of the newly admitted Mine, Mill and Smelter workers—45 per cent of their members voted and Abel outpointed Narick about five to one.

In District 4 (New York), a three-way contest was waged among Mitchel F. Mazuca, Anthony F. Barbieri, and Michael Sam. Mazuca got 8,786, Barbieri 6,825, Sam 5,199. Barbieri, considered the administration candidate, was defeated.

The Abel administration received another severe blow in the Baltimore district. There Plato defeated Simms, the black candidate, by 7,549 to 5,668. Simms's defeat was attributed, in part, to the failure of Negro steelworkers to participate in the election in sufficient numbers. It was claimed that certain Negro extremist leaders succeeded in persuading black workers to stay home on the ground that this election was not "their thing." This confirmed Baltimore's record of dissidence and internal jealousies that had long split the black constituency inside the union. Indeed, Simms's candidacy had been a grudging compromise requiring that at least one Negro candidate withdraw in order to give him the assurance of solid backing of the black workers. This was a hope that failed.

In District 15, the four-way contest seesawed between Joseph Odor-cich and Paul Hilbert, the incumbent, with the two others trailing. An investigation by the Labor Department found that more than a thousand votes had been fraudulently switched to Hilbert. Subsequently, the international tellers threw out the entire vote of U.S. Steel Local 1397, with the result that Odorcich was declared the winner with a margin of 522 votes. Later, in reviewing the tellers' report, the international executive board examined protests from Hilbert and the president of the large U.S. Steel Local 1408 at McKeesport, which had gone heavily for Odorcich and Narick. After lengthy consideration, even-handed justice was applied; that local's vote was also thrown out and Hilbert was then declared the victor by 72 votes! But Hilbert immediately resigned, "for the good of the union." To replace him, the durable Lester Thornton, who had been defeated by Joseph Angelo in the West Coast District 38, was made administrator of the district pending a special election. His victory snatched from him, Odorcich blasted the international union leadership. Members from his district picketed the union headquarters, jeering at international officers. Odorcich successfully carried his appeal to the Labor Department. Not until April 1970, however, did a rerun of the election, ordered by the federal court under the supervision of the Labor Department, give a belated victory to Odorcich by a substantial majority.

In District 20, Kay Kluz, the incumbent director, squeezed through in his run against three others: Kluz, 13,568; Walter Bachowski, 10,610; Nicholas Mamula, 8,720; and James Huntermark, 4,692. The combined total of his opponents came to two-thirds of the vote cast.

A massive setback to the administration occurred in the Youngstown district, District 26, where Leseganich defeated Griffin, 13,845 to 11,683. Griffin's ability was unexcelled by any member of the executive board. His importance as a state leader in Ohio's political affairs was widely recognized, but in the district he had led for twenty-three years, this was not enough. Kender's victory over Paul Schremp in the Cleveland district —7,021 to 5,615—contained elements of poetic justice. Barred from the ballot four years before, he had successfully fought his way through litigation that finally established additional explicit rules in the nominating procedures applicable to all districts. In the Iron Range country, District 33, incumbent Glenn Peterson barely nosed out Clarence Lawson, 4,795 to 4,401. In the West Coast and the Rocky Mountain states, Angelo had defeated Thornton, 21,860 to 17,809.

In contrast to the procedures in the 1965 international election, the protest hearings of the international tellers were not observed and reported by representatives of the Labor Department. This time the department had not been invited to do so by both sides. All told, the votes of five locals were invalidated by the tellers because of irregularities in the conduct of the election, while 120 were not counted because of technical violations; more than half of the latter had submitted their returns too late to be tabulated.

What appeared significant and disturbing was the importance of those local unions whose votes had been thrown out by the tellers on the ground of election irregularities. Two of them were Bethlehem Steel locals in District 4 that had a combined membership of more than 6,500; two were U.S. Steel locals in District 15, with a total membership of 12,000; another was a Bethlehem local in the same district with a membership of 5,000; and another was a U.S. Steel local in District 28 with a membership of about 7,000. Thus more than 30,000 voters in the basic steel locals were disenfranchised, about 9 per cent of the total membership in basic steel. In none of these cases was an objective evaluation by nonunion observers available. The locals whose votes were invalidated were carried unofficially by Narick and opposition district candidates.

In the 1969 election, the personal elation and the sense of moral ascendancy of his victory four years before were not there for Abel. The realization that a man possessing few union credentials of importance could command the votes of relatively so many brought home the humbling fact that all the speeches, all the negotiations, all the publicized kudos, could not guarantee an incumbent leader unqualified acceptance. Leadership had now become an open aspiration. By his own example, Abel himself had proved that entrenched leadership was not sacrosanct and that opposition was not treason.

The problem that faced the Steelworkers Union centered on the quality of leadership that could be developed. Where was the preparation for such leadership? The school of struggle in which many top leaders had been trained was no longer available, and to many it was no longer desirable.

Once, in recalling the election of 1965, Alex Fuller, secretary of the Abel-Burke-Molony campaign committee that year as in 1969, said: "This was an exercise in democracy I shan't forget. I'm very glad I went through it. But let's not get carried away. Let's not go through it again real soon. It takes a lot out of you." But the decision to challenge an election is not for the incumbent to make.

When Abel assembled his new executive board for formal installation in Washington on June 2, 1970 he found himself at the table with an unusually large number of comparatively new if not hostile faces. Of the 28 men on the board, only he, Molony, and Germano had served continuously since 1942, when the United Steelworkers became an established constitutional entity. The new directors, considered as a bloc, might constitute a core of opposition, and Abel had to find ways to cope with his new associates. He found some reassurance in the knowledge that in the past, newly elected district directors usually adjusted to the sense of the majority. They too were team players. Through an appeal to "close ranks," Abel was determined to develop the climate of political tranquility. Whether such a climate was enough to quiet the broadening challenge to the Steelworkers Union, and to the labor movement in general, was a question to which he, his associates, and their successors had henceforth to address themselves.

Afterword

The progress toward change in the political life of the Steelworkers Union was marked in several ways.

For the first time, the making of important decisions between conventions was placed, after Abel's election in 1965, where the union constitution said it belonged: in the international executive board. Under Philip Murray, the union's founder, the executive board had bowed to his wishes. Willing obedience under Murray, however, turned into complaisance under McDonald. Abel affected neither the airs of a liege lord nor the posture of a flamboyant bullyboy.

Along with the renovation of union democracy at the top, Abel's first administration became a time to prove respectability and responsibility in its dealings with government and management. But it did more than pay lip service to democratic procedure. At conventions there was greater participation by delegates—made up mainly of local leadership—who asserted their right to speak, even to challenge the leaders. This did not make those seated on the platform particularly happy. Top officers and district directors underwent a period of adjustment. But absent were the old familiar threats of muscle or the application of financial and political retaliations, open or secret.

Elements of opposition were as much the results of growth and change in the labor force as in the change of union climate. Members found they could dissent without feeling that they were perpetrating an act of betrayal. This sense of a more open union brought with it a feeling of expansion and easier access to higher levels of union government. The black members, making up about 15 per cent in basic steel, became more assertive of their rights. Their insistence that their time had come was soon echoed by the Mexican-Americans.

Under the pressure of numbers and out of conviction as well, the union leaders were obliged to cultivate in the newly emerging groups a belief in themselves, similar to that which leaders of other ethnic groups had acquired in preceding decades. Obviously they could not transplant into the new groups the militancy of bygone days—a militancy which was magnified if not distorted through the prism of retrospection. But on pain of losing their own right to lead, they could not gainsay the right of others to challenge. The exercise of this right is bound to inconvenience, when it does not infuriate, those who are challenged. Paradoxically, this exercise is perhaps the only way to enrich the heritage and raise the competence of free trade unionism. This confidence in asserting themselves, this mood of rebellion, was supported by an increased awareness of the protection—and perhaps the incentives—afforded by certain provisions of the Landrum-Griffin Act, some of which were necessarily incorporated into the union's constitution.

A membership, or a considerable section of it, that is stimulated to action can bring constructive pressure on a responsive leadership. In the triennial local elections of 1970, perhaps as an aftermath of the Narick-Abel campaign of 1969, there was a significantly larger overturn in the leadership of presidents in key locals. This development brought the international leadership up short. To them, perhaps, this was evidence that the educational process did not go down deeply enough, or perhaps a little learning had become a dangerous thing: The training of staff representatives was increasingly urgent; moreover, the failure to recognize the importance of greater attention and assign a larger part of the union treasury to the education of the local leadership could result in a condition where flash floods of anger rather than experience and intelligence take control of the union's political life.

A new period had begun with a new challenge to leadership. At the 1970 convention, the nation beheld an Abel roused to do battle. The militant tone of the resolutions that came pouring in before the convention furnished the overture to the Abel performance. For hundreds of delegates, this was their first convention. He caught their mood and they his. An aroused leader challenged them to prepare for the negotiations of 1971 and 1972 in the various sectors of American and Canadian industry.

The first test came several months later, in February, 1971, and with it, victory. Abel and his negotiators achieved a pattern-making contract in the can manufacturing industry. Along with a substantial wage increase and fringe benefits, a cost-of-living clause was made, for the first time, part of the agreements in this industry. It took nearly a month's strike to make the three largest can companies come around. By early April Abel made it clear that his union would move with equal determination into the negotiations with the aluminum, copper and, finally, basic steel companies.

The gathering momentum was a resultant of rank-and-file participation, local assertiveness and economic pressure. The union leadership sustained the movement which now led in the aluminum negotiations to wage increases and improved benefits, comparable to those in can manufacturing. Bargaining in copper, as in 1967 and 1968, was carried on through a coordination of the efforts of the Steelworkers and twenty-five other unions. Before the copper companies finally agreed to satisfactory settlements, a strike of nearly thirty days had ensued, a contrast with the ordeal of three years before. Then the members of the coalition of unions in the copper industry endured the rigors of an expedition into the badlands of still primitive industrial relations. But as the copper strike phased into agreements by late July 1971, the leadership of the Steelworkers Union had also to face the critical final days of negotiation with most of the basic steel companies. Despite management's last-ditch resistance, the Abel team refused to retreat from an acceptable contract. The basic steel agreement finally included the now indispensable wage increase of more than thirty percent over the life of the three-year contract, significant improvements in pensions, a distribution of vacation periods, and riding on top of it all, the shield of a cost-of-living provision, restored after a decade to the members of the United Steelworkers. And for the third time, Abel had presided over settlements in basic steel, without a strike.

But Abel placed his union's efforts in a larger context. At the 1970 convention, he had urged the delegates of more than 1,200,000 workers to understand that their union must assume a larger role in the changing world. Thirty-five years after the founding of the Steelworkers Union, he said:

"Our union must today give full consideration to the needs of the younger workers. Old slogans and old ideas are of great value and have their place—but this union must always be open and receptive to new views. . . . We must work, plan, and persevere to ensure equal opportunity in the industries in which we are employed. In part, this is to be done by collective bargaining, in part by governmental action." But, he said, "We are not going to solve the serious problems that beset us by 'burning up,' 'tearing down,' 'turning on,' or 'turning off.' We are not certainly going to solve those problems by ganging up on those with different points of view and beating them up. We will not thus solve our problems as a divided Nation. We will solve them in unity and with reason—or we won't solve them at all."

To which Manuel Sierras, the Mexican-American local leader on the West Coast, gave his amen: "You know, John, I think we did a God-damn good thing when we began changing things over with Abel in that 1965 election. We won a chance to do more, now—and from now on."

APPENDIXES

Appendix 1

"In December [1926]," wrote John Brophy in *A Miner's Life* (p. 217), describing the results of his campaign against John L. Lewis, "the tellers in the international office announced that Lewis had won, by a vote of about 170,000 to 60,000. Nobody was surprised by the outcome, but I was surprised that they had admitted to that large a vote for me.

"The constitution provided that the tellers' report be published, with figures for each local union. At the international convention in February 1927, I demanded that this be done, but it was May before I received an accounting. Reading the report, I could see the reason for the delay: it would take time to cook the figures that thoroughly. For example, in anthracite District 1, out of a reported membership of 9,262, 8,466 votes were counted for Lewis and 232 for me. District 7, also anthracite, gave Lewis 3,483 votes out of 3,704, and I got 9. More fantastic was the vote in District 20, Eastern Kentucky. The district paid per capita on one member for the first six months of 1926, and on none at all for the last six months, during which the vote was taken. But 16 locals, with an alleged membership of 2,686½, cast 2,686½ for Lewis and none for Brophy, indicating a membership not only of impressive unanimity . . . not one man failed to come out to cast a ballot.

"I was able to check the actual vote sent in to the national office from five locals in District 5 and compare it with the national report. The actual vote was: Lewis, 487; Brophy, 635. The reported vote was: Lewis, 1,473; Brophy, 158. Thus in only five locals, Lewis was given 986 stolen votes and I was robbed of 477. I secured affidavits from officers of these locals, but evidence had no effect on the international board, which rubber-stamped the report of Lewis' tellers." For thirty-four years after, until John Lewis retired, there were no presidential contests in the United Mine Workers.

Appendix 2:
The Quayle Poll

So far as is known, this is the first time that political polling techniques were employed in a presidential race in an international union. Quayle explained how he conducted his survey:

"The purpose of the survey," he said, "was to obtain an early reading on the race for President of the Union in the election scheduled for February 1965. Not only did we wish to learn the present standings, but our objective has been to find the standings among key groups that make up the Union's total membership. Membership lists were not available for random sampling by name. Hence a number of criteria were established for representation, including

1. Widespread geographic representation.
2. Representation of locals affiliated with different employer groups.
3. Representation of different industry groups.

"Accordingly, a stratified sampling design was used in conjunction with a controlled selection technique. To achieve the above-stated objectives, each local was assigned to the corporation employing its members. Employing corporations were then stratified according to the total membership in their employ. Four different size strata were then used as follows:

a. Corporations with more than 10,000 estimated Union members.
b. Corporations with 3,000 to 9,999 estimated Union members.
c. Corporations with 1,000 to 2,999 estimated Union members, and
d. Corporations with fewer than 1,000 estimated Union members.

"From each of these strata, independent samples were selected, with the total sample size in the strata proportional to the total membership within the firm and the industry. Geographic representation was achieved by assigning low probabilities to undesirable regional groupings across the four strata. The interviewing points thus selected were finally validated against the present Union districts to make certain we had a proportional representation of districts whose directors are endorsing each of the candidates in the presidential election.

"Our final selection was 50 sample points, and trained members of our field staff conducted personal interviews on a random basis at plant gates for each sample point. . . . Interviewing was scheduled to cover all shifts. In all, we completed 600 interviews on Monday, November 30, and Tuesday, December 1. Answers were recorded on a structured questionnaire. Preferences for President of the Union were marked privately on a ballot by each Union member interviewed and placed by him or her in a ballot box carried by each interviewer. All answers were returned to our office where they were coded and tabulated.

"An analysis of our sample by industry yielded the following:

Aluminum	4%
Basic Steel	50
Can	4
Non-Ferrous Metals	4
Miscellaneous	38

"Then came the analysis, with this result:

The Standings	With Undecided In	With Undecided Out
David McDonald	58%	58.6%
I. W. Abel	41	41.4
Not sure	1	—

"At this point in time, David McDonald holds a 17-point lead over his challenger, Secretary-Treasurer I. W. Abel. Only one per cent of the Union members who plan to vote in February election are at present undecided. When this one per cent is assigned to each candidate according to how all other Union members have made up their minds, the results show McDonald leading by a 58.6% to 41.4% margin."

This, then, according to Quayle, was the situation as of December 1, 1964.

Appendix 3

A month after Abel was installed as president, he appointed Lawrence Spitz as head of the union's Wage Division. Before leaving Providence, Spitz was hailed by the state's General Assembly and by Governor John H. Chafee at a huge testimonial dinner as a "man Rhode Island can ill afford to lose." Professor Philip Taft described Spitz as one who "still angers at injustice . . . and is at home in the library," while Frank Licht, then a Superior Court judge, later governor, found him a "fighter in all good causes . . . a man who has brought to this community a higher standard for us all to follow." Whatever the effect of Roy Stevens's attack on Spitz during the election, the alleged conspiracy to libel had not, in the last analysis, "degraded and disgraced him in the eyes of men, damaged and blackened his reputation."

But Spitz waited more than a year before he consented to drop the libel suits against the four local union presidents whose names had been signed to the offensive "Security Check" leaflet distributed in Stevens's behalf. In a letter of apology, they wrote him that the leaflet had been printed and circulated without their knowledge and they did not subscribe to its contents. Subsequently, at the urging of Abel and his fellow officers, Spitz instructed his lawyer to drop the legal action against Stevens himself.

Appendix 4: The Government's Scrutiny of the Steelworkers Election

That same day, April 30, the Labor Department's observers—George Avery and William T. Kane—completed their official report. It was not submitted to the contending parties. Its purpose was to provide guidance to the Secretary of Labor in determining his future course of action. Against the union's constitutional provisions, some of which reflected the requirements of the Landrum-Griffin Act, the Labor Department observers sought to measure the performance of the international tellers and the protest hearings.

What kind of violations were alleged by both sides? Many local unions filed multiple protests. Of the more than 150 protests, about 25, including the wholesale scatter-gun protest filed by McDonald that was considered on April 12 and 13, and those filed by Abel in various individual locals, were made by persons who were not members of the locals whose election results they protested. Under the strict construction of the constitution, the tellers decided that such protests could not be "properly" considered.

The variety and number of alleged violations in each category that were heard in 97 tellers' hearings from March 15 through April 13, 1965 are analyzed as follows:

Nature of Violation Alleged	Number of Alleged Violations
1. Lack of observers	19
2. No secret ballot	10
3. Inadequate records to establish voter eligibility	10
4. Return Sheet given Organizer rather than mailed directly to International Tellers	6
5. Improper selection of Local Union Tellers	4
6. Denied the right to vote because of insufficient ballots	18
7. Refusal to furnish advance information as to time and place of election	6
8. Constitutional tellers failed to serve	7
9. Improper use of union funds in campaigning	8
10. No 15-day advance notice of elections	5
11. Improper interference with voting procedure	2
12. Ballot package opened prior to Election Day	3
13. Ballots not opened in presence of observers	2
14. Ballots not tabulated at place specified in notice	4
15. Return Sheet signed in blank by Local President and Recording Secretary	2
16. Hours of voting different from those specified in notice	6
17. Nonmembers (of locals) voting	2
18. Improper campaigning in and around polling place	19
19. Improper voiding of ballot	2
20. Persons other than elected tellers ran election	4
21. General miscellaneous	49
Total alleged violations	188

In their report to Frank Kleiler, the director of the Office of Labor-Management and Welfare Pension Reports (officially designated as LMWP), Avery and Kane, the two Labor Department observers, remarked rather sharply, "The evidence presented in most instances left much to be desired with regard to completeness and clarity." For the most part, the member filing the protest stated or read his complaint and the officers of the local, or other persons whose actions were complained of, gave their version of the facts. Although witnesses were sworn, there was no cross-examination; and since the complainants on both sides were biased in favor of their slate of candidates, the true situation was frequently left in doubt.

In addition, the tellers did not invalidate the votes of any local unions whose elections were protested by a watcher who was a nonmember of that particular local, despite the fact that the protests made by nonmembers were frequently quite detailed and convincing. After consideration of all such protests, Wayne Antrim, chairman of the international tellers, stated that the tellers had decided that a protest of a local union's elections could be properly filed only by a member of that particular union. As justification for this decision, he cited Section 21, Article V, of the international constitution. He stuck to the letter of that document.

Such a decision carried with it a considerable inconsistency. Under the constitution and by regulations approved by the international executive board, a candidate for international office could authorize the appointment of a member of one local to serve as a watcher at the polling place of another local. Was it not illogical, then, to bar such a watcher from filing a complaint on matters which he observed? Such a right to complain would seem to be a necessary concomitant of his duties as an observer. All protests should have been considered on an equal basis, the government representatives argued. The failure to do so raised the question of the legality of this constitutional provision under Title IV of the Landrum-Griffin Act.

While the number of protests in behalf of Abel against the conduct of elections in what were considered McDonald districts and/or locals just about equaled those made in behalf of McDonald in protesting violations in Abel districts, the government's analysis was geared generally to an evaluation of protests made in behalf of McDonald as the aggrieved party. Was there any substantial basis for the McDonald contention that Abel's victory had not been honestly won? The Labor Department representatives examined McDonald's main contentions:

1. That union funds had been used in behalf of the Abel slate in Canada. Since the expenditure came to $13.50 and the money was readily reimbursable, this consideration was deemed minor.

2. On the confusion attending the delivery of ballots to the Puerto Rico locals, the Labor Department representatives determined that no more than 874 members in Puerto Rico could have been denied an opportunity to vote.

3. On the failure to admit observers in eleven locals, which McDonald felt operated against him, the Labor Department representatives noted that six of the locals where observers were barred were located in District 4, headed by Joseph P. Molony, a pro-Abel director, and the other five locals were located in five districts headed by pro-McDonald directors. Observers were therefore excluded by both sides. The practice was apparently a standoff.

"It is apparent," reported the Labor Department representatives, "that there were violations of both the International's Constitution and of the Labor-Management Reporting and Disclosure Act. When the magnitude of the election is considered, however, involving as it did more than 1,000,000 members in over 3,000 local unions scattered throughout the United States and Canada, it appears to have been fairly well run. In such a large and widespread undertaking, many violations are bound to occur. It is assumed that the most glaring known violations which occurred were brought to light by the protests and hearings.

"Based solely upon the evaluation of the protests, as supported by the facts presented at the hearings, the representatives of the Department are of the opinion that the violations may not have affected the outcome of the election."

"This opinion," the department representatives added, "is supported by the following:

Official Results

Abel	308,910
McDonald	298,768
Difference	10,142"

(1) If the tellers had ordered that all eligible voters in Puerto Rico who did not have an opportunity to vote be given such an opportunity, and they had *all* voted for McDonald, it would increase McDonald's vote by 874.

(2) If the tellers had counted the returns from the ten local unions with "untimely" returns and *all* had voted for McDonald, it would increase McDonald's vote by 956.

(3) If the tellers had counted returns from two local unions that had overvoted and *all* eligible voters voted for McDonald, it would have increased his vote by 41.

(4) If the tellers had not invalidated the returns from twenty locals because of lack of seal or proper signature, it would have increased Abel's total by 791 and McDonald's total by 2,281.

(5) If the tellers had not invalidated the returns of four local unions based on the protest hearings, it would have increased Abel's vote by 1,853 and McDonald's by 4,332.

(6) If the tellers had not ordered the recounts of previously voided ballots in two local unions, it would deduct 132 votes from Abel's total and 36 from McDonald's total.

The preceding arithmetic can be summed up in table form:

	Abel	McDonald	Difference
Official Count	308,910	298,768	10,142
Step (1)		874	9,268
Step (2)		956	8,312
Step (3)		41	8,271
Step (4)	791	2,281	6,781
Step (5)	1,853	4,332	4,302
Step (6)	132	36	4,206
Totals	311,422	307,216	4,206

In submitting the final report to Assistant Secretary James J. Reynolds, Jr., and to Director Kleiler of LMWP, Kane and Avery concluded that "the outcome of the election . . . could not have been affected by the actions of the Tellers in rejecting local union returns. . . . The bulk of the protests relate to situations in which returns from local unions were accepted and included in the tabulation rather than rejected." Their conclusions, carefully examined by their superiors, weighed heavily with Secretary Wirtz, who had promised McDonald at the Madison Hotel meeting to proceed on the basis of "facts."

Appendix 5:
Summary Analysis of 1965 Election

The Vote in Canada

A surprising feature of the vote was the meager participation of members— only 35.47 per cent—in the three Canadian districts.

In District 2, only 21.58 per cent of the eligible voters participated, reflecting an especially lackadaisical mood. Although the district director here was recorded for Abel, who had secured a narrow margin of local nominations, McDonald carried the district.

In District 6, Canada's largest, headed by Lawrence Sefton, participation was 34.30 per cent. Abel defeated McDonald, 16,943 to 11,536.

Only District 5 (Quebec) came up with a comparatively high vote—about 54 per cent of those eligible. The greater participation was clearly due to the spirited contest for district director. The contest between two French-speaking Québecois, plus the element of ethnic identity, produced an unusually high degree of voter interest, which spilled over into the international contest. Obviously, a local or a district contest could bring out votes that even a closely fought international election would not stimulate. District 5 proved an outstanding example: here the combined vote for the presidency came to 9,889, or 53.7 per cent of the eligible vote, while the combined vote for the two candidates for district director came to 12,835—or 70 per cent of the total eligible.

All in all, Abel's Canadian majority of 9,592, though not so great as had been expected, made the essential difference in the Abel-McDonald election. His teammates ran better than he did. Burke's majority over Whitehouse was 13,583; Molony scored 16,262 over Hague. Molony's larger vote reflected in part his active campaigning in Canada; he was better known to the local Canadian leadership.

The Vote in the United States

In contrast to the shallow Canadian vote, the U.S. participation came to 62.10 per cent.

In *District 1* (New England), with 30,149 eligible voters, the bitter contest between the incumbent Roy Stevens, the pro-McDonald director, and Lawrence Spitz, the strongly committed Abel advocate, brought out almost 70 per cent of the eligible vote. Stevens defeated Spitz by 517 votes, 10,576 to 10,059. Abel, however, won over McDonald, 10,563 to 10,365, or 198 votes. The strong turnout resulting from the district contest plus early campaigning by Abel and Molony in New England helped produce the result. While Abel won narrowly over McDonald, both his teammates outran their opponents by about 5,000 votes.

District 4 (New York), with 53,382 eligible voters, was Molony's home district. Abel carried the district by 21,176 to 11,388, a handsome margin that was a tribute to the Molony organization. The turnout of 61 per cent, however, revealed no more than average participation for the district. The margins of Burke and Molony over their opponents ran to 13,000 and to more than 14,000 respectively. As was to be expected, Molony outpolled his teammates in his own district.

District 7 (Philadelphia area), with 55,675 eligible voters, was headed by Hugh Carcella, one of McDonald's more aggressive supporters and a mainstay for McDonald and Griffin in the campaign in his own and other districts. According to the tellers' report, McDonald carried the district over Abel, 21,031 to 12,350. The tellers disqualified the vote of Local 1374—a Bethlehem Steel local with 1,597 eligible voters—for violations of Article V, Section 13, of the constitution. The tally here originally gave McDonald 559 votes against 242 for Abel. Either in a spirit of conciliation or through a misunderstanding on Abel's part, the vote of this local was restored by the executive board when it reviewed the tellers' report. As a result, there was a net gain for McDonald of 317. (The final official national vote would have to read 309,152 for Abel, 299,327 for McDonald.)

District 8 (Baltimore area), with 19,656 eligible voters, was headed by Albert Atallah, who ran unopposed. The international tellers reported that McDonald carried the district by 6,523 to 3,666 for Abel. The vote of Local 2610—the huge Bethlehem local at Sparrows Point—was disallowed by the tellers for various violations. (In this local, McDonald had been credited by the local tellers with 3,545 against 1,429 for Abel.)

District 9 (Bethlehem, Pennsylvania–New Jersey area), with 46,005 eligible voters, headed by William Moran, a pro-McDonald director who ran unopposed, gave McDonald 16,014 votes to Abel's 9,615.

District 13 (Charleroi-Johnstown, Pennsylvania), with 26,448 eligible voters, headed by Eugene Maurice, a McDonald supporter who ran unopposed, gave McDonald 10,598 to Abel's 9,007.

District 15 (Homestead-McKeesport), with 34,206 eligible voters, headed by Paul M. Hilbert, a McDonald supporter, gave McDonald 13,991 to Abel's 10,487.

District 16 (Southside-McKees Rocks), with 19,372 eligible voters, was the scene of a rancorous contest between Paul Normile, the incumbent and a McDonald supporter, and Walter Bachowski, ostensibly an Abel backer. Normile won by 7,626 to 6,539; McDonald carried the district by 9,042 to 5,509. This indicated that Bachowski ran his contest rather independently of the Abel campaign. The outstanding fact in this contest was that 75.11 per cent participated, the highest percentage of any of the twenty-nine districts.

District 19 (Tarentum, Pennsylvania), with 26,745 eligible voters, was headed by William J. Hart, an Abel supporter, unopposed. He bore the distinction of being the only one of the eight Pennsylvania directors who was anti-McDonald. Hart polled 14,644 votes, but his persuasive powers were limited; McDonald carried the district by 11,134 to 9,457. This was one of three districts whose pro-Abel directors did not carry their area for Abel—the other two were District 2 (Canada) and District 23 (Steubenville-Wheeling).

District 20 (Ambridge, Pennsylvania), with 31,395 eligible voters, headed by Kay Kluz, unopposed, a McDonald supporter, gave McDonald 11,112 to 9,457.

District 21 (Sharon, Pennsylvania), with 23,489 eligible voters, was the scene of a contest between two staff men, William Nicholson and Ray F. DeMay. Nicholson was backed by retiring director, John W. Grajciar, treasurer of the McDonald campaign committee, while DeMay was pro-Abel. Nicholson won by 9,172 to 7,014. McDonald carried the district by 10,287 to 6,547.

In *District 23* (Steubenville, Ohio–Wheeling, West Virginia), with 36,596 eligible voters, incumbent director Paul Rusen, an early Abel supporter, ran unopposed. He polled 13,715 votes, but McDonald carried the district by 11,621 to 8,883.

In this old coal-mine area, McDonald's margin over Abel was attributed to the fact that he had sentimental support among the local unions and the rank and file. "The members saw McDonald only as the inheritor of Murray's mantle," explained one close-up observer. "They knew he had been Murray's boy. He had been extravagant, maybe. He had been a supreme egoist, but in this kind of situation these people don't object to this, if they don't see skulduggery at first hand. Besides, McDonald was considered the favorite. You ride what you think is the band wagon."

In addition, Rusen himself enjoyed something less than an enthusiastic following. Like most district directors, he could gain the nomination for himself hands down, through control over the leadership of the local unions and their sparsely attended membership meetings. But once the rank and file came into the act in an international election, the results could be different. A popular and respected incumbent district director could win the ungrudging support of most of his staff representatives, the local union officers, and the rank and file. But too often a district director retains his own office, an island of power in a sea of disaffection, by not risking his resources in an uncertain international union contest.

In *District 25* (Cincinnati), with 12,075 eligible voters, Al Whitehouse retired as director in order to run on the McDonald slate for the post of international secretary-treasurer. His choice for a successor was James P.

Gallagher, who ran unopposed and polled 4,112 votes; McDonald carried the district by 3,813 to 1,677. It was a poor district, but their own.

In *District 26* (Youngstown, Ohio), with 46,197 eligible voters, the scene was a bitterly fought contest between incumbent James P. Griffin, McDonald's campaign manager, and challenger Russell Thomas, an Abel supporter. Griffin won by the rather narrow margin of 16,230 to 14,772. McDonald carried this district by 16,918 to 15,110.

In *District 27* (Canton), with 37,771 eligible voters, John S. Johns, a pro-Abel director in Abel's home district, carried the district for Abel by 12,551 to 7,641. He himself was unopposed, received 15,767 votes.

In *District 28* (Cleveland), with 32,439 voters, headed by Paul E. Schremp, an Abel supporter, Abel won by 12,251 votes to 9,437 for McDonald. Schremp ran unopposed but his election was contested in the courts by Joseph Kender. After three years of litigation, the Kender case was to be settled through a stipulated agreement with the Labor Department that established important new procedures in the nomination of district directors. Kender defeated Schremp in the 1969 election.

In *District 29* (Detroit), with 25,202 eligible voters, headed by Charles Younglove, an Abel supporter, Abel won the district by 8,336 to 4,187. Younglove, unopposed, received 8,329 votes.

In *District 30* (Indianapolis), with 23,676 eligible voters, James Robb, the retiring district director, backed Harry O. Dougherty as his successor. Robb was a McDonald backer. Although Dougherty himself was reported to have had some reservations about McDonald, he was (at least for a time) listed in the McDonald column. His opponent, Robert E. Washburn, enlisted on the Abel team, but alignments on both sides were somewhat ambiguous, if not ambivalent. Dougherty won the district by 8,763 to 4,866. Abel carried the district by 7,476 to 6,484.

District 31 (Chicago-Calumet-Gary), with 114,247 eligible voters, was the union's largest. The incumbent director for twenty-three years, Joseph Germano, Abel's campaign manager, ran unopposed and polled 43,920 votes. Abel carried this district by the unexpectedly narrow margin of 35,246 to 29,830, much to Germano's chagrin; he had predicted a much stronger showing in his district.

In *District 32* (Milwaukee), with 28,730 eligible voters, Walter J. Burke had retired as director to run for international secretary-treasurer; Bertram McNamara, unopposed, polled 14,621. Abel ran away from McDonald in this district, 14,080 to 3,525. But the vote of Local 63, the large Northwestern Steel & Wire Company, was thrown out by the tellers because of the local officers' failure to apply the seal to the return tally sheet. Here Abel had received only 324 votes to McDonald's 1,714.

In *District 33* (Minnesota and the Iron Ranges), with 22,673 eligible voters, retiring director Earl T. Bester, an Abel supporter, backed Glenn Peterson, who, unopposed, polled 11,955 votes. Abel carried the district by 9,086 to 5,291.

In *District 34* (St. Louis), with 31,635 eligible voters, retiring director Al F. Kojetinsky, an Abel supporter, backed Lloyd McBride, who, unopposed, polled 12,511 votes. Abel carried the district 9,960 to 6,370.

In *District 35* (Southeastern), with 17,602 eligible voters, retiring director Lorne H. Nelles, a McDonald supporter, backed M. C. Weston who, unopposed, polled 5,363 votes. McDonald carried the district, 5,484 to 3,164.

In *District 36* (Southern, which included the highly controversial 36-G), with 35,548 eligible voters, retiring R. E. Farr, a McDonald supporter, backed Howard Strevel, who, pro-McDonald and unopposed, polled 15,041 votes. McDonald carried the district by 13,115 to 7,585.

In *District 37* (Texas), with 24,269 eligible voters, retiring Martin Burns, an Abel supporter, backed James E. Ward, who, unopposed, polled 12,185 votes. Abel carried the district by 11,000 to 5,107.

In *District 38* (West Coast), with 63,403 eligible voters, incumbent Charles J. Smith ran unopposed and polled 31,479 votes. McDonald carried the district by 23,336 to 19,803, an unexpectedly narrow margin.

In summary, Abel carried thirteen districts. Two of them headed by McDonald directors—Nos. 1 and 30—went for Abel. Both involved contests for directorships.

McDonald carried sixteen districts. Three of them headed by pro-Abel directors—Nos. 2, 19, and 23—went for McDonald.

The Voting Phenomenon by Size of Locals

In a district whose director favored a presidential candidate, the proportion of the total vote cast for that candidate in the smaller locals of that district—those locals with under 500 eligible voters—was generally greater than the proportion of the vote cast for that candidate in the larger locals. In some districts the percentage difference between the vote cast in the larger and in smaller locals was rather striking.

For example, take the two large pro-Abel Canadian districts—Nos. 5 and 6. In the former, Abel received 64 per cent of the total vote cast in the larger locals and 79 per cent of the total vote in the smaller locals; in District 6, Abel received 51 per cent of the total vote in the larger locals and 64 per cent in the smaller ones.

In District 27, Abel's home district, headed by John S. Johns, Abel received 57 per cent of the total vote in the large locals but 71 per cent of the total vote in the smaller locals. In District 28, he received 52 per cent of the vote cast in the larger locals and 65 per cent of that cast in the smaller locals. In District 31, Abel broke a little better than even with McDonald—at 50.26 per cent—in the vote of the larger locals but he received 65 per cent of the vote in the smaller locals. In District 34, Abel received 59 per cent of the vote in the larger locals and 68 per cent of the vote in the smaller locals. In District 37, Abel received 64 per cent of the vote in the larger locals and 74 per cent of the vote in the smaller locals.

The voting pattern was the same in districts whose directors supported McDonald. In District 1, McDonald received 47 per cent of the vote in the larger locals and 51 per cent of the vote in the small locals. In District 7, McDonald received 60 per cent of the total in the larger locals and 67 per cent of the total in the smaller locals. In District 8, the McDonald vote for the larger locals was 62 per cent and 68 per cent in the smaller locals. In District 13, McDonald received 53 per cent of the vote in the larger locals and 59 per cent of the vote in the smaller ones. In Districts 15 and 16, however, McDonald received 59 and 69 per cent respectively in the large locals and carried the smaller ones by 55 and 66 per cent. In District 20, McDonald carried the larger locals by 52 per cent and the smaller locals by 61 per cent. In District 21, McDonald received 56 per cent of the vote in the large locals and 70 per cent of the vote in the smaller locals. In District 26, Griffin's district, McDonald received 50 per cent of the vote of the larger locals and 59 per cent of the vote in the smaller locals. In District 30, McDonald received 41 per cent of the vote in the larger locals and 55 per cent of the vote in the smaller locals. In District 35, McDonald received 55 per cent of the vote from the large locals and 71 per cent in the smaller locals. The hotly protested vote in District 36 broke down as follows: 58 per cent of the vote from the large locals was for McDonald, with 73 per cent of the vote of the smaller locals. In District 38, McDonald received 51 per cent of the vote in the larger locals and 63 per cent of the vote of the smaller locals.

Thus in twenty-three districts out of the twenty-nine, the percentage of votes cast in the smaller locals exceeded that cast in the larger districts. In only five districts did the percentage of the votes cast in the larger locals exceed that of the smaller ones. In District 9 alone, the same percentage of votes was cast in the large and small locals.

How to account for the larger percentage of voter participation in the smaller locals than in the larger? There are several possible explanations. It may be the result of more intensive canvassing in small locals, where communication is more direct and an election spirit can be more easily aroused by supporters of the director. Or the "machine" operations of staff representatives committed to their district director may have been more efficient, the arm twisting more intensive. Or perhaps the local officers pursued their responsibilities more diligently or implacably. Also, as is true in national, state, and municipal elections, the remote precincts often constitute the reliable "backbone" of the political machine, sometimes coming up with the necessary margins as required. Implicit in all this is the impossibility of the opposition candidates—whether in the international or the district contests— to man all the smaller locals with watchers and observers as completely as they could the larger locals. It is here that the staff representatives could exercise their greatest influence in seeing that the voters came out and their votes were counted and delivered. Here in effect their "loyalty" to the district director could best be measured. Both the Abel and McDonald forces concentrated, with their observers, on the larger locals as the target areas requiring the closest attention, since the gains or losses could be significant.

From the large locals—those with 500 or more members—Abel had received 270 nominations to McDonald's 143. But in the election, Abel carried only 189—a drop of 30 per cent—of the 270 locals which had nominated him, and captured 28 out of the 143 locals that had nominated McDonald. In the election, on the other hand, McDonald won 81 of the large locals that had nominated Abel and lost 28—20 per cent—of the 143 locals that had nominated him.

Of the 433 large locals, Abel carried 230 and McDonald 203. These 433 locals (of 500 or more) had 695,833 eligible voters, compared with a total of 323,270 in 2,591 under-500 locals.

	Voting Strength
816 locals (under 49 members)	22,753
639 locals (50-99 members)	46,293
745 locals (100-249 members)	118,769
391 locals (250-499 members)	135,455
2,591 locals (under 500 members)	323,270
433 locals (over 500 members)	695,833
	1,019,103

The final tally for district director elections showed the following:

On the Abel side, eight incumbent directors were returned without contest. In addition, five Abel supporters backed by their retiring predecessors were elected to fill vacancies. In a sixth, in Canada, retiring director Pat Burke remained aloof from the contest between two pro-Abel candidates. Thus the total number of Abel directors elected was fourteen. These directors represented a weighted total vote of 540,000.

On the McDonald side, ten incumbents were returned and five McDonald supporters to fill vacancies, backed by retirees, were elected. Thus the total number of McDonald directors elected was fifteen, representing a weighted total of 469,000 members.

All eighteen incumbent directors who sought re-election were returned to office. Only three of them were opposed. In these three contests, the incumbents were McDonald supporters and managed to retain their jobs; the totals were fairly close, especially in New England. In no district did a McDonald challenger of an Abel incumbent in a district directorship obtain enough local union nominations to be placed on the ballot.

After June 1, when the new administration took over, this was the voting strength of the international executive board:

DIRECTORS SUPPORTING ABEL			DIRECTORS SUPPORTING McDONALD		
District	*Director*	*Votes*	*District*	*Director*	*Votes*
2	James Nicholson	7	1	Roy H. Stevens	30
4	Matthew Armstrong	52	7	Hugh Carcella	54
5	Jean Gerin-LaJoie	21	8	Albert Atallah	31
6	Lawrence Sefton	86	9	William Moran	42
19	William J. Hart	26	13	Eugene Maurice	29
23	Paul Rusen	36	15	Paul Hilbert	33
27	John S. Johns	36	16	Paul Normile	19
28	Paul E. Schremp	29	20	Kay Kluz	25
29	Charles Younglove	26	21	William Nicholson	17
31	Joseph Germano	115	25	James P. Gallagher	14
32	Bert McNamara	31	26	James P. Griffin	45
33	Glenn Peterson	20	30	Harry Dougherty	23
34	Lloyd McBride	31	35	M. C. Weston	17
37	James Ward	24	36	Howard Strevel	32
		———	38	Charles J. Smith	58
		540			———
					469

National Director of Canada		
William Mahoney		86
President I. W. Abel		115
Vice-President Joseph Molony		115
Secretary-Treasurer		
Walter J. Burke		115
		———
		431

"Abel" total	971		"McDonald" total	469

Appendix 6

H. James Neary, a statistical expert in the field of union membership analysis, undertook a study on the subject of delegate representation in my behalf. He found that nearly 40 per cent of the local unions at the 14th Constitutional Convention (1968) of the United Steelworkers, were, in fact, represented by an international union officer, a district director, or a paid employee at the headquarters or the district level. The votes controlled by them, if a roll-call vote were taken, would come to about 13 per cent of the vote, weighted by membership. Perhaps the main point, however, is not the size of the vote, but the number of individual staff representatives on the convention floor, the influence they exercise on voice votes, as well as on the management of parliamentary business from the floor.

NUMBER OF DISTRICT FIELD STAFF PERSONNEL ACTING AS DELEGATES TO THE
14TH CONSTITUTIONAL CONVENTION, USWA (AFL-CIO), AUGUST 1968

District	Number of Field Staff Listed as Delegates	Number of Field Staff Recorded in 1967 Financial Statement
No. 1	21	22
2	3	3
4	27	29
5	14	29
6	49	75
7	34	37
8	8	11
9	28	31
13	15	16
15	10	14
16	11	14
19	17	20
20	13	13
21	9	10
23	17	18
25	11	15
26	24	25
27	14	16
28	13	16
29	20	26
30	14	16
31	44	44
32	16	18
33	12	14
34	15	19
35	16	19
36	17	29
37	20	26
38	50	70
TOTALS	562	695 = 80.9%

SOURCE: Cross reference between the 1967 LM-2 Financial Statement submitted by the USWA to the U.S. Labor Department's Office of Labor-Management and Welfare-Pension Reports and the convention's Credential Report.

Acknowledgments

To a considerable extent this book is a result of the interest and help of many people extending over several years. Without a generous grant from the Ford Foundation, I would not have been able to travel as extensively as this study has required. I am especially grateful to Marshall Robinson and Charles B. Warden, Jr., of the Foundation for their indispensable aid in obtaining the grant. Evan Thomas, then of Harper & Row, turned the writer's desire into a publishing possibility.

For more than twenty-five years I have reported the labor scene in all its ramifications and have seen the emergence and departure of many labor leaders. To many people, the importance of labor organizations becomes evident only at a time of imminent crisis such as a strike, whether averted or called, while the teeming political continuity of a union's life is too often disregarded or treated with indifference. To produce an intimate portrait of the internal life of the Steelworkers Union in the United States and Canada, I moved in with eye, ear, tape recorder, and a certain durability.

My effort required more than the simple compliance of many of those who played a significant part in its development. Hundreds of national and district leaders, local officers, and ordinary dues-paying members as well as professional observers talked to me at length and most often with candor. Their answers sometimes came hard because the questions put to them were not easy. But as one key union officer burst out during two days of interviewing, "We're big enough and strong enough to deserve an honest picture, and that means—may my sainted father forgive me for quoting Oliver Cromwell—'warts and all.'"

The first draft of this book ran more than twice its present length. But under the relentless guidance of three editors of Harper & Row—Norbert Slepyan, Marguerite Hoyle Glynn, and, above all, Virginia Hilu—this book achieved its present form. In the early stages of the research, I was assisted by an advisory committee, headed by my friend Dr. Thomas W. Holland and his faculty associates, Dr. Daniel R. Cloutier and Dr. Leroy Merrifield, all of George Washington University.

In the course of writing the book, I had determined to avoid the use of what Edmund Wilson, I think, has described as the "barbed wire entanglements" of excessive footnotes and references. Where material used is of sufficient importance, the sources, personal or documentary, are made part of the body of the book. In most instances, the more intimate and personal incidents and observations were recorded on tapes whose unedited transcriptions came to more than two thousand pages.

It would be impossible even if it were desirable to express or assess fully my obligation to the many people who helped me in the technical preparation of the book. At my request, H. James Neary compiled a series of tables analyzing the 1965 election that unfortunately could not be included because of limitations of space. In the typing and retyping, Mrs. Boris Levine remained efficient and enthusiastic. For more than a year and a half, Miss Connie Gray transcribed the tapes without visible physical erosion. Her comments in the process were often perceptive although not usable. Two studies of the election—one a private document by Meyer Bernstein and another, "A Documentary History of the 1965 Election," by Norris B. Woodie of Berea College, Kentucky—were exceedingly helpful. Helen Rommeihs Benedict, then of the AFL-CIO Industrial Union Department, made available several huge scrapbooks of clippings having to do with the election. My brother, Albert Herling, was very helpful, especially at critical times.

My appreciation is extended especially to the men who as the dramatis personae could have begged off for personal or official reasons, but most of them did not. President I. W. Abel and former President David J. McDonald both gave taped interviews, as did Secretary-Treasurer Walter J. Burke and Vice-President Joseph P. Molony. Joseph Germano and James P. Griffin, the rival campaign managers in 1965, were cooperative. The latter gave me full run of his campaign records, on which I spent a weekend at his home in Youngstown.

And now I shall list alphabetically the names of scores of others who were helpful, in ways often hard to describe: Ann Allen, Mike L. Baca, Emery Bacon, Charles Baker, Earl Bester, Ronald Bitonti, Nelson Bortz, Elliot Bredhoff, Horace Brock, Otis Brubaker, Pat Burke, Henry Cano, Elmer Chatak, Jacob Clayman, Dean Clowes, John A. Dean, John T. Dunlop, William J. Eaton, David E. Feller, Frank Fernbach, Ben Fischer, Alex Fuller, Herman Gadon, Bill Garvey, Leo Gatewood, Chris Gellepis, John P. Gilbert, Maurice Goyette, Harry Guenther, Violet M. Gunther, Alphonse O. Guttierez, Howard Hague, Thomas E. Harris, Monsignor George G. Higgins, Alice C. Hoffman, John A. Hogan, John S. Johns, James (Jimmy) Jones, William Kane, Frank Kleiler, Kay Kluz, Steve Lakich, John Lawrence, Bertram McNamara, Bill Moyers, Tom Murray, Patrick Nall, Emil Narick, James Cuff O'Brien, Ray Pasnick, James J. Reynolds, Jr., Lawrence Rogin, Stanley H. Ruttenberg, Gene Saari, Murray Seeger, Lawrence Sefton, Joel Seidman, Manuel Sierras, Donald Smith, Lawrence Spitz, Damon Stetson, Roy H. Stevens, David Stolberg, Ross Thomas, Tony Torres, Richard Valdez, Saul Wallen, Jane Weissman, Stephen Wexler, W. Willard Wirtz, Nicholas Zonarich, and "Hymns for the Celebration of Life," (Beacon Press).

I was sustained throughout by many persons in and out of the labor movement whose names need not be mentioned here. They constituted a kind of Greek chorus urging me over the rough spots but warning me of booby traps on and off stage. I may not always have succeeded in avoiding them.

J.H.

Index